FOURTH EDITION

MULTICULTURAL EDUCATION OF CHILDREN AND ADOLESCENTS

M. LEE MANNING
Old Dominion University

LEROY G. BARUTH
Appalachian State University

Boston ■ New York ■ San Francisco
Mexico City ■ Montreal ■ Toronto ■ London ■ Madrid ■ Munich ■ Paris
Hong Kong ■ Singapore ■ Tokyo ■ Cape Town ■ Sydney

Series Editor: *Traci Mueller*
Editorial Assistant: *Krista E. Price*
Marketing Manager: *Elizabeth Fogarty*
Production Editor: *Paul Mihailidis*
Editorial Production Service: *Omegatype Typography, Inc.*
Manufacturing Buyer: *Andrew Turso*
Composition and Prepress Buyer: *Linda Cox*
Cover Administrator: *Joel Gendron*
Electronic Composition: *Omegatype Typography, Inc.*

For related titles and support materials, visit our online catalog at www.ablongman.com.

Between the time Website information is gathered and published, some sites may have closed. Also, the transcription of URLs can result in typographical errors. The publisher would appreciate notification where these errors occur so that they may be corrected in subsequent editions.

Many of the designations used by manufacturers and sellers to distinguish their products are claimed as trademarks. Where those designations appear in this book, and Allyn and Bacon was aware of a trademark claim, the designations have been printed in initial or all caps.

Library of Congress Cataloging-in-Publication Data

Manning, M. Lee.
    Multicultural education of children and adolescents / M. Lee Manning, Leroy G. Baruth.—4th ed.
        p.   cm.
    Includes bibliographical references (p.) and indexes.
    ISBN 0-205-40263-1
        1. Multicultural education—United States.   2. Indians of North America—Education.   3. African American children—Education.   4. Asian American children—Education.   5. Hispanic American children—Education.   I. Baruth, Leroy, G.   II. Title.

    LC1099.3.M36   2004
    370.117—dc21

                                                                    2003041855

Printed in the United States of America

10   9   8   7   6   5   4   3   08   07   06

*To my family: My wife, Marianne; and my
children, Jennifer and Michael*
MLM

*To my brother, Carroll, who has devoted most
of his professional career to the education
of children and adolescents*
LGB

CONTENTS

CHAPTER TWO
An Increasingly Multicultural Society   28

CHAPTER FIVE

Understanding Arab American Children and Adolescents   111

CHAPTER SIX

Understanding Asian American Children and Adolescents   133

CHAPTER SEVEN

Understanding European American Children and Adolescents   157

CHAPTER EIGHT

Understanding Hispanic American Children and Adolescents   180

PART III   TEACHING AND LEARNING IN A DIVERSE SOCIETY   207

CHAPTER NINE
Curricular Efforts   209

CHAPTER TEN

Instructional Practices   237

CHAPTER ELEVEN
Individual and Cultural Differences 263

PART IV   THE FUTURE OF MULTICULTURAL EDUCATION   343

PREFACE

OUR NATION'S INCREASING CULTURAL DIVERSITY

Multicultural Education of Children and Adolescents is based on the premise that people from culturally different backgrounds enrich the United States and that a better understanding of people and their differences leads to higher levels of acceptance and respect for all people. This fourth edition is being published at a time when all demographic projections indicate that the number of people of differing cultures in the United States will increase.

Predictions suggest that the Hispanic American population will soon outnumber the African American population and that people of European ancestry will soon be in the minority. At this time, the Asian American population is increasing dramatically. Without doubt, the high birthrates among some cultural groups, increasing numbers of Spanish-speaking people, and the recent influxes of immigrants from Southeast Asia will increase the cultural diversity of the United States and challenge its citizens to accept and respect all people whatever their cultural background, ethnicity, race, sexual orientation, socioeconomic status, gender, or religion.

At one time during the nation's history, the "melting pot" theory proposed to erase differences and to acculturate or "melt" cultural differences. In essence, the person of a different cultural background was supposed to forsake cherished and traditional cultural values and adopt "American values," probably those of the middle-class European American population. This concept viewed differences as wrong or inferior and promoted wholesale abandonment of cultural heritage.

Realistically, for any number of reasons, the melting pot is not an accurate model—people have difficulty giving up cultural characteristics or they live in enclaves in which assimilation with the mainstream society is unnecessary. Likewise, some people chose to maintain their culture as well as to adopt American values. Regardless of the reasons, the melting pot did not account for all the citizenry as some proposed; the nation is a heterogenous mixture of different peoples.

Serious questions continue to plague educators and other concerned people: Why is there an increase in racism? After fifty years since the landmark *Brown* decision, why are schools still segregated? Why do elementary and secondary schools address primarily the needs of some learners and allow others to fall behind? Why do people fear diversity? Why are victims often blamed for their problems? These questions defy easy answers and evince many people's belief that differences are negative manifestations in need of eradication.

Rather than provoking anger or causing fear, differences in values, customs, and traditions should be celebrated and considered a means of enriching the United States. We do not claim that the people who perceive differences as enriching will eliminate racism and acts of violence. Celebrating differences, though, is a first step, especially if efforts focus on today's children and adolescents, who will lead the nation during the twenty-first century. Considering differences to be positive and enriching, however, is only a beginning. Significant change will require more comprehensive and deliberate efforts.

Elementary and secondary schools can play a major role in teaching acceptance and respect for all forms of diversity. The schools, in fact, are logical places to begin instilling feelings of acceptance for all people. Schools, however, must do more than pay lip service; effective curriculum reflects diversity, and appropriate learning materials represent all people in positive and meaningful roles. We believe wholeheartedly that multicultural education should be a total-school approach, rather than simply a unit or Multicultural Education Week approach. Although teaching about multiculturalism is an admirable concept, schools should also model acceptance and respect for cultural diversity. Schools that teach about cultural differences and celebrate diversity, but whose actions indicate racism or a lack of respect, fail in their multicultural efforts.

OUR REASONS FOR WRITING THIS BOOK

We wrote this fourth edition of *Multicultural Education of Children and Adolescents* to provide preservice and in-service educators with a knowledge of the six prevalent cultural groups and to show the components of responsive multicultural education programs. The text staunchly maintains that multicultural education programs should be a total-school effort—that is, that administrators, teachers, library media specialists, special-education teachers, counselors, and communications disorder specialists have vital roles in the multicultural education program. Similarly, we believe that multicultural efforts should be comprehensive. The curriculum, instructional strategies, materials, environment, and school practices should reflect multiculturalism and should show a genuine respect for all forms of diversity.

Our Selection of Cultural Groups

After careful consideration of and reflection on the increasing cultural diversity of the United States, we decided to focus on six broad groups of people (listed alphabetically): African, American Indian, Arab, Asian, European, and Hispanic American. These groups are, and in all likelihood will continue to be, the most populous groups in elementary and secondary schools. Choosing only these groups does not negate the importance of other cultures. We hope and expect that learning about diversity in these cultures will motivate readers to explore the values, customs, and traditions of other cultures.

A Word of Caution

Any discussion focusing on characteristics of children and adolescents and their cultural backgrounds risks stereotyping and an overdependence on generalizations. The many differences resulting from cultural, intracultural, socioeconomic, geographic, generational, gender, sexual orientation, and individuality factors among people contribute to their diversity and to the difficulty of describing individuals of various cultures. Although we based this text on current and objective information, it remains crucial for educators to understand individual children and adolescents within a culture through conscientious study and first-hand contact. Failing to understand individuals and failing to consider crucial differences may result in assuming too much cultural homogeneity—for example, that all Hispanic cultural groups share identical values, problems, and cultural expectations or that all Asian Americans fit the "model minority" label.

THE ORGANIZATION OF THE BOOK

Multicultural Education of Children and Adolescents is divided into four parts and fourteen chapters. Part I introduces multicultural education as a concept and documents the increasing cultural diversity of the United States. Part II provides a cultural portrait of children and adolescents in the African, American Indian, Arab, Asian, European, and Hispanic cultures. Part III focuses on aspects that educators should consider when planning and implementing programs that teach acceptance and respect for cultural diversity. Part IV examines issues that will continue to challenge educators in the twenty-first century.

PEDAGOGICAL FEATURES

Pedagogical features of *Multicultural Education of Children and Adolescents* include:

- *Case Studies* throughout the text show how educators have addressed the chapters' topics.
- *Implementing Research* boxes throughout the text provide readers with research studies that focus on children and adolescents of culturally different backgrounds and give practical suggestions for implementing the research. In an attempt to provide readers with a wide range of information and sources, we define research in its broadest sense.
- *Expanding Your Horizons: Additional Journal Readings and Books*, located at the end of each chapter, provides readers with resources for further study and consideration.
- *Expanding Your Students' Horizons: Appropriate Books for Children and Adolescents* is located at the end of Chapters 3, 4, 5, 6, 7, and 8.
- *Using Children's Literature*, located in Chapters 3, 4, 5, 6, 7, and 8, provides titles and a brief annotation of developmentally appropriate children's and adolescents' literature that can help learners better understand their cultural heritages.
- *For Additional Information*, located in Chapters 3, 4, 5, 6, 7, and 8, provides names and addresses of organizations and groups that promote cultural diversity and that act as disseminators of information about the respective cultures.

- *Suggestions for Collaborative Efforts*, at the end of each chapter, provides readers with opportunities to work cooperatively and collaboratively toward group goals.
- *Gender Perspectives*, located in selected chapters throughout the text, highlights current research and scholarly opinion on females and underscores the importance of understanding gender as well as cultural and other diversities.

ACKNOWLEDGMENTS

An author's only chance and hope for making a valuable contribution lies in the willingness of others to offer advice and to share their expertise. We would like to thank reviewers Gail Mosby, University of Tennessee, Knoxville, and Dilys Shourman, Florida Atlantic University, for their helpful comments. Our appreciation is also extended to people of all cultures who have contributed to the richness of our lives and the nation.

MLM
LGB

MULTICULTURAL EDUCATION AND ITS RESPONSE TO OUR NATION'S INCREASING DIVERSITY

Part I introduces multicultural education as a concept and documents the increasing cultural diversity of the United States. Chapter 1 examines the multicultural education movement and its role in elementary and secondary schools. Chapter 2 looks at our nation's increasing cultural diversity and the ways that people's differences enrich our schools. These chapters reflect a belief that educators have a professional responsibility to teach respect for diversity as well as to teach all students the concepts of justice, equality, and democracy.

CHAPTER ONE

MULTICULTURAL EDUCATION

Understanding the material and activities in this chapter will help the reader to:

- Define multicultural education and explain its fundamental purposes
- List several goals, assumptions, concepts, and principles of multicultural education
- List several myths and misconceptions about multicultural education
- Explain briefly the historical milestones and legal precedents of multicultural education
- List several characteristics of effective multicultural educators
- List several controversial issues in multicultural education

OVERVIEW

The tremendous cultural, ethnic, religious, and socioeconomic diversity in schools today calls for multicultural education programs that reflect understanding and respect for children's and adolescents' differences. The multicultural education movement has particular relevance for the new century because of the continuing influx of people into the United States and because of the enlightened and more humane perspective that diversity enriches, rather than weakens, a nation. This chapter examines the fundamentals and principles of multicultural education and considers the various aspects that make programs successful.

MULTICULTURAL EDUCATION FOR CULTURALLY PLURALISTIC SCHOOLS

In this section we describe our (the authors') preferred definition of multicultural education and examine principles, concepts, goals, and assumptions that form the basis for responsive multicultural education programs. We then look at several myths and provide an overview of historical events and court decisions that have contributed to multicultural education.

Definition

Various groups and individuals define multicultural education in numerous ways. Some definitions address the perspectives of specific disciplines, such as education,

■ ■ ■ ■ ■ ▬▬▬

FOLLOW THROUGH 1.1

**DETERMINING DIFFERENCES TO INCLUDE
IN MULTICULTURAL EDUCATION**

Consider the differences and characteristics we included in our definition. Some might disagree with nontraditional views on sexual orientation, ability/disability, and gender. What do you think? Do people whose views are nontraditional have a culture of their own? For example, each person has his or her own cultural background, but wouldn't he or she also have a "culture" of sexual orientation, a "culture" associated with a disabling condition, or a culture associated with being either male or female? How inclusive do you think multicultural education should be?

anthropology, sociology, and psychology. Other definitions represent the views of accrediting agencies and professional organizations that are concerned with what teachers need to teach and what students need to learn.

We think the following definition most effectively meets the goals and purposes of multicultural education for children and adolescents. Multicultural education is both a concept and deliberate process designed to:

- Teach learners to recognize, accept, and appreciate differences in culture, ethnicity, social class, sexual orientation, religion, special needs, and gender
- Instill in learners during their crucial developmental years a sense of responsibility and a commitment to work toward the democratic ideals of justice, equality, and democracy

Case Study 1.1 examines the importance of having a multicultural education program that considers diversity in its broadest forms.

Gender Perspectives 1.1 looks at how multicultural education should include gender studies and feminist pedagogy. We have adopted a broad definition of multicultural education, one that includes gender as an entity to be considered. Therefore, we agree with Mulvihill (2000) that multicultural education should include analysis of gender as well as feminist and critical education theories.

Principles

Appropriate multicultural education requires more than simply providing cultural information about ethnic groups. Several "fundamentals" necessary to the promotion of effective multicultural education allow learners and teachers of various cultures to maintain integrity and dignity. First, students need curricular materials appropriate to their cultural backgrounds. These materials should enhance students' self-concept, engage student interest in classroom learning, and provide examples, vocabulary, and models that relate to students' cultural backgrounds. Second, major curricular focuses should include skills in analysis and critical thinking. Third, materials, activities, and experiences should

CASE STUDY 1.1

TOWARD AN ALL-ENCOMPASSING DEFINITION OF MULTICULTURAL EDUCATION

The administration, faculty, and staff at PS 105 decided on a broad approach to their multicultural education program. This group agreed that rather than address only "cultural backgrounds," their program should direct attention to a broad range of differences, including ethnicity, race, gender, social class, and individual.

Children and adolescents of respective cultures are vastly different. Consider, for example, the many different cultures that make up the Hispanic American population, the vast differences among Asian Americans, and the diversity among African Americans.

The question for PS 105 was how to address so many differences. The committee decided first to examine each difference and its influence on learning and other school-related activities and then to look at the curriculum, instructional approaches, print and nonprint media, school policies, extracurricular activities, and cultural composition of the administration, faculty, and staff. Although this constituted a task of some magnitude, the group recognized the advantages of having a multicultural education program that genuinely addressed diversity in its broadest definition.

GENDER PERSPECTIVES 1.1

MULTICULTURAL EDUCATION AND GENDER STUDIES

Mulvihill maintained that multicultural education has always been a contested terrain because of tensions and debates over what the field includes and does not include. Although theories of multicultural education have been developed, they have not always taken into account the debates surrounding the terms "gender" and "sex," or the multiple feminist theories that focus on the more critical aspects of social justice. In fact, some believe multicultural education's influence as a change agent depends on the tensions it creates and on its success in working to resolve conflicts among various groups. In her article, Mulvihill looked at some of the tensions between gender studies and multicultural education, such as understanding gender as a category of analysis, theoretical constructions of feminism, and building an educational agenda for social justice.

Mulvihill focused attention on gender as well as feminist and critical education theories, especially as to how they relate to social justice. She proposed that multicultural education has an obligation to take advantage of the contributions of women and gender studies, especially because feminist pedagogy deals consistently with all the central issues inherent in multicultural education.

Source: Mulvihill, T. M. (2000). Women and gender studies and multicultural education? Building the agenda for 2000 and beyond. *Teacher Educator, 36*(1), 49–57.

■ ■ ■ ■ ■ ▬▬▬▬▬▬

FOLLOW THROUGH 1.2
SURVEYING FOR GENDER BIAS

Visit several elementary or secondary schools to determine gender bias. Prepare a survey that examines (but is not limited to) such items as teacher–student interactions, instructional methods, grouping strategies, questioning strategies, and classroom environment. What evidence do you see that teachers recognize and address gender differences? Are boys and girls being treated equally and equitably? How might multicultural education address the bias in treatment of boys and girls (if, in fact you find evidence of bias)?

be authentic and multidimensional to help students understand ethnic differences and cultural diversity. They should include both cognitive and affective skills.

Concepts

It is especially important for teachers to understand three concepts of multicultural education, because it is the educator's concept of the term that determines his or her program's direction and issues.

First, multicultural education is a product in which there is emphasis on the study of ethnicity—for example, the contributions or characteristics of a group of people. This concept, which addresses teaching about different ethnic and cultural groups, may be best described as *ethnic studies.*

Second, multicultural education emphasizes the role of oppression of one group by another and the oppressors' atonement or compensation for past injustices. Dealing primarily with targeted oppressed groups (and possible solutions to their problems), this concept considers multicultural education a concern only of minorities.

The third concept views multicultural education as a teaching process and includes aspects such as product and entitlement. It extends even further than product and entitlement, because teachers focus on the concept of culture as an entity separate from ethnicity. It emphasizes the intrinsic aspects of culture and its influence on teaching and learning processes. Such a concept of multicultural education recognizes the entitlement aspect in the belief that to obtain what one is entitled to requires a fair system and an equal chance to acquire social and academic skills. It incorporates the product view in that (1) certain historical facts and events must be taught and (2) an adequate understanding of present conditions, as well as general human behavior, comes about with knowledge of historical facts. This idea of multicultural education as a process includes all educational variables, such as methodology, curriculum, and instructional techniques (Payne, 1984).

Goals

An integral aspect of all multicultural education focuses on the development of skills and attitudes necessary for people to function in a culturally diverse society. Not only

■ ■ ■ ■ ■ ▬▬▬▬▬▬▬▬▬▬▬▬▬▬▬▬▬▬▬▬▬▬▬▬▬▬▬

FOR ADDITIONAL INFORMATION
INTERNET ADDRESSES

Multicultural Pavilion
http://curry.edschool.Virginia.edu/go/multi
cultural   Provides conceptualizations and goals
of multicultural education as well as resources
for teachers.

**National Association
for Multicultural Education**
www.inform.umd.edu/NAME   Provides
information on the purposes, design, and implementation of effective multicultural education
programs.

*STANDARDS: The International Journal
of Multicultural Studies*
http://stripe.colorado.edu/~standard   Focuses
on multiculturalism in education; includes online
syllabi, lesson plans, and book reviews.

ED334 320
www.msue.msu.edu/msue/imp/moddp/1118016.
html   Provides a paradigm for examining multicultural education.

ED 240 224
http://eric-web.tc.columbia.edu/abstracts/
ed240224.html   Describes how educators can
move multicultural education to higher levels of
effectiveness and sophistication.

Infoseek: Multicultural Education
http://guide-p.infoseek.com/Education/K_12/
Resources_for-educators/Multicultural_ education   Provides multicultural educational resources for grades K–12.

should educators learn about other cultures, they should also develop the attitudes and skills to function in multicultural situations, including an awareness, understanding, and acceptance of cultural differences. Additionally, educators may need to develop empathy with members of other cultures and modify their own cultural values.

One goal of multicultural education is to change the total educational environment so that it promotes a respect for a wide range of cultural groups and enables all cultural groups to experience equal educational opportunities (Banks, 1987, p. 29). Developing cross-cultural competency is another goal and includes an awareness of the skills, attitudes, and knowledge necessary to live within the individual's own ethnic culture and the universal American culture, as well as within and across ethnic cultures (Banks, 1987, pp. 35–36).

Educators need to be enlightened on the social, political, and economic realities they will encounter in a culturally diverse and complex society. Other goals of multicultural education include recognizing and respecting the nature of cultural differences and similarities; understanding intracultural differences as well as individuals' many differences; developing a better understanding of the nature and impact of racism and of the implications for positive or negative influence; and developing a positive attitude toward one's own cultural background.

Ramsey (1987) offers several goals that differ slightly from those of Banks and the professional organization. First, in her goals for teaching from multicultural perspectives, Ramsey feels it necessary "to help children develop positive gender, racial, cultural, class, and individual identities, and to recognize and accept their membership in many different groups" (p. 3). Another goal is to encourage social relationships in which there is "an openness and interest with others, a willingness to include others, and a desire to cooperate" (p. 4). A third, different goal is to "empower children to become autonomous and critical analysts and activists in their social environment" (p. 4). Another difference, a major focus of this text, is the inclusion of immediate and extended families, as Ramsey wrote, "to promote effective and reciprocal relationships between schools and families" (p. 5).

Assumptions

Several assumptions underlie multicultural education and are, in fact, the philosophy on which this book, *Multicultural Education of Children and Adolescents*, is based.

Assumption 1. Cultural diversity is a positive, enriching element in a society because it provides individuals increased opportunities to experience other cultures and thus to become more fulfilled as human beings (Banks, 1988). Rather than perceiving it as a weakness to be remediated, educators should view cultural diversity as a strength with the potential for helping individuals better understand their own cultures. Similarly, as people reach higher levels of understanding and acceptance of other cultures, we hope that they will achieve similar heights of understanding and sensitivity in areas such as racism, sexism, and classism.

Assumption 2. Multicultural education is for all students (Hernandez, 1989). Some people believe that multicultural education is only for minority children and adolescents. For example, some states require multicultural education only in districts having at least one school with a 25 percent minority student population (Hernandez, 1989). This and similar policies are based on the odd notion that only minority youngsters need multicultural education. This notion completely fails to recognize that majority cultures can benefit from a better understanding of cultural differences and, eventually, of their own cultural backgrounds.

Assumption 3. Teaching is a cross-cultural encounter (Hernandez, 1989). All teachers and students have their own cultural baggage—their backgrounds, values, customs, perceptions, and, perhaps, prejudices. These cultural aspects play a significant role in teaching and learning situations and can have a substantial effect on behavior and learning. Socioeconomic status, ethnicity, gender, and language have a powerful and dynamic effect on one's outlook and attitude toward school and on one's actual school achievement (Hernandez, 1989).

Assumption 4. Multicultural education should permeate the total school curriculum rather than be doled out in a "one-course" or a teaching-unit approach. Responsive multicultural education programs cannot accomplish lasting and worthwhile goals through "one-shot" approaches. The school must be genuinely multicultural. Multiculturalism must embrace the curriculum, as defined in the broadest sense (every aspect of the school with which learners come in contact); the composition of the administration, faculty, and staff; expectations that reflect an understanding of different cultural groups, their attitudes toward school success, and their learning styles; and the recognition of all other aspects that may affect both minority- and majority-culture learners. A school that appears to address only majority needs and expectations will cause learners from culturally different backgrounds to feel like "intruders" or "outsiders."

Assumption 5. The education system has not served all students equally well (Hernandez, 1989). Generally speaking, members of minority groups, students from low-income families, and students who are culturally different or speak a language other than English have not fared well in U.S. school systems. Any number of reasons may account for such students' lack of achievement: differing achievement orientations; problems resulting from language barriers; differing learning styles; curricula and school policies that are unresponsive to minority student needs; testing and assessment procedures that may be designed for middle-class white students; and a lack of understanding or acceptance of cultural differences. In any event, the high dropout rate among American Indians, African Americans, and Hispanic Americans substantiates the position that learners from culturally different backgrounds often do not succeed in U.S. schools.

Assumption 6. Schools will continue to experience and reflect increasing cultural diversity because of influxes of immigrants and refugees and the high birthrates of some cultural groups. To say that U.S. society continues to grow more diverse is an understatement. The arrival in this country of increasing numbers of people from culturally different backgrounds is one example. Increasing recognition of differences in gender, religion, socioeconomic group, sexual orientation, and geography are others. Multicultural education programs have the responsibility to reflect the rich diversity that characterizes U.S. society.

Assumption 7. Elementary and secondary schools have a responsibility to implement appropriate multicultural education programs. These programs must contribute to a better understanding of cultural differences, show the dangers of stereotyping, and reduce racism, sexism, and classism. Families are unquestionably children's first teachers of values, opinions, and attitudes. Ideally, families teach acceptance and respect for all people and their differences. Realistically speaking, however, children may learn that their culture, race, or ethnic backgrounds are "right" but that those of others are "wrong" or "inferior." Because considerable cultural diversity characterizes the U.S. educational

■ ■ ■ ■ ■ ▬▬▬▬▬▬▬▬▬▬▬▬▬▬▬▬▬▬▬▬

FOLLOW THROUGH 1.3
ACCOMMODATING THE NEEDS OF DIVERSE STUDENT POPULATIONS

Most people agree that the population of the United States will continue to grow more and more diverse. Schools will be challenged to address the needs of students from many backgrounds. What mindsets must educators change to accommodate the needs of a diverse student population? Name several specific recommendations that might improve the educational experience, such as making the curriculum more culturally relevant and responsive.

system, the transmission of understanding and respect for cultural diversity is most feasible in elementary and secondary schools. Responsive programs must teach genuine respect and must work toward reducing racism, sexism, and classism. Admittedly, this is an undertaking of considerable magnitude; the teaching and modeling of respect for all people, however, may have the most dramatic impact during children's formative years.

Myths and Misconceptions

At one time or another, most people have probably heard someone voice concerns about the dire consequences of multicultural education. Banks (1993), an acknowledged leader in the multicultural education movement, identifies and debunks several misconceptions about multicultural education.

Misconception 1: Multicultural education is for others. Some people argue that multicultural education is an entitlement program and a curriculum movement for African Americans, Hispanics, the poor, women, and other victimized groups. Banks debunks this misconception. In fact, multicultural education as designed during the 1980s called for a restructuring of educational institutions so that all learners will acquire the knowledge, skills, and attitudes necessary to function effectively in a culturally diverse nation. Rather than focus only on specific gender and ethnic movements, multicultural education tries to empower all students to become knowledgeable, caring, active citizens (Banks, 1993).

Misconception 2: Multicultural education is opposed to the Western tradition. Banks (1993) maintains that multicultural education is not anti-West, because many writers from culturally diverse backgrounds, such as Rudolfo Anaya, Paula Gunn Allen, Maxine Hong Kingston, Maya Angelou, and Toni Morrison, are Western writers. In fact, multicultural education is a thoroughly Western movement, which grew out of the civil rights movement and is grounded in such democratic ideals as freedom, justice, and equality (Banks, 1993).

Misconception 3: Multicultural education will divide the nation and undercut its unity. This misconception is based partly on questionable assumptions about the nature of U.S. society and partly on a mistaken understanding of multicultural education. The claim that multicultural education will divide the nation assumes an already united nation. Without doubt, the United States is one nation politically; sociologically, however, our nation is deeply divided along lines of race, gender, and class. Multicultural education seeks to unify a deeply divided nation rather than to divide a highly cohesive one.

Traditionally, U.S. society and the schools tried to create unity by "assimilating" students from diverse racial and ethnic groups into a mythical Anglo American culture. Assimilation would require a process of self-alienation. But, even when students from different backgrounds became culturally "assimilated," they continued to experience exclusion from mainstream society (Banks, 1993).

Maintaining multicultural education is plagued with misconceptions, Lane F. Birkel (2000) examined a number of unclear and sometimes erroneous notions. In Implementing Research 1.1, Birkel (2000) explains what multicultural education is and is

■ ■ ■ ■ ■ ▬▬▬

IMPLEMENTING RESEARCH 1.1
MULTICULTURAL EDUCATION: IT IS EDUCATION

Birkel maintains that "multicultural" (p. 22) has many meanings. To some, it means the acceptance and appreciation of diversity (an opinion emphasized throughout this book); to others, it means, an association with "political correctness" (p. 22). The term is also misunderstood as a program on race relations, as an affirmative action vehicle, and as a civil rights movement. It has also been charged as an attack on Western thought. Birkel sought to clarify the true meaning of multicultural education and to refute some of the fallacious ideas that have limited its success.

Birkel's major points include that multicultural education is neither political nor an attempt to establish blame or instill guilt. Such actions would negate the purpose of the movement, which is to promote unity rather than division among the American people. Another point is that, rather than advocating the eradication of ethnicity and diversity, multicultural education advocates the teaching of factual and complete knowledge about the cultural groups that comprise the United States.

According to Birkel, multicultural education is, first of all, education concerned with the teaching/learning processes and the acceptance and appreciation of diversity. Primarily, multicultural education is a way of teaching and learning. Three elements include the skills of intercultural understanding and interaction, the integration of cultural content, and the building of positive attitudes.

Birkel thoughtfully explains what multicultural education is and what it is not. Some may argue with a few of the misconceptions (e.g., multicultural education promotes unity rather than division among the American people), but Birkel proposes a sound defense of multicultural education as a movement to promote the acceptance and appreciation of diversity.

IMPLEMENTING THE RESEARCH
1. Educators need to clarify as many misconceptions about multicultural education as possible in order to promote the real causes of the movement.
2. Educators in their daily interactions with students should remember and emphasize Birkel's contention that multicultural education is, first of all, education.
3. Proponents should have a defense ready when approached by critics who claim that multicultural education is only a program on race relations, an affirmative action vehicle, and a civil rights movement.

Source: Birkel, L. F. (2000). Multicultural education: It is education first of all. *Teacher Educator, 36*(1), 23–28.

not. It is a particularly useful article because it clarifies misconceptions that we think have limited the success of the multicultural education movement.

A Brief Historical Overview

Before 1978 the Education Index did not include multicultural education in its listings; few pedagogical journals addressed the topic. During the 1970s and 1980s, however, increasing numbers of articles and books focused on multicultural education (Tiedt & Tiedt, 1995). Three forces contributed to the emergence of the multicultural education movement: (1) the civil rights movement came of age, (2) school textbooks came under critical analysis, and (3) assumptions underlying the deficiency orientation were changed to a more positive perspective.

The civil rights movement began as a passive, nonviolent means of changing laws that oppressed specific racial groups. By the late 1960s, the movement had matured into an energetic coalition uniting all Americans of color and directed toward self-determination and power. The movement severely criticized the U.S. school system because of its segregation and curricula that focused attention only on Western culture. Similarly, few teachers knew about minority groups, their rich cultural diversity, their individual strengths and weaknesses, and their learning styles. In fact, schools considered cultural and ethnic differences primarily weaknesses in need of remediation (Sleeter & Grant, 1988).

The 1970s saw the development of multicultural education into a more comprehensive approach. With cultural diversity and equal opportunity serving as an impetus, the multicultural education movement encouraged educators to examine and consider the relationships among culture, ethnicity, language, gender, disabling conditions, and social class in developing educational programs. Multicultural education that takes a social reconstructionist tack is a recent and controversial approach that represents an extension of multicultural education toward more definitive social action. This approach incorporates a curricular emphasis on (1) active student involvement in social issues such as sexism, racism, and classism; (2) the development of problem-solving ability and political action skills; and (3) the implementation of curricular adaptations, cooperative learning, and decision-making skills (Hernandez, 1989).

Payne and Welsh (2000), in Implementing Research 1.2, argue that the term "multicultural education" has been evolving throughout the world for centuries, although the actual term first appeared in the United States.

Banks (1988) described phases that place multicultural education in its proper historical perspective. During Phase I (monoethnic studies), the black civil rights movement began and African Americans demanded more African American teachers, more control of community schools, and the rewriting of textbooks to provide a more accurate portrayal of African Americans, their culture, and their contributions. Phase II (multiethnic studies) provided courses that focused on several minority groups and viewed experiences of ethnic groups from comparative perspectives. During Phase III (multiethnic education), an increasing number of educators recognized that the mere reforming of courses was insufficient to result in genuine educational reform.

In Phase IV (multicultural education), some educators became interested in an even broader development of pluralistic education that focused on reform of the total school environment. *Multicultural education* emerged as the preferred concept because it enabled educators to broaden their perspective to include a wider range of groups rather than maintain a limited focus on racial and ethnic minorities. Phase V is a slowly occurring process that includes strategies designed to increase the pace and scope of

■ ■ ■ ■ ■ ▬▬▬▬▬▬▬▬▬▬▬▬▬▬▬▬▬▬▬▬▬▬▬▬▬▬▬▬▬▬▬▬

IMPLEMENTING RESEARCH 1.2

THE PROGRESSIVE DEVELOPMENT
OF MULTICULTURAL EDUCATION

Although some people assume that multicultural education resulted from the social-political climate of the 1960s, Payne and Welsh (2000) believe that it resulted from 2,500 years of arduous struggles for dignity, duty, equality, freedom, and fundamental human rights. In fact, Payne and Welsh propose that the Code of Hammurabi (1,750 B.C.), the Magna Carta (A.D. 1215), and the British Bill of Rights (A.D. 1689) provide examples of "the spirit of struggle" (p. 30). Still, Payne and Welsh believe that the concept of multicultural education was created in the United States. One reason is that since the adoption of the U.S. Constitution, a major goal has been the creation of democracy and a more perfect union.

Particularly interesting points in the Payne and Welsh article include their historical perspective of multicultural education, discussion of court cases leading to desegregation, policies and practices used when schools faced the reality of desegregation, and federal initiatives that influenced the course of multicultural education.

IMPLEMENTING THE RESEARCH

1. Educators need to realize that the antecedents of multicultural education go back many centuries rather than stemming entirely from the 1960s.
2. Multicultural education needs to extend beyond racism, discrimination, prejudice, and oppression to an examination of culture and cultural similarities and differences.
3. Research into multicultural education will be necessary to achieve or work toward dignity, duty, equality, freedom, and fundamental human rights.

The article by Payne and Welsh (2000) offers considerable information on the struggles for equality and should interest all readers wanting to promote the causes of multicultural education.

Source: Payne, C. R., & Welsh, B. H. (2000). The progressive development of multicultural education before and after the 1960s: A theoretical framework. *Teacher Educator, 36*(1), 29–48.

the institutionalization of multiethnic and multicultural education within schools (Banks, 1988).

The two world wars, mass immigrations to the United States, the intercultural movements, and racial disturbances all contributed to the emergence and development of multicultural education.

The Influence of Court Decisions

Ruling in favor of equal opportunity and human rights, several court decisions and laws also contributed to the present multicultural education movement. The U.S. Supreme Court, in *Brown v. Topeka Board of Education* (1954), ruled unconstitutional the segregation of black and white learners. In 1957, the U.S. Commission on Civil Rights was established to investigate complaints that alleged the denial of civil rights. In 1968, the federal Bilingual Education Act (BEA) was passed as part of Title VII of the Elementary and Secondary Education Act.

The U.S. Commission on Civil Rights issued a report in 1975 called *A Better Chance to Learn: Bilingual–Bicultural Education*, designed for educators as a means of providing equal opportunity for language-minority students. This report provides only a brief listing of a few representative events that recognized cultural diversity and equal rights. These and other events, however, were the forerunners of the movement to recognize and teach respect for people from culturally different backgrounds. Schools continue to have a major responsibility in breaking down stereotypes, promoting multicultural understandings, and making a difference in the lives of individual learners (Tiedt & Tiedt, 1999).

Some educators believe that if racial problems are not visible, then multicultural education programs are not necessary. Case Study 1.2 examines just such a situation.

Interdisciplinary Approaches

Multicultural education should be an integral aspect of all curricular areas, rather than just be administered through the social studies course. Likewise, a once-a-year Multicultural Week or unit focusing on African American history, tacos, and Oriental dress and customs will not suffice. Such approaches have not worked and will not work, because diversity awareness does not necessarily result in acceptance of and respect for individuals within a cultural group. The curriculum, learning environments, and mindset of learners, faculty, and staff should become genuinely multicultural in nature and should reflect the cultural diversity of the school. Second, well-meaning multicultural education programs may serve only cosmetic purposes if students and school personnel harbor long-held cultural biases and stereotypes. In essence, to be effective, responsive multicultural education programs must recognize the need both to inform and to change negative attitudes and long-held prejudices.

Case Study 1.3 shows the advantages of an interdisciplinary approach to multicultural education.

■ ■ ■ ■ ■ ▬▬

CASE STUDY 1.2
"WE DON'T NEED A MULTICULTURAL EDUCATION PROGRAM."

After the faculty meeting at which the principal formed a committee to plan a multicultural education program, you hear Mr. Brown say, "But we don't need a multicultural program in our school. We do not have any racial problems." School professionals and parents sometimes feel that multicultural education is not necessary unless racial problems exist. But Mr. Brown is missing an important goal of multicultural education. First, students in his school need a better understanding of each others' cultural backgrounds. Second, if the school waits to form a multicultural education program until after racial disturbances emerge, it may be too late. The school may hurriedly implement the program without giving it sufficient thought.

■ ■ ■ ■ ■

FOLLOW THROUGH 1.4
PLANNING INTERDISCIPLINARY APPROACHES

Talk with several teachers who are experienced with interdisciplinary curricular approaches (in fact, several might be students in your class). Ask them to offer suggestions for integrating multiculturalism into the curriculum. Your specific questions should focus on culturally appropriate topics, for example, and on materials that offer diverse perspectives and show respect for diversity, instructional methods that cater to diverse learning styles, and culturally appropriate assessment techniques.

■ ■ ■ ■ ■

CASE STUDY 1.3
INTERDISCIPLINARY APPROACHES

The administrators, faculty, and staff at Browning High School worked conscientiously toward developing their multicultural education program. The committee had decided to fully support an interdisciplinary program. They had decided the goals, curriculum content, instructional practices, school policies, and how best to evaluate both print and nonprint media. Although the committee recognized the legitimacy of approaches and that regard multicultural education as a single subject, it also recognized that an interdisciplinary approach would be most effective for several reasons. Specifically, the interdisciplinary approach could:

1. Function as a means of including multicultural education experiences in all subject areas—showing, for example, the contributions of all cultural groups in the various disciplines.
2. Ensure broad involvement of all educators responsible for the various discipline areas.
3. Show students from culturally different backgrounds as well as majority-culture learners that the school is committed to serious multicultural education efforts.
4. Provide a wide variety of instructional approaches and learning experiences.
5. Empower all school personnel to be a part of the multicultural education program and responsible for its success.

The educators at Browning felt good about their multicultural education efforts: Everybody was involved. Teachers and administrators examined curricular and instructional practices, they reconsidered school policies, and efforts crossed discipline lines.

THE EFFECTIVE MULTICULTURAL EDUCATOR

Competencies for effective multicultural educators fall into three categories—knowledge, skills, and attitudes—each necessary to the existence of the other. We briefly examine several examples here. Chapter 10 takes a more in-depth look at knowledge, attitudes, and skills and more specific teaching behaviors.

Knowledge includes an understanding of individual learners' cultures. American Indians, for example, place great importance on the concept of sharing. African Americans value the extended family and have a unique language usage. Asian Americans have a unique concept of generational and family relationships. *Machismo* is an integral part of Hispanic American culture, as is commitment to the Spanish language.

Skills include recognizing and responding appropriately to learners' strengths and weaknesses and responding to the relationship between learning styles and culture. Skills-based teaching provides school experiences that embrace learners' orientations toward school and academic success. It requires teachers to select standardized tests and evaluation instruments with the least cultural bias and to use teaching methods that have proven especially appropriate for children and adolescents from culturally different backgrounds.

Attitudes include developing positive outlooks and values, creating culturally appropriate learning environments, and modeling for children respect and concern for all people. See Chapter 10 for a more detailed analysis of effective teaching behaviors in multicultural settings.

Challenges of Designing Multicultural Education Programs

History constantly reminds us how many people have been on the receiving end of cruel and inhumane treatment primarily because of cultural differences. Just a few examples include the injustices that American Indians and their land suffered at the hands of colonists and other immigrants; the racism and discrimination in education, employment, and housing that have affected the progress of African and Hispanic Americans for centuries; and the cruel treatment of Asian Americans upon their arrival in the United States. Twenty-first-century educators face the challenge of molding a more humane and equitable society by providing multicultural education programs that teach respect for cultural differences. They have the opportunity to address the need for positive cultural identities and respond with decisive action to the often disastrous effects of racism and stereotyping.

Although considerable racism and discrimination continue to exist and to restrain minority entrance into mainstream America, the turn of the century can be a

■ ■ ■ ■ ■ ▬▬▬▬▬▬▬▬

FOLLOW THROUGH 1.5
ACQUIRING KNOWLEDGE, SKILLS, AND ATTITUDES

Most teachers trained in the past ten to fifteen years have had experience with multicultural education because state and national accrediting associations have required such training. Other teachers, however, probably graduated before the required training, and some may have graduated from programs that provided only the minimum. How might a teacher develop the knowledge, skills, and attitudes necessary to become an effective educator in multicultural situations? Specifically, how might the teacher acquire such knowledge, skills, and attitudes?

■ ■ ■ ■ ■

FOLLOW THROUGH 1.6
CHANGING ATTITUDES THROUGH MULTICULTURAL EDUCATION

Several areas that multicultural education programs need to address include: (1) teaching respect for cultural differences, (2) addressing the need for positive cultural identities, and (3) responding appropriately to racism, stereotyping, and all forms of injustice and discrimination. These are indeed lofty goals and will be more difficult to implement than to espouse. Choose at least one of the three topics and list four or five ways to achieve effective implementation. Name several other areas that you think should be included with these three.

time for recognition and acceptance of cultural diversity. Factors and events that may contribute to such recognition include the increasing numbers of people from culturally diverse backgrounds, the efforts directed at children and adolescents in elementary and secondary schools (e.g., multicultural education courses); the multicultural emphasis of the National Council for Accreditation of Teacher Education; the increasing recognition that the nation actually benefits from cultural diversity; and increasing numbers of organizations working to instill cultural pride.

Ethnocentrism

Ethnocentrism is the belief that one's own cultural ways are not only valid and superior to those of others but also universally applicable in evaluating human behavior (Hernandez, 1989, p. 25). People with strong ethnocentric attitudes and beliefs—especially unconscious ones—may have difficulty appreciating and accepting the range of cultural differences that exist in societies (Hernandez, 1989).

Because culture influences the way we think, feel, and act, it is our means of judging the world (Gollnick & Chinn, 2002). Culture becomes the only natural way to function in the world. It gives us the notion that our own common sense is the norm for common sense in other cultures of the world. As a result, we evaluate other cultures by our cultural standards and beliefs and find it virtually impossible to view another culture as separate from our own.

In essence, ethnocentrism is a universal characteristic in which one views one's own cultural traits as natural, correct, and superior and perceives those of others' cultures as odd or inferior (Gollnick & Chinn, 2002).

Case Study 1.4 examines the problem of ethnocentrism and suggests several ways to address it.

The challenge for educators in multicultural situations is to understand ethnocentrism, to recognize its dangers, and to respond appropriately. Textbooks and other instructional materials can perpetuate ethnocentrism in subtle ways that educators may find difficult to recognize. Because we are likely to accept without question a perspective consistent with our own vantage point, attitudes, and values, we may not even be aware that another cultural perspective exists (Gollnick & Chinn, 2002).

■ ■ ■ ■ ■

FOLLOW THROUGH 1.7
ADDRESSING ETHNOCENTRISM

Belief in the superiority of and universal applicability of one's culture is the direct cause of considerable injustice and discrimination. In all cultures are people who believe their culture is the "best" or the standard by which to evaluate others. List several ways to convince people to consider their enthnocentric beliefs. What could you do to get them to engage in an objective examination of their cultural beliefs?

■ ■ ■ ■ ■

CASE STUDY 1.4
REDUCING ETHNOCENTRISM

People all too often believe that their culture and cultural traditions are "correct" and that those of all others are "wrong." Dr. Farnsworth (let's call him) was one of these people. He either misunderstood or was unwilling to accept that people from culturally diverse backgrounds have different opinions of what is important, different perceptions of immediate and extended families, and different degrees of allegiance to the elderly. Such opinions and perceptions may have become ingrained early in Dr. Farnsworth. He never considered his ethnocentrism objectively.

Educators like Dr. Farnsworth and those who teach ethnocentric children and adolescents should take action. First, educators must address their own ethnocentrism and that of their colleagues. Second, they must seek ways to reduce their own ethnocentrism and that of their colleagues and students. Although reducing ethnocentrism is difficult, educators can use several approaches to further this goal with children and adolescents.

1. Instill in children and adolescents the idea that one should not consider cultural differences right or wrong, superior or inferior.
2. Arrange teaching and learning situations (e.g., cooperative learning and cross-age tutoring) in which learners of varying cultures can have first-hand experiences with each other.
3. Model acceptance of and respect for all people.
4. Respond appropriately to statements indicating a lack of understanding or acceptance of cultural differences.
5. Encourage respect for all differences—cultural and ethnic, socioeconomic, differences in ability/disability, gender, and other characteristics that contribute to diversity.

Developing Positive Cultural Identities

Identity is a person's sense of place in the world; it is the meaning we attach to ourselves in the broader context of life. Identity answers questions such as "Who am I?" and "Who am I to be?"

It is important for educators to show children and adolescents that people may have several identities at once; that is, an individual might be Hispanic American, a member of any of the Spanish-speaking cultures, someone's brother, a Catholic, and an inhabitant of a specific geographic region in the United States.

The educator's first challenge is to view students as unique individuals rather than as a homogeneous group. Educators who assume too much homogeneity among students often fail to address individual and cultural differences and then fail to provide experiences that lead to positive cultural identities.

Second, educators must understand that all individuals need to clarify personal attitudes toward their cultural and ethnic backgrounds. Educators' goals can be to teach self-acceptance, to instill in learners an acceptance and understanding of both the positive and negative attributes of their cultural groups, and to teach learners the importance of acquiring genuine pride. Individuals who have positive ethnic, national, and global identifications value their ethnic, national, and global communities highly and are proud of these identifications. They desire and are able to take actions that support and reinforce the values and norms of these communities (Banks, 1988).

In some situations, people of differing cultural backgrounds might feel they have to give up their identities in order to be accepted and successful in the majority society. Nevertheless, people of differing cultural backgrounds might not view the attitudes and behaviors of the dominant group appropriate for them. People who adopt attitudes and behaviors of the dominant group might experience an identity crisis or an internal opposition to giving up their cultural beliefs. The relationship between identity and school success can result in students believing that "for a minority person to succeed, academically, he or she must learn to think and act white" (Ogbu, 1988, p. 177).

To avoid situations in which students feel they must "act white," educators need to redesign teaching–learning experiences. Students must be able to feel that they can maintain their cultural identities and still experience school success. Educators need to demonstrate their respect for students' cultural identities, understand that students'

■ ■ ■ ■ ■

FOLLOW THROUGH 1.8
CLARIFYING MULTIPLE IDENTITIES

Ask children and adolescents to consider their identities. For example, a child or an adolescent may have a number of different and changing identities. He or she might be

- African, Asian, European, Hispanic, or American Indian (just to mention a few in a world full of national origins)
- A person of the specific cultural background
- A member of a minority group
- Male or female
- Gay or lesbian; bisexual or heterosexual
- A member of a particular school and grade
- A son or daughter, a grandchild, and a nephew or niece
- Someone's best friend
- A person with a disability

perceptions of motivation may vary with culture, and allow students to learn in cultur-ally relevant ways (i.e., working collaboratively rather than competitively). Educators must also provide curricular content and learning materials that show the contribu-tions of various cultural groups, and help students to feel they are accepted in the majority-culture school system.

Racism

Often defined as the domination of one social or ethnic group by another, racism is an ideological system used to justify discrimination by some racial groups against others. Although we continue to hope that the twenty-first century will bring greater accep-tance and recognition of cultural diversity, we must acknowledge that discrimination, racism, and bigotry continue in the United States. As victims of overt racism and dis-crimination as well as the more covert forms that often deny them employment and housing opportunities, African Americans and other minorities continue to experience inequities and inequalities. Racial injustices, perhaps not as visible as they were several decades ago, nonetheless continue to affect people's progress and well-being. Educa-tors of all cultures may have to deal with problems resulting from these realities in the United States and may have to sort through their own personal biases and long-held cultural beliefs.

Racism and its negative effects have been with us for centuries, and unfortu-nately, little evidence suggests this evil will ever be eliminated. How can multicultural education programs respond to the racism that has affected people for centuries? Multi-cultural education should not focus only on past events, it must provide an impetus for changing the future. Educators are challenged to reduce the ignorance that breeds racism and to develop and support antiracist understanding and behavior in their stu-dents. The goal of multicultural education is founded on these tenets:

1. It is worthwhile for educators to focus on the reduction of racial and ethnic prej-udice and discrimination.
2. It is appropriate for schools to teach certain humanistic values, such as the nega-tive effects of racism, prejudice, and discrimination.
3. It is possible to reduce racial and ethnic prejudice and discrimination through ap-propriate educational experiences (Bennett, 1986).

White Privilege

"White privilege" can be defined as "unearned assets" (Lucal, 1996, p. 247) that help whites in all daily activities. Jackson refers to white privilege as a club that only enrolls certain people at birth, without their consent, and brings them up according to rules and expectations (Jackson, 1999). White privilege is an entrenched and powerful sys-tem that makes itself appear natural and benign and therefore perpetuates itself (Vera, Feagin, & Gordon, 1995).

Both historically and in contemporary society, the relationships between racial and ethnic groups in the United States are framed within a context of unequal power. People of European descent generally assume the power to claim the land, claim the resources, and claim the language. They even claim the right to frame the culture and identity of who we are as Americans. Sleeter (2000/2001) noted that even now, people of European descent, particularly the wealthy, continue to benefit from white privilege. Sleeter admits that she also knows white people who are disenfranchised in many ways (Sleeter, 2000/2001).

White privilege brings several advantages. Whites can feel confident when they look at the newspaper or television that they will see other whites. Having white skin allows people to assimilate into the dominant culture in a way that most people of color cannot. Whites are fairly sure they will not be followed or harassed in a store. Having white skin protects people from degrading, distasteful experiences. In general, whites do not have to spend the psychological effort or economic resources recovering from others' prejudices (Lucal, 1996). Whites accept the dominant culture simply as a given, a perspective that obscures and reproduces unequal power relations (Vera et al., 1995).

Examples of preferences shown for being white include "flesh"-colored bandages (Lucal, 1996, p. 247), "nude" or "natural" (Pence & Fields, 1999, p. 151) white hose color and "natural" (Pence & Fields, 1999, p. 151) hair, portrayed as shoulder length with a gentle curl (Pence & Fields, 1999).

Race for many whites is invisible, just as gender is for men, sexuality for heterosexuals, and class for the middle class (Lucal, 1996). Since they personify the cultural categories privileged in Western cultures as human, those who are white, male, and heterosexual can think of themselves as individuals (Lucal, 1996). Some people argue that not viewing oneself as having a race is also an example of privilege. Members of the dominant group use race to distinguish others from themselves and thus ascribe race only to others.

Most white Americans either do not think about their whiteness or do not consider it a privilege (Vera et al., 1995). Racial privilege is lived but not seen. White people are often unaware or unwilling to acknowledge that they are privileged (Willis & Lewis, 1999). Still, white privilege exists regardless of a particular white person's attitudes. A white skin in the United States opens many doors, regardless of whether the whites themselves approve of the way dominance has been given to them (Lucal, 1996). White people often deny the suggestion that privilege exists. In order for an individual to deny something, he or she must be aware that it exists (Jackson, 1999). White people often fail to understand the privileges and advantages of their racial membership in a dominant cultural group.

Once white people recognize their advantages, they need to acknowledge that institutionalized inequality exists and favors them. In fact, some white people see inequality only as a black or Latino/a issue. Others think that because they are white, they do not have anything to add to discussions on racial issues. Many race- and ethnicity-based privileges are invisible to and taken for granted by most whites and even some people of color (Pence & Fields, 1999). Racial inequality is explained in ways that do not implicate white society; white responsibility for the persistence of racism is obscured. As a result, whites can look at racial discrimination with detachment (Lucal, 1996).

There needs to be some effort for people of European descent "to unlearn practices and tenets that sustained White dominance" (Palmer, 2000, p. 131). The goal should be for whites to recognize some of the institutional elements of their dominant racial position and to adopt a vision of a community without white dominance (Palmer, 2000).

Stereotypes, Prejudices, and Generalizations

Stereotyping can be defined as holding attitudes toward a person or group that supposedly characterize or describe an entire age group, gender, race, or religion. It is discussed in more detail in Chapter 2. Stereotypes produce a generalized mental picture that usually results in a judgment (negative or positive) of a person or an entire culture.

It is imperative that educators approach all stereotypes with skepticism and acknowledge that most are based on prejudice—like or dislike, approval or disapproval of a culture or even an age group. Recognizing that stereotypes all too often contribute to people's benefiting from or being victims of discrimination, effective multicultural educators seek to understand and respond appropriately to others' and their own beliefs about people.

How can educators counter biases and stereotypes? How can teachers design multicultural education programs to encourage understanding and reduce stereotypical beliefs?

1. Educators should be aware of their own biases and stereotypes.
2. Educators should have equal, high expectations of all students, whatever their cultural background.
3. Educators should examine and confront the biases and stereotypes their students hold.
4. Educators should ensure that library materials and other instructional materials portray characters in a realistic, nonsexist, nonracist, nonstereotypical manner.
5. Educators should arrange heterogeneous class mixes that allow students an opportunity to build long-term, sustained interethnic and interracial relationships.
6. Educators should provide role-playing situations and simulation activities that allow students a better understanding of their own stereotypes (Garcia, 1984).

Cultural stereotypes and generalizations have the potential to severely damage interpersonal counseling and the outcome of educational efforts. Whatever one's prejudice—that all learners from different cultural backgrounds are underachievers or that all adolescents are involved in drugs and sex—stereotypes and generalizations can be detrimental to learners, educators, and the student–teacher relationship. Too often, cultural stereotypes and generalizations are considered "facts" and become the basis for professional decisions that affect people's lives.

■ ■ ■ ■ ■ ▬▬▬▬▬▬▬▬▬▬▬▬▬▬▬▬▬▬▬▬▬▬▬

FOLLOW THROUGH 1.9
CLARIFYING STEREOTYPES

List several stereotypes that people might harbor about each other. How do you think these stereotypes originated? Is there any objective basis for them? How might such stereotypes affect educational decisions? List several ways educators can gain a better understanding of people rather than rely on stereotypical generalizations.

Myths and Realities

We must eliminate myths and misconceptions that influence attitudes and actions toward those who are culturally different. Examples of current myths and misconceptions include both negative and positive stereotypes:

> All children of the same ethnic background have the same needs and intellectual abilities.
>
> All children who speak broken English or a dialect are intellectually deficient.
>
> All minorities are disadvantaged, lazy, and on welfare.
>
> All Asian American children are academically gifted.
>
> All minorities are inferior.

Other myths and misconceptions exist about people from different cultural and socioeconomic backgrounds. Clearly, cultural stereotyping tends to encourage negative attitudes about oneself and others and diminishes perception and appreciation of individual cultures.

Understanding Learners from Culturally Different Backgrounds

Recognizing the diversity in cultural backgrounds challenges all educators, especially those with a powerful sense of ethnocentrism and a steadfast belief that their culture is superior to others. Prejudiced educators may assume that learners should surrender their unique cultural values and beliefs.

All educators must understand individual learners and cultural diversity. Professionals who have a genuine caring attitude are on the right track, but they must also understand learners' families, language, religion, and other significant aspects of their lives. Educators are continually challenged to learn what it is like to be a child or adolescent in a specific culture, how it feels to attend a school that often appears to have strange rules and expectations, and how it feels to experience communication problems. Educators can meet the challenge by

1. Reading textbooks, journal articles, Internet articles, and other material on cultural diversity and teaching and learning in multicultural settings
2. Requesting information from organizations that disseminate objective information and promote various cultures
3. Meeting on a first-hand basis learners and their families (perhaps in their homes) to gain a better understanding of what it means to be a learner from a different cultural background
4. Attending conferences that focus on cultural diversity and working with children and adolescents from various cultures
5. Reading about cultural diversity in books and magazines written primarily for children and adolescents

CONTROVERSIAL ISSUES IN
MULTICULTURAL EDUCATION

We examine multicultural education as a concept in more detail in Chapter 14, but we must explain several issues at this point. Although the last several decades have seen multicultural education emerging as a means of promoting understanding, acceptance, and goodwill among people, it is somewhat ironic that some circles have not whole-heartedly accepted multicultural programs. In some cases, multicultural education has evoked criticism and controversy. It is important for educators to recognize several controversial areas and the claims of the critics of multicultural education.

Serious limitations plague the various approaches to multicultural education. Education for the culturally different is basically a condescending approach; it assumes that a student's failure in school results from cultural differences. Education about cultural differences is designed to teach their value, an understanding of the concept of culture, and acceptance of others' differences. It also leads, ironically, to a kind of stereotyping that ignores similarities among all groups and neglects differences within any one group. Also, multicultural education has underestimated the impact of racism; one cannot assume that developing ethnic literacy and cultural appreciation will end racism, prejudice, and discrimination.

A second criticism of multicultural education is based on the belief that in the United States, society does not promote sufficient love and interpersonal caring for a fulfilling existence (Sleeter & Grant, 1999). This criticism holds that by emphasizing cognitive knowledge about cultural groups over the exploration of interpersonal feelings multicultural education becomes misdirected. Although multicultural education might provide students a broad knowledge base, educators must also stress and experience interpersonal relationships in order to effect change in attitudes and prejudices (Sleeter & Grant, 1999).

A third criticism arises because the words *culture*, *race*, and *class* have multiple interpretations. Some people perceive these words as accusatory, connoting prejudice, fears of job or housing discrimination, and isolation and alienation from the larger society. Ramsey (1987) wrote:

> One Head Start teacher talked about the resistance of her low-income white parents whenever she said the word *multicultural*. It appeared from the parents' comments that the term meant glorifying "those people who get all the jobs and services." Because the teacher knew the community and was aware of the controversies and cutbacks related to jobs and welfare, she understood that, before the parents could hear anything positive about other groups of people, they had to explore and share their own feelings of economic and social threat. After some of their anger was dissipated, she tried to help them feel more personally powerful and optimistic, through activities designed to foster their feelings of self-appreciation and confidence. After several sessions, the parents were more receptive to the idea of multicultural education. (p. 176)

Ramsey (1987) also pointed out that some parents who identify with mainstream society feel threatened by the arrival of different people and may resent schools' efforts to have their children think positively about these groups. Responsive educators recognize that these problematic situations have the potential to limit the success of

■ ■ ■ ■ ■ ▬▬▬▬▬▬▬▬▬▬▬▬▬▬▬▬▬▬▬▬▬▬▬▬▬▬▬▬▬▬▬▬▬▬▬▬▬▬

FOLLOW THROUGH 1.10
DETERMINING CONTROVERSIAL ISSUES

What other controversial issues surround multicultural education? Do you think the definition should embrace sexual orientation and disabling conditions? Should it include European Americans? Is it discriminatory to unrepresented groups? How might the issues you have selected be resolved? How do unresolved issues affect the progress of multicultural education?

multicultural programs. They also realize the crucial need for planning appropriate ways to help change parental and community attitudes.

SUMMING UP

Educators planning and implementing multicultural education programs should remember to:

1. Address the wrongs of the past, such as racism, prejudice, and discrimination, but maintain the primary focus on the present understanding, respect, and acceptance of people of differing cultural backgrounds.
2. Consider multicultural education as an emerging concept that will continue to evolve as necessary to meet the needs of a society that is becoming increasingly diverse culturally.
3. Transmit facts and knowledge (including an awareness of cultural diversity) to help learners develop the skills necessary to interrelate positively with people of culturally diverse backgrounds.
4. Consider a total school curricular approach that integrates multicultural education in all teaching and learning situations.
5. Recognize multicultural education as an endeavor that has received considerable recognition and respect. Several areas of controversy and criticism continue to exist, however, and deserve attention.
6. Direct attention to issues such as sexism, agism, and classism, create more positive attitudes toward the disabled, and eliminate the racism, prejudice, and discrimination that plague U.S. society.
7. Address the ethnocentrism of learners and educators both.
8. Insist on multicultural education programs in all schools, rather than just in schools that have a culturally diverse student population.

SUGGESTED LEARNING ACTIVITIES

1. Outline a multicultural education program for a school that has a population 50 percent European American, 25 percent African American, 20 percent Hispanic American, and

approximately 5 percent other culturally diverse groups. Respond specifically to such areas as the extent of emphasis on each culture; a determination of the content of the program and examination of attitudes; appropriate in-service sessions for administration, faculty, and staff; appropriate curriculum and instruction methods and materials; and methods of assessing the program.

2. Read several definitions of multicultural education and then, on the basis of these definitions and your opinions, write your own definition of multicultural education. Should multicultural education include more than just "culture," for example, and should the definition include diversity in religion, gender, social class, and sexual orientation?

3. As a potential or practicing educator in our increasingly multicultural society, how should you attempt to address racism? Do you think you have ever been a victim of racism? Do you address racism when you see or hear it, or do you just ignore it? Name three or four ways you could help reduce racism in your school.

SUGGESTIONS FOR COLLABORATIVE EFFORTS

Form groups of three or four people that, if possible, represent our nation's cultural and gender diversity. Working collaboratively, focus your group's attention toward the following efforts:

1. In your group, discuss the following statement: "There are more differences in social class than there are differences in culture. For example, middle- or upper-class people of various cultures may be more alike (e.g., in terms of preferences in food, clothing, customs, traditions, and religion) than people of a given culture or race. In essence, social class may be the distinguishing factor among people." Have several members of your group interview people from different social classes and several people from different cultural backgrounds to compare and contrast differences and similarities.

2. Have one or two of your group members visit a school to examine and compare the multicultural education programs. How do schools differ in philosophy, commitment, approaches (unit or total curriculum integration), goals and objectives, treatment of holidays, and overall attempts to have a truly "multicultural" school?

3. Select a school known for its diverse student population. Have your group formulate an instrument (survey or checklist) to assess the school's efforts in multicultural education. Make sure it examines the cultural, racial, and ethnic composition of faculty, staff, and other professional personnel; whether organization and grouping methods segregate learners by race; and whether the curriculum and instruction materials reflect cultural diversity.

EXPANDING YOUR HORIZONS: ADDITIONAL
JOURNAL READINGS AND BOOKS

Gay, G. (2000). Multicultural teacher education for the 21st century. *Teacher Educator, 36*(1), 1–16.
Gay presents a strong argument for teacher education programs that prepare European Americans to teach ethnically diverse students of color, especially the fear of diversity and dealing with race and racism.

Palmer, P. (2000). Recognizing racial privilege: White girls and boys at National Conference of Christians and Jews summer camps. *Oral History Review, 27*(2), 129–155.

Palmer looks at the changed circumstances and moral climate brought into being by the civil rights and racial freedom movements, which sought to unlearn practices and tenets that sustained white dominance.

Payne, C. R., & Welsh, B. H. (2000). The progressive development of multicultural education before and after the 1960s: A theoretical framework. *Teacher Educator, 36*(1), 29–48.

These authors offer many interesting points as they explain the development of multicultural education.

Rodriguez, A. P. (2000). Adjusting the multicultural lens. *Race, Gender, and Class, 7*(3), 150–177.

Rodriguez maintained multicultural education is "ripe for attack, demonization, exaltation, and dismissal" (p. 150) and called for consideration of feminist, postmodern writers in discussions of identity.

Singer, A. (2001). Wanted: Theories and research that explain privilege and oppression in education and U.S. society. *Race, Gender, and Class, 8*(1), 27–38.

Singer discusses the social construction of race and ethnicity, race and class, whiteness and white privilege, unity of the oppressed, and dealing with racism.

Warren, S. R. (2002). Stories from the classrooms: How expectations and efficacy of diverse teachers affect the academic performance of children in poor urban schools. *Educational Horizons, 80*(3), 109–116.

Warren describes a study designed to determine whether teachers hold the same expectations of all students, especially students of color and lower socioeconomic status, and also whether they think they can make a difference in these students' lives.

CHAPTER TWO

AN INCREASINGLY MULTICULTURAL SOCIETY

Understanding the material and activities in this chapter will help the reader to:

- Grasp the historical and contemporary perspectives toward cultural diversity—that is, the melting pot and salad bowl ideologies, respectively
- Provide a cultural classification of populations presently living in the United States
- Explain concepts such as culture, ethnicity, race, socioeconomic status, and gender; and explain why understanding these concepts is important when working with children and adolescents from various cultures
- Explicate perspectives toward cultural diversity such as cultural deficit and cultural mismatch and provide a rationale for adopting a positive and enriching perspective that appreciates cultural difference or cultural diversity
- Explain how racism, discrimination, and stereotypes can hurt children and adolescents who are culturally different; and how elementary and secondary schools can provide appropriate responses
- Provide concrete evidence that the United States is becoming increasingly culturally diverse, and explain the roles of elementary and secondary schools in addressing the needs of learners from differing cultural backgrounds

OVERVIEW

The increasing cultural diversity of the United States challenges elementary- and secondary-school educators to understand differing values, customs, and traditions and to provide responsive multicultural experiences for all learners. The melting pot theory, once thought to be a model of the assimilation of immigrants into the United States, obviously is not valid. People do not lose their differences when they immigrate to the United States. In fact, the diversity of their cultural backgrounds deeply enriches the nation.

The melting pot theory is no longer considered a model, much less a means of achieving a just, equal, and accepting society. Educators need a sound understanding of cultural, ethnic, racial, socioeconomic, gender, and individual differences, especially in light of the wealth of cultural diversity of the nation that increases daily. This chapter examines cultural diversity in the United States and suggests that responsive multicultural education programs can address many challenges.

HISTORICAL AND CONTEMPORARY PERSPECTIVES

The melting pot metaphor used to describe the cultural composition of the United States, does not, in reality, describe it accurately. People who immigrate to the United States are increasingly reluctant to forsake their cultural traditions and values to become like mainstream society. Asians and Hispanics are often reluctant to give up ethnic customs and traditions in favor of middle-class European American habits that might appear to contradict beliefs they were taught early in life. The United States is hardly a melting pot resulting in a homogeneous group of people; many people continue to hold onto Old World traditions and cherished values.

Some cultural assimilation has undoubtedly taken place as people have adopted majority culture customs and standards. Generally speaking, however, the melting pot concept has given way to a perspective in which each group holds onto its unique identity and culture. This latter perspective is more realistic and far more humane. Whether they arrive from Southeast Asia, one of the Spanish-speaking countries, or Europe, people should not have to forsake their cultural heritages and traditions. Although some degree of assimilation might be necessary to survive economically and to cope with the challenges of everyday life, people can nevertheless hold fast to time-honored cultural traditions and customs. The more contemporary perspective views differences not as elements to be "melted away," but as personal characteristics that enrich U.S. society.

Table 2.1 shows a breakdown of cultural groups and documents in an increasingly multicultural society. We will give more detailed information with the discussion of each cultural group.

A survey in *Newsweek* revealed that attitudes toward immigration are changing. For example, 59 percent of people in the past thought immigration was a good thing, and 31 percent considered it a bad thing. However, 60 percent of people today think immigration is a bad thing, compared with 29 percent who consider it good. Sixty-six percent of respondents felt that immigrants seek to maintain their identity, while only

TABLE 2.1   Selected Cultural Groups in the United States (in thousands)

GROUP	POPULATION NUMBERS	PROJECTED POPULATION NUMBERS 2025	PROJECTED POPULATION NUMBERS 2050
American Indians, Eskimos, Aleuts	2,434	3,399	4,405
African Americans	35,307	47,089	59,239
Arab Americans	3,000	Unavailable	Unavailable
Asian Americans	11,157	22,020	37,589
European Americans	226,232	265,306	302,453
Hispanic Americans	32,440	61,433	98,229

Source: U.S. Bureau of the Census. (2001). *Statistical abstracts of the United States* (121th ed.). Washington, DC; demographics, www.aaiusa.org/demographics.html, retrieved September 18, 2002.

■ ■ ■ ■ ■

FOLLOW THROUGH 2.1
EXAMINING YOUR FEELINGS

Clearly, as Morganthau's *Newsweek* survey showed, attitudes toward immigration are changing. People do not feel as positive about immigration as they did in the past. Do you think these changes of attitudes are justified? How do you perceive immigration? Do you think it should be tougher for people to immigrate to the United States? Offer several possible reasons that attitudes might be growing more negative toward immigration. How might the change in attitudes toward immigration affect attitudes toward children and adolescents (e.g., the push to end or limit affirmative action or to end bilingual programs)?

20 percent still felt that the nation is a melting pot. Also, 62 percent think immigrants take jobs from U.S. workers; 78 percent felt immigrants work hard and accept jobs that Americans do not want; and 59 percent felt that immigrants end up on welfare, thus raising taxes for Americans (Morganthau, 1993).

Cultural pluralism can pose problems for educators who, on the one hand, are to infuse multiculturalism into their subject matter and, on the other hand, are to produce graduates who are culturally literate in the traditional sense. Teachers also face difficult choices among many topics and curriculum materials, which may take either assimilationist or pluralistic perspectives. Table 2.2 shows the five states with the largest percent of a specified cultural group.

Case Study 2.1 shows how Mrs. Rowe helped the teachers in her school better understand the advantages of adopting a "salad bowl" perspective toward cultural diversity.

THE CULTURALLY DIFFERENT: DEMOGRAPHICS

Present trends and projections for the United States indicate that the influx and growth of diverse cultural groups will continue. While many different cultural groups enter the United States each year, space allows us to mention only representative

TABLE 2.2   Five States with Largest Percent of a Specified Group

EUROPEAN AMERICAN	AFRICAN AMERICAN	ASIAN AMERICAN	AMERICAN INDIAN, ALASKAN NATIVE	HISPANIC AMERICAN
ME (97%)	DC (60%)	HI (42%)	AK (16%)	NM (42%)
VT (97%)	MS (36%)	CA (11%)	NM (10%)	CA (32%)
NH (96%)	LA (33%)	NJ (6%)	SD (8%)	TX (32%)
WV (95%)	SC (30%)	NY (6%)	OK (8%)	AZ (25%)
IA (94%)	GA (29%)	WA (6%)	MT (6%)	NV (20%)

Source: U.S. Bureau of the Census. (2001). *Statistical abstracts of the United States* (121th ed.). Washington, DC.

■ ■ ■ ■ ■

CASE STUDY 2.1
TOWARD A "SALAD BOWL" PERSPECTIVE

Mrs. Rowe, a fourth-grade teacher, realized early that her school expected learners to assimilate middle-class European American values and customs. Textbooks emphasized middle-class white characters while downplaying other cultural groups; teaching styles and instructional strategies addressed the needs of white learners. School rules and policies, however, applied to all learners; school environments did little to celebrate cultural or gender diversity; and the ethnic composition of the administration, faculty, and staff indicated that the school system had not sought to employ professionals from a variety of cultures. Learners from culturally different backgrounds who were unable or unwilling to adopt middle-class white values suffered the consequences of low achievement, poor self-esteem, and a feeling of nonacceptance in the school.

Mrs. Rowe thought of ways to move the school toward a more "salad bowl" perspective, in which learners from all cultures could retain cultural values and traditions and in which the school could address the needs of all learners. Mrs. Rowe sought the administration's advice and support. The administration then formed a committee consisting of Mrs. Rowe, a speech correctionist, a special educator, a guidance counselor, several classroom teachers, and several parents representing different cultural groups.

The committee decided to take deliberate action to make the entire school more responsive to learners from differing cultural backgrounds. They made plans to examine all phases of the school: textbooks and other curricular materials, the overall curriculum, instructional strategies, the efforts of special school personnel, the school environment, and efforts designed to celebrate diversity. Mrs. Rowe and the committee realized the need to be realistic—changing the school would take time, commitment, and the efforts of all educators. They had, however, taken two crucial steps: The school had realized the need for change and decided to take planned and deliberate action.

groups. Interested readers are referred to the many readily available Census documents that provide a more comprehensive examination of many cultural groups.

Hodgkinson (2000/2001), in Implementing Research 2.1, looks at the changing demographics of our nation and schools and offers demographic tips for teachers.

Maintaining that diversity is unevenly distributed in the United States, Hodgkinson (2000/2001) wrote that the 65 percent increase in diverse populations will be absorbed in only about 230 of our 3,068 counties. California, Texas, and Florida will get about three-fifths of the population increase. Although we talk of "minority majorities" (p. 9), it is possible in only a few counties (Hodgkinson, 2000/2001).

African Americans

As Table 2.1 indicates, the African American population totaled approximately 33,503,000 in 1997. Although most of the population growth (percentage increase shown in the right-hand column of Table 2.1) resulted from a natural increase, immigration from Caribbean and African countries also contributed to the growth.

■ ■ ■ ■ ■

IMPLEMENTING RESEARCH 2.1
CHANGING DEMOGRAPHICS

Hodgkinson (2000/2001) maintains that the field of demographics over the last two decades has become vitally important to teachers and education policymakers. He explains that race, religion, age, and fertility are unevenly distributed in the United States. For example, we hear about increases in school enrollment, but only about five states will have a 20 percent increase in school enrollments.

Hodgkinson looked at a number of demographic facts, but we will look only at his observations about race. His conclusions concerning race included: First, the nature of race is changing, that is, about 65 percent of the U.S. population growth in the next two decades will be "minority" (p. 8), particularly Hispanic and Asian immigrants. These groups have higher fertility rates than Caucasians, whose fertility level is too low even to replace the current population. Second, the 2000 Census allows people to check as many race boxes as they wish. Questions arise such as whether the person counts as two or more people or only one. Can a person be counted as white for housing surveys and black for civil rights actions? Third, 3 million black Hispanics in the United States, mostly dark-skinned Spanish speakers from the Caribbean, checked *black* (italics Hodgkinson's) on the Census, because Hispanic is not a race. Fourth, at least 40 percent of all Americans have had some racial mixing in the last three generations, but only 2.4 percent admit it on Census surveys.

IMPLEMENTING THE RESEARCH
Hodgkinson offers several demographic tips for teachers:

- Check to see what country Hispanic students' families are from, what language is used in the home, and whether the parents speak English and how well.
- Be patient if a child will not look you in eye in the first week of school—discuss in private with the student.
- Learn which students are new to the area, to determine whether they need help getting settled.
- Strive for a "culture fair" (p. 11) rather than a "color-blind" classroom.
- Give close attention to students who receive free lunches, because they might not get enough to eat on the weekends.
- Try to use as many visual presentations as possible, because pictures convey meanings that words do not.

Source: Hodgkinson, H. (2000/2001). Educational demographics: What teachers should know. *Educational Leadership, 58*(4), 6–11.

The African American birthrate is slightly above replacement levels (the death rate) and will bring the total African American population from 11.5 percent of the total U.S. population in 1980 to 13 percent in 2020 (The Hispanic Policy Development Project, 1997).

When the government took the first Census in 1790, African Americans in the United States numbered about 760,000. By 1860, as the Civil War began, the African American population had increased to 4.4 million. By 1900, population numbers had

■ ■ ■ ■ ■

FOLLOW THROUGH 2.2
DETERMINING PREFERRED DESIGNATIONS

To show respect for cultural backgrounds and to promote cultural identities, educators need to call African Americans (who have been called black, black American, Afro-American, Negro, and colored) by the term that best describes their cultural heritage. Some do not like *African American* because they feel a stronger allegiance to the United States than to Africa; others respect *African American* because it reflects their cultural heritage. It is essential for educators (indeed all people) to show genuine respect by referring to people by the term they prefer. Survey a number of African Americans to determine their preferred term.

doubled and reached 8.8 million. By 1950, population numbers of African Americans reached the 15 million mark, and they were close to 27 million in 1980.

Table 2.3 categorizes the African American school-age population by age.

African Americans for the most part live in metropolitan areas—nationally, 84 percent. At least 95 percent of all African Americans in the Northeast, Midwest, and West regions live in metropolitan areas. The ten cities with the largest African American population in 1990 included New York, Chicago, Detroit, Philadelphia, Los Angeles, Houston, Baltimore, Washington, Memphis, and New Orleans. The 1990 Census indicated that African Americans live in every state of the Union, from about 2,000 in Vermont to 2.9 million in New York. Sixteen states in that Census had an African American population of 1 million or more. California and New York each have African American populations exceeding 2 million (U.S. Bureau of the Census, 1993b).

American Indians

A number of different names have been used to identify the first Americans: "Original Americans," "Native People," "American Indians," and "Native Americans."

The most reliable population numbers, which the U.S. Bureau of the Census supplies, include Eskimos and Aleuts in the American Indian population. There have been estimates of American Indian population numbers since the founding of the nation, but it was not until 1860 that the federal government actually counted American

TABLE 2.3   African American Children and Adolescents (in thousands)

AGE	POPULATION 2000	PROJECTED POPULATION 2005	PROJECTED POPULATION 2010
Under 5 years	2,792	2,907	3,103
5–9 years	3,086	2,829	2,953
10–14 years	3,172	3,246	2,977
15–19 years	3,053	3,370	3,444

Source: U.S. Bureau of the Census. (2001). *Statistical abstracts of the United States* (121st ed.). Washington, DC.

Indians, including them in the Census only if they had left the reservations and were living among other Americans. The 1890 Census was the first to obtain a complete count of American Indians throughout the country.

Data from the U.S. Bureau of the Census report the American Indian population at approximately 1.95 million in 1997. Projections suggest that the American Indian population will reach 4.6 million by 2050.

Nearly one-half of the American Indian population lived west of the Mississippi River in the 1990 Census. Two of every three American Indians (including Eskimos and Aleuts) live in ten states. Of these states, only North Carolina, Michigan, and New York are east of the Mississippi River. As of 1990, more than half of the American Indian population lived in just six states: Oklahoma, California, Arizona, New Mexico, Alaska, and Washington.

Table 2.4 categorizes the American Indian school-age population by age and gender.

Arab Americans

Arab Americans constitute a diverse, multifaceted, productive, and growing community. Arab Americans have settled in all fifty states and the District of Columbia, but the heaviest concentrations are in California, Michigan, Ohio, Illinois, Massachusetts, New York, New Jersey, Pennsylvania, Virginia, and Texas. They are considered one of the fastest growing groups of immigrants, settling mainly in big cities. Michigan has one of the largest Arab American communities, with over 250,000 in the Detroit–Dearborn area alone. Also, New York and California have the largest and most visible Arab American populations in the United States. Most Arab Americans would say that the "Arab Nation" includes all people who speak the Arabic language and claim a link with the nomadic tribes of Arabia, whether by descent, affiliation, or by appropriating the traditional ideals of human excellence and standards of beauty. This definition includes reference to a historical process that began with the preaching by Mohammed of a religion called Islam, a process in which all Arabs play a leading part and by virtue of which they can claim a unique role in the history of mankind (Wertsman, 2001).

Arab Americans constitute an ethnicity made up of several waves of immigrants from the Arabic-speaking countries of southwestern Asia and North Africa. Their re-

TABLE 2.4   American Indian Children and Adolescents (in thousands)

AGE	POPULATION 2000	PROJECTED POPULATION 2005	PROJECTED POPULATION 2010
Under 5 years	206	222	240
5–9 years	212	212	232
10–14 years	254	238	237
15–19 years	239	259	242

Source: U.S. Bureau of the Census. (2001). *Statistical abstracts of the United States* (121st ed.). Washington, DC.

■ ■ ■ ■ ■ ▬▬▬▬▬▬▬▬▬▬▬▬▬▬▬▬▬▬▬▬▬▬▬▬▬▬▬▬▬▬▬

FOLLOW THROUGH 2.3
DETERMINING A SCHOOL'S DIVERSITY

Survey an elementary or secondary school in your area to determine its cultural composition. To what extent has each culture increased or decreased over the last ten years? Give several examples of how the school has responded to cultural differences. Also, give several examples of other ways the school can better address cultural diversity.

■ ■ ■ ■ ■ ▬▬▬▬▬▬▬▬▬▬▬▬▬▬▬▬▬▬▬▬▬▬▬▬▬▬▬▬▬▬▬

FOR ADDITIONAL INFORMATION
INTERNET ADDRESSES

Main
http://funnelweb.utcc.utk.edu/~csma/main.html
Provides learning opportunities for people interested in the study of multicultural societies.

ANU—Centre for Immigration
& Multicultural Studies
http://coombs.anu.edu.au/SpecialProj/CIMS/
CIMSHomePage.html   Provides information and research on social sciences and Pacific and Asian studies.

IUME: The Institute for Urban
and Minority Education
http://iume.tc.columbia.edu   Provides research to better understand the experiences of diverse urban and minority-group populations.

Asian Americans—Tables, Figures, Boxes
www.prb.org./pubs/bulletin/bu53-2/tfb.htm   Provides a summary of Asian Americans' diversity and increasing numbers.

USDLC 1995–96 Program Series
www.esc20.tenet.edu/star/prog.html   Provides information on how educators in today's classrooms of changing demographics can address cultural diversity.

gional homeland includes twenty-two Arab countries, stretching from Morocco in the west to the Arabian (Persian) Gulf in the east. Table 2.5 provides a look at the origins of Arab Americans. Unfortunately, the U.S. Census Bureau does not provide identical data for all cultural groups; however, Table 2.6 looks at selected Arab American demographics.

Although not as much is known about Arab Americans as the other populous cultural groups, there is interesting and educational information on this cultural group. Educationally, 82 percent of Arab Americans have at least a high school diploma. Those with a bachelor's degree are 36 percent, and 15 percent hold graduate degrees. Of school-age children, 7 percent are in primary school, 53.6 percent are enrolled in elementary or secondary school, and 38.5 percent are enrolled in college. Occupationally, approximately 65 percent are in the labor force; only 5.9 percent are unemployed. Nearly 73 percent of these working adults are employed in managerial, professional, technical, and sales or administrative fields. Most Arab Americans work in the private

TABLE 2.5   Arab Americans: Demographics

COUNTRY OF ORIGIN	PERCENT	COUNTRY OF ORIGIN	PERCENT
Jordan	2	Palestine	6
Syria	15	Lebanon	47
Iraq	3	Other	18
Egypt	9		

Source: Demographics, www.aaiusa.org/demographics.html, retrieved September 18, 2002.

TABLE 2.6   Arab Americans: Demographics

- 3 million Arab Americans live in all fifty states and the District of Columbia
- 66 percent of Arab Americans live in ten states
- 33 percent live in California, Michigan, and New York
- 48 percent live in twenty metro cities
- The largest Arab American populations are Los Angeles, Detroit, Chicago, and Washington, DC, respectively

Source: Demographics, www.aaiusa.org/demographics.html, retrieved September 18, 2002.

sector (77 percent); 12.4 percent are government employees. Interestingly, the majority of Arab Americans are Christian: 12 percent are Protestant, 42 percent are Catholic, 23 percent are Muslim, and 23 percent are Orthodox (demographics, www.aaiusa.org/demographics.html, retrieved September 18, 2002).

Asian Americans

The Asian American population includes a wide array of people from Asia and the Pacific Islands. Census documents include Chinese, Filipinos, Koreans, Asian Indians, Japanese, Vietnamese, Cambodians, Laotians, Hmong, and Thai people in the Asian populations. They also include people of Polynesian (Hawaiians, Samoans, Tongans, and Tahitians), Micronesian (primarily Guamanians or Chamorros but also Mariana Islanders, Marshall Islanders, Palauans and several other groups), and Melanesian (primarily the Fijian people) descent.

Asians constitute the most rapidly growing minority group percentage in the United States. It is estimated that by 2020, Asians will account for 6.5 percent of the total U.S. population (The Hispanic Policy Development Project, 1997).

In three decades, the numbers of Asians and Pacific Islanders in the United States nearly quintupled—growing from 1.5 million in 1970 to 3.7 million in 1980 to 7.3 million in 1990. The percentage of Asians and Pacific Islanders in the total population also nearly doubled during the 1980s, from 1.5 to 2.9 percent (U.S. Bureau of the Census, 1993f).

The 1990 Census counted nearly 7 million Asians living in the United States, a 99 percent increase over the 1980 count. The largest proportion of Asian Americans

■ ■ ■ ■ ■

FOLLOW THROUGH 2.4
DEVELOPING OBJECTIVE UNDERSTANDINGS

The fact that many Asian Americans have been very successful in U.S. schools and society has stereotyped them as the "model minority." Not all Asian Americans have fared equally well, however. Some experience culture-related problems, socioeconomic difficulties, and language problems. How can educators gain an accurate and objective understanding of Asian Americans (such as getting to know individual Asian groups as well as individual Asian Americans)?

were Chinese (24 percent) and Filipino (20 percent), followed by Japanese (12 percent). New immigration groups, including Laotian, Cambodian, Thai, and Hmong, each accounted for 2 percent or less of the Asians in the United States.

Immigration contributed significantly to the growth of the Asian population in the 1970s and 1980s, but the percentages who are foreign-born differ considerably from group to group. Sixty-six percent of Asians were born in foreign countries. Among Asian groups, Vietnamese, Laotian, and Cambodian groups had the highest proportion of foreign born and Japanese had the lowest proportion. Most of the Asian populations live in the West. Approximately 66 percent of Asians live in just five states: California, New York, Hawaii, Texas, and Illinois. The population is highly concentrated in California, New York, and Hawaii.

Asians had a median age of thirty years in 1990, younger than the national median of thirty-three years. Only 6 percent of the Asian population were sixty-five years old or older, compared with 13 percent of the total population. The Japanese were the eldest of the Asian populations, with a median age of thirty-six years, in part because fewer Japanese were foreign-born. The Hmong and Cambodian, with their large numbers of recent immigrants, were the youngest Asians, with a median age of thirteen years and nineteen years, respectively. In 1990, Asian males were younger than Asian females, with median ages of twenty-nine years and thirty-one years, respectively (U.S. Bureau of the Census, 1993a). Table 2.7 categorizes the Asian American school-age population by age group and gender.

TABLE 2.7   Asian American Children and Adolescents (in thousands)

AGE	POPULATION 2000	PROJECTED POPULATION 2005	PROJECTED POPULATION 2010
Under 5 years	917	1,042	1,147
5–9 years	904	1,006	1,126
10–14 years	851	1,073	1,187
15–19 years	844	957	1,187

Source: U.S. Bureau of the Census. (2001). *Statistical abstracts of the United States* (121st ed.). Washington, DC.

The Pacific Islander population of the United States shares many similarities with the other Asian populations. Hawaiians, of course, who are native to the United States, represent 58 percent of the total Pacific Islander population. Samoans and Guamanians were the next largest groups in the 1990 Census, representing 17 percent and 14 percent, respectively, followed by Tongans and Fijians, who were 5 percent and 2 percent, respectively, of all Pacific Islanders. Other Pacific Islanders such as the Palauans, Northern Mariana Islanders, and Tahitians each constituted less than one-half of 1 percent of Pacific Islander Americans (U.S. Bureau of the Census, 1993d; U.S. Bureau of the Census, 1993f).

Eighty-six percent of all Pacific Islanders live in the West. Approximately 75 percent of Pacific Islanders live in just two states, California and Hawaii. These two states had more than 100,000 Pacific Islanders each. Other states with significant populations of Pacific Islanders include Washington, Oregon, Texas, and Utah. Also, like the other Asian populations, Pacific Islanders are relatively young. They had a median age of twenty-five years in 1990. Only about 4 percent were sixty-five years old and over, compared with 6 percent of all Asians and Pacific Islanders and 13 percent of the entire population. Hawaiians have the oldest median age among Pacific Islanders, twenty-six years, followed by Guamanians with a median age of twenty-five. Samoans, at twenty-two years, had the youngest median age among Pacific Islanders (U.S. Bureau of the Census, 1993d; U.S. Bureau of the Census, 1993f).

European Americans and Other Cultural Groups

European and Australian peoples also inhabit the United States, adding to its diversity. Table 2.8 provides population numbers of children and adolescents.

As the earlier discussions of cultural groups illustrated, most immigrants today come from Asia and Latin America. This pattern contrasts significantly with that of previous decades. Of the nearly 42 million people who immigrated between 1820 and 1960, for example, 34 million were European. In the forty years since then, only 2.7 percent of the 15 million immigrants entering the United States have been from Europe. In 1900, 85 percent of the immigrants were from Europe; in 1990, only 22 percent came from Europe (U.S. Bureau of the Census, 1993d). By 2050 at the latest, the majority of U.S. citizens will no longer be white. The white population is not replacing itself, and the numbers of nonwhite groups are growing at higher than replacement

TABLE 2.8   European American Children and Adolescents (in thousands)

AGE	POPULATION 2000	PROJECTED POPULATION 2005	PROJECTED POPULATION 2010
Under 5 years	15,020	15,041	15,609
5–9 years	15,566	15,074	15,127
10–14 years	15,621	16,077	15,506
15–19 years	15,744	16,405	16,804

Source: U.S. Bureau of the Census. (2001). *Statistical abstracts of the United States* (121st ed.). Washington, DC.

rates through both natural increase and immigration (The Hispanic Policy Development Project, 1997).

It is interesting to note that some cultural groups actually lost population between 1980 and 1990. Of the forty groups with more than 100,000 foreign-born people in 1990, fourteen declined in size. With the exception of Canadians, all of these groups were European. Italians, followed by Scottish, Hungarians, Germans, and Greeks had the largest declines.

Hispanic Americans

Hispanic people trace their origins to Spain, Mexico, Puerto Rico, Cuba, and many other Spanish-speaking countries of Latin America. Hispanic people share many similarities such as history, customs, the Spanish language, and sometimes country of origin; but the wide diversity within Hispanic culture requires educators to consider, whenever possible, people as individuals.

Hispanic populations have not always appeared in the Census as a separate ethnic group. In 1930, the government counted the number of Mexicans who had immigrated to the United States, and in 1940 the Census included "persons of Spanish mother tongue." The 1950 and 1960 Censuses enumerated "persons of Spanish surname." The 1970 Census asked people about their "origins," and listed several Hispanic cultures. In the 1980 and 1990 Censuses, the categories constituting people of "Spanish/Hispanic" origin included Mexican, Puerto Rican, Cuban, and "other Hispanic." The 1990 Census accounted for about thirty additional groups of Hispanic origin.

Hispanics—the most rapidly growing U.S. immigrant group in terms of absolute numbers—increased by 53 percent between 1980 and 1990. By 2015, the number of Hispanics in the United States will equal or slightly exceed the number of African Americans. It is estimated that by 2020, Asians, African Americans, and Hispanics will account for 16 percent of the total U.S. population. Today, there are 27 million Hispanics in 7.6 million households concentrated predominantly in five states—California, Texas, Florida, New York, and Illinois. By 2050, Hispanics will represent the second largest racial and ethnic group in the U.S. population—their numbers will have risen to 84 million (The Hispanic Policy Development Project, 1997).

Several factors have contributed to the tremendous increase in Hispanic population in the United States. Among them are birthrates higher than those of the rest of the population and a substantial immigration from Mexico, Central America, the Caribbean, and South America. In fact, in 1990, there were 22.4 million Hispanics in the United States, almost 9 percent of the nation's 250 million people. The Hispanic population in 1990 numbered slightly less than the entire U.S. population in 1850. Also, the Census Bureau's 1992 middle series projections suggest that rapid population growth may continue into the twenty-first century. The population could rise from 24 million in 1992 to 31 million by the year 2000, 59 million by 2030, and 81 million by 2050.

People of Hispanic heritage come from many different origins. Although Hispanic people have much in common, many differences exist between groups that deserve understanding. Interesting for educators is the number of Hispanic children and adolescents attending schools today. Table 2.9 categorizes the Hispanic American school-age population by age and gender.

TABLE 2.9   Hispanic American Children and Adolescents (in thousands)

AGE	POPULATION 2000	PROJECTED POPULATION 2005
Under 5 years	3,451	4,027
5–9 years	3,343	3,681
10–14 years	2,874	3,622
15–19 years	2,842	3,307

Source: U.S. Bureau of the Census. (2001). *Statistical abstracts of the United States* (121st ed.). Washington, DC.

UNDERSTANDING DIVERSITY

Culture

Culture can be defined in a number of ways; but recent definitions, while worded differently, basically connote similar meanings. We define *culture* as people's values, language, religion, ideals, artistic expressions, patterns of social and interpersonal relationships, and ways of perceiving, behaving, and thinking. People's basis for perceptions as well as their actual perceptions differ culturally. How we feel, think, respond, and behave reflects our cultural background.

It is important to say that all people have culture. Such a statement might appear strange, but a century or so ago *culture* was thought to be the province of only some people. Educated people, well read, literate, and knowledgeable in areas such as music, the arts, and drama had culture; those who did not were thought to lack culture. Today, we recognize that all people have culture.

People referred to as *bicultural* have competencies and can function effectively in two cultures. These people have mastered the knowledge of and are able to function effectively in two cultures. They feel comfortable in two cultures and have a strong desire to function effectively in them.

The reasons for and levels of biculturalism vary. Some African Americans, for example, learn to function effectively in the European American culture in an attempt to attain social and economic mobility during the formal working day. In their private lives, however, these same individuals may be highly African American and monocultural (Gollnick & Chinn, 2002).

■ ■ ■ ■ ■

FOLLOW THROUGH 2.5
DETERMINING "CULTURE"

Consider your culture—how many do you have? You have a "cultural background," but you also have a culture of region, sexual orientation, socioeconomic status, and professional status: Are you a preservice or an in-service teacher?

Race

Although the term *race* refers to biological differences among people, it has long been used to differentiate groups of people. Determining racial categories often proves difficult because of the wide variety of traits and characteristics people and groups share. Society has generally recognized differences between races (e.g., physical differences), but these differences satisfy only biological aspects and do not explain differences in social behavior.

There are several important points concerning race. First, despite the movements of large numbers of people from one geographic region to another and the influence of intermarriage across racial groups, the concept of race today still has a significant social meaning. Second, race contributes few insights to cultural understanding. There is seldom cultural correspondence between a person's nationality, geography, language, and religion and his or her racial category. Therefore, knowledge of a person's racial identity does not reveal much about his or her nationality, religion, and language.

Difficulties the U.S. Bureau of the Census experienced in its documents show the confusion regarding race and ethnicity. For example, the Census may ask people to define themselves in categories that are not mutually exclusive; that is, a person can have more than one racial or ethnic designation.

Ethnicity

The definition of *ethnicity* takes into consideration people's national origin, religion, race, and any combination thereof. Attributes associated with ethnicity include group image and sense of identity derived from contemporary cultural patterns; shared political and economic interests; and involuntary membership, although individual identification with the group may be optional. The extent to which individuals identify with a particular ethnic group varies considerably, and some may identify with more than one. Strong ethnic identification suggests a sharing and acceptance of ethnic group values, beliefs, behaviors, language, and ways of thinking.

The definition of ethnicity also includes a community of people within a larger society who are set apart by others or who set themselves apart primarily on the basis of racial identity and cultural characteristics such as religion, language, or tradition. The central factor is the notion of being set apart because of physical or cultural attributes or both.

Gender

The term *gender* describes masculinity and femininity—the thoughts, feelings, and behavior that identify one as either male or female (Butler & Manning, 1998). A multicultural education text would be remiss if it failed to address gender differences. Although many similarities exist between males and females, differences also exist, which educators should recognize and for which they should plan gender-appropriate educational experiences. Likewise, educators have a responsibility to clarify stereotypical beliefs about males and females.

We have included gender as a difference to be recognized in multicultural education because of the gender inequality that has long limited females' potential. While gender inequality is mostly considered during the adult years, Baunach (2001), in Gender Perspectives 2.1, maintains that gender inequality actually begins during childhood. We think that Baunach's article provides a good argument for including gender in multicultural education efforts.

How might females differ from males? Research on gender and its effects have focused mainly on health concerns, social networks, self-esteem, achievement, self-image, and sex role attitudes and behaviors.

1. Females and males report the same number of best friends; attributes they considered important in themselves and their same-sex friends differed according to sex. Males had larger social networks than females.

2. Females feel less positive about their bodies than males feel about theirs, and assign more different values than males do to different aspects of their bodies. Changes affecting the female body may make girls disappointed in their bodies. Boys, by contrast, may be less concerned with physical appearance and more interested in task mastery and effectiveness.

■ ■ ■ ■ ■ ■

GENDER PERSPECTIVES 2.1
GENDER INEQUALITY DURING CHILDHOOD

In an excellent article, Baunach proposes that women's lower status is universal, although variation exists in the character and degree of gender inequality across different societies. Gender inequality affects females and males throughout their lives. It does not suddenly materialize with entrance into adulthood. Baunach seeks to answer several questions: Is gender inequality in childhood different from gender inequality in adulthood, and if so, how is childhood inequality different?

Adults are positioned to better take advantage of available resources and use power to their advantage. Because of their age, adults have accumulated advantages over time that children have not had the opportunity to accumulate. Also, children's economic utility is at its lowest in infancy and early childhood; therefore, gender inequality may be most severe at earlier ages.

Baunach offers several possible explanations (childhood, cultural, political, familial, and economic) for gender equality during the childhood years. In her conclusions, she maintains that children's gender inequality can have serious repercussions for adults. For example, educational differences generated during childhood, adolescence, and early adulthood have important effects on labor-force inequalities in adulthood. What females experience at the earlier ages is reinforced and sometimes enhanced later in life and then revisited on the next generation. Efforts should be made within school systems, because schools are one place where childhood inequality begins, is taught, and is learned.

Source: Baunach, D. M. (2001). Gender inequality in childhood: Toward a life course perspective. *Gender Issues, 19*(3), 61–86.

3. Females who have curricular choices often choose fewer mathematics courses than do males. The reason for this difference, however, is attributed to educators and counselors who steer females away from mathematics and science, and not to actual weaknesses in females' native ability.
4. Females prove significantly more nontraditional in their sex-role behaviors. Both genders demonstrate more nontraditionalism in sex-role attitudes than in actual sex-role behaviors.
5. Females benefit more from group-oriented collaborative learning projects (e.g., cooperative learning) rather than individualistic and competitive projects, which many males prefer (Butler & Manning, 1998).

Schmuck and Schmuck (1994) consider the treatment of girls in high schools today. They cite the American Association of University Women (AAUW) study, *How Schools Shortchange Girls*, which reviews more than 450 studies and concludes that girls are "invisible in our nation's schools" (p. 23). Schmuck and Schmuck provide a detailed list of resources on gender equity in schools. They maintain that exclusionary high schools promote the status quo and, in fact, exclude the experiences of girls and other minorities. Girls are shortchanged, often without being aware that they are. Principals who want to be nondiscriminatory try to comply with legal mandates of nondiscrimination by examining curricular and extracurricular offerings, reviewing policies that may unintentionally discriminate, and actively seeking changes in school policy and practice to reduce discriminatory policy. In essence, principals and other educators should attempt to include all members in a democratic society (Schmuck & Schmuck, 1994).

Sexual Orientation

One debate among multiculturalists concerns the inclusiveness of the definition of multiculturalism. One side favors an inclusive definition of multiculturalism (including race, ethnicity, and sexual orientation); the other side supports an exclusive definition, or one favoring only ethnic and racial minorities (Pope, 1995).

Some people think the definition of multiculturalism should be restricted to cultural and ethnic differences. While W. M. L. Lee (1996) directs attention solely toward multicultural counseling, she maintains that in defining multiculturalism, some oppose a more inclusive definition, especially when dealing with differences involving males and females, gays and lesbians, elderly people, and people with physical disabilities.

■ ■ ■ ■ ■

FOLLOW THROUGH 2.6
SCHOOL PRACTICES AND GENDER

Make a list of school practices or education-related issues that might fail to address gender differences. Why do you think educators sometimes use school practices and harbor expectations that fail to address gender differences?

Others contend that unequal treatment and discrimination are not limited to racial and ethnic differences (Lee, 1996).

We believe that multicultural education should include people of differing sexual orientation. We believe that gays and lesbians share specific cultural characteristics, experience injustices and discrimination the way racial and ethnic minorities do, and deserve educators capable of providing effective educational experiences. We also believe those with physical disabilities should be included in the definition because they have a "culture" of their own and often experience injustices in U.S. society. Such a position does not imply that these people do not share many similarities with others. It simply implies that, because of their differences and potential as targets of injustice, they should be included in the definition of multiculturalism and in multicultural education programs.

Gays, lesbians, and bisexuals have their own culture and experience many of the same problems as minorities. Educators teaching gay and lesbian students need to understand the special challenges (e.g., loneliness, isolation, ridicule) that gays and lesbians experience. We feel that sexual orientation should be perceived as a cultural difference, just as gender, race, ethnicity, and social class are considered differences. Teaching gay and lesbian students requires trying to understand these students' worldviews and perspectives on life.

Researchers have generally accepted consistently that 10 percent of the population is gay or lesbian and that this portion represents every race, creed, social class, and degree of disability. In fact, estimates suggest there are 2.9 million gay or lesbian adolescents in the United States. These students are from all cultural groups and from rural as well as urban schools. They have for the most part sat passively through the years of schooling where their identities as gay and lesbian people have been ignored or denied. They have done so because of their own fears and isolation and because of the failure of society, full of taboos and fear of controversy, to take up their cause (Bailey & Phariss, 1996).

Educators and others in the helping profession are beginning to realize that these "invisible" (Bailey & Phariss, 1996, p. 39) students are becoming more visible each day through increased numbers of referrals to school counselors, school social workers, substance-abuse personnel, and various other support staff. Individual reasons for these referrals are diverse, but among the most common are efforts to clarify sexual orientation, anxiety, suicide attempts, substance abuse, low self-esteem, family conflict, and emotional isolation.

Bailey and Phariss recommend (1) providing factual information about youth sexuality, (2) abandoning the myth that discussing homosexuality will cause young people to grow up to be gay or lesbian, (3) promoting and protecting the human and civil rights of all people in the classroom, and (4) encouraging the hiring of and supporting gay and lesbian educators who can provide healthy role models (Bailey & Phariss, 1996).

Implementing Research 2.2 looks at GLBTQ (gay, lesbian, bisexual, transgendered, queer, and questioning) adolescents.

Individual

Children's and adolescents' individual differences are yet another form of diversity that educators need to understand so that they may plan appropriate educational experi-

■ ■ ■ ■ ■

IMPLEMENTING RESEARCH 2.2
LESBIAN AND GAY ADOLESCENTS

MacGillivray and Kozik-Rosabal, in their introduction to a special issue of *Education and Urban Society*, provide an excellent discussion of terminology in which they define LGBTQ as gay, lesbian, bisexual, transgendered, queer, and questioning. They describe the terms they prefer and provide rationales. In their article, they look at sexual orientation as "simply a state of being" (p. 289). Other topics explored include gender identity, the roles schools play in the creation and perpetuation of discrimination directed toward GLBTQ students, the difficulty of determining demographics of GLBTQ students, and the fact that being GLBTQ is not just an urban issue.

Interesting aspects that MacGillivray and Kozik-Rosabal offer include:

1. The term itself, GLBTQ, which seems to support the inclusion the authors want— no adolescent is being left out due to his or her sexual orientation
2. The assertion that GLBTQ is not just an urban issue—these students also attend schools in rural and suburban schools
3. Schools, in addition to meeting the needs of GLBTQ students, need to prepare heterosexual students for democratic citizenship in communities with significant populations of politically active and "out" GLBTQ people

MacGillivray and Kozik-Rosabal suggest that educators have an enormous task before them as they make schools safe for GLBTQ students. Undoubtedly, counselors also will play significant roles, both helping GLBTQ students as well as helping heterosexual students accept diversity among people.

Source: MacGillivray, I. K., & Kozik-Rosabal, G. (2000). Introduction. *Education and Urban Society*, *32*(3), 287–302.

ences. It is an equally serious mistake to assume too much cultural homogeneity among learners; one should not, for example, assume that all Hispanic learners are alike simply because they all speak Spanish. Likewise, there is great variety among African American learners according to socioeconomic background and geographic location.

For an objective and clear understanding of learners, educators should consider individual differences when they plan teaching and learning experiences: overall abilities, interests, intelligence, problem-solving abilities, critical-thinking skills, motivation, previous academic backgrounds, and the ability to use English or the language in which educators provide instruction. Likewise, it is important to consider intelligence and motivation from a cultural perspective—that is, perceptions of intelligence and motivation may vary from culture to culture. Educators should not view intelligence and motivation from only a middle-class white perspective.

Teachers may address individual differences in several ways: individualized instruction, cooperative learning, use of materials of varying levels of difficulty, the timed and untimed pacing of study, and changing the levels of learning, that is, mastery, understanding, and application.

■ ■ ■ ■ ■ ■

FOLLOW THROUGH 2.7

DETERMINING OTHER INDIVIDUAL DIFFERENCES

We have looked at culture, race, ethnicity, gender, sexual orientation, and socioeconomic status—what might other "individual" differences be? What other forms of diversity might an elementary or secondary student bring to educational situations? Divide a sheet of paper into halves—on the left side list differences, and on the right, ways you might address these individual differences.

Socioeconomic Factors

Hodgkinson (2000/2001) maintained that 20 percent of children in the United States live below the poverty line—the exact same percentage as 15 years ago—even though most of the nation is less sergregated and wealthier. Socioeconomic differences play a significant role in determining how a person acts, thinks, lives, and relates to others. Differences in values between students and educators basically represent social class differences, because many minority group learners come from the lower socioeconomic classes. Educators coming from middle- or upper-class backgrounds may have difficulty understanding the social and economic problems facing children and adolescents from lower-socioeconomic homes. Many educators are far removed from poor people's experience of poverty, low wages, lack of property, and indeed of the most basic needs. The accompanying differences in values, attitudes, behaviors, and beliefs among the various socioeconomic groups warrant the professional's consideration (Atkinson, Morten, & Sue, 1993).

Remember that a person's social class is sometimes thought to indicate his or her ambitions or motivation to achieve. It is a serious mistake, however, to stereotype people by social class—to assume, for example, that the lower classes lack ambition and do not want to work or improve their education status. It is not unreasonable to suggest that lower-class families, regardless of cultural background, want to improve their social status in life but meet with considerable frustration when faced with poverty and its accompanying conditions.

Social class differences in some cases may be more pronounced than differences resulting from cultural diversity. For example, lower-class African Americans may have more cultural commonalities with lower-class European Americans than they do with middle- or upper-class African Americans. Table 2.10 shows the number and percent of individuals under age 18 living below the poverty level, categorized by selected cultural groups.

CHALLENGES IN A CULTURALLY DIVERSE SOCIETY

Educators and other professionals need to examine their perspectives toward diversity and to determine if diversity appears as a "cultural deficit" (implying the need for change), a "cultural mismatch" (implying that learners from different cultural back-

TABLE 2.10   Selected Groups (Under Age 18) Below Poverty Level by Selected Characteristics (in thousands)

GROUP	NUMBER	PERCENT
European American	7,568	13.5
African American	3,759	33.1
Asian American and Pacific Islander	361	11.8
Hispanic American	3,506	30.3

Source: U.S. Bureau of the Census. (2001). *Statistical abstracts of the United States* (121st ed.). Washington, DC.

grounds fail because their traits are incompatible with schools' teaching practices), or as "culturally different" (implying that differences enrich the classroom and make individuals unique). This is more important than just an academic question; educators' perception of diversity determines their philosophical beliefs toward learners and toward their own instructional practices.

The Cultural Deficit Model

In the cultural deficit model, students who are culturally different are thought of as "deprived," "disadvantaged," and "socially deprived" only because their behavior, language, and customs are different from those the middle-class values. The notion that some cultures do not seek to advance themselves because of a cultural deficit results in "blaming the victim." The individual is at fault for not being more successful (educationally, socially, etc.). The cultural deficit model has failed to address the implicit cultural biases that shape negative perceptions and inhibit the understanding of the roles of sociopolitical forces.

The Cultural Mismatch Model

In contrast to the cultural deficit model, the cultural mismatch perspective assumes that cultures are inherently different but not necessarily superior or inferior to one another. It assumes that people from culturally different backgrounds fail to achieve academically because their cultural traits do not match those of the dominant culture reflected in schools. Thus, in the mismatch model, the educational performance of diverse groups is related to the degree of incongruence between group values and traits and those of the educational system: The better the match, the greater the likelihood of academic success. Efforts to improve the performance of students from culturally different backgrounds aim at increasing the congruence between the schools and the various cultures (Hernandez, 1989).

Case Study 2.2 examines one teacher's opinions about diversity and another teacher's attempts to provide a more positive perspective.

The Culturally Different Model

The "culturally different" model recognizes differences as strengths that are valuable and enriching to schools and to society as a whole. Its proponents believe nonetheless

■ ■ ■ ■ ■

CASE STUDY 2.2
THE IMPORTANCE OF PERSPECTIVE

Mrs. Williams overheard a conversation in the teacher's lounge: "Those minorities—I don't know what to do—are different and so difficult to change, so far behind, can't do so many things; they are just not suited for my classes." Mrs. Williams considered what she had heard and thought about what she had learned in a recent multicultural education course. This teacher is expressing the cultural deficit, or cultural mismatch model, she thought. Realizing such an attitude could hurt students' chances of learning, she decided to speak with this teacher about his attitudes about diversity.

Mrs. Williams met with the teacher and tried to make him aware of the dangers of harboring such perspectives. Believing that people must eliminate or change their differences reveals negative attitudes toward diversity—attitudes that undoubtedly affect feelings toward learners of differing cultural backgrounds. Likewise, expecting learners to change to meet the teacher's instructional strategies is in opposition to what is known about effective education. A student's achievement and behavior can also be affected by a teacher's expectations of poor performance and behavior. In reality, Mrs. Williams knew how hard it is to change such thinking toward diversity.

Mrs. Williams wondered how many other teachers in the school harbored such feelings toward cultural differences. She decided to design an informal assessment device to determine other teachers' perspectives and to ask the principal if it would be possible to arrange in-service activities designed to help teachers adopt appropriate perspectives toward diversity.

that all children and adolescents need to learn mainstream cultural values and knowledge. Researchers have begun to establish a research base documenting that differences in learning styles and language are not deficiencies. The differences can be a foundation to facilitate learning.

A certain degree of cultural compatibility is necessary as teachers and students become increasingly aware of each others' cultural differences, whether differences relate to school or home expectations. The situation for children and adolescents might be even more acute than for teachers, especially because learners must switch from home to school cultures and vice versa. In any event, educators should not condemn learners for their language or culture, and they should encourage the students to retain and build on these differences, whenever possible (Gollnick & Chinn, 2002).

■ ■ ■ ■ ■

FOLLOW THROUGH 2.8
DETERMINING SCHOOL OPINIONS TOWARD DIFFERENCES

Visit an elementary or secondary school to learn about its educational philosophy, grouping practices, curricular and library materials, and extracurricular activities. Do you think the school's practices and policies indicate an acceptance of a cultural deficit, mismatch, or difference model? What are the implications of the model the school chooses?

UNDERSTANDING AND REDUCING RACISM

Racism or a general dislike of others who are different sometimes results in crimes committed against people based on their culture, sexual orientation, or other differences. Since 1985, hate crimes has come to include acts of violence in sexual orientation, gender, and disability. Figure 2.1 shows the number of hate crimes occurring in recent years.

Incidents of racism continue to plague U.S. society and, in some cases, appear to be increasing in number and severity. Evidence of racism fills the popular press and the news media: Hate groups spread their opinions and literature, people are attacked solely because of cultural and racial heritage, and people are denied opportunities simply because their culture is different from the prevailing culture.

Eight common patterns of racism in schools include: hostile and insensitive acts toward others; bias in the use of punishment; bias in giving attention to students; bias in curriculum materials; inequality in the amount of instruction; bias in attitudes toward students; failure to employ educational professionals from various cultural backgrounds; and denial of racist acts (Murray & Clark, 1990).

Evidence (Duncan, 1993) suggests that other forms of racism occur during a typical school day. For example, if a student seeks a teacher's assistance, the request is usually a sign of motivation, an indication that the student wants to learn and perhaps even excel. If African American students seek help from a teacher, however, the teacher may perceive the request as an indication of African Americans' inability to learn or to cope with academic tasks. Hence, when such perceptions reinforce a general perception of African American children's low achievement, the teacher's expectations begin to limit the learning opportunities of these students. Equally damaging are perceptions of African and Latino/a students that cause some educators to dilute curriculum and institute austere classroom management procedures (Duncan, 1993).

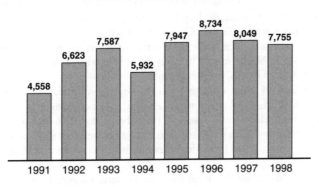

FIGURE 2.1   Number of Hate Crime Incidents, 1991–1998

Source: Grattet, Y. (2000). "Hate crimes: Better data or increasing frequency?" *Population Today, 28*(5), 1, 4.

Racism also has the potential to attack children's developing sense of group membership as well as their individual and cultural identities. In fact, children are often more susceptible to racism's harm than are adults.

Implementing Research 2.3 looks at how privileges differ for cultural groups and the effects of privileges.

A Chinese American girl, for example, enrolled in a kindergarten. Her teacher, deciding her name was too difficult to pronounce, renamed her "Mary." Now that the child had an "American" name, it would be easier for the teacher to deal with her. But the teacher did not consider the effects on the child. The young girl asked, "What is wrong with my name? What was wrong with my parents to give me such a name?"

UNDERSTANDING AND DISPELLING STEREOTYPES

Stereotyping can be defined as holding attitudes toward a person or group that supposedly characterize or describe an entire group, gender, race, or religion. Stereo-

■ ■ ■ ■ ■ ▬▬▬▬▬▬▬▬▬▬▬▬▬▬▬▬▬▬

IMPLEMENTING RESEARCH 2.3
FORTY ACRES AND A MULE

Conley selected his title from the Freedman's Bureau set up to help slaves after the Emancipation. Blacks were promised "40 acres and a mule" (p. 21); however, even then, blacks experienced institutional restraints as they tried to accumulate property. Conley maintains that in 1965, the last of a series of laws was passed that capped the civil rights movement in the United States. Even today, however, blacks are half as likely to graduate from college as whites, twice as likely to be unemployed, and earn about 55 percent of what whites earn. Even with these dismal numbers, improvements have been made, but Conley maintains that they obscure the real nature of racial inequality of property and class. He believes the typical white family enjoys a net worth of about ten times as much as its nonwhite counterparts. Latinos—a very diverse group—fare slightly better than African Americans but fall far short of whites on the net worth indicator. Conley offers a number of injustices that hurt blacks throughout history. More recently, the devaluation of blacks' property occurred after the "white flight" (p. 23). As blacks started to make inroads in white communities, whites moved out, and devaluation of blacks' property began.

Conley suggests several policy options, such as integration insurance, which would protect property owners from devaluation when a neighborhood changes from white to black; a national wealth tax that would result in funds being redistributed to the asset-poor; loosening of restrictions in the welfare system so that welfare recipients can save money without being penalized; and Individual Development Accounts that foster savings through matching funds.

In closing, Conley maintains that until the United States takes some action to close the asset gap, the nation will still be two societies, "separate and unequal" (p. 24).

Source: Conley, D. (2000). 40 acres and a mule. *National Forum*, 80(2), 21–24.

■ ■ ■ ■ ■

FOLLOW THROUGH 2.9
ADDRESSING RACISM

There is a serious need to address racism in all its forms: hostile and insensitive acts, bias in use of punishment, bias in giving attention, bias in curricular materials, and inequality in quality of instruction. Unfortunately, racism is a societal ill that will never be totally eliminated. It can, however, be reduced. List several forms of racism teachers might encounter and suggest ways to reduce this evil.

types usually tend to emphasize differences between ourselves and other individuals or groups. They tend to be negative. Unfortunately, many people base their first impressions of others on stereotypes, which can result, consciously or unconsciously, in negative attitudes and a lack of overall interpersonal understanding and communication.

Stereotyping can have at least two negative results. First, an over general perception of people usually results in a judgmental negative or positive image of people or their entire culture. Second, stereotypes have the potential to influence educators' professional decisions about students. When teachers use stereotypes to group students, to prescribe their course of study, and to help them plan their extracurricular activities, they do individuals a disservice. For example, when educators or counselors use culture or gender as the basis to advise students—some to join the chess club and others to a study block, some to play on the basketball team and others on the tennis team, and some to take literature instead of mathematics and science subjects—educators might be basing educational decisions on stereotypes. Students need careful and thoughtful guidance; decisions about them need to be based on accurate and objective information, not stereotypical generalizations about their culture and gender.

The dangers of stereotyping learners are all too clear: Educators do students a terrible misservice when they use stereotypes to conclude that African American learners misbehave and are slow learners; that Asian Americans are all high-ability learners and that all are "bright and motivated"; that Hispanic Americans have reading and behavior problems. Although we mention stereotyping here only briefly, Chapters 3, 4, 5, 6, 7, and 8 on children and adolescents have sections on the respective cultures.

■ ■ ■ ■ ■

FOLLOW THROUGH 2.10
PROMOTING CULTURAL IDENTITIES

All people, whatever their cultural background, need to have a positive cultural identity—they need to understand and appreciate their cultural heritages. List six to eight ways you can help children and adolescents have a positive cultural identity.

HELPING LEARNERS DEVELOP POSITIVE CULTURAL IDENTITIES

Among the significant challenges educators face daily is the fact that children and adolescents are constantly developing perceptions of their individual and cultural identities. Learners' perceptions of cultural differences and their opinions of others' perceptions play significant roles in their degree of self-worth and self-image. For example, a student who comes from a different culture and a lower socioeconomic level than the teacher may, indeed, understandably consider "differences" as inferior or wrong. Perceptive educators recognize the disastrous consequences such feelings can have on learners' sense of personal worth.

Educators can help learners from majority and from culturally different backgrounds as well to understand "culture," recognize how culture affects peoples' lives, and understand that one cannot readily place values on culture. Likewise, educators can work toward providing all children and adolescents with accurate and objective materials and lead discussions of culture and cultural differences that lay to rest as many myths, distortions, and stereotypes as possible.

SUMMING UP

Educators who wish to plan an appropriate response to our nation's cultural diversity and to provide effective multicultural education programs should:

1. Understand the melting pot ideology and the more realistic contemporary perspectives toward cultural diversity
2. Understand that cultural differences have value and are enriching to the United States
3. Understand terms such as *culture, ethnicity, race, social class,* and *gender*
4. Address and stand against racism in all forms, regardless of the victim's cultural and racial backgrounds
5. Form a perspective on culture and cultural diversity that perceives differences as "positives" rather than disadvantages that must be eliminated

SUGGESTED LEARNING ACTIVITIES

1. Suggest several methods of helping children and adolescents develop positive individual and cultural identities. What would be your response to an educator who stated, "My work is teaching content—improving cultural identities is not my job!"

2. Give at least four examples of racist acts and offer a solution (a difficult task indeed) to each racist act. To what extent should reducing racism be a role of the school?

3. Name four or five stereotypical images of American Indian, African, Asian, Hispanic, or European American children or adolescents. Suggest how such images may have originated and how schools can provide appropriate responses.

SUGGESTIONS FOR COLLABORATIVE EFFORTS

Form groups of three or four that, if possible, represent our nation's cultural and gender diversity. Working collaboratively, focus your group's attention toward the following efforts:

1. Survey a number of elementary, middle, or secondary schools to determine the cultural composition of the student body. What has been the school's response to meeting the needs of students' cultural differences? What efforts has the school made to teach majority cultures about minority cultures and vice versa?

2. Increasingly, gender and gender differences are important topics in multicultural education programs. Does your group feel gender should be a minor or major emphasis in multicultural education programs? Does your group feel that there is a "culture of gender" or that there is an overemphasis of gender differences? What role should educators play (or not play) in making gender an integral component of multicultural education programs?

3. How inclusive should multicultural education be? Originally, the idea prevailed that the term *multicultural education* included only culture, ethnicity, and race. Now, it has been expanded to include cultures of gender, sexual orientation, and ability/disability. How inclusive does your group think multiculturalism should be? Have scholars taken the "inclusiveness" idea too far? Or do we need to make "multiculturalism" even more inclusive?

EXPANDING YOUR HORIZONS: ADDITIONAL JOURNAL READINGS AND BOOKS

Baunach, D. M. (2001). Gender inequality in childhood: Toward a life course perspective. *Gender Issues, 19*(3), 61–86.

In this thought-provoking article on gender, Baunach offers several possible explanations (childhood, cultural, political, familial, and economic) for gender inequality during the childhood years.

Gerber, D. A. (2001). Forming a transnational narrative: New perspectives on European migrations to the United States. *The History Teacher, 35*(1), 61–77.

Gerber explains transnational narrative, or the model that posits the existence of modes of understanding and of behavior that span homelands and destinations and defy time and space, especially national boundaries.

Hodgkinson, H. (2000/2001). Educational demographics: What teachers should know. *Educational Leadership, 58*(4), 6–11.

Hodgkinson provides a wealth of information demographics and how these demographics affect elementary and secondary schools.

Martin, P., & Martin, S. K. (2001). U.S. immigration policy and globalization. *Insights on Law and Society, 1*(3), 4–6, 31.

Martin and Martin propose remedies for immigration problems and suggest fine-tuning immigration policies rather than radical change.

Olney, M. F., & Kennedy, J. (2002). Racial disparities in VR use and job placement rates for adults with disabilities. *Rehabilitation Counseling Bulletin, 45*(3), 177–185.

These authors maintain racial and ethnic disparities exist in the access to vocational rehabilitation services and efficacy of services.

UNDERSTANDING LEARNERS AND THEIR CULTURAL BACKGROUNDS

To understand, accept, and respect learners from all cultural backgrounds is of primary importance, as is to provide them with culturally relevant educational experiences. Part II includes Chapters 3, 4, 5, 6, 7, and 8 and provides a portrait of children and adolescents in African, American Indian, Arab, Asian, European, and Hispanic American cultures.

■ ■ ■ ■ ■

CHAPTER THREE

UNDERSTANDING AFRICAN AMERICAN CHILDREN AND ADOLESCENTS

Understanding the material and activities in this chapter will help the reader to:

- Describe the cultural, gender, socioeconomic, familial, and language characteristics of African American children and adolescents

- List several stereotypes of African American children and adolescents, and explain how these beliefs affect curriculum and school practices

- Describe the educational achievement of African American children and adolescents and be able to explain the importance of self-esteem to learning achievement

- Understand African American English dialect as a valued cultural trait, and be able to explain its importance to achievement in school and development of self-esteem

- Explain the importance of understanding learning styles and the uniqueness of African American learning styles

- List several points educators should remember when planning educational experiences for African American children and adolescents

- Incorporate practical activities, suggest appropriate children's literature, implement research findings, and respond appropriately in school situations involving African American learners

OVERVIEW

A responsive multicultural curriculum recognizes the cultural diversity of African American children and adolescents and provides appropriate educational experiences based on an understanding of both the individual and the culture. The culture of African American children and adolescents as well as socioeconomic class, family, and language play significant roles and interact in a complex fashion to create unique learners with individual strengths and needs. Providing appropriate teaching and learning experiences for African American learners requires an understanding of the individual's development, learning styles, achievement levels, and self-esteem. This chapter examines African American children and adolescents and explores educational issues germane to these learners.

ORIGINS

African American people have lived in United States for many centuries. Arriving in North America either as explorers or as slaves, African American people have experienced a long history of struggle. The first Africans in the Americas were explorers: Columbus's last voyage to the Americas included an African man, Balboa's crew brought an African man, and an African explored the territory that is now Kansas with Coronado. Africans were among the first non-native settlers. African people were part of the ill-fated South Carolina colony, San Miguel de Guadalupe, in 1526; and African people helped to establish Saint Augustine, Florida, in 1665.

One important distinction deserves understanding: Many multicultural groups elected to immigrate to the United States in hopes of improving their lives, to seek religious freedom, or to get away from oppressive conditions or war-torn areas. Most Africans, on the other hand, were transported against their will to a foreign land and forced to work and live in cruel and inhumane conditions.

AFRICAN AMERICANS TODAY

African Americans presently constitute the largest U.S. ethnic minority group. The latest annual population estimates indicate that African Americans total nearly 30 million, or 13 percent of the nation's population. The African American population has been growing at a faster rate than the total population. About one-third of the African American population in 1990 was under eighteen years old. Most African Americans live in metropolitan areas, but the number of suburban African Americans today stands at about 7 percent of the U.S. suburban population. Educators in city schools

■ ■ ■ ■ ■

USING CHILDREN'S LITERATURE
UNDERSTANDING SLAVERY AND RACISM

These Newbery Award winners offer an excellent representation of slavery and racism.

Armstrong, William. *Sounder.* Delacorte, 1983.
   This story describes the racism and prejudice a black sharecropper and his family experience. (Reading Level: 6; Interest Level: Ages 10 and above.)

Fox, Paula. *The Slave Dancer.* Bradbury, 1973.
   A young boy plays the fife on a slave ship. (Reading Level: 7; Interest Level: 12 and above.)

Taylor, Mildred D. *Roll of Thunder, Hear My Cry.* Dial, 1976.
   A black family in 1933 Mississippi experiences humiliating experiences yet retains its pride. (Reading Level: 6; Interest Level: 10 and above.)

■ ■ ■ ■ ■ ▬▬▬▬▬

USING CHILDREN'S LITERATURE
NONFICTION BOOKS ABOUT THE AFRICAN AMERICAN EXPERIENCE

Patterson, Lillie. *Frederick Douglass: Freedom Fighter.* Garrand, 1965.
The story of Douglass's life in slavery, protest against slavery, escape from slave owners and slave hunters, and his championing of the rights of all people. (Reading Level: Grade 3; Interest Level: Age 8 and above.)

Dekay, James T. *Meet Martin Luther King.* Random House, 1969.
Dekay stresses King's tremendous work and his reasons for fighting against injustice and prejudice. (Reading Level: Grade 4; Interest Level: Ages 7–12.)

work with significant numbers of African Americans, but educators in suburban schools will increasingly work with African Americans as more and more move away from the inner city.

Decades after the civil rights movement forced the United States to confront racial inequities, disturbing disparities remain on one of the most basic human levels: Blacks get sick more easily, stay sick longer, and die sooner than whites. From birth, a black baby's life expectancy is six and one-half years shorter than a white baby's. Blacks are more likely to be born weighing too little and less likely to survive their first year. Blacks face a higher risk of asthma, hypertension, and cancer. They are nearly twice as likely as whites to die of a stroke, 40 percent more likely to die of heart disease, and they face a 35 percent higher cancer rate than whites.

Blacks are more than twice as likely to be without health insurance. People cite many reasons for blacks' health predicament: Blacks face extra stresses living in a racist society, blacks have an unhealthy diet (it can be difficult to find fresh vegetables and produce in many inner-city grocery stores), and blacks often mistrust doctors and other health care providers; only 63 percent of blacks say they trust the medical profession (Blacks are slipping through the health gap, 1998).

African Americans have not shared equally in the nation's prosperity. They earn less than whites, and they possess far less wealth. The black-to-white median income ratio has hovered in the mid-50 to mid-60 percentage range for the past twenty years. Fluctuations have been minor. In some respects, the United States has grown accustomed to this benchmark of inequality. In fact, for every dollar whites earn, African American households earn 62 cents (Oliver & Shapiro, 1998).

The loss of community has hit poor and African American people hard. The decline of manufacturing has dried up the pool of well-paid jobs for the unskilled. Racial discrimination prevails in both hiring and housing, and the value of income supports is decreasing. The often inferior and overwhelmed schools and public services, the flight of the middle class to the suburbs, the easy availability of drugs—all have contributed to inner-city problems and unhealthy human development (Schorr, 1998).

STEREOTYPING OF AFRICAN AMERICAN CHILDREN AND ADOLESCENTS

To be a child or adolescent as well as an African American in a predominantly European American society is to bear a double stigma. Stereotyping has produced negative images of the African American culture and its young people. Youth is the time of identity formation; for this reason it is especially important that everyone objectively accept social, cultural, and age differences among young people. Young African Americans need fair opportunities to develop identities appropriate for their culture and age. Categorizing African American young people as language-deficient because they speak dialectical English or as low achievers and behavior problems negates diversity and individual differences. Educators must take a closer and more objective look at the child and the adolescent in the African American culture to improve their understanding of the learner and the world in which she or he lives. Such knowledge and understanding gives educators an objective and sound foundation for a multicultural curriculum.

Case Study 3.1 shows the detrimental effects of stereotypical statements.

CULTURAL CHARACTERISTICS

African American children and adolescents are considerably diverse (Table 3.1). Differences exist between lower, middle, and higher socioeconomic groups, between younger and older generations, between African Americans residing in the various geographic locations of the United States, and between urban and rural African Ameri-

■ ■ ■ ■ ■ ▬▬▬▬▬▬▬▬▬▬▬▬▬▬▬▬▬▬▬▬▬▬▬▬▬

CASE STUDY 3.1
DEALING WITH STEREOTYPICAL SITUATIONS

Mrs. Lewis overhears someone at the grocery store say, "African American students have ruined that school. Their achievement is low. They speak a language nobody can understand. They are always misbehaving. That school has gone to the dogs. It used to be such a nice school, too."

If Mrs. Lewis confronts the person in the grocery store directly, she will probably be unsuccessful. She can, however, politely tell the person of the school's many accomplishments.

What can you do? Perhaps you could launch a community-wide campaign to change the school's image. Make public the school's accomplishments, encourage the school's young people to take an active role in the community, and encourage business leaders to take a greater role in schools and to publicize successful efforts.

Even though such efforts may improve the school's image, stereotypical statements are nonetheless a serious problem. These problems require people to have more objectivity toward and acceptance of differing cultures, as well as to make a larger-scale effort and change of attitude.

■ ■ ■ ■ ■ ▬▬▬▬▬▬▬▬▬▬▬▬▬▬▬▬▬▬▬▬▬▬▬▬▬▬▬▬▬▬▬▬▬▬▬

FOLLOW THROUGH 3.1
APPRECIATING AFRICAN AMERICAN CONTRIBUTIONS

Make a list of historical and contemporary African Americans who have contributed to their culture and to the United States. Include such leaders of the past as George Washington Carver and Frederick Douglass and contemporary African Americans such as Jesse Jackson and Colin Powell. List their achievements and the ways their actions have contributed to the betterment of all cultures.

TABLE 3.1   **Selected Characteristics of African American Children and Adolescents**

CATEGORY	CHARACTERISTICS
Behavioral/emotional expressiveness	High-context, rely on nonverbals
Verbal	Affective, emotional, interpersonal
Nonverbal	Preference for closer space; importance placed on nonverbal behavior
Concept of time	Oriented more to situation than to concrete, tangible, and immediate goals
Social orientation	Sense of "peoplehood" and collective concern

Developed from: Rivera, B. D., & Rogers-Adkinson, D. (1997). Culturally sensitive interventions: Social skills training with children and parents from culturally and linguistically diverse backgrounds. *Intervention in School and Clinic, 33*(2), 75–80.

cans. An educator who understands this diversity among African American children and adolescents can make a valuable contribution to the multicultural curriculum, and base choices on objective and factual information.

African American children daily face two cultures: the African American culture of the home and neighborhood and the European American culture of schools and other social institutions. African American children and children from other cultures need opportunities to learn about one another's cultures and to understand that "different" does not imply "wrong."

■ ■ ■ ■ ■ ▬▬▬▬▬▬▬▬▬▬▬▬▬▬▬▬▬▬▬▬▬▬▬▬▬▬▬▬▬▬▬▬▬▬▬

FOLLOW THROUGH 3.2
IDENTIFYING CULTURAL DIFFERENCES

Make a list of cultural differences between African and European Americans. Then, keeping in mind the characteristics you listed, make another list of social class differences. How are the cultures alike and different? Are the social class differences more alike or different between the two groups? Are African and European American members of the same social class more alike than African American members of differing social classes?

Education has focused for many years solely on historical and contemporary whites. Educators sometimes justifiably complain that their education did not provide them with examples of the contributions of African Americans. During the past several decades, attempts to instill pride and a better understanding of the African American culture have given rise to learning materials that emphasize the many positive aspects and leaders of the culture.

Although educators should make cultural generalizations cautiously, African Americans *tend* to have large families and respect for immediate and extended families. They also *tend* to have a nonverbal communication style that differs from that of the European American culture (for example, an African American feels comfortable interrupting a speaker to show support and does not find it necessary to look the speaker in the eye). African American children are generally highly expressive emotionally, assertive, and verbal in dealings with peers and adults (Rotheram-Borus & Phinney, 1990). African American children and adolescents are taught respect for the elderly, kinship and extended family bonds, and authoritarian child-rearing practices. Once

■ ■ ■ ■ ■ ▬▬▬▬▬▬▬▬▬▬▬▬▬▬▬

USING CHILDREN'S LITERATURE
THE AFRICAN AMERICAN EXPERIENCE IN CHILDREN'S BOOKS

Keats, Ezra Jack. *The Snowy Day*. Viking, 1962. Keats captures the mood of the African American experience in this book. Illustrated with collage. (Reading Level: Grade 2; Interest Level: Ages 2–7.)

Steptoe, John. *Stevie*. Harper & Row, 1969. Robert is unhappy when Stevie wants to play with his toys. (Reading Level: Grades 3–7; Interest Level: Ages 2–8.)

Hamilton, Virginia. *Zeely*. Macmillan, 1967. Geeder is convinced that her neighbor is a Watusi queen. (Reading Level: Grade 4; Interest Level: Ages 7–12.)

■ ■ ■ ■ ■ ▬▬▬▬▬▬▬▬▬▬▬▬▬▬▬

USING CHILDREN'S LITERATURE
CONTRIBUTIONS OF AFRICAN AMERICANS TO THE FINE ARTS

Byran, Ashley. *I'm Going to Sing: Black American Spirituals*, vol. 2. Atheneum, 1982. This book includes words and music that help African American children understand their heritage. (Interest Level: All ages.)

Haskins, James. *Black Theater in America*. Crowell, 1982. This text traces the contributions of African Americans from minstrel shows through contemporary protest plays. (Reading Level: 7; Interest Level: Age 9 and above.)

again, we remind readers that individuals within a culture differ and that cultural characteristics vary with socioeconomic class and geographic region.

A difficult situation exists when African Americans want to retain their cultural heritage, the culture of their ancestors, and the culture with which they can relate and feel comfortable. Some African Americans, however, may also feel that some acculturation with the European Americans is necessary for economic and psychological survival. It is important to attain a middle ground on which African American adolescents can not only retain their African heritage but also feel successful in contemporary society.

Gender

The recent emphasis on gender differences and gender-appropriate education suggests educators should consider African American females and males from different perspectives. Undoubtedly, educators need to consider females' different learning styles, perceptions of motivation, and ways of responding to educators' efforts. Females, however, may need to give special attention to socially acceptable behaviors such as modulating their voices, proper grooming, and developing assertive demeanors (Young, 1994). Such a proposal does not suggest that African American males (as well as males from other cultures) do not need educational experiences in similar areas; when addressing these points, however, educators need to consider the female perspective.

Teachers also should consider gender differences when planning actual educational experiences for African American females. For example, African American females might learn better through cooperative efforts rather than in competitive atmospheres. Also, they might benefit more from behavior management systems promoting positive consequences rather than negative ones. Positive environments also contribute to African American females' academic achievement and social development.

Mitchell, Bush, and Bush (2002) maintained that the plight of African American males calls for alternative schools to address their specific needs. They offered disturbing statistics about African American males: The leading cause of death for black males between the ages of fifteen and twenty-four is homicide; one in twenty black males is in federal or state prison; black males' unemployment rate is sometimes twice that of white males; and African American males have higher suspension, expulsion, retention and dropout rates, and dramatically lower grade-point averages (Mitchell et al., 2002).

■ ■ ■ ■ ■ ▬▬▬▬▬▬▬▬▬▬▬▬▬▬▬▬▬▬▬▬▬▬▬▬▬▬

FOLLOW THROUGH 3.3
HELPING AFRICAN AMERICAN URBAN MALES

Design a strategy to help African American urban boys in either elementary or secondary schools. First, decide on a method of determining their needs (either a case study, some diagnostic device, interviews, or observation); second, select instructional methods that reflect their learning styles; third, select curricular materials to which they can relate; fourth, select culturally appropriate assessment devices; and fifth, decide what other guidance or advising topics might address their needs. In addition to these five approaches, what else might you suggest to help African American urban boys?

■ ■ ■ ■ ■ ▬▬▬

FOR ADDITIONAL INFORMATION

National Black Child Development Institute, 1463 Rhode Island Ave. NW, Washington, DC 20005.
This organization is dedicated to improving the quality of life for African American children and youth, and focuses on issues such as health, child welfare, education, and child care.

Minority Caucus of Family Services America, 34 Beacon Street, Boston, MA 02108.

This organization participates in policy-making groups and works toward the needs of minority families.

National Black Youth Leadership Council, 250 W. 54th Street, Suite 800, New York, NY 10019.
This council provides training and motivation workshops, resources, information, skills, and strategies for fostering leadership development.

As early as 1790, Africans in the United States created alternative ways to school themselves. Reasons included lack of access to public schools, a threat of miseducation, and a belief that they were responsible for their own education. More recent impetuses to the independent schooling tradition and the black studies movement of the 1960s and 1970s included the black power, civil rights, and pan-American movements. The result has been an emergence of schools designed to focus on African American students, such as African-centered public schools, African American immersion academics, and black male academies (Mitchell et al., 2002).

In Gender Perspectives 3.1, Mitchell, Bush, and Bush (2002) describe the African American Males Program, an effort to provide alternative schooling to African American males.

Socioeconomic Status

Within a complex society, social class and ethnicity are two major sociologic structures that produce diversity in human lifestyle and development (Hale-Benson, 1986). Six determinants provide indications of socioeconomic status: income, wealth, occupation, education, prestige, and power (Gollnick & Chinn, 2002). The discrimination African American people experience has resulted in a lack of educational and employment opportunities and has prohibited significant social mobility. Because they have long been deprived of equal opportunities and the chance to improve themselves educationally and economically, African American people find themselves disproportionately represented in the lower socioeconomic classes.

Socioeconomic class continues to be a powerful indicator of academic success for American children. Children from higher socioeconomic status (SES) backgrounds score higher on standardized achievement tests, are more likely to finish high school, and are more likely to attend college and do postgraduate work than their less advantaged peers. Because poor children are less likely to pursue higher education, it is difficult to break them out of the cycle of poverty. The relationship between poverty and academic achievement is complicated by ethnicity; a disproportionate number of the

■ ■ ■ ■ ■ ▬▬▬▬

GENDER PERSPECTIVES 3.1

A MODEL FOR AN AFRICAN AMERICAN MALES PROGRAM

The MAAT (Motivated Action towards Achievement and Transformation) Academy has twenty-two African American mentors. Eight serve as full-time MAAT academic teachers, while fourteen, from a variety of professions, serve as mentors. The program holds meetings twice a week after school, from 2:45 to 4:00 P.M. The meetings consist of:

- Academic lessons in language arts, reading, and math designed to increase basic skills
- Study skills development
- Cultural-enrichment activities and curricula designed to enhance cultural knowledge through thought-provoking historical, sociopolitical, and biographical lessons
- Counseling and mentorships designed to increase self-esteem and the development of intrinsic motivation
- Parent-education workshops, which provide parents with parenting strategies
- Sports-related activities to encourage the development of healthy relationships with peers and adult mentors

Mitchell et al. (2002) describe each of the above areas in more detail. They also describe the selection criteria and explain that the main purpose is to seek the most "at-risk" (p. 143) African American populations. Fifty African American males in grades 6–8 were selected based on their reading, language, and math scores, cumulative grade-point averages, and office referrals.

Results have been promising: Office referrals have decreased; general classroom behavior has improved; students are spending less time outside the classroom; about three-fourths of the students have experienced academic gains (e.g., higher course grades and standardized test scores); and parents have reported improved relationships with their sons.

Source: Mitchell, K., Bush, E. C., & Bush, L. (2002). Standing in the gap: A model for establishing African American male intervention programs with public schools. *Educational Horizons 80*(3), 140–146.

poor are members of ethnic minority groups whose long history as victims of discrimination has impeded their chances of academic and material success (Halle, Kurtz-Costes, & Mahoney, 1997).

The odds that African Americans will encounter obstacles to academic success are high. African American children are three times more likely to live in poverty than are white children in the United States. Significant numbers of low-income African American children get off to a bad start, lag behind in the early elementary years, and are twice as likely to drop out of school than their more advantaged white peers. These distressing disparities exist despite a long-standing commitment among African Americans to the belief that education can eliminate poverty and eventually end racial discrimination.

Not that many African American success stories don't exist; many disadvantaged parents—of minority as well as majority cultural groups—are successful in translating their high academic aspirations for their children into reality. Along this line of thinking, it should be noted although some economic hardships and social discrimination provide

■ ■ ■ ■ ■ ▬▬▬▬▬▬▬▬▬▬▬▬▬▬▬▬▬▬▬▬▬▬

USING CHILDREN'S LITERATURE
FAMILIES IN AFRICAN AMERICAN CHILDREN'S BOOKS

Flournoy, Valerie. *The Patchwork Quilt.* Dial, 1985.
This is the story of a grandmother's and a granddaughter's developing relationship while constructing a quilt. (Reading Level: Grade 4; Interest Level: Ages 5–10.)

Greenfield, Eloise. *She Come Bringing Me That Little Baby Girl.* Lippincott, 1974.
Kevin dislikes all the attention his new baby sister receives. The book shows changing emotions in a warm, loving story. (Reading Level: Grade 3; Interest Level: Ages 6–9.)

Mathias, Sharon Bell. *The Hundred Penny Box.* Viking, 1975.
This story focuses on the life and love of great-great-Aunt Dew, an aged African American woman, and Michael, a young boy. (Reading Level: Grade 3; Interest Level: Ages 6–10.)

Yarbrough, Camille. *Cornrows.* Putnam, 1979.
An African American great-grandmother braids a young girl's hair and relates the history of her people. (Reading Level: Grade 3; Interest Level: Ages 6–10.)

difficult obstacles to overcome, parents' behaviors, beliefs, attitudes, and goals may circumvent the detrimental effects of poverty (Halle, Kurtz-Costes, & Mahoney, 1997).

When working with African American learners, elementary and secondary educators should:

1. Understand the effects of being a member of a lower socioeconomic group
2. Understand that children from lower socioeconomic groups might not understand words like *physician, lavatory, wraps,* and *pens* (pens for writing versus pens for confining animals)
3. Understand that language differences are "differences"—not "deficits"
4. Understand the need to work first on concrete learning and then move on to abstract learning
5. Understand the need to provide positive reinforcement during the learning process, rather than expecting learners to stay motivated by focusing on some faraway goal
6. Understand the need to involve parents and extended families in the learning process
7. Understand each learner's individual strengths and needs, and plan teaching and learning experiences that always challenge and instruct

Today African Americans have more equality of opportunity, better access to education, and more equitable salaries than they did in the 1960s. Through civil rights legislation, affirmative action programs, and equal employment opportunity, African Americans are able to obtain an education and seek employment. Such gains will result in improved conditions for children. The problem of poverty, however, continues for many people and requires the attention of government, school, and other organizations concerned with the welfare of children.

■ ■ ■ ■ ■

FOLLOW THROUGH 3.4
ADDRESSING POVERTY'S EFFECTS

Although educators can do little to alleviate the poverty and poor socioeconomic conditions of students, what might schools do to address the needs of these students? How
might educators better understand the effects of poverty? How can they understand these
students and their mindsets toward long-term goals and success?

Families

Educators who work with African American learners need a historical understanding
of and perspective on the African American family. To gain such knowledge might
prove difficult, because U.S. scholarship has mistreated, ignored, and distorted the
African American family. Often, the misconceptions of majority-culture educators may
cause them to question African American cultural traditions. Throughout centuries of
cultural oppression and repression, for example, African Americans have developed,
perhaps as much through necessity as choice, a network of "significant others" who
have close ties to and are willing to assist the individual family. Understanding and accepting this African American family tradition continues to be a prerequisite for educators to help students make effective educational decisions.

America had 8.1 million African American families in 1996. Of these, 3.7 million
(46 percent) were married-couple families; 3.8 million (47 percent) were families maintained by women (no spouse present). Forty-two percent of African American families
had two or more wage earners; about 57 percent had children under age eighteen.
Heads of household in African American families were younger than householders of
other ethnic backgrounds. Almost 60 percent were younger than forty-five years old;
only 22 percent were fifty-five or over. African American families had a real median income of $25,970 in 1995. Married-couple families had a real median income of $41,750.
Women who maintained households without a spouse present had a real median income
of $15,500. Fifty-six percent of all African American families lived in the South.

African American children grow up in homes that are very different from the
homes of European American children and adolescents. Minority extended families
function on the principles of interdependence and an extensive reliance on networks of
people including blood relatives and close friends called kinsmen. A young African
American child might be taken into the household of elderly grandparents. In such
arrangements children have a sense they belong to an extended family clan, not merely
to their parents. Uncles, aunts, cousins, and grandparents have considerable power
within the family unit and may take responsibility for the care and rearing of children
and for teaching appropriate skills and values.

These strong kinship bonds probably originated from two guiding principles of
the African ethos: the survival of the tribe and the oneness of being. Children see early
that their families develop a kinship in the African American community and that African Americans refer to each other as "sister," "brother," "cousin," "blood brother," or
"homeboy" to imply a family closeness even where actual kinship does not exist (Hale-
Benson, 1986, p. 49).

■ ■ ■ ■ ■

FOLLOW THROUGH 3.5

INTERVIEWING AFRICAN AMERICAN FAMILIES

Interview several African American families (maybe you can include extended-family members, too) to determine their expectations of the schools. What do they want for their children? What questions do they have? What do they feel good about? What are their frustrations? On the basis of this information, suggest ways the schools can become more responsive to the educational needs and expectations of African American families.

Religion

Religion is a powerful aspect of the African American family orientation that has almost never had empirical documentation. Rather than study the church and religion in relation to children, writers usually focus attention on the role of religion in the civil rights movement, economic leadership, and the quest for equal opportunity. Children, however, undoubtedly perceive the African American church as a socializing and peer-group institution, a hub of social life, and a means to aspire to community leadership. Rather than simply a Sunday-morning experience, church membership for children is an integral aspect of African American family life (Hale-Benson, 1986).

The most rapidly growing religion in the United States is Islam. In 1960 there were no mosques in this country; in 1998 there were over 1,000. Muslims are a rapidly increasing part of the American religious scene. The United States needs to appreciate the gifts—their culture, their music, their food, and their philosophy—they bring to U.S. society. It is in the schools that people first start adapting to Muslim cultures and Muslims begin adapting to other U.S. cultures (Hodgkinson, 1998).

Language

The language of African American children is a function of their culture and plays a significant role in their self-esteem, school achievement, and social and psychological development. Although the child may not experience communication difficulties at home or in the neighborhood, language differences may cause problems when significant variations exist between home and neighborhood and school languages. Children's language skills are crucial in their education, and much of what educators measure as "intelligence" and "achievement" is actually language and communication skills (Hale-Benson, 1986).

Aspects of African American oral tradition are observable in African American student behavior. In telling stories, African Americans render abstract observations about life, love, and people in the form of concrete narrative sequences that may seem to meander from the point and to take on an episodic framework. In African American communication styles, we often find overt demonstration of sympathetic involvement through movement and sounds; a prescribed method for how performer and audience react; total involvement of the participants, the tendency to personalize by incorporating personal pronouns and references to self (African American students tend to use first-person singular pronouns to focus attention on themselves); and use of active verbs coupled with adjectives and adverbs with potential for intensification (called features of elongation and variable stress). Prosodic structure of speech often reflects the way information is organized for presentation. All of those observable aspects of the African American communication style provide leads for teaching innovations (Anokye, 1997).

Educators can benefit from objective and reliable information about African American language. Although the child may not experience difficulty at home or in the neighborhood, language differences may cause problems when the child gets to school. The dilemma for African American children is that their language, which is "worthy" at home, may be "different" and unworthy in school.

Considerable diversity exists in the degree to which children speak an English dialect. Dialect use varies with socioeconomic class, geographic location, and the acculturation of the child and the parents. Children of educated and socially mobile urban African American parents may not speak the dialect of rural and less fortunate parents. African American English is used in varying degrees depending on the individual and the situation.

African Americans have developed effective nonverbal communication that other cultures may question. For example, African American children may learn early that active listening does not always require looking the speaker in the eye. Neither is it necessary to nod one's head or make little noises to show that one is listening.

The language of African American children, albeit an excellent means of communication in the African American culture, may result in communication difficulties and other problems generally associated with not being understood outside one's social community. Furthermore, children who hear negative statements about their language and who are urged to change to a more "standard" form of English undoubtedly have a lower self-esteem and opinion of cultural backgrounds.

The grammatical structure of African American speech patterns frequently leads listeners to conclude that a genuine structural pattern does not exist. Linguists acquainted with the various vernaculars of African American English realize the fallacy of such thinking. African American speakers who say "Carl hat" and "she book" might have knowledge of possessives in grammar like the speaker who says "Mary's hat" and "his book."

■ ■ ■ ■ ■

FOLLOW THROUGH 3.6

UNDERSTANDING AFRICAN AMERICANS'
LANGUAGE "PROBLEMS"

Are African Americans' language "problems" actually problems, or is the real problem the schools' reluctance to accept their grammatical structures? In other words, do the problems result from African Americans' lack of standard English or from others' reluctance to accept African American English and dialects? What will happen if African American students are expected to speak one language at school and another at home?

■ ■ ■ ■ ■

CASE STUDY 3.2

DIALECTAL DIFFERENCES AND STANDARD ENGLISH

"I ain't got no pencil!" "That Paul pencil—I seen him with it!" Mrs. Johnson, a teacher for many years, gets irritated when learners do not speak the standard English that she and the textbooks try to present. Although these language dialects annoy Mrs. Johnson, she really does not know what to do. She has tried to "change" the students' language to a more acceptable dialect, but nothing seems to work.

First, Mrs. Johnson should avoid a perspective that promotes a "blame the victim" attitude. Second, her attempts to "change" the students' language (which has resulted only in frustration for her and her students) shows a lack of understanding of the students and their cultural heritages. Rather than trying to change language habits, or considering "differences" as "deficits," Mrs. Johnson needs to understand that the students' language dialects and communication patterns work perfectly well in their homes and neighborhoods. It is only in schools and outside the African American community that "others" have difficulty understanding.

■ ■ ■ ■ ■

FOR ADDITIONAL INFORMATION
INTERNET ADDRESSES

MEL: Multicultural & ESL Resources
http://mel.lib.mi.us/education/edu-mc.esl.html
Provides information and resources for teaching African Americans (and about African Americans).

The Faces of Science: African Americans in the Sciences
www.lib.lsu.edu/lib/chem/display/faces.html
Provides information on African Americans who have made significant contributions in the field of science.

Black Americans of Achievement Inside
www.baoa.com/index.html   Provides a look at one of the few traded companies that is owned and operated by African Americans.

The Black People of America's First Official National Flag
www.blacknationalflag.com   Provides information on African American struggles across the world and that the U.S. flag deals only with the colonial experience.

Black Americans for Life
www.nrcl.org/outreach/bal.html   Provides information on the problems African Americans face and ways this organization tries to help.

Case Study 3.2 illustrates how Mrs. Johnson becomes annoyed with dialectal differences and how she should consider such differences.

ACHIEVEMENT LEVELS

By the time children begin their formal school career at five years of age, they already have internalized rules and procedures for acquiring knowledge and demonstrating their skills. These cognitive processing protocols are learned from their cultural socialization. They may be refined and elaborated over time, even superseded on occasion for the performance of certain tasks. But the core of these culturally influenced rules and procedures continues to *anchor* how individuals process intellectual challenges for the rest of their lives (Gay, 2000).

Objectivity is fundamental in considering the African American child's achievement (which is closely related to self-esteem). There is no room for stereotypes of achievement expectations. Nationally, the school dropout rate for African American youth is almost 28 percent, and it approaches 50 percent in some areas. African American pupils lag behind European American pupils on standardized tests, and the debate rages over where the responsibility for low academic performance lies. School officials too often blame the child's "disadvantaged" or "culturally deprived" home, although many African American educators point out that generations of European American and Oriental immigrants have performed successfully in schools and have achieved social mobility. These African American educators call for effective schools in which teachers have an objective understanding of African American children and have similar expectations for both African American and European American children (Clark-Johnson, 1988).

African American children's lower performance in the academic areas may be evidence of "blaming the victims" instead of examining the underlying causes of the problem. On national assessments in reading, writing, mathematics, and science, African American students' performance continues to lag behind that of white students, with uneven progress in closing the gap. Several possible reasons exist for this gap, ranging from increased family and community stresses (e.g., poverty, poor health, family difficulties, and community violence) to lower rates of in-school and out-of-school reading among learners, and the declining quality of urban areas where most African American students attend school. Another possibility is that the curriculum in inner-city schools is outdated, inadequate to meet the demands of new curricula experiences and assessment. Many urban systems have focused their curricula more on rote learning of basic skills than on thoughtful examination of serious literature or assignments requiring frequent and extended writing (Darling-Hammond, 1998).

Despite the rhetoric of equality and efforts of many involved in school desegregation and finance reform, problems continue to plague schools attended by many African Americans. African Americans have school experiences substantially separate from and unequal to those of other groups; the physical condition of many schools is poorer; and shortages of funds make it more difficult for rural and urban schools to employ qualified teachers and to provide the equipment that students need (Darling-Hammond, 1998).

Many African American parents have stressed to their children the importance of exceeding European American children's achievement and behavior, because falling short reflects unfavorably on the whole group. In fact, evidence indicates that achievement orientation is a strength of African American families: Most African American college youths came from families whose members were not college-educated. One poll indicated that over 75 percent of African American children said that their mothers wanted them to be one of the best students in the class; interestingly, there appears to be a correlation between maternal warmth (i.e., use of reinforcement, consultation

■ ■ ■ ■ ■ ▬▬▬▬▬▬▬▬▬▬▬▬▬▬▬▬▬▬▬▬▬▬▬▬

FOLLOW THROUGH 3.7

INCREASING AFRICAN AMERICANS' ACHIEVEMENT

Brainstorm in groups of three or four *specific* ways to increase African Americans' achievement levels. Consider the academic backgrounds of the students, school practices (such as the curriculum, instructional practices, and school environment), and educators' mindsets toward African American learners.

Remember, you are looking for ways to improve *African Americans' achievement* rather than achievement in general. You will need, therefore, to consider African Americans' cultural background and the characteristics described in Table 3.1.

with the child, and sensitivity to the child's feelings) and intellectual achievement (Hale-Benson, 1986).

Although statistics reveal lower academic achievement among African Americans, it is important to understand the situation in its historical perspective. For years, many African Americans attended segregated schools in which instruction and materials were often substandard. Substantial progress has been made toward the provision of educational resources to African Americans, but educational opportunities are still not generally equal. Standards of academic performance in schools that serve predominantly African American learners are not equivalent to those that serve predominantly European American learners. Likewise, the amount of encouragement and support the schools provide for educational achievement and attainment are not equal (Jaynes & Williams, 1989).

African American learners face a brighter and more optimistic future. First, African Americans now attend the same schools as their European American counterparts and are receiving more equitable educational opportunities. Second, more opportunities in employment, education, and housing will allow their families an improved standard of living. Third, educators are better trained in diagnostic and remediation approaches and individualized education. Fourth, educators are translating the research on effective teaching, which has grown considerably during the past twenty years, into practical application.

Case Study 3.3 looks at improving academic achievement among African American learners.

Suggestions for working with elementary and secondary learners include:

1. Get to know individual children and their strengths and weaknesses. Hold high expectations for *all* your students.
2. Administer interest inventories to determine needs and areas in which instruction might be most effective.
3. Administer culturally appropriate diagnostic tests to determine which areas require remediation.
4. Work to improve self-esteem and convince learners that they can learn and achieve.
5. Work to improve the learner's attitude about the African American culture.
6. Teach, evaluate, and reteach basic skills.

■ ■ ■ ■ ■ ▬▬▬▬▬▬▬▬▬

CASE STUDY 3.3
IMPROVING ACADEMIC ACHIEVEMENT AMONG AFRICAN AMERICAN LEARNERS

Miss Carter, a new teacher in your school, comments, "I just graduated from the teacher ed. program, and they didn't teach me about all this! I taught students in a nearly all-white school in the suburbs. Now, I have all these African American students. I looked at their achievement test scores and I am floored. What can I do?"

Here are several suggestions for Miss Carter.

1. First and foremost, Miss Carter should understand the dangers of believing generalizations and making blanket statements that downplay the academic performance of an entire cultural group in the school.
2. She needs to understand African American students, their culture, and the dangers of labeling a whole culture's students academically slow.
3. She needs to consider individual students to determine those who are behind academically, and she should make lists of individual strengths and weaknesses.
4. She needs to plan diagnostic–remediation efforts for individuals who have documented learning problems.
5. She needs to plan developmentally and academically appropriate instruction for average and above-average learners, and to seek assistance from administrators, remedial and resource personnel, and special district personnel as she plans instruction for students who are behind academically.

CampbellJones and CampbellJones (2002) maintain that the overwhelming majority of teachers are white, yet schools continue to grow more diverse. One question deserves to be answered: If we believe that all students can learn, then why are disproportionate numbers of African American children having difficulty in school? In Implementing Research 3.1, CampbellJones and CampbellJones (2002) call for teachers to have high expectations for African American children and to learn their culture better, so that educational experiences will be more relevant and successful.

LEARNING STYLES: CULTURAL CONSIDERATIONS

Educators have long recognized that learners respond differently to instruction. While some students learn most efficiently reading alone in a quiet atmosphere, others learn best in a group or cooperative learning project that discusses issues. The "means or conditions" under which a student learns most effectively and efficiently can be termed his or her *learning style*. In essence, learning styles are a complex blend of personal, social, cultural, and behavioral elements that varies from individual to individual and from culture to culture.

■ ■ ■ ■ ■ ▬

IMPLEMENTING RESEARCH 3.1

EDUCATING AFRICAN AMERICAN CHILDREN

CampbellJones and CampbellJones (2002) begin their article by explaining that African Americans often feel "a crisis of credibility" (p. 133) due to many broken promises. Then, they briefly explain several amendments and court cases that have been unproductive in helping African Americans reach their potential.

African American children continue to face teachers with low expectations and schools where covert discrimination is common. In school, more than any other place in society, African American children are socialized that their culture is unimportant, especially compared to that of their European American counterparts. This often results in African American children disidentifying with school—for example, participating in school activities, academics, and eventually dropping out of school.

CampbellJones and CampbellJones (2002) encourage teachers to engage in self-reflection in order to improve their teaching. Teachers often face the intense challenge of reflecting on behavior, feelings, and attitudes that affect their perceptions of others. Such reflection is one of the best ways to gain a better understanding of oneself and others.

IMPLEMENTING THE RESEARCH

CampbellJones and CampbellJones offer several strategies to improve teaching practices and create a more credible education system for African American students.

■ Videotape instruction for critical analysis of teacher interaction with African American students—for example, look for wait times, expectations, and opportunities for higher-level thought.
■ Visit in the homes of African American students in an effort to establish relationships and to become knowledgeable about their lives.
■ Use parents as resources to learn about their children, and use their expertise to provide a culturally relevant curriculum.
■ Consider classroom materials to ensure that students are honored with literature that reflects positively on their culture.
■ Facilitate learning by increasing variety, space, and opportunity for social interaction and movement.
■ Build on the students' use of dialect in the classroom as a means of teaching language flexibility.

We recommend this article to readers because it brings important issues to light and offers specific strategies for helping African American students.

Source: CampbellJones, B., & CampbellJones, F. (2002). Educating African American children: Credibility at the crossroads. *Educational Horizons 80*(3), 133–139.

Although the relationship between culture and learning style is not fully understood, it is an important one: "Culture shapes the way we think (cognition), the way we interact (behavior), and the way we transmit knowledge to the next generation (education)" (Collier & Hoover, 1987, p. 7). Hernandez (1989) explains that cultural and cognitive development are closely intertwined, that social and environmental factors that influence cognitive development are closely intertwined, and that social and environmental factors influence cognitive and affective preferences. These, in turn, reflect themselves in incentives, motivation, interpersonal relationships, and patterns of intellectual abilities (Hernandez, 1989).

Selected instructional strategies appropriate for African Americans include:

- Affirming the strong personal voice in African American informal interactions and formal writings
- Building on oral discourse habits and interpretation
- Incorporating performance and role playing as regular features of teaching and learning
- Validating African American dialect and expressive modes as a functional communication system and assisting students in analyzing and appreciating them
- Valuing and using African American culture habitually, rather than just on special occasions
- Developing a sense of trust, community, and mutual responsibility for learning among students and with teachers
- Consistently combining individual and group efforts and accountability for task performance
- Creating classroom climates and opportunities for collaborative composing, revising, and editing writing tasks
- Using a system of peer response, tutoring, and study buddies
- Affirming personal responses to reading (Gay, 2000)

Knowing African American learners' cultural characteristics and their learning styles represents an essential first step when planning and implementing a multicultural curriculum that meets the needs of African American learners. In Implementing Research 3.2, Howard (2001) focuses on African Americans and culturally relevant teaching.

SCHOOL PRACTICES IMPEDING AFRICAN AMERICANS' PROGRESS

Educators sometimes develop and implement curricula that either overlook or ignore cultural diversity. African American learners may find themselves in a world of European American rules, expectations, and orientations. Rather than recognize cultural diversity and teach learners as individuals, educators treat learners as groups with homogeneous characteristics. School practices that may impede learning achievement and appropriate behavior include the following.

1. Failing to understand African American learners and expecting all learners to conform to European American standards and expectations
2. Grouping by homogeneous ability, which may result in the segregation of learners by culture and by social class

■ ■ ■ ■ ■

IMPLEMENTING RESEARCH 3.2
AFRICAN AMERICANS AND CULTURALLY RELEVANT TEACHING

Howard (2001) maintains that research examining African Americans' perceptions and interpretations of learning environments has been minimal. In his article, Howard explains the findings from a study that sought to assess African American elementary students' interpretations of culturally relevant teachers in urban contexts. Student responses indicated that culturally relevant teaching strategies had a positive affect on student effort and engagement in class content and were consistent with culturally relevant pedagogy. The students' perceptions and interpretations of their teachers' pedagogy reveal critical insights into the dynamics of young African American learners.

IMPLEMENTING THE RESEARCH
- Teachers can make "school feel like home" (p. 145), for example, creating a school environment that is not in conflict with the students' cultural background.
- Teachers can demonstrate caring in as many ways as possible, for example, providing positive reinforcement, emphasizing high expectations, giving praise for student accomplishments, and asking about students' lives outside the classroom.
- Teachers can establish a sense of community, for example, encouraging kindred relationships among students that will lead to more cooperative learning situations.
- Teachers can create stimulating and exciting classroom environments that generate student interest and enthusiasm.

Source: Howard, T. C. (2001). Telling their side of the story: African American students' perceptions of culturally relevant teaching. *The Urban Review, 33*(2), 131–149.

3. Providing insufficient or inappropriate positive reinforcement
4. Downgrading or even punishing learners for using English dialects
5. Providing for African American learners too many worksheets and drill times without a meaningful purpose
6. Using European American–oriented textbooks and curricular materials
7. Basing academic and behavior standards and expectations on stereotypical expectations

The importance of culturally responsive learning environments is explored in Implementing Research 3.3.

School practices related to the assessment of children and adolescents is another area that can impede African American learners' progress. Assessment devices designed primarily for middle-class white learners do not always provide an accurate assessment of African American learners.

Isen (1983) recommends four tests for African American learners. See Table 3.2.

Case Study 3.4 shows that educators should listen to and offer a response to parents' concerns.

■ ■ ■ ■ ■

IMPLEMENTING RESEARCH 3.3

CULTURALLY RESPONSIVE LEARNING ENVIRONMENTS

Howard-Hamilton (2000) maintains that teachers have the power to make the learning environment for all students more inclusive and supportive rather than isolating and exclusionary. To understand African American students' meaning-making and learning process in the classroom, teachers need to understand who the student is and what the student believes in. First, Howard-Hamilton provides an excellent explanation of several racial identity theories. Then, she provides a discussion of effective dialogue and teaching practices. She believes that recognizing the diverse and unique backgrounds of all students in the classroom enhances the learning experiences for everyone. Designing a culturally responsive curriculum should include:

- Coursework that emphasizes human need or interest so students can feel a sense of relevancy
- Teachers who are collaborative with learners, helping them to understand the meaning of their learning as well as the virtue of their own thinking
- Students working collaboratively as a community of learners
- Students and teacher assuming a blame-free and trusting belief in people and their potential to be transformed
- Students being treated equally in the classroom and invited to address behaviors, practices, and policies that are prejudicial

IMPLEMENTING THE RESEARCH
- Teachers should be willing to empower students and be comfortable with the disagreements that come with extensive dialogue, which eventually leads to dissonance.
- Teachers should be willing to allow students to engage in self-exploration through journal writing and through raising and answering their own questions.
- Teachers should be comfortable with affective dialogue that can lead to students venting frustration, anger, guilt, and shame when delving with issues of racial consciousness.
- Teachers can use small-group discussions to evoke moral dilemma decision-making skills and multiple perspective taking.
- Teachers should revise their curriculum to include reading selections that have a multicultural perspective.

Source: Howard-Hamilton, M. F. (2000). Creating a culturally responsive learning environment for African American students. *New Directions for Teaching and Learning, 82,* 45–53.

PROMOTING POSITIVE SELF-ESTEEM AND CULTURAL IDENTITIES

Several studies have sought to ascertain the effects of minority group status on personality development during identity formation. These studies provide concrete evidence for long-held opinions that the society and the culture in which African Americans live adversely affects their personality development, self-esteem, and educational achievements.

■ ■ ■ ■ ■ ■

CASE STUDY 3.4
RESPONDING TO PARENTS' DEMANDS

A vocal and militant group of parents presents a list of demands for improving the school system. They feel that the education their children are receiving does not meet the needs of African Americans. One of their demands is to create all-male classes and to have African American male teachers for kindergarten through grade 3.

It is clear that some action is necessary to change the attitudes of these parents toward their school and to have a school that better meets the needs of African American learners. Failing to listen and respond appropriately to the parents' concerns whenever possible can only result in frustration for parents, school officials, and the children attending the school. The school's response should include these steps.

1. Assess how well the school is meeting African American students' needs in the areas in which the parents perceive it to be failing. Encourage educators to listen to the parents' demands in an atmosphere free of hostility and defensiveness.
2. Complete a multicultural assessment of the overall school curriculum and environment to determine how effectively educators are addressing the needs of African American learners.
3. Form an advisory committee consisting of parents, an administrator, teachers from the school, and several community members to discuss the concerns of the African American parents.
4. Explain that having black male teachers in kindergarten through third grade has not been conclusively proven beneficial and that there are not enough black male teachers willing to teach the lower grades.

TABLE 3.2 Assessing African American Children

The Black Intelligence Test of Cultural Homogeneity (BITCH) is a test whose major objectives are to identify early indicators of intelligence in black children. Test items include black American folklore, history, life experiences, and dialect, which Isen feels are more relevant and fairer to the black culture than other standardized tests.

Themes of Black Awareness (TOBA) is a forty-item sentence-completion instrument that elicits thematic material relating to an individual's level of black awareness.

Themes Concerning Black (TCB) is a personality inventory for blacks.

Multicultural Pluralistic Assessment (SOMPA) is a battery of tests to be used with culturally diverse five- to eleven-year-olds. It is based on the fundamental assumption that U.S. society is pluralistic, both culturally and structurally. The battery includes an interview with parents, a medical examination, and a Wechsler IQ test.

Lee and Lindsey (1985) maintain that racism and oppression hinder the positive development of the African American child's self-esteem.

Self-esteem may be the most influential factor in a learner's development. The African American child or adolescent's self-perception influences not only his or her academic achievement but also many other social and psychological aspects of development. Distinctive aspects affecting self-esteem include children's perception of themselves, how others perceive them to be, and how the children perceive others. The negative feelings and discrimination African American children and adolescents perceive are devastating to their self-esteem. Historically, African Americans have experienced much to lower their self-esteem, but civil rights efforts and recent decades of progress have helped raise it.

African American parents can help foster self-esteem development in their children. The phrase "You're just as good as anybody else" may help sooth anxieties that arise when their children engage in a social comparison with European American children (Hale-Benson, 1986, p. 64).

Suggestions for educators working with African American children and adolescents include the following.

1. Be open and honest in relationships with African American children.
2. Learn as much as possible about your own culture.
3. Seek to respect and appreciate culturally different attitudes and behaviors.
4. Take advantage of all available opportunities to participate in activities in the African American community.
5. Keep in mind that African American children are members of their unique cultural group and are unique individuals as well.
6. Eliminate all behaviors that suggest prejudice or racism.
7. Implement practices that acknowledge the African American culture.
8. Hold high expectations of African American children, and encourage all who work with African American children to do likewise.
9. Ask questions about the African American culture.
10. Develop culture-specific strategies, mechanisms, techniques, and programs to foster the psychological development of African American children (Locke, 1989).

The identity formation of the African American adolescent has been a source of considerable concern, especially in poverty-ridden households and single-parent homes. New evidence, however, indicates that this concern may be ill-founded, that the African American adolescent might not be as detrimentally affected as once believed. Specifically, single mothers do not usually perceive their families as "broken," because fathers and the extended family and kinship network continue to play a role in their lives. The physical presence or absence of adult males in the home says little about the availability of other male models. Adolescent males living in single-parent households often identify male role models in their neighborhoods and classrooms, and even in instruction from their mothers (Bell-Scott & McKenry, 1986).

Gay African American and Hispanic youths (ages 14–19) have a unique set of stressful life events, low self-esteem, emotional distress, and multiple problem behaviors (alcohol use, drug use, and risky sexual behavior). Admitting their sexual orientation or having it discovered by others can expose a gay or lesbian to ridicule. Gay and lesbian youth cannot anticipate how others may respond to knowledge of their sexual identity. Stressful events related to being gay or lesbian have been shown to cause significant emotional distress, multiple problem behavior, and low self-esteem. In fact, even good

■ ■ ■ ■ ■ ▬▬▬

FOLLOW THROUGH 3.8
COMPARING AND CONTRASTING LEARNERS

Using the case study method, compare and contrast two learners, one with self-esteem and one without. What are the differences in such areas as attitudes toward self, school, and the teacher; academic achievement; and overall mental health and psychosocial development? What might you do to help learners with low self-esteem? What might you suggest to parents and extended family members?

■ ■ ■ ■ ■ ▬▬▬

CULTURAL PORTRAIT
PAUL—AN AFRICAN AMERICAN LEARNER

Paul J., a ten-year-old African American learner, attends a large urban elementary school that is approximately half African and half European American. Paul is a low achiever, speaks an English dialect, and has low self-esteem. When speaking of Paul's lack of academic achievement, Mrs. Smith, Paul's teacher, feels he does not listen. "He looks away when I talk to him. I have tried to get him to look at me," Mrs. Smith states. Paul claims he is listening, even though he does not look directly at Mrs. Smith as she speaks. Paul knows Mrs. Smith does not approve of his English dialect, but his language works fine at home and in the playground, so he doesn't see any need to change.

Paul feels he is in a bind: He tries to make higher grades but just cannot seem to do so. He sees himself in the "middle." Some African American students make better grades than he does, and others make worse. Paul feels the frustration of coping in a school that appears to cater to white students and appears to expect African Americans to conform to European American expectations.

HOW PAUL'S TEACHER CAN RESPOND
Mrs. Smith's response can take several directions.

1. First and foremost, she needs to understand that the people of the African American culture do not feel it is necessary to look someone in the eye when listening to him or her.
2. Mrs. Smith also needs to recognize that Paul's English dialect works well for him at home, in the playground, and in the neighborhood.
3. As for Paul's seeing himself in the "middle," Mrs. Smith's response should be to administer the proper diagnostic tests to determine Paul's achievement and to identify any special strengths and weaknesses.
4. The fourth response extends further into the school itself. Mrs. Smith can focus the administration's attention on the school's European American orientation and try to change it. Rather than the school's being genuinely multicultural in nature (and celebrating cultural diversity), it might be continuing an orientation toward European American perspectives and dealing with Paul (and other African American learners) as just another of those liabilities one can expect in urban schools.

self-esteem does not buffer the relationship between gay-related stressful life events and emotional stress or between these life events and multiple problem behaviors (Rosario, Rotheram-Borus, & Reid, 1996).

SUMMING UP

Educators planning a culturally responsive curriculum and school environment for African American learners should:

1. Understand the African American culture and its people from a historical and contemporary perspective.
2. Understand the close correlation between socioeconomic class and academic achievement among African American learners (and learners of other cultures).
3. Address the dilemma of African American English, which needs understanding and appropriate action: African Americans understand one another in home and community situations, yet they sometimes experience difficulty in school and teaching and learning situations. Remember that "different" does not equate with "wrong" or "inferior."
4. Promote the self-esteem and cultural identities that are crucial to African American learners' academic achievement, psychosocial development, and general outlook on life.
5. Consider and address African American students' learning styles when planning teaching and learning experiences.
6. Consider intracultural, geographic, socioeconomic, urban and rural, and other differences that result in "individuality," rather than categorizing all African American learners as a homogeneous group.
7. Understand several factors (appropriate diagnostic and remediation procedures, improving self-esteem, basic skills instruction) that have the potential for improving African American academic achievement.
8. Adhere to the commitment that educators should not stereotype African American learners or label them as slow learners. Educators also must not group learners in organization patterns that result in segregation by either culture or social class.

SUGGESTED LEARNING ACTIVITIES

1. Complete a case study of two African American learners, each from a different social class—for example, one from a lower class and one from a higher social class. Compare and contrast differences in culture, language, familial traditions, food, and life expectations.

2. Using an actual student achievement permanent record (with academic grades, standardized test scores, and anecdotal comments), outline what appear to be the learner's strengths and weaknesses. Administer two different diagnostic instruments designed to determine strengths and weaknesses. With this information, outline a teaching and learning plan designed to improve academic achievement and self-esteem.

3. The family, both immediate and extended, is a valued aspect of the African American culture. How can educators use this resource? What can educators do to involve African American families? What special concerns should educators keep in mind during parent conferences?

SUGGESTIONS FOR COLLABORATIVE EFFORTS

Form groups of three or four that, if possible, represent our nation's cultural and gender diversity. Working collaboratively, focus your group's attention toward the following efforts.

1. Conduct an in-depth study of English dialects. Divide learning assignments in such a manner that each group member has an individual task such as providing specific examples of dialectical differences, providing names of textbooks and other curricular materials that positively reflect dialects, and reviewing the literature on dialects. Working collaboratively, discuss how children and adolescents who are able to communicate in home and community situations may experience difficulties communicating in school.

2. Design a study (case studies, interviews, anecdotal records) to learn more about several African American families. Determine cultural, intracultural, and social class differences. How do these families differ in dress and food preferences, customs, and family behaviors? What other evidence can you find of tremendous diversity among African American families? How can the school provide a curriculum that responds to the African American family?

3. African Americans sometimes want segregated all-black schools for their children and adolescents. They believe that African Americans receive better treatment in such schools and learn more about the African culture. They also believe that educators in such schools address their cultural characteristics and learning styles. Have a discussion in your group as to the advantages and disadvantages of "separate culture" schools. Also, how do these schools differ from the segregated schools that fueled the civil rights movement? Will "separate culture" schools prepare African Americans to live and work with people from other cultures? How can schools address the concerns of parents who want to send their children to all-black schools?

EXPANDING YOUR HORIZONS: ADDITIONAL JOURNAL READINGS AND BOOKS

Constantine, M. G., & Blackmon, S. M. (2002). Black adolescents' racial socialization experiences: Their relations to home, school, and peer self-esteem. *Journal of Black Studies, 32*(3), 322–335.
Constantine and Blackmon explored the relationship between parental racial socialization messages and home, school, and peer self-esteem among African American adolescents and found parental racial socialization messages positively associated self-esteem.

Hollie, S. (2001). Acknowledging the language of African American students: Instructional strategies. *English Journal, 90*(4), 54–59.
As the title implies, Hollie looks at language and literacy backgrounds and describes strategies for success in Los Angeles.

Joshua, M. B. (2002). Inside picture books: Where are the children of color? *Educational Horizons, 80*(3), 125–132.
Joshua, an author who has rewritten two classics using African and African American illustrations, maintains that picture books lack children of color and offers a number of worthwhile recommendations to remedy this unfortunate situation.

McCollough, S. (2000). Teaching African American students. *The Clearing House, 74*(1), 5–6.
McCollough maintains that teachers continue to mistreat, misunderstand, and misassess African American students.

Perez, S. A. (2002). Using Ebonics or Black English as a bridge to teaching standard English. *Contemporary Education, 71*(4), 34–37.

>As the title implies, Perez looks at the Ebonics controversy and proposes that it can become an effective bridge to standard English.

Texeira, M. T., & Christian, P. M. (2002). And still they rise: Practical advice for increasing African American enrollments in higher education. *Educational Horizons, 80*(3), 117–124.

>Texeira and Christian (2002) maintain that teacher attitudes and institutional racism (or teachers' tendency to respond from racist- and class-biased paradigms) seem to be stumbling blocks for teachers teaching students of color.

EXPANDING YOUR STUDENTS' HORIZONS: APPROPRIATE AFRICAN AMERICAN BOOKS FOR CHILDREN AND ADOLESCENTS

Barboza, Steven. *Door of No Return: The Legend of Goree Island*. Cobblehill, 1994.

Belton, Sandra. *May'naise Sandwiches & Sunshine Tea*. Four Winds, 1994.

Belton, Sandra. *From Miss Ida's Porch*. Four Winds, 1993.

Berry, James. *Celebration Song*. Simon & Schuster, 1994.

Bogart, Jo Ellen. *Daniel's Dog*. Scholastic, 1990.

Bray, Rosemary L. *Martin Luther King*. Four Winds, 1994.

Coleman, Evelyn. *The Foot Warmer and the Crow*. Macmillan, 1994.

Coles, Robert. *The Story of Ruby Bridges*. Scholastic, 1994.

Cummings, Pat. *Clean Your Room, Harvey Moon*. Bradbury, 1991.

Gilchrist, Jan Spivey. *Lift Ev'ry Voice and Sing*. Scholastic, 1994.

Hamilton, Virginia. *Jagurundi*. Blue Sky, 1994.

Howard, Elizabeth Fitzgerald. *Aunt Flossie's Hats (Crab Cakes Later)*. Clarion, 1991.

Hudson, Wade. *Five Brave Explorers*. Scholastic, 1994.

Johnson, Angela. *Toning the Sweep*. Orchard, 1993.

Johnson, Delores. *Seminole Diary*. Macmillan, 1994.

Katz, William Loren. *Breaking the Chain: African American Slave Resistance*. Atheneum, 1990.

Kurtz, Jane. *Fire on the Mountain*. Simon & Schuster, 1994.

Lester, Julius. *The Man Who Knew Too Much*. Clarion, 1994.

Lyons, Mary E. *Raw Head, Bloody Bones: African American Tales of the Supernatural*. Atheneum, 1995.

Meltzer, Milton. *Frederick Douglass: In His Own Words*. Harcourt, Brace, 1994.

Miller, William. *Zora Hurston and the Chinaberry Tree*. Lee and Low, 1994.

Myers, Walter Dean. *The Dragon Takes a Wife*. Scholastic, 1994.

Pinkney, Andrea Davis. *Hold Fast to Dreams*. Morrow, 1995.

Pinkwater, Jill. *Tales of the Bronx*. Macmillan, 1991.

Pitts, Mildred. *Mississippi Challenge*. Aladdin, 1995.

Quackenbush, Robert. *Arthur Ashe and His Match with History*. Simon & Schuster, 1994.

Rinaldi, Ann. *Wolf by the Ears*. Scholastic, 1991.

Ritter, Larence. *Leagues Apart: The Men and Times of the Negro Baseball Leagues*. Morrow, 1995.

Rochelle, Belinda. *When Joe Louis Won the Title*. Houghton-Mifflin, 1994.

Woodson, Jacqueline. *I Hadn't Meant to Tell You*. Delacorte, 1994.

CHAPTER FOUR

UNDERSTANDING AMERICAN INDIAN CHILDREN AND ADOLESCENTS

Understanding the material and activities in this chapter will help the reader to:

- Describe the cultural, socioeconomic, and familial characteristics of American Indian children and adolescents

- Explain special problems and challenges that confront American Indian children and adolescents

- Describe American Indian learners and their development, achievement levels, language problems, and learning styles

- List several educational practices that impede the American Indian learners' educational progress

- Offer several suggestions and strategies for improving American Indian learners' self-esteem and cultural identities

- List several points that educators of American Indians should remember when planning teaching and learning experiences

- Suggest appropriate children's literature, implement research findings, and provide culturally appropriate experiences for American Indian learners

OVERVIEW

American Indian children and adolescents have special needs that warrant educators' understanding: cherished and unique cultural characteristics, language problems, familial traditions, and learning problems, which present schools with special challenges. Yet teacher education programs traditionally have not prepared prospective teachers to understand multicultural populations and the special characteristics and learning problems of American Indian learners or, in reality, any other multicultural group. This chapter examines American Indian learners—their culture, language issues, families, achievement levels, learning styles, and overall school programs.

ORIGINS

Scholars do not know exactly when people first came to the Americas. While many archaeologists have concluded that the lack of fossils rules out the possibility of men and women having evolved in the Western hemisphere, some American Indian believe that they originated in the Americas. Archaeologists believe that the ancestors of American Indians came from Asia.

Portman and Herring (2001) offer an excellent description of American Indian history. (It is important to note that Portman and Herring preferred the term Native American Indian rather than Native American or American Indian.) The long history of interaction between Native American Indians and European Americans can be divided into five time periods, which have been determined largely by the interaction of the federal government with Native American Indians: (1) removal (seventeenth century to the 1840s), characterized as saying, "the only good Indian is a dead Indian" (Portman & Herring, 2001, p. 186); (2) reservation (1860s to 1920s), characterized by the saying, "kill the Indian, but save the person"; (3) reorganization (1930s to 1950s), when schools were allowed on the reservation, which eased cultural repression; (4) termination (1950s to1960s), characterized by attempts at sociocultural integration and end of dependence on the federal government, which led to the sale of large tracts of Native American Indian lands and increased poverty; and (5) self-determination (1973 to present), characterized by increased tribal sovereignty due mainly to the militant struggles of many Native American Indians in the early 1970s. Portman and Herring (2001) maintain that these time periods cannot be considered exclusive of each other because of the oral histories that were passed from one generation to the next in Native American Indian cultures. The experiences of past generations are continued in some degree by those Native American Indians who have maintained cultural and familial ties (Portman & Herring, 2001).

AMERICAN INDIANS TODAY

American Indians number more than 500 tribes of varying sizes. The larger tribes (those with more than 100,000 members) include the Cherokee, Navajo, Chippewa, and Sioux. Tribes in the range of 50,000 people include the Choctaw, Pueblo, and Apache. Fourteen tribes have populations between 10,000 and 21,000. Most tribes have less than 10,000. Nearly one-half of American Indians today live west of the Mississippi River. In fact, more than half of the American Indian population lived in just six states in 1990: Oklahoma, California, Arizona, New Mexico, Alaska (with large numbers of Aleuts), and Washington.

The U.S. Bureau of the Census offers other facts about American Indians and their demographics. First, they are a young and growing population. Thirty-nine percent of the American Indian population (which also includes Eskimos and Aleuts) was under twenty years of age in 1990, compared with 29 percent of the nation's total population. Second, their educational attainment improved during the 1980s. Increasingly, American Indians are finishing high school, and about 9 percent complete a bachelor's

■ ■ ■ ■ ■ ▬▬▬▬▬▬▬▬▬▬▬

FOLLOW THROUGH 4.1

LEARNING ABOUT AMERICAN INDIANS—
THEIR TRIBES AND INDIVIDUALS

The American Indian population represents many different tribes and peoples—it is difficult to offer generalizations and conclusions. Bearing in mind tribal and individual differences, suggest four or five ways you could learn about the American Indian students in
your class.

degree or higher. Third, more American Indians lived below the poverty lines. Fourth,
about 22 percent, or about 437,431, lived on reservations and trust lands in 1990 (U.S.
Bureau of the Census, 1993c).

Over the past three decades, American Indians have been progressively moving
off reservation lands. As a result, over 70 percent of American Indians live in non-In-
dian communities. Movement from reservation to off-reservation settings can harm
family relationships and increase the likelihood of risk-taking behaviors that endanger
health and well-being. Because educational behaviors and attitudes may result from
other stresses in students' lives, off-reservation adolescents may be even more prone to
educational problems than their on-reservation peers (Machamer & Gruber, 1998).

STEREOTYPING OF AMERICAN INDIAN
CHILDREN AND ADOLESCENTS

Although stereotypical images often accompany the term American Indian children and
adolescents, this culture and these developmental periods constitute a highly diverse
group. Differences in developing children and adolescents vary significantly. Not all
American Indians are slow learners, shy, and undependable; likewise, not all adolescents
are rebellious and experience difficult and stressful times. Although some common
characteristics emerge from the study of American Indian children and adolescents, we
must use caution not to oversimplify or ignore individual differences.

Case Study 4.1 shows the importance of understanding American Indians.

CULTURAL CHARACTERISTICS

American Indian culture plays a major role in the shaping of children and adolescents.
Educators must make the extra effort to seek accurate information and to understand
American history and the American Indian culture from the point of view of the American Indian and from the child and adolescent's perspective. Educators should also
think through their own cultural beliefs and realize the dangers of *cultural substitution*,
in which American Indian learners are expected to change cultural viewpoints to coin-
cide with European American, middle-class ones. Table 4.1 provides a look at selected
cultural characteristics of American Indian children and adolescents.

■ ■ ■ ■ ■ ▬▬

CASE STUDY 4.1

ACCURATE PERCEPTIONS OF AMERICAN INDIANS

On completing her teacher education program in the East, Ms. Stein joined several friends who went to a Western state in hopes of finding teaching positions. Ms. Stein accepted a position teaching eighth-grade social studies in a school that was predominantly American Indian.

Trying to be as objective as possible, Ms. Stein questioned her beliefs about American Indian learners. She asked herself and her friends, "Are American Indians really different? Are they all poor? What will I do about their lower achievement?" She had heard so many stories. She wondered whether they were true and how she should separate facts from stereotypes.

Ms. Stein and her future students are fortunate in at least one aspect—Ms. Stein realizes that she does not know what to believe, and she is willing to question stereotypical generalizations. Miss Stein decided on the following strategy:

1. Speak with several professionals in the school—teachers, administrators, and special-services personnel, such as the speech therapist and the librarian. Obtain an objective cultural portrait; base opinions on objective information about the American Indian culture, families, religions, socioeconomic status, and language.
2. Look at each student's permanent record to learn academic strengths and weaknesses.
3. Learn as much as possible about the learners' families and their role in the education process.
4. Read about the American Indian culture, its contributions, and its proud heritage.
5. Read nonfiction and basic informational children's books that provide insights into the American Indian culture.
6. Talk to American Indian learners and express an interest in their cultural backgrounds.
7. Seek information from organizations that promote American Indians, their overall welfare, and their determination for equality.

TABLE 4.1   Selected Characteristics of American Indian Children and Adolescents

CATEGORY	CHARACTERISTIC
Behavioral/emotional expressiveness	Introverted
Verbal	Indirect gaze when listening or speaking
Nonverbal	Preference for close personal space
Concept of time	Time and place viewed as permanent and settled
Social orientation	Group-centered; cooperative rather than competitive

Developed from: Rivera, B. D., & Rogers-Adkinson, D. (1997). Culturally sensitive interventions: Social skills training with children and parents from culturally and linguistically diverse backgrounds. *Intervention in School and Clinic 33*(2), 75–80.

■ ■ ■ ■ ■

USING CHILDREN'S LITERATURE
INFORMATIONAL BOOKS

Aliki. Corn Is Maize: *The Gift of the Indians.* Crowell, 1976.
Aliki provides an interesting and excellent history of corn, how it grows, and its first uses. (Reading Level: 2; Interest Level: 5–9.)

Ashabranner, Brent. *To Live in Two Worlds: American Indian Youth Today.* Dodd, Mead, 1984.
Ashabranner provides true accounts as Indian youths tell about their own lives. (Reading Level: 7; Interest Level: 11 and above.)

Ashabranner, Brent. *Morning Star, Black Sun: The Northern Cheyenne Indians and America's Energy Crisis.* Dodd, Mead, 1982.

This informative text traces the history of the Northern Cheyenne and discusses their fight to save their lands. (Reading Level: 7; Interest Level: 11 and above.)

Poatgieter, Alice Hermina. *Indian Legacy: Native American Influences on World Life and Culture.* Messner, 1981.
This text provides readers with an informative account of North and South American Indian contributions to democratic attitudes and culture. (Reading Level: 5–7; Interest Level: 9 and above.)

American Indians esteem values and beliefs that differ from those of European Americans. European Americans believe that individuals have freedoms as long as their actions remain within the law; American Indian children are taught that all actions must be in harmony with nature. Other values conveyed to children and adolescents include a degree of self-sufficiency and being in harmony with knowledge they gain from the natural world. Adults teach youth to respect and protect the aged, who provide wisdom and acquaint the young with traditions, customs, legends, and myths (Axelson, 1999).

Achievement in the European American culture may not equate with achievement in the American Indian culture, and vice versa, and to place a value judgment on one or the other constitutes a serious mistake. Sanders (1987) hypothesizes that this cultural conflict and incompatibility contribute significantly to the academic failure of many American Indian children. American Indian children function in the average to superior range until the fourth grade. Thereafter, academic achievement typically declines each year, so that by the tenth grade, American Indian students are doing below-average work.

American Indian tribes, organizations, and communities play vital roles in the improvement of educational opportunities for American Indian children. More than one hundred tribes operate Head Start programs that serve 16,548 American Indian children. Many public schools, the Bureau of Indian Affairs, and tribal schools also strive to provide special education and culture-related learning designed to assist the development and early education of American Indian children (Walker, 1988).

Societal and cultural beliefs and traditions of the American Indian people particularly influence developing adolescents and their evolving identities. Adolescents living in American Indian families and attending European American schools, whether

■ ■ ■ ■ ■ ▬▬▬▬▬▬▬▬▬▬▬▬▬▬▬▬▬▬▬▬▬▬▬▬▬▬▬▬▬▬▬▬▬

USING CHILDREN'S LITERATURE
BIOGRAPHIES

Tobias, Tobi. *Maria Tallchief.* Crowell, 1970.
    The biography of Maria Tallchief, a world-
    renowned ballerina born in Fairfax, Okla-
    homa. (Reading Level: 4; Interest Level:
    8–12.)

Fall, Thomas. *Jim Thorpe.* Crowell, 1970.
    A biography for young children, this story
    focuses on Jim Thorpe, a great athlete and
    Olympic hero. (Reading Level: 2; Interest
    Level: 7–10.)

Grant, Matthew. *Squanto: The Indian Who Saved
    the Pilgrims.* Publications Associates, 1974.

This is an illustrated biography of the
Wampanoag Indian who played an impor-
tant role in the lives of early settlers in
New England. (Reading Level: 3; Interest
Level: 6–10.)

Brown, Marion Marsh. *Homeward, The Arrow's
    Flight.* Abington, 1980.
    The story of the first female American
    Indian to become a doctor of Western
    medicine. (Reading Level: 6; Interest
    Level: 9–11.)

on or off the reservation, experience degrees of cultural confusion and often question allegiance to a cultural identification. Such a dilemma can pose a particularly serious problem for adolescents who want to retain their rich cultural heritage while seeking acceptance in European American schools and society.

American Indian adolescents must also resolve cultural differences surrounding the concept of sharing. Sharing represents a genuine and routine way of life in the American Indian culture. Yet this cultural belief, which is so deeply ingrained in the American Indian culture, does not equate with the European American custom of accumulating private property or savings.

The accumulation of material possessions is the measure of most people's "worth" and social status, but the American Indian considers the ability and willingness to share to be most worthy (Lewis & Ho, 1989). While younger children may wish to share only with adults, an acceptance and allegiance to the cultural tradition of sharing increases as the child or adolescent develops. Adolescence is a unique time to develop a concept of sharing that is congruent with American Indian cultural expectations. Case Study 4.2 shows the need for teachers to understand the American Indian concept of sharing.

Several reasons exist for adolescents' becoming increasingly cognizant and ac-cepting of this cultural expectation. Adolescents have more advanced intellectual abil-ities that enable them to recognize that it is possible for two people to want the same thing at the same time, that shared possessions often return, and that sharing can be reciprocal. Developing intellectual skills allows an adolescent to understand the differ-ence between sharing temporarily and donating permanently. The adolescent can understand, as well as make clear to others, his or her intent (Kostelnik, Stein, Whiren, & Soderman, 1988).

■ ■ ■ ■ ■ ▬▬▬

CASE STUDY 4.2
THE AMERICAN INDIAN CONCEPT OF SHARING

Mrs. Jason was upset with eight-year-old Bill, an American Indian, when she learned that he had taken a pencil off another child's desk. The week before he had taken a pencil off her desk. What's wrong with Bill? she wondered. She asked a friend, "I told him about taking other people's things. I just cannot understand him. Why does he continue to take things that do not belong to him?"

Her friend thought that the problem might be more Mrs. Jason's than Bill's. Although Mrs. Jason needs to discuss with Bill that whites can misconstrue taking things as stealing, Mrs. Jason also needs to understand Bill's perception of the situation and his cultural concepts of sharing. Bill had forgotten his pencil, and in his culture taking another's pencil is not a problem (she had others, didn't she?). He would not have objected if someone had taken his pencil when he had more than one.

When she heard Bill's explanation, Mrs. Jason realized that what she had perceived as stealing was Bill's concept (culturally permissible and encouraged) of sharing. She decided that two steps would be appropriate: First, she needed a better understanding of sharing in the American Indian culture, and second, she needed to explain to others in the class that Bill was not stealing their pencils.

Other notable cultural characteristics of American Indians that become an integral part of children's and adolescents' evolving identity are the tendencies toward patience and passive temperaments. American Indians are taught to be patient, to control emotions, and to avoid passionate outbursts over small matters. As the American Indian adolescent develops an identity, cultural characteristics such as poise and self-containment become ingrained.

These cultural habits conflict with European American impatience and competitiveness and often result in the mistaken perception that the American Indian is lazy, uncaring, and inactive (Lewis & Ho, 1989). This demeanor or personality trait is also demonstrated in American Indians' tendency to lower their voices to communicate anger, unlike European American adolescents, who learn to raise their voices to convey a message (Kostelnik et al., 1988).

■ ■ ■ ■ ■ ▬▬▬

FOLLOW THROUGH 4.2
UNDERSTANDING THE AMERICAN INDIAN CONCEPT OF SHARING

Talk to American Indian children and adolescents about sharing. Learn specifically how they feel and why. See how they perceive European American attitudes toward possessions and ownership.

■ ■ ■ ■ ■ ▬▬▬▬▬▬▬▬▬▬▬▬▬▬▬▬▬▬▬▬▬▬

FOLLOW THROUGH 4.3
UNDERSTANDING AMERICAN INDIAN VALUES AND BELIEFS

Learn more about American Indian students by asking about their values and beliefs. For example, question how they feel about competition, achievement, and self-sufficiency, and ask for their opinions of school rules.

Noninterference with others and a deep respect for the rights and dignity of individuals constitute basic premises of American Indian culture. Although such practices may have allowed people of other cultures to think of American Indians as uncaring or unconcerned, the actual case is quite the contrary. American Indians are taught early to respect the rights and privileges of other individuals and the responsibility to work together toward a common goal in harmony with nature.

Gender

Gender is another difference that makes American Indian children and adolescents unique. As in other cultures, American Indian females differ from males in their ways of thinking, behaving, and learning. Undoubtedly, American Indian females are also taught certain cultural and tribal beliefs from birth that influence their roles. Educators working with American Indians need to address females' particular gender differences, rather than assuming too much homogeneity between males and females. While research studies focusing specifically on American Indian females are virtually nonexistent, it is obvious that gender differences exist (Grossman & Grossman, 1994). As

■ ■ ■ ■ ■ ▬▬▬▬▬▬▬▬▬▬▬▬▬▬▬▬▬▬▬▬▬▬

FOR ADDITIONAL INFORMATION

Indian Youth of America, 609 Badgerow Building, P.O. Box 2786, Sioux City, IA 51106. This American Indian organization sponsors cultural enrichment projects, summer camp programs, and a resource center in its attempt to improve the lives of American Indian children.

Council for Indian Education, 517 Rimrock Rd., Billings, MT 59102. The CIE seeks to improve and secure higher standards of education for American Indian children, promotes high-quality children's literature in the Indian culture, and publishes books about American Indian life, past and present.

Natural Indian Education Association, 1819 H St., NW, Suite 800, Washington, D.C. 20006. This organization designs programs to improve the social and economic well-being of American Indians and Alaskan natives. The primary emphasis is on an exchange of ideas, techniques, and research methods among participants in American Indian education.

with other differences that multicultural educators work to address, gender differences also deserve consideration.

Portman and Herring (2001) offer several generalizations about American Indian women today. While they are useful in providing a glimpse of Native American Indian women, it is also important to consider tribal and other differences.

First, Native American Indian women continue to maintain a respect for power of words. They are socialized to use words positively (e.g., to inform, think, reconcile others) as well as negatively (e.g., insult or threaten). Many also use disclaimers to their humbleness and limitations prior to expressing an opinion. Native American Indian women also were encouraged to be strong and resilient in the face of tragedy (Portman & Herring, 2001).

Second, Portman and Herring (2001) also maintain that there are some indications of a positive correlation between the number of Native American Indian women in the labor force and the suicide rate of Native American Indian women. As more American Indian women entered the labor force, their suicide rates increased.

Third, the effects of forced assimilation have destroyed the complementary nature of female–male relations and have resulted in a general increase of Native American Indian male control over women. Women held many complementary positions in the tribes, as did men. When European men colonized the New World, they imposed a male-dominated system of "gynocide" (Portman & Herring, 2001, p. 193).

Gender Perspectives 4.1 looks at the Pocahontas paradox, or the historical and contemporary stereotypes of Native American Indian women.

Socioeconomic Status

Statistically, American Indians in the United States are among the poorest economically, the least employed, and the unhealthiest. Their education and income levels are low, and they are among the worst-housed ethnic groups. There are, however, signs of improvement in each area.

Civil rights legislation and the strong will and determination of the American Indian population are enabling these people to improve their lot in life. Some of their lands contain rich energy resources. Specifically, the Southern Utes in Colorado, the Uinta-Ouray Utes in Utah, and the Blackfeet in Montana have gas and oil reserves, as do the Shoshones and Arapaho in Wyoming. Similarly, the Bannocks and Shoshones, whose reservations are in Idaho, own one of the largest phosphate deposits in the West. The Navajo and Hopi reservations in the Southwest contain vast oil and gas fields as well as uranium reserves (Dorriss, 1981).

Attempting to break the bonds of poverty, other American Indians today are making notable achievements. With such attitudes as "we never, never give up" (Dorriss, 1981, p. 40), some American Indians have engaged in business ventures that have had considerable successes. The Navajo nation produces electronic missile assemblies for General Dynamics; the Choctaws of Mississippi build wire harnesses for Ford Motor Company; the Seminoles in Florida own a 156-room hotel; and the Swinomish Indians of Washington state plan a 60-acre boat basin, an 800-slip marina, and a three-story office and commercial headquarters.

Newsweek reports that such aggressive approaches to business were previously unheard of on the reservations. High unemployment, high rates of alcoholism, and

■ ■ ■ ■ ■

GENDER PERSPECTIVES 4.1
DEBUNKING THE POCAHONTAS PARADOX

Historical and contemporary stereotypes of Native American Indian (Portman's and Herring's choice of terminology) women have resulted in inaccurate and insensitive images. Mass media, movies, and printed materials continue to portray Native American Indian women as either princesses or savages. Portman and Herring strive to provide a more humanistic perspective of this population.

Although tremendous differences exist among Native American Indian tribes and nations, traditional perspectives of these women can be generalized. Generally, Native American Indian women value being mothers and rearing healthy families. Spiritually, they are considered to be extensions of the Spirit Mother and continuators of their people. Socially, they serve as transmitters of cultural knowledge and caretakers of children and relatives.

Portman and Herring provide an excellent overview of Native American Indian history. Particularly interesting facts include that Native American Indian women:

- Contributed to community survival—they were successful agriculturalists, made clothing, reared children, preserved food, did bead and quill work, and trapped fur-bearing animals
- Contributed to economic and social survival of their nations and tribes—for example, they provided guidance and influenced governance decisions and served as leaders and advisors
- Educated Native American Indian children about traditional ceremonies and practices
- Accepted responsibility for keeping the oral traditions alive and passing them on to future generations
- Emphasized the spirituality aspects that many Native American Indians felt essential

Portman and Herring also included an excellent section on Native American Indian female stereotypes. They were often viewed in a dual-faceted manner, that is, either as strong, powerful, dangerous women or as beautiful, exotic, lustful women. Both facets merged into one representation of Native American Indian women through the stereotype of Pocahontas.

Source: Portman, T. A. A., & Herring, R. (2001). Debunking the Pocahontas paradox: The need for a humanistic perspective. *Journal of Humanistic Counseling, Education and Development, 40,* 185–199.

poverty-level living conditions have characterized the American Indian people for many decades. Critics charge that these successful business ventures have not helped the entire culture: Unemployment affects 35 percent of some tribes, young people often must leave home to find work, and some critics worry that economic development will threaten the cultural identity of American Indians (*Indian Tribes, Incorporated,* 1988).

Families

American Indian adolescents place a high priority on both the immediate and the extended family. The immediate and extended families, tribe, clan, and heritage all contribute to the child's cultural identity and play a significant role in overall development.

Grandparents retain an official and symbolic leadership in family communities. Children seek daily contact with grandparents, who monitor children's behavior and have a voice in childrearing practices (Lum, 1986). Although the adolescent's social consciousness and awareness doubtlessly cause a transition from a family-centered to a more peer-centered environment, the traditional American Indian respect and commitment to the family continues (Lum, 1986).

Adult perceptions of childhood and childrearing practices also influence the developing person significantly. The American Indian family considers children to be gifts worthy of sharing with others, while the white perception holds that children constitute private property to be disciplined when necessary. In essence, children in the Indian family have few rules to obey, but white children have rules with strict consequences.

American Indian parents provide children with early training in self-sufficiency. Whereas European Americans prize individualism, the American Indian family places importance on group welfare (Axelson, 1999).

Any crisis in the home or within the family precipitates an absence from school until the crisis ends and the family situation returns to normal. American Indian children and adolescents are taught obedience and respect for elders, experts, and those with spiritual power. They also learn the importance of the family as well as responsibility to family members. In fact, supportive nonfamily members are often considered to be an integral part of the family network (Rivera & Rogers-Adkinson, 1997).

American Indian child-rearing practices and differing cultural expectations for behavior can result in confusion and frustration for the children. American Indians who confront an incompatibility with their European American counterparts appear to demonstrate growing feelings of isolation, rejection, and anxiety, which can result in alienation, poor self-image, and withdrawal. Such feelings undoubtedly affect the behavior and aspirations of American Indian children and adolescents.

Young people seek social acceptance and approval from older members of the family as well as from younger family members. Unlike adolescents in the European American culture, which emphasizes youth and the self, American Indian adolescents place family before self and have great respect for elders and their wisdom. The wisdom of life is received from the older people, whose task it is to acquaint the young with the traditions, customs, legends, and myths of the culture. All members of a family care for the old and consider death an accepted fact of life (Axelson, 1999).

The early training in self-sufficiency that American Indians receive from their families and other significant adults continues to have an impact during the adolescent years. Although the adolescent continues to recognize the loyalty and dependence on the im-

■ ■ ■ ■ ■

FOLLOW THROUGH 4.4
TALKING ABOUT PARENTS AND EXTENDED FAMILIES

Talk with American Indian learners about their parents and extended families. Try to understand the American Indian concept of family and the role of extended family members in the lives of children and adolescents.

mediate and surrounding family, adolescents develop independence and confidence in their abilities to deal with the world outside the family. We must consider this attitude of self-sufficiency, however, from the American Indian point of view. For example, not sharing with one's fellows and the accumulation of great wealth and possessions would not be included in the American Indian self-sufficiency concept. The cultural expectation must be compatible with knowledge of the natural world and in harmony with others. Achieving self-sufficiency and self-gain cannot be at the expense of family or tribal members or at the expense of harming any aspect of the natural world (Axelson, 1999).

Religion

According to American Indian belief, the world is interconnected, and everything, including humankind, lives according to the same process. Each being has its power, function, and place in the universe. Every part of nature has a spirit that many tribes believe possesses intelligence, emotion, and free will. Praying, in fact, is praying to one's own power. Because the Great Spirit is everything in all of nature, there is no need to question the existence of a god. Because nature is the essence of God, nature would stop if God no longer lived (Axelson, 1999).

God is the great power above everything. It is "the force which is responsible for action, and which can actually have control over man's destiny" (Zychowicz, 1975, p. 15). God created man, nature, and the universe, and God instructs on how to live on the land. The inner spiritual power, or the word *God*, was "orenda" to the Iroquois, "manitou" to the Algonkian tribes, "alone" to the Powhatans, and "wakan" or "wakonda" to the Sioux. The Sioux also used the expression "wakan tanka," meaning all of the "wakan" beings.

The spiritual God of the American Indians is positive, benevolent, and part of daily living. God's knowledge and advice are transmitted through traditional American Indian wisdom. Ideal action toward God is accomplished by helping others understand and get along with people and by comprehending the natural world of which everything (living and nonliving) is a part. The American Indian respects all of nature's objects equally as both physical and spiritual entities (Axelson, 1999).

As in any other culture, the American Indian culture contains norms and standards for behavior, but American Indians are inclined to judge each person as a separate individual, taking into consideration the reasons for actions ahead of the norms of the society. The dominant society judges behavior as right or wrong, good or bad, and considers how things "should" be and not necessarily how they are. The practice of judging the behavior of others is an important value in mainstream society (Axelson, 1999).

For American Indians there exists a close relationship between spiritual realization and unity and their cultural practices. Catholic and Protestant clergy have sought to Christianize American Indians, but there has been a continuation of indigenous religious rituals and beliefs in the healing power of nature. Natural forces are associated with the life process itself and pervade everything that the believing American Indian does.

Community religious rites are a collective effort that promote this mode of healing and increase inward insight and experiential connection with nature. American Indian individuals can utilize the positive experiences resulting from ceremonial events, power-revealing events (omens, dreams, visions), and contact with a tribal medicine

man in the healing process. Helping to discover and reinforce the therapeutic significance of American Indian religious and cultural events can be a learning task for social
workers (Axelson, 1999).

Language

Language and communication, whether verbal or nonverbal, may constitute the most
important aspects of an individual's culture and characterize the general culture, its values, and its ways of looking and thinking. Educators should develop a consciousness and
appreciation for the many American Indian languages and recognize the problems that
may result when educators and school children have differing language backgrounds.

The cultural mannerisms and nonverbal communication the American Indian
child demonstrates add another personal dimension to both culture and language. Professionals should recognize communicational differences (both verbal and nonverbal)
between American Indian and European American children. American Indians tend to
speak more softly and at a slower rate, to avoid direct identification between speaker
and listener, and to interject less frequently with encouraging communicational signs
such as head nods and verbal acknowledgements (Sanders, 1987).

American Indian adolescents, like adolescents of all cultures, need the security
and psychological safety that a common language provides, yet they experience significant language problems during this crucial period of development. Self-esteem and
the identity are formed during the transition from the family-centered world of the immediate and extended home. No longer is communication possible only with elders,
parents, and siblings. American Indian adolescents' ability to reach out to a wider
world depends greatly on the ability to speak and understand the language of the majority and other cultures.

American Indian children and adolescents often have to decide which language
to speak. This may be an even more difficult task for American Indians than for other
cultures, because American Indians view language as a crucial aspect of the culture and
a cherished gift that should be used whenever possible. Such a belief conflicts with the
European American opinion that English is American Indians' means to success and
that English should be the predominant language.

That American Indians speak about 2,200 different languages further compli-
cates the language problem. This broad and diversified language background, albeit
personal and sacred to American Indians, has not provided the rich cultural and language experiences that contribute to European American definitions of school success.

■ ■ ■ ■ ■

FOLLOW THROUGH 4.5
OBSERVE AMERICAN INDIAN NONVERBAL COMMUNICATION

Observe American Indian nonverbal communication patterns. How might communication be misunderstood? Discuss with American Indians how nonverbal communication is
important for all cultures and the importance of considering nonverbal mannerisms not
only from one's own cultural perspective.

■ ■ ■ ■ ■ ▬▬▬▬▬▬

FOR ADDITIONAL INFORMATION
INTERNET ADDRESSES

American Indians
http://chariott.com/~schmidt/spiel/general/indian.
html   Provides information on the Indian Child
Welfare Act of 1978, which entitles adoptees of
American Indian heritage to specific rights.

**SI Antho Outreach subpage: American
Indian Resources**
www.nmnh.si.edu/anthro/outreach/resource.html
Provides a look at elementary school explorations
of American Indian cultures and maintains that ed-

ucational activities focus too much on traditional
arts and crafts.

Choctaw Home Page
www.choctaw.com/   Provides an examination of the
Choctaw people and their lives and contributions.

Anth Outreach Indian Languages
www.nmnh.si.edu/anthro/outreach/indian_html
Provides information on the many American Indian languages north of Mexico as well as in Mexico and Central and South America.

Wide-scale differences exist in American Indians' ability to speak English. In some
cases, as few as 4 percent of American Indians speak "excellent" English; a far greater
percentage speak either "good" or "poor" English. Children who have attended
English-speaking schools, of course, speak better English than their elders.

Attending a school staffed with European American teachers and facing daily the
academic and social problems associated with not being understood and not understanding the language of others significantly affects an adolescent's self-perception.
Language may be a contributing factor in the adolescent's tendency to decline in academic achievement. Lack of cognitive and academic skills does not appear to be a
major factor (Sanders, 1987). Case Study 4.3 looks at how a fifteen-year-old boy experiences difficulty because of his language problems.

ACHIEVEMENT LEVELS

As stated earlier, several studies suggest that tests and teacher reports show that American Indian children function at the average-to-superior range until the fourth grade.
After the fourth grade, academic functioning typically declines each year so that by
grade ten, American Indian learners' academic achievement falls below that of their European American peers. Several complex factors may contribute to this predicament,
such as growing feelings of isolation, rejection, and anxiety that American Indian learners feel as they confront the incompatibility of their cultural value system with that of
their European American peers. These feelings contribute to alienation, poor self-
image, and withdrawal (Sanders, 1987).

How can the clash of values between American Indians and European Americans
affect educators? European American teachers view some behaviors that American Indian students exhibit as rude or insulting. For example, if these students avoid the
teacher's gaze, do not volunteer answers, or delay response as their cultural background has taught them to do, they are seen as lazy or uncomprehending.

■ ■ ■ ■ ■ ▬▬▬▬▬▬

CASE STUDY 4.3
AMERICAN INDIAN LANGUAGE PROBLEMS

Harry, a fifteen-year-old boy, has several problems that result, at least in part, from his lack of proficiency in English. He is faced with functioning in a bilingual world.

His family continues to rely on the language it has spoken for centuries, but he must speak English at school. (Some of his friends have been punished for not speaking English.) Meanwhile, his grades are failing, he does not always understand the teacher (and vice versa), and he experiences difficulty as he ventures outside the social confines of his culture.

Harry's teacher, Mrs. Rivers, can take several steps to assist him. She can:

1. Arrange for Harry to visit the language specialist or a bilingual teacher who can determine the extent of his problem and plan an appropriate course of action.
2. Seek the services of the remedial or resource teacher to provide Harry with appropriate remedial assistance.
3. Arrange for Harry to visit the guidance counselor, who may be able to help him widen his circle of friends.
4. Talk with Harry to let him know that she and other school personnel are interested in him as a person and as a learner.

European Americans see American Indian students as lacking time-management skills or being self-centered because of their present-time orientation. The American Indian concept of time is that what is happening now is more important than what is not happening now; that what is happening now deserves full attention; and that what one will be doing at this time tomorrow will be more important than what one is doing now or what one will not be doing tomorrow (Sanders, 1987).

Whether or not the educational problems American Indian adolescents experience are caused by "cultural teachings" or the "cultural differences" in European American schools, the result is the same: Americans Indians continue to have one of the highest dropout rates of any ethnic group at the high-school level, regardless of region or tribal affiliation (Sanders, 1987). The reasons for dropping out of school include: (1) school rules are not enforced uniformly; (2) factors pertaining to teacher–student relationships, for example, teachers' not caring about students and not providing sufficient assistance; (3) disagreements with teachers; and (4) the content of schooling, which the students perceive as not important to what they want to do in life.

Perceptive educators should demonstrate genuine care, understanding, and encouragement with which American Indian learners can identify; ensure that the curriculum addresses American Indian needs and provides culturally relevant experiences; and understand the home problems of some American Indians, such as separations and divorces, unemployment, alcoholism, and child abuse.

Nel (1994) suggests that educators who understand American Indians' cultural characteristics can help prevent school failure in American Indian learners. A significant factor in American Indians' academic underachievement appears to be feelings of isolation, anxiety, and rejection as they confront the incompatibility of their cultural

■ ■ ■ ■ ■ ■

FOLLOW THROUGH 4.6

INCREASING AMERICAN INDIANS' ACADEMIC ACHIEVEMENT

While understanding the reasons for the decline in American Indians' academic achievement after fourth grade is important, it is even more important to think of strategies for increasing their academic achievement. Suggest a number of steps (e.g., culturally appropriate diagnostic tests, culturally relevant curricular materials, instruction that reflects learning styles) that educators might take to increase American Indians' academic achievement.

values with those of their mainstream classrooms. Often forced to renounce their own culture, these learners are torn between two worlds and often withdraw as a result.

Nel (1994) offers several American Indian cultural characteristics that often conflict with mainstream school systems:

■ American Indians often place emphasis on generosity, sharing, and cooperation. These cultural characteristics sometimes conflict with mainstream school systems, which emphasize competition.

Educators can take two directions: (1) reassure American Indian learners that mainstream society accepts and encourages personal achievement and that peers will not blame them or think less of them for excelling in classwork or even in the playground, and (2) provide teaching and learning experiences that emphasize teamwork and cooperation.

■ American Indians often experience discomfort when teachers single them out for praise for accomplishments, because they often do not want to excel at others' expense.

Educators can (1) let students know that praise is a form of acknowledging accomplishments and mainstream schools' students expect it, and (2) offer private recognition and praise for those learners who continue to feel uncomfortable.

■ American Indians' sense of generosity and cooperative efforts makes it difficult not to help a friend in need, for example, a fellow student needing help on a test or graded exercise.

Educators should understand American Indians' concept of generosity and should take special care in handling these situations. Educators can (1) avoid situations in which they strictly prohibit lending assistance, and, for situations in which individuals must work alone, (2) try to explain the necessity of working alone, so they can determine individual achievement.

■ American Indians have more flexible concepts of time than do some other cultures; that is, students might not arrive at class on time and might be late with assignments. They often do not regard time and punctuality as important concerns.

Educators need to take several directions: (1) avoid judging American Indians using middle-class white perspectives, by realizing that students being late or submitting assignments late might not be signs of "laziness" or "unconcern," and (2) help students to understand that their cultural orientations are not wrong but that mainstream U.S. schools and society expect punctuality in many cases.

■ American Indians often demonstrate nonverbal behaviors that suggest (at least to middle-class mainstream educators) a lack of interest in school or respect for people in authority.

Educators can take at least two directions: (1) understand that learners working slowly, looking unconcerned or unmotivated, and being at ease during supposedly hectic times are not signs of disinterest; instead, American Indian learners might be very motivated and interested but do not show traditional middle-class indicators of motivation and interest; and (2) give an impression of being unhurried and at ease when dealing with American Indian learners, who do not want to feel they are imposing on others or are consuming their time (Nel, 1994).

Educational and societal factors, as well as the clash of cultures, during these crucial developmental years have the potential for developing feelings of frustration and hopelessness that often result in alienation. Such alienation may have been a factor to the American Indians' general loss of confidence and decline in motivation. These feelings during adolescence may also result in considerable confusion in the classroom. The American Indian adolescent may demonstrate behavior that teachers perceive as excessive shyness, inactivity, or lack of motivation. Adolescents whose teachers misunderstand or culturally misconstrue these characteristics (along with the adolescent's usual steady decline in achievement) may develop feelings of hopelessness and alienation.

Educators can benefit from understanding the American Indians' predicament in predominantly white schools.

1. In contrast to people in other cultures, American Indians often harbor significant feelings of suspicion and distrust of professionals and institutions and especially of European Americans.

2. Communication problems may result in an inability to understand, trust, and build rapport with peers and professionals of other cultures. Differences in "home language" and "school language" or American Indians' nonverbal communication might hinder educational efforts. American Indian learners may appear to be unconcerned with educational progress when, in fact, they may be painfully shy and over sensitive to strangers because of language problems and mistrust of European Americans.

3. American Indian adolescents develop in an often unique and difficult situation. They must reconcile allegiance to the values and customs of both the American Indian and the European American cultures. They also encounter the usual problems of adolescence, for example, the possibility of experiencing role confusion or differences associated with building a positive identity.

4. American Indian learners have to decide whether the Indian or the European American culture (or some "cultural combination") should provide the basis for the identity. They need to attempt proficiency in both the Indian language and English and learn how to maintain harmony with family and nature while surviving in the European American world. They also face the problem of how to accept the vast cultural differences in situations in which the European American is unlikely to attempt cross-cultural understandings or acceptance.

Implementing Research 4.1 looks at urban American Indians and traditional high schools, and in particular, Spotted Eagle High School, an alternative high school in the Milwaukee Public School System.

■ ■ ■ ■ ■ ▬▬▬▬▬▬▬▬▬▬▬▬▬▬▬▬▬▬▬▬▬▬▬▬▬▬▬▬▬

IMPLEMENTING RESEARCH 4.1
URBAN AMERICAN INDIANS AND
TRADITIONAL HIGH SCHOOLS

Jeffries, Nix, and Singer (2002) reported the record-breaking dropout rate for American Indians in Spokane, Washington. In fact, the American Indian dropout rate was the highest of any ethnic group enrolled in the Spokane public school system. In this article, Jeffries et al. (2002) use case analyses of three American Indian high school students who chose to leave the traditional school setting due to (1) lack of comfort with the traditional school environment; (2) lack of education among their families that often leads to economic and social instability; and (3) the need to earn respect, which translates into financial independence.

The authors tell about Spotted Eagle High School, an alternative high school in the Milwaukee Public School System. Spotted Eagle was created in 1994 by concerned American Indian professionals, parents, and other interested parties in response to the high dropout rate of American Indian students from traditional schools.

Barriers include (1) dropping out of the traditional school was a slow, deliberate process rather than a momentous decision; (2) traditional high schools provided discomfort—for example, students reported unsafe and large schools; and (3) family values impacted students' educational outcomes—for example, while none of the parents wanted their children to drop out, some home and family situations did not contribute to students staying in school.

Bridges identified by Jeffries et al. (2002) include, first, that the goal of Spotted Eagle was not to "rehabilitate" (p. 45) students so they could be sent back to the traditional schools. Instead, the intent was to provide a comfortable learning environment for the remainder of the students' secondary education. Second, wellness was addressed in culturally specific ways—for example, a week of Medicine Wheel activities occurred. Third, Spotted Eagle provided a school-to-work transition program in which high school students received academic credit for hours spent working at approved jobs. Fourth, educators at Spotted Eagle required 100 hours of community service, so students could better understand the program and the benefits of working with and helping others.

IMPLEMENTING THE RESEARCH
1. Dropout-prevention programs should begin prior to high schools—they should begin in middle schools—and educators should identify potential dropouts and provide appropriate assistance.
2. Parent-education programs, especially for American Indians, should be provided, so parents and families will understand how some home and family situations contribute (or do not contribute) to students staying in school.
3. Schools need to be more reflective of and responsive to the American Indian culture and its traditions.

Source: Jeffries, R., Nix, M., & Singer, C. (2002). Urban American Indians "dropping out" of traditional high schools: Barriers & bridges to success. *The High School Journal, 85*(3), 38–46.

■ ■ ■ ■ ■ ▬▬▬▬▬▬▬▬▬▬▬▬▬▬▬▬▬▬▬▬▬▬▬▬▬▬▬▬▬▬▬▬▬▬▬▬▬▬▬

FOLLOW THROUGH 4.7
EXAMINE CURRICULAR MATERIALS FOR RELEVANCE

Examine several curricular materials to determine how useful they would be for American Indian learners. Do the materials recognize American Indians and convey a respect for Indian values such as sharing and noninterference with others?

In an investigation of study habits and attitudes of American Indian learners, Gade, Hurlbert, and Fuqua (1986) studied students in grades 7 to 12. They found a correlation between poor study habits and attitudes, especially in junior high school years and among boys, and teacher evaluations that cited low achievement, insufficient cooperation, and poor work habits.

Gade et al. (1986) drew several inferences for professionals in today's schools. First, they emphasized the importance of understanding that study habits and atti-

■ ■ ■ ■ ■ ▬▬▬▬▬▬▬▬▬▬▬▬▬▬▬▬▬▬▬▬▬▬▬▬▬▬▬▬▬▬▬▬▬▬▬▬▬▬▬

CASE STUDY 4.4
HELPING THE LOW ACHIEVER

Mr. Thomas pondered his class—the achievers, the low achievers, and those who seemed to be in a constant struggle just to make passing grades. As Mr. Thomas thought about his students, he also wondered whether his lack of knowledge of how American Indians learn actually contributed to their learning difficulties. Mr. Thomas asked himself, "What can I do and what should I know about the way American Indians learn to improve their academic achievement?"

Mr. Thomas went to several authorities on American Indian children and adolescents to seek advice on how he could better understand his students, make his teaching more effective, and maximize teaching and learning efforts. Advice he received included:

1. Understand the short-term time orientations of many American Indians.
2. Understand the need to learn about families and involve them in school activities and their children's learning.
3. Understand the need to improve the American Indian learners' self-esteem and their belief in their ability to learn.
4. Understand the need for genuinely positive and caring relationships between teachers and students.
5. Understand the need to design curricula that reflect American Indians' backgrounds and contemporary needs.
6. Understand American Indian learning styles and how the curricula and teaching methods can be changed to match students' learning styles.

tudes involve all school personnel, not just classroom teachers. Second, students' poor opinions of teachers and their classroom behaviors and methods indicate the need for recruitment of more American Indian teachers and counselors. Third, American Indian learners need direct instruction in study skills and attitudes toward their education.

Case Study 4.4 shows how Mr. Thomas realized that the low-achieving students in his classes needed additional assistance and how he helped them.

Many American Indian students who are gifted are either not identified or not served in schools. As Implementing Research 4.2 shows, the underrepresentation of American Indians in gifted programs can be attributed to several factors and can be addressed through carefully planned and implemented programs.

■ ■ ■ ■ ■ ▬▬▬▬▬▬▬▬▬▬▬▬▬▬▬▬▬▬▬▬▬▬▬▬▬▬▬▬▬▬▬

IMPLEMENTING RESEARCH 4.2
AMERICAN INDIANS, GIFTED PROGRAMS, AND RURAL SCHOOLS

Montgomery (2001) maintains that American Indians are neither identified nor served in gifted programs at the same rates as their counterparts. The underrepresentation of American Indians in gifted programs can be attributed to several factors: need for appropriate measures, need for cultural responsiveness, need for appropriate language and relevant cultural responsiveness, need to accommodate predominantly rural schools providing education to American Indian children, and the need to address alternative learning styles. Montgomery maintains that rural schools traditionally have had difficulty offering a range of programs necessary to meet the needs of gifted American Indians. The main reasons for this difficulty include the heavy reliance on standardized achievement tests and the limited number of culturally and linguistically diverse school professionals. Increasing the number of Indian teachers, administrators, paraprofessionals, and psychologists may provide Indian children with greater access to educational opportunity.

To address the challenges facing American Indians in gifted programs, Montgomery explains Project Leap, which includes four program initiatives: Leadership, Excellence, Achievement, and Performance. The program focuses on collaboration, identification, curriculum, and community and parent involvement, all designed to help gifted American Indian students discover and nurture gifts, talents, or high potential.

IMPLEMENTING THE RESEARCH

1. Use culturally appropriate assessment measures, that is, tests that are more culturally relevant and reflect how American Indians think and learn.
2. Encourage more collaboration of parents, community members, and educators to identify gifted American Indian students.
3. Realize that an effective program needs to be multifaceted, one that includes a number of efforts such as collaboration, identification, curriculum, and community and parent involvement.

Source: Montgomery, D. (2001). Increasing Native American Indian involvement in gifted programs in rural schools. *Psychology in the Schools, 38,* 467–475.

LEARNING STYLES: CULTURAL CONSIDERATIONS

Effective education for American Indian learners requires consideration of each individual's learning styles—the strategies the learner uses to acquire knowledge, skills, and understanding. Myriad differences exist among the American Indian peoples. To assume that all Indians have similar learning styles shows a disregard for nations, tribes, and individuals, as well as for varying educational and socioeconomic backgrounds. Table 4.2 provides a brief overview of several learning areas and their implications for American Indian learners.

Although Table 4.2 provides representative examples of learning styles and implications, perceptive educators can see the need to consider individual learners, teaching and communication styles, internal cognitive processes, and the external conditions that affect learning outcomes. Teachers must use appropriate diagnostic instruments and learning style inventories and get to know individual learners and their learning styles.

SCHOOL PRACTICES IMPEDING AMERICAN INDIANS' PROGRESS

Because some techniques taught to educators are incompatible with American Indian cultural traditions, it is imperative that educators use strategies that are appropriate for the culture. What specifically should educators avoid?

1. Methods that increase positive self-talk, such as "something I like about myself" or "a sport I can play well," often work well with white or black children but not with American Indian children.

TABLE 4.2   American Indians Learning Styles

AREA	IMPLICATIONS
Many American Indian learners prefer to learn by visual, perceptual, and spatial rather than verbal means.	Present new or different material in a visual, perceptual, and spatial mode; many students need to improve their skills in the verbal mode.
Many American Indian learners use mental images rather than word associations to remember or understand words and concepts.	Present metaphors, images, or symbols rather than dictionary-style definitions or synonyms when teaching difficult concepts.
Many American Indian learners process information in a global, analytic manner; that is, they focus on the whole rather than the part.	Present material in a manner in which overall purpose and structure are clear, rather than in small, carefully sequenced bits.

Source: Swisher, K., & Deyhle, D. (1989). The styles of learning are different, but the teaching is just the same: Suggestions for teachers of American Indian youth. *Journal of American Indian Education, Special Issue,* August, 1–11.

2. Attempts to convince American Indians to be competitive (such as being the first, best, fastest, or smartest) are incompatible with their cultural values.
3. Educators often expect eye contact and perceive the American Indian's tendency to look the other way as a sign of withdrawal, embarrassment, or discomfort.
4. Educators and counselors often rely extensively on verbal participation by children in the class. Although verbal interaction is valued by Anglo, African, and Hispanic cultures, it is not valued by American Indians.

Implementing Research 4.3 looks at the Navajo Indian experience and the overrepresentation of American Indians diagnosed as having learning disabilities.

■ ■ ■ ■ ■ ▬▬▬▬▬▬

IMPLEMENTING RESEARCH 4.3
LESSONS FROM THE NAVAJO NATIVE AMERICAN EXPERIENCE

Wilder, Jackson, and Smith (2001) provide information that educators can use to better individualize transition services to all students with disabilities. First, they discuss the Individuals with Disabilities Act of 1990 (IDEA), P.L. 101-476, and the IDEA amendments of 1997, P.L. 105-17, which mandate a transition-planning program for all students with disabilities aged fourteen and older and transition-planning services for students sixteen and older. Then, they focus on cultural differences, especially multicultural awareness and recognizing biases and mistrust.

After the introductory material, Wilder et al. (2001) direct attention to the experience of Navajo American Indians. They maintain that Navajo American Indians provide striking examples of challenges inherent in making transitions. For example, there is an overrepresentation of American Indians diagnosed as having learning disabilities. The unemployment rate for individuals living on Navajo reservations is about 30 percent. Approximately 41 percent of those living on reservations have a high school diploma; only about 5 percent of Navajos have a college degree. Plus, 58 percent of the population live below the poverty level.

Wilder et al. (2001) offer implications for educators, especially special educators. Their focus includes the importance of supportive relationships; educational and vocational perceptions; connection to cultures and homelands; and discrepancies between high school culture and postsecondary cultures.

IMPLEMENTING THE RESEARCH
Both general and special educators should:

1. Attend to significant relationships that affect the students' transitions
2. Demonstrate awareness of and respect for students' cultural backgrounds
3. Provide clear information to the world of work
4. Provide supportive services and helping students to recognize and utilize these services

Source: Wilder, L. K., Jackson, A. P., & Smith, T. B. (2001). Secondary transition of multicultural learners: Lessons from the Navajo Native American experience. *Preventing School Failure, 45*(3), 119–124.

PROMOTING SELF-ESTEEM AND POSITIVE CULTURAL IDENTITIES

Educators working with American Indian learners readily recognize the many personal and social factors that affect children's and adolescents' self-esteem and cultural identities. Injustice and discrimination, poverty, low educational attainment, and perhaps growing up on reservations, in foster homes, or in a predominantly white society may cause American Indian learners to question their self-worth and the worth of their culture.

Although self-esteem scales reveal little difference in the levels of self-esteem between preschool American Indian and European American children, other evidence suggests that Indian learners experience conflict on entering school (Little Soldier, 1985).

■ ■ ■ ■ ■ ▬▬▬▬

CULTURAL PORTRAIT
JOHN—AN AMERICAN INDIAN LEARNER

Fourteen-year-old John attends school off the reservation. The student population is a mix of American Indians, some Hispanic Americans, a few black Americans, and some European Americans. Although the school population includes several culturally diverse groups, most teachers are European American, and the school environment and educational program indicate an orientation toward traditional white expectations.

John has several academic and social problems: He makes below-average grades, feels he does not have many friends, and generally feels uncomfortable in school. Everything is rushed, cooperation is second to competition, his teachers feel he is not trying, and the overall curricular emphasis makes little sense to him. He has an interest in the ancient traditions of his people, but his teachers rarely address his cultural needs or, in fact, any of his individual needs. He realizes that his grades need to improve, but he does not always understand the teacher or the way she teaches. Although he has American Indian friends, he has few friends among the students of the other cultures. School days are often frustrating for John as he strives to make it through another day.

WHAT JOHN'S TEACHER CAN DO
John's teacher can take several specific steps to help him improve his academic and social progress.

First, she can spend some time alone with John to determine his strengths, weaknesses, and interests. Second, she can consult the language specialist to determine whether John's academic (or social) problems are attributable to his using a second language. Third, she can arrange for John to have individual assistance from the remedial specialist. Fourth, she can reassess her teaching techniques to see whether her teaching methods match John's learning styles. Finally, she can build on John's interest in his cultural heritage through appropriate reading and other curricular materials. Reading and studying about his own cultural background might show John that the curriculum values his American Indian culture and recognizes his individual needs and interests. Just as important, the teacher will provide a curriculum that gives other learners an appropriate multicultural understanding of the American Indian culture.

Almost any number of suggestions could help John and improve his feelings about school and himself. John's teacher should recognize though how important it is to show interest in John and provide first-hand and individual help in improving his academic and social progress.

■ ■ ■ ■ ■ ▬▬▬▬▬▬▬▬▬

FOLLOW THROUGH 4.8
INVOLVING AMERICAN INDIAN CHILDREN

Ask young American Indian children to make a drawing or a silhouette of an Indian child. Ask them to write words or draw symbols to illustrate their favorite foods, favorite games, favorite sports, and perhaps some things they like to think about.

Ask the American Indian children to explain their pictures to the other children in the group. Indian children may prefer to simply look at their pictures, together, as a group. They may look for some similarities in their pictures to identify their group's favorite foods or some things their group likes to think about.

After sharing, the children may combine their pictures to create a "group personality" collage. The purpose of this type of self-disclosing activity for Indian children is twofold: First, they see a type of collective group personality emerge, and second, they begin to think of themselves as a part of the group. They do not compare themselves individually with other members of the group. Instead, they gain a sense of their contribution to the group and of the ways in which they belong and identify, not with individuals in the group but with the group as a whole.

One study compared American Indian and European American children and concluded that children of various tribes (e.g., Cree, Miccosukee, Seminole) score lower on self-esteem scales (Rotenberg & Cranwell, 1989). Such measures and conclusions, Rotenberg and Cranwell (1989) warn, may be misleading, because the self-esteem scales may be more culturally relevant for European Americans than for American Indians.

SUMMING UP

Educators who plan teaching and learning experiences for American Indian children and adolescents should:

1. Remember that American Indian people have a proud history of accomplishments and notable contributions and that these should be part of school curricula.
2. Avoid providing curricular and instructional practices that indicate only white, middle-class expectations and that might seem alien to American Indian learners.
3. Remember that educators who understand American Indians and the possible cultural basis for educational problems must address achievement levels and school dropout rates.
4. Promote positive self-images and cultural images among American Indian learners, which may be one of the most effective means for improving academic achievement and school-related problems.
5. Adapt teaching styles and other school practices to meet the American Indian's learning styles, demonstrating that educators are caring and interested in improving school achievement and overall school success.

6. Understand the American Indian culture and the learners' cultural characteristics, religious orientations, and socioeconomic backgrounds.
7. Provide learning experiences so that learners of other cultures can develop a better understanding of their Indian peers.
8. Understand the learner's development, and provide school experiences based on developmental and cultural characteristics.
9. Consider American Indians as individuals who come from different nations, tribes, socioeconomic levels, and levels of educational attainment.

SUGGESTED LEARNING ACTIVITIES

1. Observe an American Indian learner and record the cultural mannerisms that might be contrary to the behaviors that schools expect. How might a teacher misinterpret the behavior of American Indians? How might educators better understand Indian learners and their behaviors?

2. List several stereotypical beliefs about American Indians. What is the basis of those beliefs? How might those beliefs affect educators' perceptions of these learners? What steps can multicultural educators take to lessen the effect of stereotypical beliefs?

3. Sanders (1987) wrote: "American Indians continue to have the highest dropout rate of any ethnic group at the high-school level, regardless of region or tribal affiliation" (p. 81). In a plan to reduce this dropout rate, address the following points:
    - Extent of the problem
    - Reasons for the problem (be sure to examine cultural factors)
    - Possible solutions or plans to reduce the dropout rate
    - Ways to involve parents, administrators, and special school personnel

SUGGESTIONS FOR COLLABORATIVE EFFORTS

Form groups of three or four, which, if possible, represent our nation's cultural and gender diversity. Working collaboratively, focus your group's attention toward the following efforts:

1. Study (observe, examine school records, talk with, test) two American Indian learners, one who has attended reservation schools and one who has attended white schools. What differences can you list? What has been the effect of acculturation? What differences might you attribute to social class or tribal affiliation? Considering all these differences, how can educators gain an accurate perception of the American Indian learner?

2. Talk with several teachers of American Indian learners to see what first-hand experiences they have to offer. Specifically, learn their perceptions of cultural characteristics, the influence of families, achievement levels, and language problems. What advice can these teachers offer?

3. American Indians experience academic problems, including low academic achievement, low reading scores, and high dropout rates. Design a remediation plan to address Indians' academic problems. Specifically, look at learning styles, curricular materials, instructional strategies, classroom environments, and motivation (be sure to consider that American

Indian indicators of motivation might differ from others'). In other words, how does your group believe schools can better address the needs of American Indian learners?

EXPANDING YOUR HORIZONS: ADDITIONAL JOURNAL READINGS AND BOOKS

Asher, N. (2002). Class acts: Indian American high school students negotiate professional and ethnic identities. *Urban Education, 37*(2), 267–295.
> Asher focuses on how Indian American high school students deal with ethnic identities and the challenges associated with high schools.

Jones, K., & Ongtooguk, P. (2002). Equity for Alaska Natives: Can high-stakes testing bridge the chasm between ideals and realities? *Phi Delta Kappan, 83*(7), 499–503, 550.
> Jones and Ongtooguk maintain that Alaska, like many other states, remains steadfast in planning to use test scores as a primary indicator of student and school success.

Portman, T. A. A., & Herring, R. (2001). Debunking the Pocahontas paradox: The need for a humanistic perspective. *Journal of Humanistic Counseling, Education and Development, 40,* 185–199.
> Portman and Herring provide an excellent article on the history of Native American Indians and especially the role played by women in the culture.

Sparks, S. (2000). Classroom and curriculum accommodations for Native American students. *Intervention in School and Clinic, 35*(5), 259–263.
> In this informative article, Sparks explores ways to enhance the classroom and curriculum to meet the learning and social needs of Native American Indian learners.

Yurkovich, E. E. (2001). Working with American Indians toward educational success. *Journal of Nursing Education, 40*(6), 259–269.
> While Yurkovich writes primarily about nursing education, her insights on working with Indian Americans are commendable and should benefit most educators.

EXPANDING YOUR STUDENTS' HORIZONS: APPROPRIATE AMERICAN INDIAN BOOKS FOR CHILDREN AND ADOLESCENTS

Bierhorst, John. *The way of the earth: Native America and the environment.* Mulberry, 1995.
Bierhorst, John. *The Mythology of Mexico and Central America.* Mulberry, 1990.
Bierhorst, John. *The white deer and other stories told by the Lenape.* Morrow, 1995.
Bruchac, Joseph (retold by). *Gluskabe and the four wishes.* Cobblehill, 1995.
Carter, Alden R. *The Shoshoni.* Franklin Watts, 1991.
DeFelice, Cynthia. *Weasel.* Macmillan, 1990.
Girion, Barbara. *Indian summer.* Scholastic, 1990.
Goble, Paul. *Adopted by the eagles.* Bradbury, 1994.
Hillerman, Tony. *Coyote waits.* HarperCollins, 1990.
Joosse, Barbara M. *Mama, Do You Love Me?* Chronicle Books, 1991.
Landau, Elaine. *The Sioux.* Franklin Watts, 1991.
Lawlor, Laurie. *Shadow Catcher: The Life and Work of Edward S. Curtis.* Walker, 1994.
Levin, Betty. *Brother moose.* Greenwillow, 1990.
McDermott, Gerald. *Coyote: A trickster tale of the American Southwest.* Harcourt Brace, 1995.
McDermott, Gerald. *Raven: A trickster tale of the Pacific Northwest.* Bradbury, 1993.
Mead, Alice. *Crossing the starlight bridge.* Bradbury, 1994.
Riley, Patricia. *Growing up Native American.* Tupelo, 1993.
Robinson, Margaret. *A woman of her tribe.* Scribner, 1990.
Rodanas, Kristina. *Dance of the sacred circle: A Native American tale.* Little, Brown, 1994.

Stewart, Elisabeth Jane. *On the long trail home.* Clarion, 1994.

Stroud, Virginia A. *Doesn't fall off his horse.* Dial, 1994.

Thomson, Peggy. *Katie Henio: Navajo sheepherder.* Cobblehill, 1995.

Van Lann, Nancy. *In a circle long ago: A treasury of native lore.* Apple Soup Books, 1995.

Wangerin, Walter. *The crying for a vision.* Aladdin, 1994.

Welsch, Roger. *Uncle Smoke stories: Nehawka tales of Coyote the trickster.* Knopf, 1994.

Wisniewski, David. *The wave of the seawolf.* Clarion, 1994.

Wisniewski, David. *Rainplayer.* Clarion, 1994.

CHAPTER FIVE

UNDERSTANDING ARAB AMERICAN CHILDREN AND ADOLESCENTS

Understanding the material and activities in this chapter will help the reader to:

- Understand the Arab American people, their origins, and what they are like today
- List several stereotypes of Arab American children and adolescents
- Describe Arab Americans' cultural, gender, socioeconomic, familial, religious, and language diversity
- Suggest appropriate children's literature and provide culturally appropriate educational experiences for Arab Americans
- Name several culturally responsive educational practices that promote Arab Americans' educational progress, self-esteem, and cultural identities

OVERVIEW

Although articles, books, and instructional materials may deal with the cultural heritages of African American, American Indian, Asian American, European American, and Hispanic American children and adolescents, Arab American learners and their cultures are often ignored. "The kids from the Middle East are the lost sheep in the school system. They fall through the cracks in our categories" (Wingfield & Karaman,

FOLLOW THROUGH 5.1
HELPING THE LOST SHEEP IN THE SCHOOL SYSTEM

Suggest four or five ways educators can avoid letting Arab Americans become the "lost sheep in the school system." Specifically, what can educators do to avoid children from the Middle East becoming lost in the school system? Determine ways educators can recognize them, identify their strengths and weaknesses, and provide them with culturally appropriate educational experiences.

1995, p. 8). We agree wholeheartedly that Arab American children and adolescents are often forgotten or ignored in U.S. schools.

THE ARAB AMERICAN PEOPLE

Origins

The *Detroit Free Press*, in its "100 Questions and Answers about Arab Americans: A Journalist's Guide" (www.freep.com/jobspage/arabs), maintains that Arab Americans and their culture are too often described in simplistic terms. Table 5.1 provides a list of definitions to assist educators understand Arab Americans and the Arab culture.

Arab Americans is a generic term for people with ethnic roots in Asian and African Arabic-speaking lands—Algeria, Bahrain, Egypt, Iraq, Jordan, Kuwait, Lebanon, Libya, Morocco, Oman, Palestine, Qatar, Saudi Arabia, Sudan, Syria, Tunisia, the United Arab Emirates, and Yemen. Arab Americans are U.S. citizens and permanent residents who trace their ancestry to or who immigrated from Arabic-speaking places in southwestern Asia and northern Africa, a region known as the Middle East. Most Arab Americans were born in the United States (www.freep.com/jobspage/arabs).

Arab Americans represent a wide range of diverse cultures, languages, religions, ethnic and racial backgrounds. An Arab can be Muslim, Christian, Jew, or of some other belief. Although most Arab Americans are generally categorized as Caucasian, ethnic and racial diversity are two salient features of this unique group. For example, Arab Americans can be black, interracial, or white. Also, not everyone who comes from the Arab countries is an Arab. For example, people can originate from Kildanis, Kurds, Druze, Berbers, and others.

Arab Americans and Arabs can be described as a heterogeneous group that is a multicultural, multiracial, and multiethnic mosaic population (Abudabbeh, 1996). As a result, Arab Americans are diverse in country of origin, religion, and reasons for immigration. For instance, of the approximately 3 million Arab Americans, most are Christians of Lebanese or Syrian descent. However, Arab Muslims are increasing in number among recent immigrants. They share a common language, Arabic, and many other cultural traits (Suleiman, 2001).

The Arab American population in the United States is currently estimated to be nearly 3 million people, considered to have arrived in the United States in two distinct waves. The first wave, which came between 1890 and 1940, consisted mostly of merchants and farmers who emigrated for economic reasons. Ninety percent of this first-wave immigration population was Christian and originated from the regions known today as Syria and Lebanon. They seem to have assimilated in their new country with considerable ease.

The second wave of Arab immigrants began after World War II and continues today. Unlike their predecessors, this group consists mostly of people with college degrees or those seeking to earn degrees. It also differs in that these immigrants came from all over the Arab world, from regions of post-European colonization, and from sovereign Arab nations. This wave, dominated by Palestinians, Egyptians, Syrians, and Iraqis, arrived with an "Arab identity" that was absent in the first wave of immigrants.

TABLE 5.1   Definitions

Allah—means God and is used by Arabic-speaking Christians, Muslims, and Jews.

Arab—a person whose native language is Arabic and who lives according to Arab cultural traditions and values.

Arab Americans—immigrants and their descendants with ethnic roots in Asian and African Arabic-speaking lands.

Arab Nation—all peoples who speak the Arabic language and claim a link with the nomadic tribes of Arabia, whether by descent, affiliation, or by appropriating the traditional ideals of human excellence and standards of beauty.

collective or collectivism—people who are more oriented toward the group.

Bedouin—a nomadic desert-dwelling Arab.

fundamentalist—one who follows the fundamentals of a religion.

galabiya—a body-length robe

hadith—the Prophet's own traditional sayings.

hajj—the pilgrimage to Mecca by millions of Muslims once each year; for men it is called *hajji*, and for women it is called *hajjah*.

hijab—scarf worn to cover the hair on a woman's head.

imam—the leader of prayer at the mosque—he is sometimes called a sheik.

individualistic or individualism—people who are more oriented toward individual concerns.

Islam—the Arabic word means "submission" and is derived from the word meaning "peace."

jihad—every Muslim exercises strenuous intellectual, physical, and spiritual efforts for the good of all.

Muslim (not Moslem)—a believer in the religion Islam, who may or may not be an Arab.

Pillars of Islam—(1) oral testimony that there is only one God and that Mohammed is His prophet; (2) ritual prayer practiced five times a day with certain words and certain postures of the body; (3) the giving of alms; (4) keeping a strict fast of no liquid or food from sunrise to sundown during the month of Ramadan; and (5) holy pilgrimage to Mecca once in a lifetime at a specific time of year.

Quran—the holy book for Muslims, who believe it is the literal word of God revealed by the prophet Muhammad.

Ramadan—the ninth month of the calendar year, the month of fasting, self-discipline, and purification.

sunna—the Prophet's own traditional practices.

umma—a belief that all Muslims are brothers and sisters.

With the crystallization of an Arab identity came the practice of traditions and customs that affected either a hyphenated identity as "Arab Americans" or sometimes alienation from the majority of society. By the 1970s, the trend of easy assimilation began to change into a cultural separateness, built on political ideology centered on the Arab–Israeli conflict and rejection of Western norms and customs (Abudabbeh, 1996).

■ ■ ■ ■ ■

FOR ADDITIONAL INFORMATION
INTERNET ADDRESSES

Q & A on Islam and Arab Americans
www.usatoday.com/news/world/islam.html   Provides a question-and-answer format to answer questions on Islam, Quran, roles of women, Muslims, and Islam's views on terror.

**The National Association
of Arab Americans**
www.cafearabica.com/organizations/org12/orgnaaa.html   Works to strengthen U.S. relations with

Arab countries and to promote an even-handed U.S. policy based on justice and peace for all parties in the Middle East.

The *Detroit Free Press*
www.freep.com/jobspage/arabs   Provides the comprehensive "100 Questions and Answers about Arab Americans: A Journalist's Guide."

Arab Americans Today

Erroneously perceived as a unified single ethnic group, Arab Americans' diversity is grossly overlooked. Arabs in the United States come from different countries with different allegiances and interests. In addition, variations in skin, hair, and eye color are wide-ranging. There is no "typical-looking" Arab man or woman. Dark skin is not a characteristic of all Arabs and certainly not of all Muslims (Suleiman, 2001).

Arab Americans have a higher educational achievement level and significantly higher number of high school and college graduates than the U.S. population as a whole and more than most ethnic groups. Moreover, their adherence to their cultural values has been a powerful motivational force for educational success. For example, the religious and social stratification stresses seeking knowledge as the duty of every individual; it is a social and religious asset to become educated (Suleiman, 2001).

Implementing Research 5.1 brings attention to comparative and critical analysis of leading reference sources on Arab Americans.

Arab American Christians' tendency to enrich their lives through effective interaction with others appears to have assisted them as they entered mainstream U.S. culture. However, in contrast to the Arab Christians, assimilation was much more difficult for the Arab Muslims because of their strong adherence to Islamic faith and law (Suleiman, 2001).

STEREOTYPING OF ARAB AMERICAN
CHILDREN AND ADOLESCENTS

The Arab community is one of the most heterogeneous in the United States, yet it is also the most misunderstood. It is the negative images and stereotypes of Arabs that are the most prevalent. The popular images of Arabs as rich sheiks, religious zealots, or terrorists are gross stereotypes. Stereotypes also surround the roles of Arab American men and women.

■ ■ ■ ■ ■ ▬▬

IMPLEMENTING RESEARCH 5.1
LEADING REFERENCE SOURCES ON ARAB AMERICANS

Wertsman (2001), in this beneficial article, defines what he means by Arab Americans, lists countries of origins, and states where Arab Americans are most populous. Also, Wertsman gives a brief breakdown of when Arabs entered this country. Second, Wertsman discusses Arab Americans' religions and provides a breakdown of their religions. Third, he maintains that Arab Americans have made multiple contributions in over two dozen areas.

Most impressive and helpful about Wertsman's article is that he provides a comparative and critical analysis of leading reference sources on Arab Americans. He provides an analyses of information on Arab Americans that has been written in *One America, Harvard Encyclopedia of American Ethnic Groups, The Encyclopedia of New York City, American Immigrant Cultures, Gale Encyclopedia of Multicultural America, Encyclopedia of Associations,* and *Standard Periodical Directory.*

IMPLEMENTING THE RESEARCH
1. Readers can consult these and other reference sources (e.g., *American Demographics, Arab American Biography, Before the Flames: A Quest for the History of Arab Americans,* and *Arab American Today: A Demographic Profile of Arab Americans*).
2. Readers should understand the benefits of reading from more than one source rather than concentrating solely on one source—issues addressed in one reference might not be addressed in another (and vice versa).
3. Readers should consult books and periodicals that document the prejudice and discrimination faced by many Arab Americans.

Source: Wertsman, V. F. (2001). A comparative and critical analysis of leading reference sources. *Multicultural Review, 10*(2), 42–47.

■ ■ ■ ■ ■ ▬▬

FOLLOW THROUGH 5.2
CONSIDERING YOUR IMAGES OF ARAB AMERICANS

Think about your images of Arab Americans—be honest with yourself and admit possible stereotypical images. Second, determine the basis for your beliefs. Third, ask yourself, "How true is the image?" Last, decide what you can do to dispel your stereotypical images and gain a more accurate perception of this cultural group.

The fantasy film *Aladdin* has proven immensely popular with American children and their parents and is one of the few U.S. films to feature an Arab hero or heroine. Still, a closer look provides disturbing evidence of stereotyping. The film's light-skinned lead characters, Aladdin and Jasmine, have Anglicized features and Anglo American accents. This is in contrast to the other characters, who are dark-skinned, swarthy, and villainous—cruel palace guards or greedy merchants with Arabic features,

■ ■ ■ ■ ■ ▬▬▬▬▬▬▬▬▬▬▬▬▬▬▬▬▬▬▬▬▬▬▬▬▬▬▬▬▬▬▬▬▬▬

FOLLOW THROUGH 5.3
REACTING TO OFFENSIVE READING MATERIALS

Consider what you will do if a sixth-grade student brings a comic book or some other magazine to class that portrays Arab American men as dark-skinned, swarthy, villainous, and violent; and Arab women dressed as belly dancers and harem girls. Will you take the magazine and give it back at the end of school? Will you condemn the child for even bringing such offensive material to school? Will you try to talk to him or her about more accurate images of Arab Americans?

Arabic accents, and grotesque facial features. The film characterizes the Arab world as alien and exotic. Other offenders also use negative images to cast Arabs. For example, children and adolescents develop negative images of their culture when they see Arab women dressed as belly dancers and harem girls, and Arab men as violent terrorists, oil "sheiks," (p. 7), and marauding tribesman who kidnap blond Western women. Even on Saturday-morning cartoons, Arabs are portrayed as fanatic and dark-complexioned, with sabers and rifles, allies of some force plotting to take over the world. Comic books are equally troubling. Tarzan battles with an Arab chieftain who kidnaps Jane, Superman foils Arab terrorists hijacking a U.S. nuclear carrier, and the Fantastic Four combat a hideous oil sheik supervillain. Computer games often feature cartoon Arab villains, and children rack up high scores and win games by killing Arabs (Wingfield & Karaman, 1995).

Implementing Research 5.2 looks at Arab stereotypes among educators and some ideas for minimizing stereotypes.

Because many Arabs are Muslims, their dress and traditions are sometimes misunderstood. People sometimes stereotype men with a *galabiya* or body-length robe and women wearing a *hijab*, a scarf covering the head, as religious fundamentalists. As with robes, wearing *hijab* is a personal choice. Many women wear *hijab* because of cultural traditions. A devout Muslim woman does not necessarily wear a *hijab* (Suleiman, 2001). Wearing the *hijab* is a religious practice rather than a cultural practice and is rooted in the Islamic emphasis on modesty. Interestingly, some Arab women say veiling denigrates women; others say the practice liberates them. Covering is not universally observed by Muslim women and varies from region and class. In American families, a mother or daughter might cover her head, while the other one does not. Educators meeting students' parents should understand that covering is a religious practice rather than a cultural practice (www.freep.com/jobspage/arabs).

Schools should recognize other Arab American religious practices. Many Arab Americans adhere to restricted diets—for example, Islamic law forbids eating pork and drinking alcohol (www.freep.com/jobspage/arabs). Teachers should recognize the month of Ramadan, in which many Muslim students participate in fasting.

Case Study 5.1 looks at the harassment one middle-school student experienced simply because he was Arab American.

IMPLEMENTING RESEARCH 5.2
ARAB AMERICAN STEREOTYPING

Although this article is about a decade old, it continues to be one of the most informative pieces on stereotyping of Arab Americans. As just mentioned, Arabs are often stereotyped in demeaning ways. Unfortunately, the negative images of Arabs are not only in the media; some educators also hold stereotypical images. Educators who have not yet been alerted to the problems associated with stereotyping and racism are unaware of the potential harm being done to Arabs.

Problems related to stereotyping include:

- History and geography textbooks have "an over-portrayal of deserts, camels, and nomads" (p. 8) in the chapter on the Middle East. Some teachers use the Bedouin images to typify Arab cultures.
- U.S. textbooks are often Eurocentric, while Arab points of view regarding such issues as the nationalization of resources or the Arab–Israeli conflict are presented inadequately or not at all.
- Some textbooks link Islam and violence, while ignoring its similarities to Christianity and Judaism.
- Overt anti-Arab discrimination occurs, for example, when a teacher encourages children and adolescents to socialize only with children of similar cultural backgrounds.

IMPLEMENTING THE RESEARCH
Appropriate action for educators working with Arab American children and adolescents includes:

- Consider using the Arab language and literature in bilingual programs, to make students from homes in which Arabic is spoken feel comfortable.
- Work to eliminate stereotypes (both conscious and unconscious) as well as negative and ill-informed media images of the Arab people.
- Learn about students' individual histories and cultures, and be prepared to teach about them in classes.

Source: Wingfield, M., & Karaman, B. (1995). Arab stereotypes and American educators. *Social Studies and Young Learners*, 7(4), 7–10.

FOR ADDITIONAL INFORMATION
INTERNET ADDRESSES

Teaching Tolerance
www.tolerance.org/teach/expand/act/activity. jsp?cid=155   The Teaching Tolerance site provides a wealth of information on Arab Americans, Islam, and bias against Arab and Muslim Americans.

Anti-Defamation League
www.adl.org/terrorism_america/adl_responds.asp The ADL provides information on Arab Americans, combating hate, hate crimes, Nation of Islam, and terrorism.

American-Arab Anti-Discrimination Committee
www.adc.org/index.php?id=248   The ADC provides "Facts about the Arabs and the Arab World," "How to Respond to Incidents of Discrimination in Schools," and "Arab Contributions to Civilization."

■ ■ ■ ■ ■ ▬▬▬▬▬▬

CASE STUDY 5.1
ADDRESSING HARASSMENT

A thirteen-year-old Arab American boy was on the receiving end of considerable harassment after a terrorist incident thousands of miles away. Still, the media reported the incident and speculated that Arab Americans might be at fault. His middle-school peers called him names (e.g., "terror-boy" and "sheik"). During breaks and at lunch, they generally aggravated and taunted him, trying to get him to fight. No matter where he went at school in attempts to be alone, the other boys found him and continued their harassment. One teacher said, "He is a strong kid—he will survive that teasing, maybe he should just fight it out with those guys to show them what he can really do." Another teacher disagreed and stated that harassment did not have a place in their school. The boy had done nothing wrong and should not be punished for something in which he was not involved. He only happened to be from the same culture as the terrorists.

The teacher who was more perceptive of the young boy's predicament spoke with his harassers, told them the boy had nothing to do with the incident, and he should be left in peace. Did she think her admonishment would work? She had her doubts, but she knew something had to be done—she had taken only a temporary step and she was aware that she (and the administrators and counselors) would have to do more.

CULTURAL CHARACTERISTICS

It is difficult to generalize about all cultures, but it is particularly difficult with Arab Americans because of the many different countries from which they come. Still, some generalizations can be made, provided one considers factors such as generational status, socioeconomic status, commitment to one's religion, and the actual country of origin.

Generally speaking, Arab Americans have a powerful commitment to both immediate and extended family; they are collective in nature (compared to European Americans' individualism); and they have a strong respect and allegiance to their language. Even then, perceptive educators realize the only way to learn about Arab Americans is to know them individually.

Readers acquainted with the concepts of individualism–collectivism will probably not be surprised to learn that research (Buda & Elsayed-Elkhouly, 1998) suggests that Arabs are more collective or more oriented toward the group and that Americans are more individualistic or more oriented toward individual concerns. In other words, many Arab Americans believe that individuals have the right to take care of themselves. They are self-oriented and emotionally independent, and their emphasis is on individual initiative, the right to privacy, autonomy, and individual decisions. Arabs believe in a more collectivist orientation. Their identity is based on their social system. They are emotionally dependent on institutions and other people. Their lives are influenced by social and familial groups to which they belong (Buda & Elsayed-Elkhouly, 1998).

Educators who understand Arab American learners and the Arab culture quickly realize the importance of the individualism–collectivism issue and of the necessity to learn about individual Arab American students. Generally speaking, the

U.S. school system has focused on individualism. Educators expect learners, both elementary and secondary, to fend for themselves. Students are expected to have goals, to work individually toward those goals, to compete with others for academic achievement and for the teacher's time, and to claim personal and individual pride in their accomplishments. Individualistic mindset changed somewhat with the inception of cooperative learning, but still, the U.S. school system is individual-oriented. Educators working with Arab Americans (as well as some American Indians and Hispanic Americans) might see more tendencies toward collectivism. Such a statement does not imply, however, that all Arab Americans are collective. To some, when considering education, the theory of collectivism does not make sense and therefore, they feel a need to compete.

Even considering the research on individualism–collectivism, educators who are sensitive to cultural concerns realize the need to consider students' individuality—undoubtedly, there are Americans who have orientations toward collectivism and Arabs who prefer to work individually toward learning goals. Perceptive educators see the need to know individual students and then to plan culturally responsive educational experiences.

Gender

Gender roles differ for Arab Americans. Some factors affecting gender roles include country of origin, whether the family came from a rural or urban area, and how long the family has been in the United States. Rather than assume a gender stereotype, it is better to ask the person about his or her own experiences (www.freep.com/jobspage/arabs).

Arab American women and girls sometimes experience "double jeopardy" for being young and female, and almost constantly feel victimized by stereotypical images in the media. Females often feel obligated to fight the media images in positive ways, showing a more accurate context of their religious and social climate (Bing-Canar & Zerkel, 1998).

Boys and girls are treated differently in Arab cultures. Also, as explained later in the "Families" section, Arab parental discipline and child-rearing methods are often gender-specific. While child-rearing methods vary among Arab cultures and among parents, a great deal of unconditional love usually accompanies discipline, especially for sons. Differential treatment of boys and girls is not uncommon. Educators working with Arab Americans need to remember that their equal treatment of boys and girls as well as the

■ ■ ■ ■ ■

FOLLOW THROUGH 5.4
DETERMINING "COLLECTIVE" OR "INDIVIDUALISTIC"

Develop several questions or an informal instrument that you can use to determine whether students are "collective" or "individualistic." This list or instrument will help you avoid the trap of assuming Arab Americans are "collective" and European Americans are "individualistic." Describe what you will look for, such as characteristics, behaviors, and mannerisms.

school's efforts to promote egalitarianism might be misunderstood by children and parents. While some acculturation might have occurred toward more equal sex roles, it is a mistake to assume that children and adolescents who have lived in the United States for a number of years have adopted Western norms of gender and equality.

According to Abu-Ali and Reisen (1999), Muslim girls living in the United States often live in a subculture with different attitudes and beliefs from those of the host culture. They are exposed to varied and sometimes discrepant values and expectations, which can affect the development of their gender schema. For example, Muslim girls may be exposed to conflicting ideas about the roles of women from their culture and from their religion. In Gender Perspectives 5.1, Abu-Ali and Reisen (1999) summarize their research on gender role identity among adolescent Muslim girls.

Case Study 5.2 looks at how assumptions were made about a Muslim girl and how a perceptive teacher worked to change the direction of the girl's education.

■ ■ ■ ■ ■

GENDER PERSPECTIVES 5.1
ADOLESCENT MUSLIM GIRLS AND GENDER ROLE IDENTITY

Abu-Ali and Reisen (1999) maintain that gender role identity is acquired through exposure to societal expectations and beliefs about behaviors and characteristics appropriate for males and females. They examined influences on gender identity among ninety-six Muslim adolescent girls living in the United States and attending an Islamic high school.

In their discussion, Abu-Ali and Reisen (1999) found that their study:

■ Contradicted the common Western stereotype of Muslim women as being submissive and passive—Muslim girls in their study had higher scores on the masculinity scale than did U.S. college women.
■ Reported that greater exposure to Western culture, as measured by years in the United States, was associated with increased masculine attributes.
■ Reported that girls with a stronger sense of belonging to their ethnic group identified themselves as possessing more stereotypically feminine traits.

IMPLEMENTING THE RESEARCH
■ Educators need to understand the complexity of cultural influences on gender because some aspects can affect gender role development and identity.
■ Educators should recognize the effects of acculturation on the acquiring of male attributes.
■ Educators should recognize that gender role identity is affected by identification with one's culture, adherence to religious practices, and exposure to foreign cultural values.
■ Educators should avoid making assumptions about Arab Americans' gender role development and should try diligently to learn individual learners.

Source: Abu-Ali, A., & Reisen, C. A. (1999). Gender role identity among adolescent Muslim girls living in the U.S. *Current Psychology, 18,* 185–192.

■ ■ ■ ■ ■ ▬▬▬▬▬▬▬▬▬▬▬▬

CASE STUDY 5.2
THE SUBMISSIVE AND PASSIVE STEREOTYPE

A sixteen-year-old girl entered a new high school because her parents moved to a different part of the city. The teachers at her new school recognized that she was an Arab American girl and made some quick assumptions: She would be submissive and passive and would demonstrate traditional or fundamental Arab feminine characteristics.

The teachers did not realize, however, that she had been in the United States since she was five; she was from an upper-class family, with parents who had worked diligently to be socially and economically successful. Such success required a high degree of acculturation. To gain social and economic success in the United States, they had chosen to acculturate or, as some might say, "They had whitened." Both her parents were fluent in English. Plus, her parents had sent her to public schools (and had lived in neighborhoods with "good" schools). While she was indeed Arab American, she had also acculturated toward Western cultural standards and had in some ways, like her mother, been influenced by the feminist movement.

One perceptive European American teacher at the new school (who was actually married to an Arab American) recognized the fallacies of some of the other teachers' assumptions. In a meeting, she suggested they do the following:

- Recognize that the student had been in the United States since she was five—she had "grown up" in U.S. schools and considerable acculturation had occurred.
- Review her previous school records to see that she was involved in a number of school activities, which suggested that she was not as submissive and passive as they thought.
- Realize that their assumptions about her traditional cultural femininity might be wrong because her school records indicated she had been involved in mixed-gender soccer teams.

■ ■ ■ ■ ■ ▬▬▬▬▬▬▬▬▬▬▬▬

FOLLOW THROUGH 5.5
HELPING ARAB AMERICAN GIRLS

Consider special steps you can take to help Arab American girls—for example, addressing stereotypes, understanding collectivism (if, indeed, they are collective), providing culturally and gender-responsive curricular materials, and providing a helpful learning environment.

Socioeconomic Status

Although many Arab immigrants were peddlers and merchants, the new immigrants reflect a greater variety of professions. Whereas household income averages for Arab Americans tend to be higher than the national average, there is a greater percentage of Arab American households below the poverty level than for the U.S. population as a whole. This is because a large number of Arab immigrants earn less than poverty income and have a higher unemployment rate (Suleiman, 2001).

Individually, Arab Americans are at every economic strata of U.S. life. Nationally, Arab American households have a higher-than-average median income. Like occupational patterns, this varies by geographic location (www.freep.com/jobspage/arabs).

Families

Arab Americans value the family and take pride in extended family members. They share several familial traits, such as generosity, hospitality, courage, and respect for the elderly. Most important, Arab Americans invest in their children through education, which is seen as a social asset and religious duty necessary for both the survival of both individuals and groups (Suleiman, 2001).

Arab American families are, on the average, larger than non-Arab American families and smaller than families in Arab countries. Traditionally, more children meant more pride and economic contributors for the family. The cost of having large families in the United States, however, and adaptation to American customs seems to encourage smaller families (www.freep.com/jobspage/arabs).

If the Quran is the soul of Islam, then the family can be described as the body. Islam focuses on the *umma* and considers all Muslims as brothers and sisters belonging to the same *umma*. With the *umma*, families are given importance as units. Men are given specific duties toward their wives and children, wives are given instructions as to how to treat their husbands, and children are advised to honor their mothers. The empowerment of the family unit reassures women of economic and emotional support within their social position in the world. Both men and women support and maintain the family unit and are responsible for childrearing. In crisis, both are expected to view the good of the family above the fulfillment of individual wishes. Strains on the familial system include industrialization, urbanization, war and conflict, and Westernization. Despite these pressures, the family remains the primary support system for Arabs. For the majority of Arabs, as for virtually all other cultural groups, no institution has replaced the family as a support system (Abudabbeh, 1996).

The Arab family can be described as patriarchal and hierarchial with regard to age and sex, and extended. Despite the moves toward a more Westernized nuclear family, the extended family remains important. Although families may have established their own households, they nevertheless consider their own kin as being worthy of the most attention, of being confided in, and of being worthy of allegiance.

Children in Arab families perpetuate familial customs and traditions. This relationship leads to communication between parents and children in which parents use anger and punishment and the children respond by crying, self-censorship, covering up, or deception. Methods of discipline vacillate between mild punishment for unacceptable behavior and putting fear in the child with warnings of what happens to those who do bad things. This is often accompanied by a great deal of unconditional love, especially for sons. Differential treatment of boys is not uncommon, and the instilling of traditional expectations in girls is common practice. Still, for both genders, it is more likely in the Arab family for parents to use an authoritarian style in interactions with their children. It is likely that children respect the father's authority and, therefore are encouraged to obey orders as opposed to exploring ideas or thoughts with him. Likewise, it is likely that children will spend more time with the mother, and are likely to be more open with her, at times using her as a messenger to their father. Although these trends are changing, Arab children are encouraged to maintain close ties with their families and are not encouraged, as Westerners often are, to be individualistic and separate from their parents (Abudabbeh, 1996).

How can educators best respond to Arab American families? Schwartz (1999) reminds educators that Arab Americans from different countries differ from each other in culture, socioeconomic status, Muslim and Christian Arabs, and newly arrived second and third generations. To accommodate the individuality of Arab families, it is important for teachers and counselors to take the lead from students and their parents when discussing school and other related issues, and to be knowledgeable about Arab culture. Educators also can recognize that family life and harmony are crucial to Arabs, so educators need to demonstrate respect for the sanctity of the nuclear and extended family and the familial role of elders. When Arab American students seem troubled, it may be productive to determine whether their problems stem from intergenerational differences within their family or another source. Inviting parents' input in problem solving can be helpful. Because Arabs are sensitive to public criticism, teachers should be careful how they express concerns to Arab American students and parents. Last, helping families cope with varying levels of acculturation, language differences, and conformity to tradition can enable students to develop a positive identity that is both personally satisfying and respectful of their heritage (Schwartz, 1999).

Religion

Arabs do not share a common religion. Instead, they belong to many religions, including Islam, Christianity, Druze, Judaism, and others. There are additional distinctions within each of these, and some religious groups have evolved new identities and faith practices in the United States. Educators should be careful to distinguish religion from culture. Although Arabs are connected by culture, they have different faiths. Common misperceptions are that all Arab traditions are Islamic, or that Islam unifies all Arabs. Most Arab Americans are Catholic or Orthodox Christians, but this is not true in all parts of the United States. In some areas, most Arab Americans are Muslim (www.freep.com/jobspage/arabs).

■ ■ ■ ■ ■

FOLLOW THROUGH 5.6
INTERVIEWING ARAB PARENTS AND FAMILIES

First, write six to eight carefully crafted interview questions that reflect what you have just learned about Arab families. As you develop the interview questions, be sure to consider the parents' generational status (i.e., how long they have been in the United States), socioeconomic status, and their commitment to their religion. Then, interview several Arab American parents, preferably both parents at the same time about their experiences in the United States and reactions to Western culture, their experiences with discrimination, prejudices, and others' stereotyping. Also, learn about their children and child-rearing and disciplinary practices.

One must differentiate between two terms: Arab and Muslim. An Arab is a person whose native language is Arabic and who lives according to Arabic cultural traditions and values. He or she is not tied to any particular religion. Religious diversity is characteristic of both the Arab world and the Arab American population. In the United States, where the majority of Arab Americans are Christians, there are still several thousand who belong to the Jewish faith. On the other hand, a Muslim is an adherent to Islam and may or may not be an Arab. Arabs are a minority in the Muslim community. Muslims are from many different parts of the world, including China, Indonesia, Turkey, Russia, and even the United States. To label all Arabs as Muslim is a sweeping false generalization (Suleiman, 2001).

In the United States, about 50 percent of Arab Americans are Muslims and Druzes, and the other half are of various Eastern and Western rites. These include Antiochians, Maronites, Melkites, Chaldeans (Catholics from Iraq), Syriacs/Jacobites, Copts, Greek Orthodox, and Protestants. Despite the disproportionate number of Christians Arabs, the influx of Muslim Arabs has contributed to Islam becoming one of the fastest-growing religions in the United States (Wertsman, 2001).

The essence of Islam, as preached by the Prophet Mohammed, was transmitted through the Quran, which is believed to be the literal word of God. In addition to the Quran, religious guidance also includes the Prophet's own traditional sayings (*hadith*) and his practices (*sunna*). Except by implication, the Quran does not contain explicit doctrines or instructions; basically, it provides guidance. The *hadith* and *sunna*, however, contain some specific commands on issues such as marriage. They also address such daily habits as how often the believer should worship God and how all people should treat each other.

Based on the general guidance of the Quran, five basic obligations of Muslims emerged in the form of the "Pillars of Islam." These consist of (1) oral testimony that there is only one God and that Mohammed is His prophet; (2) ritual prayer practiced five times a day with certain words and certain postures of the body; (3) the giving of alms; (4) keeping a strict fast of no liquid or food from sunrise to sundown during the month of Ramadan; and (5) holy pilgrimage to Mecca (*hajj*) once in a lifetime at a specific time of year. *Jihad* carries the universal meaning that every Muslim must exercise strenuous intellectual, physical, and spiritual efforts for the good of all (Abudabbeh, 1996).

Language

The Arabic language is one of the great unifying and distinguishing characteristics of Arab people. Albert Hourani (1970), as cited in Abudabbeh (1996), describes the relationship between Arabs and their language as "more conscious of their language than any people in the world" (p. 337). Arabic is spoken by 130 million people and is the fourth most widely spoken language in the world (tied with Bengali). Although spoken Arabic is as varied as the different parts of the Arab world, classical Arabic and written Arabic are the same in all Arab nations. While many people feel an affection for their native language, Arab feelings for their language are much more intense. The Arabic language is one of the greatest Arab cultural treasures. Plus, because of its complexity, a good command of the Arabic language is highly admired (Abudabbeh, 1996).

Arab schools usually teach more than one language. It is more common for Arab Americans to speak more than one language than it is for non-Arab Americans. Many immigrants come to the United States having learned two or three languages in their country of origin (www.freep.com/jobspage/arabs).

Case Study 5.3 tells about a school that was unprepared for an influx of Arab American students.

ACHIEVEMENT LEVELS

Arab American students are among the new sizable ethnic groups comprising the student population in the United States. Arab American students have generally been an invisible minority in many ways. Their immigration to the United States has been relatively smooth. Most important, Arab students have not suffered any significant failures in schools, as have some other ethnic groups (Nieto, 2000; Suleiman, 2001). Still, elementary- and secondary-school educators should not assume that Arab Americans have experienced "an easy success" in U.S. schools. Arab Americans' academic progress

■ ■ ■ ■ ■

CASE STUDY 5.3
A SCHOOL FACES A LANGUAGE DILEMMA

The educators at the K–5 school in this medium-sized Southern city were somewhat startled when they learned that 28–30 Arab American children planned to enroll in their school in less than a week. The school was predominantly European American, but there were a handful of African and Asian American students. The school had neither planned nor implemented language services for Arab learners because there had never been a need. Still, the school had a commitment to diversity, and they faced a problem: How would they accommodate the language needs of 28–30 Arab American children who would be entering the school in less than a week? The children, ranging in age from five to nine, had differing English-language abilities. None were fluent, but some had a meager knowledge of the English language.

A committee of teachers, administrators, and counselors met to decide how to meet the challenge. Fortunately, one teacher knew a person who had grown up in the country from which the children were coming and could speak the language. The committee made several quick decisions. First, they decided to see if she would volunteer as a translator several days a week. Second, they contacted the local university to see if its student services expert (who had considerable experience working with diverse populations) would come to the school to discuss Arab cultural mannerisms and traditions. Third, they had the foresight to ask a local religious leader to speak to the teachers and other teachers about religious customs—he agreed, but cautioned them to avoid making assumptions about the new students' religious allegiances.

Would all schools offer such a commitment to an influx of Arab students? Unfortunately, some would not have the initiative or available resources to make the effort, but still some effort needs to be made to help young Arab American learners.

■ ■ ■ ■ ■ ▬▬▬▬▬▬▬▬▬▬▬▬▬▬▬▬▬▬▬▬▬▬▬▬▬▬▬

FOLLOW THROUGH 5.7
IDENTIFYING REFERENCES AND INFORMATION

Because there is little information about Arab Americans, their culture, school experiences, or learning styles, make a list of informational sources on children and adolescents in the Arabic culture. Your list might include Internet sites, books, journals, and experts you might contact.

has not undergone the scrutiny that other cultural groups have experienced. Because the cultural group has been an invisible minority, data to prove or disprove their academic achievement are not available.

Several factors are known that have the potential for limiting their academic achievement. First, Arab Americans often experience racism and discrimination and are subject to stereotyping. Second, some schools have not yet acknowledged Arab culture and history or even tried to transform curricular and instructional experiences and to infuse culturally pedagogical experiences conducive to Arab American needs (Suleiman, 2001). Third, curricular materials might contain only negative images.

SCHOOL PRACTICES IMPEDING ARAB AMERICANS' PROGRESS

Teachers and curriculum designers should integrate culturally relevant materials that can enrich the lives of mainstream students while learning about other ethnic and cultural groups. Although a lot has been written about various ethnic groups, schools have little information about Arab Americans, their culture, school experiences, or learning styles (Nieto, 2000). At the same time, teachers must engage in the unteaching of myths, stereotypes, and false images incubated in the minds of Arab American students' peers (Suleiman, 2001).

Placed in mainstream classrooms, Arab American students are often confronted by a biased curriculum and literature. As a result of negative media images, perceptions of Arab American students and their families range from the overly romanticized to the harmfully negative. Schools can make sure that Arabs are accurately and fairly represented in the curriculum and school activities.

Schools can take action against prejudice, discrimination, and incidences of racism. They can also provide professional training for staff and teachers and provide accurate textbooks and curricular materials. Schools can avoid discrimination by increasing awareness about various social patterns and traditions. As for Arab American students, knowledge of their culture and history should help educators to construct a more realistic picture of their students. For example, by being aware of food taboos, dress codes, and restrictions on male and female interaction, teachers reach out to their students in a meaningful way. Teachers can enhance pride in Arab American students by learning about Arab contributions in fields such as algebra, science, linguistics, astrology, art, and architecture. Teachers can also increase Arabic-speaking students' self-image through affirming their language (Suleiman, 2001).

■ ■ ■ ■ ■ ▬▬▬▬▬▬

FOLLOW THROUGH 5.8
BEING PROACTIVE

Make a list of strategies and plans you can implement when political events appear to involve Arab Americans. Specifically, what can you do to reduce or eliminate harassment, both psychological and physical, to students who are not to blame for the world's problems?

Implementing Research 5.3 offers suggestions for educating and helping Arab American students in public schools.

PROMOTING POSITIVE SELF-ESTEEM AND CULTURAL IDENTITY

It is recognized that the more positive a student's self-esteem, the higher is her or his achievement level. Teachers use various techniques to make students feel worthwhile and capable of handling everyday academic and social tasks. Arab American students need to see positive images of their culture and cultural backgrounds (Wingfield & Karaman, 1995).

One special challenge to educators of Arab American learners is how to provide educational activities that improve self-esteem, those activities that acknowledge and respect students' Arab culture and cultural traditions. While one approach is to attempt to employ counselors and teachers from Arab cultural backgrounds, that may be difficult in some areas. Another approach is to provide training sessions focusing on Arab cultural characteristics, worldviews, and perceptions of school success and motivation. Whatever the approach, the focus should be on improving self-esteem. As a result of the training, educators might learn that all students do not perceive events through a European American (or whatever the majority culture) lens. With the increasing number of learners from Arabic cultures, educators should understand students' cultural orientations and worldviews and use culturally responsive teaching–learning strategies that promote self-esteem.

The following Cultural Portrait tells about Abdullah Salaam, a thirteen-year-old Arab American learner.

SUMMING UP

Educators who plan teaching and learning experiences for Arab American children and adolescents should:

1. Remember that Arab Americans are not a unified single ethnic group; making such an assumption will grossly overlook their tremendous diversity.
2. Clarify stereotypes, myths, and misconceptions about the Arabic cultures.

■ ■ ■ ■ ■ ▬

IMPLEMENTING RESEARCH 5.3

ARAB AMERICAN STUDENTS IN PUBLIC SCHOOLS

Schwartz (1999) notes that Arab Americans in U.S. schools represent more than twenty countries. They share many similarities with other immigrant groups seeking to establish an ethnic identity in a heterogeneous nation. They face at least four challenges: negative stereotyping; racism and discrimination; widespread misinformation about their history and culture; and for the majority who are Muslim, the need to find ways to practice their religion in a predominantly Judeo-Christian country. As the number of Arab Americans students in public schools has increased, so have the strategies and materials for working with these students. Still, many schools have not yet acknowledged Arab culture and history or counteracted Arab stereotyping (Schwartz, 1999).

School policies and practices that contribute to Arab Americans feeling positive about schools and the United States include:

- Represent the Middle East, Arabs, and Muslims accurately, completely, and fairly in curriculum and school activities.
- Ensure that Arab American students are treated equitably and without prejudice by teachers and peers, and that teachers respond to incidents of racism and discrimination with prompt and appropriate action.
- Respect the customs of the native culture and religion of Arab students (Schwartz, 1999).

IMPLEMENTING THE RESEARCH
Educators can take appropriate action to:

- Represent the Arab American culture in multicultural courses and activities to validate their culture and educate all students about the Middle East.
- Work to eliminate prejudice and discrimination against Arab Americans, especially when political events result in additional harassment.
- Avoid discrimination against Arab Americans, for example, not enforcing dress codes or showering requirements that violate Muslim traditions of modesty or requiring students to engage in mixed-gender physical education classes.
- Avoid scheduling tests on major Islamic holidays, and allow fasting students to visit the library instead of the cafeteria during Ramadan.
- Infuse Arab references and content throughout the curriculum to familiarize students with the Middle East culture and to dispel myths.
- Evaluate textbooks and other curricular materials to be sure that Middle East topics are treated fairly and accurately.

Source: Schwartz, W. (1999, March). Arab American students in public schools. ERIC Digest (EDO-UD-99-2), http://eric~web.tc.columbia.edu/digests/dig142.htnml, retrieved July 22, 2002.

3. Avoid letting Arab American children and adolescents become the lost sheep of the school system.
4. Consider acculturation factors among Arab Americans; for example, the length of U.S. residence, age at immigration, visits to one's homeland, and being of the Christian religious persuasion affect acculturation.

■ ■ ■ ■ ■ ▬▬

CULTURAL PORTRAIT
ABDULLAH SALAAM—A THIRTEEN-YEAR-OLD ARAB AMERICAN BOY

Abdullah Salaam is a thirteen-year-old Arab American boy whose parents had moved from Saudi Arabia. Abdullah's father worked for a company that wanted to expand its international operation. His family was reluctant to move to the United States, but they realized the economic and other benefits of the move.

Abdullah faced several challenges, which the school addressed with varying degrees of success. First, his English speaking skills were good, but he still had difficulty understanding the teacher and communicating with other students. Second, he received a little abuse from other middle-school students, who sometimes mocked his language. They spoke to him using what they considered an "Arab accent." Third, his social development was lacking, perhaps because of his language proficiency and fear of others mocking him. He had few friends and usually stayed alone.

Most of the teachers, unfortunately, ignored Abdullah's school situation, but two teachers realized that he needed help. They enlisted the aid of the guidance counselor to come up with a plan. They decided on a four-prong approach. First, they asked the language specialist to work with Abdullah in an effort to improve his language abilities. Second, they decided to address "mocking and other forms of harassment" in the advisor–advisee program (an essential middle-school concept), to try to show the effects of such negative behaviors. Third, they decided to try cooperative learning activities that would bring Abdullah into social contact with other students. Fourth, they agreed to work informally with him to improve his self-esteem.

Admittedly, they had doubts about whether these approaches would have positive and long-term effects, but they thought Abdullah's problems deserved to be addressed in some way.

5. Remember differences—cultural, gender, generational, and socioeconomic—that contribute to Arab American children's and adolescents' diversity.
6. Recognize the essential need for Arab American learners to develop positive self-esteem and cultural identity.
7. Provide a learning environment that respects Arabic American cultural backgrounds and languages.
8. Provide curricular and instructional practices that reflect the Arab American culture as well as their accomplishments, art, and literature.

SUGGESTED LEARNING ACTIVITIES

1. Choose an Arab American learner with a language problem. Evaluate the extent of the problem, list several ways educators might address the language difficulty, and devise a plan to remediate the language problem.
2. Buda & Elsayed-Elkhouly (1998), in their discussion of individualism–collectivism, state that Arabs are more collective or more oriented toward the group, and Americans are more individualistic or more oriented toward individual concerns. How will you address this issue during learning activities? For example, how will you allow Arab Americans to be "collective" and European Americans to be more "individualistic"?

3. Make a list of specific ways you can improve Arab Americans' self-esteem, especially students who are not doing well academically, students with language difficulties, and maybe girls who feel inadequate in a predominantly white and male-dominated classroom. As you compile your list, how can you make it as culturally responsive as possible, that is, as responsive to the Arab culture as possible?

SUGGESTIONS FOR COLLABORATIVE EFFORTS

Form groups of three or four, which, if possible, represent our nation's cultural and gender diversity. Working collaboratively, focus your group's attention toward the following efforts.

1. Schwartz (1999) suggests that educators should infuse Arab references and content throughout the curriculum to familiarize students with the Middle East culture and to dispel myths. Working in groups of three or more, have each student compile a list of Arab music, Arab art, and Arab children's and adolescents' literature (and other curricular materials) that portrays Arab Americans in a positive light and that dispel myths and stereotypes.

2. Design a one-hour school orientation program that can be presented to Arab American parents and families. Brainstorm in your group what these parents might need to know about the U.S. public school system—for instance, its egalitarian treatment of both genders, the emphasis on individualism, teacher and school expectations, parents' responsibilities and rights, and student rights. Let each person in your group take one aspect and tell what will benefit Arab American parents the most.

3. Interview a first-, second-, and third-generation parent (only two will suffice, if your group cannot locate three) to determine the challenges they face in dealing with the school and society in general. List the challenges on the left and what your group thinks will help the parents on the right.

EXPANDING YOUR HORIZONS: ADDITIONAL
JOURNAL READINGS AND BOOKS

"100 Questions and Answers about Arab Americans: A Journalist's Guide." *Detroit Free Press* (www.freep.com/jobspage/arabs).
Using a question-and-answer format, this Internet site is the single best source of information on Arab Americans—overview, origins, language, demographics, family, customs, religion, politics, and stereotypes.

Ajrouch, K. J. (2000). Community living and ethnic identity among Lebanese American adolescents. *Small Group Research, 31,* 447–469.
Ajrouch studied the social ties and examined the process of acculturation and the negotiation of ethnic identity of adolescent children of Lebanese immigrants.

Kulczycki, A., & Lobo, A. P. (2002). Patterns, determinants, and implications of intermarriage among Arab Americans. *Journal of Marriage and the Family, 64,* 202–210.
This study discusses ethnic options for children of intermarried couples, mainly U.S.-born and their non-Arab spouses.

Naber, N. (2000). Ambiguous insiders: An investigation of Arab American invisibility. *Ethnic and Racial Studies, 23,* 37–61.
In an excellent article exploring paradoxes shaping Arab American identity, Naber maintains that Arab Americans are a complex, diverse community, but have been represented as a monolith in media images.

Schwartz, W. (1999, March). Arab American students in public schools. ERIC Digest (EDO-UD-99-2), http://eric~web.tc.columbia.edu/digests/dig142.html
> In this highly recommended ERIC Digest, Schwartz provides practical suggestions for helping Arab Americans in school.

Wertsman, V. F. (2001). A comparative and critical analysis of leading reference sources. *Multicultural Review, 10*(2), 42–47.
> Wertsman provides a helpful resource and comparative analysis of leading reference sources on Arab Americans—beneficial for readers wanting additional information on Arab Americans.

EXPANDING YOUR STUDENTS' HORIZONS: APPROPRIATE ARAB AMERICAN BOOKS FOR CHILDREN AND ADOLESCENTS

This list of books was developed from: Lems, K. (1999). The Arab world and Arab Americans. www.ala.org/BookLinks/v09/arab.html.

ALGERIA
Schwartz, Howard, & Rush, Barbara. *The Sabbath Lion: A Jewish Folktale from Algeria*. Linnet, 1992.

ARMENIA
Hogrogian, Nonny. *The Contest*. Greenwillow, 1976.
Kherdian, David. *The Golden Bracelet*. Holiday, 1998.
San Souci, Robert D. *A Weave of Words*. Orchard, 1998.

EGYPT
Clements, Andrew. *Temple Cat*. Clarion, 1996.
Climo, Shirley. *The Egyptian Cinderella*. HarperCollins, 1989.
Heide, Florence Parry, & Gilliland, Judith Heide. *The Day of Ahmed's Secret*. Lothrop, 1990.
Lattimore, Deborah Nourse. *The Winged Cat: A Tale of Ancient Egypt*. HarperCollins, 1992.
McDermott, Gerald. *The Voyage of Osiris: A Myth of Ancient Egypt*. Harcourt, 1995.

IRAQ
Heide, Florence Parry, & Gilliland, Judith Heide. *The House of Wisdom*. DK INK, 1999.
Hickox, Rebecca. *The Golden Sandal: A Middle Eastern Cinderella Story*. Holiday, 1998.
Laird, Elizabeth. *Kiss the Dust*. Puffin, 1994.

LEBANON
Heide, Florence Parry, & Gilliland, Judith Heide. *Sami and the Time of the Troubles*. Houghton, 1992.
Lovelace, Maud Hart. *The Trees Kneel at Christmas*. Abdo, 1994.

MOROCCO
Czernecki, Stefan. *Zorah's Magic Carpet*. Hyperion, 1996.
Lewin, Ted. *The Storytellers*. Lothrop, 1998.
London, Jonathan. *Ali, Child of the Desert*. Lothrop, 1997.

PALESTINE
Holliday, Laurel. *Children of Israel, Children of Palestine: Our Own True Stories*. Pocket, 1998.
Nye, Naomi Shihab. *Habibi*. Simon & Schuster, 1997.
Nye, Naomi Shihab. *Sitti's Secrets*. Simon & Schuster, 1994.

SAHARA–TUAREG
Kesler, Cristine. *One Night: A Story from the Desert*. Putnam/Paperstar, 1995.

TURKEY
Walker, Barbara K. *A Treasury of Turkish Folktales for Children.* Shoe String, 1988.

PAN-ARAB OR NONSPECIFIC LOCATIONS
Al-Saleh, Khairat. *Fabled Cities, Princes and Jinn from Arab Myths and Legends.* Schocken, 1985.
Ben-Ezae, Ehud. *Hosni the Dreamer: An Arabian Tale.* Farrar, 1997.
Child, John. *The Rise of Islam.* NTC/Contemporary, 1995.
George, Linda S. *The Golden Age of Islam.* Benchmark, 1998.
Ghazi, Suhaib Hamid. *Ramadan.* Holiday, 1996.
Husain, Shahrukh. *What Do We Know about Islam.* NTC/Contemporary, 1996.
Johnson-Davies, Denys. *Goha.* Hoopoe, 1993.
Kimmel, Eric. *Rimonah of the Flashing Sword: A North African Tale.* Holiday, 1995.
Lewin, Betsy. *What's the Matter, Habibi?* Clarion, 1997.
MacDonald, Finoa. *A 16th Century Mosque.* NTC/Contemporary, 1994.

CHAPTER SIX

UNDERSTANDING ASIAN AMERICAN CHILDREN AND ADOLESCENTS

Understanding the material and activities in this chapter will help the reader to:

- Describe the cultural, gender, socioeconomic, familial, and language characteristics of Asian American children and adolescents
- Explain the "model minority" stereotype and its effects on Asian American children and adolescents
- Describe Asian American learners and their development, achievement levels, language problems, and learning styles
- List several practices that impede Asian American learners' educational progress
- Offer several concrete suggestions for improving Asian American learners' self-esteem and cultural identities
- List several points that educators of Asian Americans should remember
- Suggest appropriate children's literature, implement research findings, and provide culturally appropriate experiences for Asian American learners

OVERVIEW

Planning teaching and learning experiences for Asian American learners requires an understanding of their developmental characteristics, achievement levels, language problems, learning styles, and cultural characteristics. The diversity among Asian American learners also requires a consideration of their geographic, generational, and socioeconomic differences, as well as intracultural and individual characteristics.

Stereotyping, which plagues learners from all cultures, is a particular problem for Asian Americans. The notable successes of the Asian American people have resulted in a "model minority" stereotype that sometimes leads educators to expect exemplary achievement and behavior of all Asian American learners. This chapter examines the cultural characteristics of Asian American children and adolescents, and then focuses attention on these learners in teaching and learning situations.

ORIGINS

Asian Americans include a number of national, cultural, and religious heritages and more than twenty-nine distinct subgroups, each with unique language, religion, and customs. The four major groups of Asian Americans include East Asian, such as Chinese, Japanese, and Korean; Pacific Islander; Southeast Asian, such as Thai and Vietnamese; and South Asian, such as Indian and Pakistani. Undoubtedly, similarities exist among these cultures, but educators working with Asian Americans need to remember Asians' different origins, ecological adaptations, and histories.

The term *Asian American* is an artificial one, originating as an imposed entity by non-Asians and later adopted by Asian American activists in the 1960s. Since the immigration act of 1965, the Asian American population has become more diverse ethnically, and with immigration legislation giving preference to those with more schooling, Asian Americans have been more fragmented socioeconomically (Tamura, 2001).

Asian Americans have lived in the United States for over one-and-a-half centuries: Chinese and Asian Indians since the mid-nineteenth century, Japanese since the late nineteenth century, and Koreans and Filipinos since the first decade of the twentieth century. An earlier group of Filipinos settled near New Orleans in the late eighteenth century. Because of exclusion laws that culminated with the 1924 Immigration Act, the Asian American population was relatively small before the mid-twentieth century. As late as 1940, Asian immigrants and their descendants constituted considerably less than 1 percent of the U.S. population. With the passage of the 1965 immigration law, the United States opened its doors to formerly excluded groups. As a result, East Asians, South Asians, and Southeast Asians began arriving in increasing numbers. Whereas they constituted 1.5 percent of the country's population in 1980, their percentage increased to almost 3 percent ten years later, and was expected to grow to 4.3 percent by the year 2000 and 10 percent by the year 2050 (Tamura, 2001).

Tamura (2001) divides Asian Americans' history into four broad time periods. The first period, spanning from the late 1800s to 1940, can be seen as a time of labor, discrimination, and exclusion. Asians worked in dangerous jobs, such as railroad building, factories, salmon canning, fishing, and farming. During this time, laws prevented Asians from applying for citizenship, and other laws were passed to close the doors to further Asian immigration. The second period, from 1941 to 1945, emerged during America's involvement in World War II, and was dominated by the incarceration of Japanese Americans. The third period, from 1943 to the 1950s, was one of changing attitudes and the gradual liberalization of immigration and naturalization laws. In 1943, Congress repealed the Chinese Exclusion Act and allowed immigrant Chinese immigrants to apply for citizenship. The act was followed by another that allowed Japanese and other Asians to apply for naturalization. The fourth period, from 1965 until the present, dismantled the discriminatory barriers of earlier immigration laws. Congress did not foresee the tremendous flow that would come from Asian, with Chinese, Koreans, Asian Indians, Filipinos, Vietnamese, and other Southeast Asian groups arriving in unprecedented numbers (Tamura, 2001).

Individual differences also exist in reasons for immigration and related hopes and expectations. Some immigrants are refugees from war-torn countries, and others are from the middle class of stable countries. Some came with nothing, and others came with skills and affluence.

Asian Americans constitute a rapidly growing, diverse population of the United States. Between 1980 and 1990, the number of Asians living in the United States increased by 99 percent. In 1990, the largest proportions of Asian Americans were Chinese (24 percent) and Filipino (20 percent), followed by Japanese (12 percent). Newer immigrant groups such as Laotian, Cambodian, Thai, and Hmong each accounted for 2 percent or less of the Asians in the United States. Sixty-six percent of Asians were born in foreign countries. Among Asian groups, Vietnamese, Laotian, and Cambodian groups constituted the highest proportion of foreign-born, Japanese the lowest (U.S. Bureau of the Census, 1993a).

ASIAN AMERICANS TODAY

Several indicators provide a portrait of Asian Americans today: 54 percent lived in the West in 1990, compared to 21 percent of the total population; their median age was thirty years, younger than the national median of thirty-three years; their educational attainment varied widely by group; 67 percent of the Asian populations, compared with 65 percent of all Americans, were in the workforce; and many work in higher-paying occupations, partly because of higher educational attainment (U.S. Bureau of the Census, 1993a).

There are several characteristics of the cultures of Southeast Asian countries, differences that professionals working with children can misunderstand. Many people refer to any Southeast Asian child as "Vietnamese" without realizing that they may be insulting him or her because of a different cultural heritage. Such labeling fails to realize the bitter feelings among various nationalities and ethnic groups:

> Children may not know one another's language. They may not be of the same religion; their parents may have been opposing enemies; or they may harbor feelings of superiority, inferiority, or resentment toward one another. (West, 1983, pp. 85–86)

Although Asian Americans are a small group compared with other minority groups, such as African American and Latinos, their potential for growth is enormous in the next decade, given that Asian Americans currently represent approximately 38 percent of all immigrants (Kim, Rendon, & Valadez, 1998).

In a very informative article, Tamura (2001), in Implementing Research 6.1, points to a number of important works on Asian Americans.

STEREOTYPING OF ASIAN AMERICAN CHILDREN AND ADOLESCENTS

Asian Americans are often called the "model minority" because of their remarkable educational, occupational, and economic successes. Yao (1988), reflecting on the model minority stereotype, describes Asian American children thus:

> Not all of them are superior students who have no problems in school. Some have learning problems; some lack motivation, proficiency in English, or financial resources;

■ ■ ■ ■ ■ ▬▬▬▬

IMPLEMENTING RESEARCH 6.1

ASIAN AMERICANS IN THE HISTORY OF EDUCATION

Tamura (2001) focuses on several aspects of Asian Americans, such as their history and their designating term. After an interesting historical overview, Tamura recommends a number of important books, essays, and book reviews on Asian Americans and their history in the United States. She makes clear that before World War II, most research focused on Europeans rather than Asians and Asian immigrants.

Tamura (2001) offers a brief description of many important works on Asian Americans and explains the time period during which they were written. Educators, researchers, and scholars interested in the Asian populations will find Tamura's article beneficial. Tamura calls for more historical studies of the pre- and post-1965 periods to illuminate the diversity of experiences as well as the common patterns in Asian American education. The paucity of studies on educational history of Asian Americans in the decades before 1965 poses a challenge to historians.

IMPLEMENTING THE RESEARCH

1. Educators working with Asian Americans should understand Asians' history and the challenges they have faced—it is also interesting to understand the pre- and post-1965 periods.
2. Asian American students benefit when educators know common patterns, experiences, and expectations in Asian American education.
3. Educators and other readers interested in the history of Asian Americans and the Asian culture will find Tamura's comprehensive listing of books both interesting and informative.

Source: Tamura, E. H. (2001). Asian Americans in the history of education: An historical essay. *History of Education Quarterly, 41*(1), 58–71.

and some have parents who do not understand the American school system, because of cultural differences, language barriers, or their own single-minded quest for survival. (p. 223)

The media like to portray the contemporary image of Asian Americans as a minority that has achieved great success in the European American society. For example, some reports applaud the educational achievements of Asian Americans and generally stereotype them as successful, law-abiding, and high-achieving minorities. The success of many Asian students has created the "model minority" stereotype. The popular and professional literature often labels them as "whiz kids," and as "problem free." Some claim that Asians are smarter than other groups; others believe there is something in Asian culture that breeds success, perhaps the Confucian ideas that stress family values and education (Feng, 1994).

Other stereotypes include viewing Asian Americans as proficient in mathematics and not competent with verbal tasks. Such stereotypes might lead educators to hold high expectations of their Asian American students in some areas and low expectations in

■ ■ ■ ■ ■ ▬▬▬▬▬▬

FOLLOW THROUGH 6.1
ADDRESSING ASIAN AMERICAN DIVERSITY

Visit an elementary or secondary school that has a significant number of Asian American student subgroups. What are the educators in the school doing to address the diversity among the Asian groups? What else might they do?

■ ■ ■ ■ ■ ▬▬▬▬▬▬

FOR ADDITIONAL INFORMATION

Chinese Cultural Center, 159 Lexington Ave., New York, NY 10016.
The Cultural Center provides classes and library and information services to promote better understanding of the Chinese culture.

Chinese Cultural Association, P. O. Box 1272, Palo Alto, CA 94302.
This worldwide organization promotes communication and better understanding between the Chinese and people of other cultures.

Southeast Asian Center, 1124–1128 W. Ainslie, Chicago, IL 60640.
The Southeast Asian Center promotes the independence and well-being of Lao, Hmong, Cambodian, Vietnamese, and Chinese people.

others. Both kinds of expectations can produce bored, frustrated students who are afforded few opportunities to learn at their ability and motivational levels. Educators must remember to view each child as an individual with unique strengths and weaknesses.

The academic successes of some Asian Americans have led to a perception that all Asian Americans are exceptional in all pursuits. To assume, however, such scholarly expertise on the basis of culture alone does not have any greater validity than does saying that all African Americans are incapable of high academic achievement or that all American Indians live on reservations. Cultural misconceptions of oneself can have a detrimental effect on the forming identity and can result in undue and unrealistic pressures and demands. Case Study 6.1 shows steps that one can take to learn about Asian Americans as individuals, rather than assuming the "model minority" stereotype.

CULTURAL CHARACTERISTICS

Teachers often think of Asian American children as studious, high-achieving, and well-behaved students (Yee, 1988), whom educators expect to excel in the U.S. culture and yet retain Asian American cultures, values, and traditions. Conforming to both Asian American and European American cultures results in high expectations and considerable

■ ■ ■ ■ ■ ▬▬▬▬▬

USING CHILDREN'S LITERATURE
THE ASIAN AMERICAN EXPERIENCE

Children of all cultures can read developmentally appropriate books about the Asian American culture for more enhanced knowledge and better understanding.

Yep, Laurence. *The Rainbow People.* Harper & Row, 1989.
This book of folktales presents a lively and enjoyable picture of Chinese culture.

Clark, Ann Noland. *To Stand against the Wind.* Viking, 1978.
An eleven-year-old Vietnamese boy's memories of his beautiful land before war destroyed it.

Yagawa, Sumiko. *The Crane Wife.* Morrow, 1981.
In this traditional Japanese tale, greed and its consequences become clear.

■ ■ ■ ■ ■ ▬▬▬▬▬

CASE STUDY 6.1
THE "MODEL MINORITY" STEREOTYPE

Ms. Carter, a European American and a first-year teacher, has a large percentage of Asian American learners in her class. She has heard about the excellent reputation of some Asian American learners and wants to challenge them to excel in as many areas as possible. She is also realistic, however, in the sense that she knows not all Asian Americans are "model students," "problem free," and "whiz kids," She wonders how she can have high expectations for learners capable of excelling yet not be too demanding of students unable to excel.

It is good that Ms. Carter recognizes possible discrepancies between stereotypes and realities, but now she has to determine a means of discovering which students can excel and which need assistance. What can she do?

1. Check permanent records to determine previous achievement and areas of strengths and weaknesses.
2. Request a diagnostic or achievement test (as free from cultural bias as possible) from the district assessment personnel.
3. Meet with each student to discuss achievements and areas in which the student needs help.
4. Request that the school language specialist meet with each student for an individual language assessment.
5. Seek any assistance the guidance counselor can offer regarding tests, inventories, and scales to determine capabilities.

problems for developing personalities and identities. Emphasizing the need to recognize and understand cultural differences, Divoky (1988) writes:

> Too often we forget that those whose roots are in Asia are not necessarily alike; a recently arrived Hmong refugee has virtually nothing in common with an affluent Japanese American student whose parents were born and raised in the Midwest. (p. 220)

Differences between the European American culture of the United States and the many long-accepted traditions, customs, and values of Asian American families (both immediate and extended) contribute to the developing child's sense of confusion regarding role expectations. Children growing up in such a multicultural setting may develop an ethnic identity problem as two major role expectations confront them. Developing children can, indeed, become confused as their identities form. Educators who work with Asian Americans should remember the personality differences between these children and European American children. These differences deserve recognition as cultural variations and should be in proper perspective. For example, people have described Japanese Americans as quiet, reticent, or aloof in interethnic situations and as more dependent, conforming, and obedient to authority and more willing to place family welfare over individual wishes (Feng, 1994).

Table 6.1 looks at selected cultural characteristics of Asian American children and adolescents.

Distinct differences also exist in respect to education and to teachers. West (1983) tells the story of a teacher who felt that she was not "reaching" a Vietnamese student. Although he was not disruptive, he was not participating fully in class. When she requested a parent–teacher conference, the father came to school feeling disgraced and sure that his son had done something terrible. The teacher repeatedly explained that she liked the student and that she was only trying to improve communication. The father ordered the boy to apologize, which he did. However, the father struck the child and ordered him to kneel during the apology. The boy immediately obeyed, only to be joined by the teacher, who informed him and his parents that no one in this country had to kneel to anyone.

Other cultural differences that warrant educators' attention (West, 1983) include: (1) Physical contact between members of the same sex is permissible but is not acceptable between members of the opposite sex, and (2) Vietnamese rarely touch their heads (either because of a religious belief or the fear of damaging their heads).

Recently arrived Asian children and adolescents may experience particularly acute conflicts. They are caught between their parents' culture and the school and have little

TABLE 6.1   Selected Characteristics of Asian American Children and Adolescents

CATEGORY	CHARACTERISTICS
Behavioral/emotional expressiveness	Control of emotions and feelings, self-effacement, modest
Verbal	Formal, one-way communication from authority figure to individual
Nonverbal	Preference for distance between speaker and listener
Concept of time	Traditional, living with the past
Social orientation	Mutual interdependence; collective responsibility; cooperative rather than competitive

Developed from: Rivera, B. D., & Rogers-Adkinson, D. (1997). Culturally sensitive interventions: Social skills training with children and parents from culturally and linguistically diverse backgrounds. *Intervention in School and Clinic, 33*(2), 75–80.

■ ■ ■ ■ ■ ▬▬▬▬▬

FOLLOW THROUGH 6.2
UNDERSTANDING ASIAN AMERICAN FAMILIES

Meet with a group of Asian American parents and extended family members to discuss their perceptions and expectations of educators and schools. Allow sufficient time for questions and discussions. Do not be dismayed if parents do not express themselves, because they sometimes perceive teachers as authority figures or place teachers on a pedestal.

---

power to influence either. These young people often serve as translators, and adults may call on them to complete forms, applications, and licenses (Chen, 1987; Kitano, 1989).

Gender

As in all cultures, particular differences distinguish females from males in the Asian cultures. First, in Asian families, females do not receive the respect that males receive; they are valued less than males. Similarly, they do not receive the opportunities afforded to males. Although these differences are only in cultural *expectations*, they can have far-reaching effects on Asian females' worldviews, motivation, and perception of their "place" in the world and their ability to perform in the home, community, and society.

Second and related, Asian females might show less motivation to succeed in ventures outside the home; they might be more reluctant to participate in class discussions and less willing to excel academically when the opportunity arises. In summary, just as we cannot classify all Asians in a single cultural group, it is equally dangerous to label all males and females as one homogeneous group.

Socioeconomic Status

The accumulation of wealth allows people more options, opportunities, and increased amounts of leisure time. A change in economic circumstances also influences a person's

---

■ ■ ■ ■ ■ ▬▬▬▬▬

FOLLOW THROUGH 6.3
HELPING ASIAN AMERICAN FEMALES
UNDERSTAND U.S. PERSPECTIVES

Consider how females are perceived in the Asian culture—they receive less respect than males and generally are valued less. They do not receive opportunities accorded to males and often show less motivation toward success in ventures outside the home. What problems might Asian American females experience in U.S. school systems because of their culture's perspective toward females? How can educators help Asian American females to understand U.S. perspectives toward females—equality and respect?

social expression, values, and patterns of thinking and behaving. A learner's socioeconomic status is undoubtedly one of the most significant factors affecting his or her learning and achievement. Educators can readily understand the educational and social implications of a learner's socioeconomic status and the danger of basing curricular and instructional decisions on stereotypical beliefs and assumptions.

Trying to determine the socioeconomic level of Asian Americans proves difficult at best, because of the diversity among the Asian cultures and the lack of current information on their earning power and social class. Educators must be careful not to rely on the "model minority" stereotype by assuming that all Asian Americans experience social and economic success—at least not according to the common U.S. perception of success as the accumulation of material wealth. In all likelihood, some Asian Americans—like members of other cultures—have achieved socioeconomic successes, and others have not.

Some immigrants received high levels of education in their home countries and have come to the United States to seek greater professional opportunities. For example, over 40 percent of foreign-born Filipinos have received bachelor's degrees, and over one-quarter are employed in professional, managerial, and executive positions (Fuligni, 1997).

Families

Child-rearing techniques of Asian American families, founded in cultural expectations, emphasize loyalty to the family. The culture sends a powerful message of the importance of not bringing embarrassment or shame to the family. The inculcation of guilt and shame is the principal technique that controls the behavior of family members. Parents emphasize their children's obligation to the family and their responsibility for abiding by family expectations. Adults consider children who act contrary to the family's wishes as selfish, inconsiderate, and ungrateful. The behavior of individual members is a reflection on the entire family. For example, aberrant behavior is great shame and is usually hidden from the public and handled within the family. Outstanding achievement in some aspect of life is a source of great pride for the child and for the entire family as well. Such a standard of morality sometimes causes confusion for children

■ ■ ■ ■ ■

FOLLOW THROUGH 6.4
HELPING ASIAN AMERICAN FAMILIES
UNDERSTAND U.S. SCHOOLS

Asian American families, especially first-generation, might not understand U.S. schools. These families have traditionally placed greater value on sons than on daughters and feel considerable shame when children's achievements or behavior does not meet the family's expectations. List several ways—such as parent-education programs or orientation sessions—in which you can help Asian American families to understand U.S. schools better.

who are attempting to satisfy the expectations of two cultures, but it emphasizes the importance of unity and honor in the Asian American family (Sue & Sue, 1999).

Asian American children and adolescents learn early in life that the family is the primary unit and that considerable value should be placed on family solidarity, responsibility, and harmony. Communication with adults is usually one-way, primarily adults speaking to children. Children also learn loyalty to authority (Mathews, 2000).

In summary, the family is central to the Asian culture. Individual conflicts may arise, because parents and family reflect traditional ways and children see another way of life (Mathews, 2000). Case Study 6.2 looks at the powerful influence of the Asian American family and shows what educators can do to learn about families.

Family allegiance and respect for parents and family play a significant role in the value system, achievements, and behavior of the developing Asian American child. In many East and Southeast Asian cultures, Confucian ideals, which include respect for elders and discipline, are a strong influence. Most Asian American parents and families teach their children to value educational achievement, respect authority, feel responsible for relatives, and show self-control. Asian American children tend to be more dependent, conforming, and willing to place family welfare ahead of their own individual wishes than are other American children (Mathews, 2000).

Asian American parents seem to structure their children's lives for academic success more than Caucasian parents do. Asian parents are more likely to decide whether their children should go to college, to discuss SAT/ACT plans and preparation with their chil-

■ ■ ■ ■ ■ ▬▬▬▬▬▬▬▬▬▬▬▬▬▬▬▬▬▬▬▬▬▬▬▬▬▬▬▬▬▬▬

CASE STUDY 6.2

UNDERSTANDING THE FAMILY

Mr. Jones looked at the research on Asian American families. Without a doubt, the family plays a major role in determining learners' attitudes, behavior, and academic achievement. He read the following (Hartman & Askounis, 1989): "The family is the primary socializing influence in the Asian culture; parents are responsible for interpreting appropriate and inappropriate behaviors" (p. 110).

He wondered how we, as educators, can better understand the Asian family and its influence on children and adolescents. He jotted down a list to consider.

1. Meeting families first-hand (in their homes, if possible) is the best means of learning family values, customs, and traditions.
2. Arrange small-group sessions with families (both immediate and extended), perhaps at Parent–Teacher Association (PTA) meetings or other school functions, to learn what families expect of schools and children and to explain school expectations to parents.
3. Learn about families from a variety of Asian cultures for a better understanding of intracultural and individual differences.
4. Learn about generational differences among families, for example, variations in first-, second-, and third-generation immigrant families in the United States.
5. Learn about families from differing socioeconomic groups to gain an understanding of values, traditions, and beliefs.

dren, and limit television and video games. In general, it appears that Asian parents organize and structure their children's lives to facilitate academic success. Another important point, however, needs to be explained. People often have an authoritarian image of Asian parents. That is, Asian parents are less likely to be involved in children's actual academic activities. For example, they are less likely to decide what classes their children should take and to check on the completion of homework. They help their children with homework less often and discuss school progress less.

Researchers have concluded that Asian parents structure their children's lives for success, yet leave the actual work and achievement to the children themselves. On the other hand, Asian American parenting practices are more like a combination of "authoritarian" and "permissive" styles (Asakawa & Csikszentmihalyi, 1998, p. 160).

In the traditional family, age, sex, and generational status are the primary determinants of the child's role behavior. Ancestors and elders are greatly revered and respected and are actively involved with child-rearing. Families are patriarchal. The primary duty of the son is to be a good son, and his obligations as a good husband or father come second to his duty as a son. The role of the female in the family is that of subservience to the male, the performance of domestic chores, and the bearing of children. Such generalizations may vary depending on socioeconomic class and generational status (Mathews, 2000).

Implementing Research 6.2 looks at Mathews' (2000) work on South Asian and Southeast Asian Americans, especially their families and family values.

Religion

The recent influx of Indochinese, Chinese, Koreans, and other groups has increased the religious pluralism in the United States. Laotians and Cambodians are primarily Buddhists, as are the Vietnamese. Some Vietnamese, however, are Taoists or Roman Catholic. Some embrace the philosophy of Confucianism, as do the majority of Korean immigrants. Most Koreans are likely to be Buddhists. A minority, however, are Protestant, and a smaller, but still significant, group are Roman Catholic. The majority of Hong Kong immigrants are Buddhists; some are Taoists. Many of these immigrants are also likely to adhere to the teachings of Confucius (Gollnick & Chinn, 2002).

Asian Americans tend to practice values such as respect for ancestors, filial piety, and avoidance of shame. These moral principles define a person's obligation, duty, and loyalty to others. Good performance and achievement bring honor to the family. Shame and dishonor are powerful preventives to unacceptable behavior. This standard of morality may seem harsh and rigid to the outsider, but to many Asian Americans it maintains honor and harmony in the family (Mathews, 2000).

Language

For a better understanding of Asian American learners, educators should recognize the problems Asian Americans have with English. Without doubt, the language barriers and problems confronting Asian American learners make achievements and educational attainments even more significant. Although many Asian American parents encourage the use of English, many adolescents still live in homes where the native

■ ■ ■ ■ ■ ▬▬▬▬▬▬

IMPLEMENTING RESEARCH 6.2

SOUTH ASIAN AND SOUTHEAST ASIAN AMERICANS

Mathews (2000) provides excellent information on South Asian and Southeast Asian Americans, their increasing numbers, and the value that many Asians place on families and family relationships. She focuses on respect for age, social interaction and behavior, communication style, family expectations of success, humility, school situations, decision making, and socialization barriers. She also states that cultural traits among South Asian and Southeast Asian Americans differ with age, acculturation, and whether the student was an immigrant or was born in the United States.

IMPLEMENTING THE RESEARCH

1. *Awareness*—Teachers should recognize and respect cultural variations and their impact on different ethnic groups' thinking and attitudes.
2. *Nonverbal sensitivity*—Teachers should avoid the assumption that students and their parents do not or cannot understand teachers' attitudes and nonverbal behaviors because South Asian and Southeast Asian Americans have a high sensitivity to nonverbal communication.
3. *Role of humility in cultural identity*—Teachers should not assume the student has a poor self-image based on U.S. cultural expectations.
4. *Guidance-nurturant-oriented intervention*—Teachers should assume an active role and give Asian parents and families directions on how they and their children can address problems.
5. *Awareness of the fear of family rejection*—Teachers should understand that Asian parents and families sometimes think sharing a family problem brings shame on the family; therefore students and their parents might be reluctant to share family problems and conflicts.

Source: Mathews, R. (2000). Cultural patterns of South Asian and Southeast Asian Americans. *Intervention in School and Clinic, 36*(2), 101–104.

language is the primary language. This results in learners who speak and understand two languages.

Understanding the spoken word and being understood while speaking English often pose difficult situations for Asian American learners, especially in school systems that forbid learners from speaking their native languages. For example, of the 4.1 million Asians five years and older, 56 percent did not speak English "very well," and 35 percent were linguistically isolated.

Percentages of Asians reporting "do not speak English very well" were as follows: Chinese, 56; Filipino, 60.4; Japanese, 57.7; Asian Indian, 31.0; Korean, 63.5; and Vietnamese, 65 (U.S. Bureau of the Census, 1993a). Even with these difficulties, many Asian American children have, however, overcome many language problems, and have demonstrated educational successes. Educators, however, need to recognize the tremendous diversity in Asians' ability to speak English.

Japanese American and Chinese American boys and girls scored lower than European American children on the verbal sections of an achievement test. The reasons for language difficulties may include that Asian Americans often come from bilingual backgrounds and that cultural traditions and customs often restrict or impede verbal communication. Many Asian American families, for example, encourage one-way communication; that is, parents speak to children.

Educators working in multicultural settings with such children can avoid several of the pitfalls that may lead to stereotypical thinking. Educators must remember that Asian American students may be communicating in a second language. Although English may be the predominant language, these children may continue to hear their parents' native language.

Educators who work with Asian American learners readily recognize the language and communication problems. One of the authors taught a Japanese American learner who excelled over all others in the class. Her language problems, however, required that she study far longer and more diligently than her classmates. During tests and other written work, she relied extensively on her Japanese–English dictionary and requested extra time. Despite all her language difficulties, her persistence and determination overcame her deficiencies in English. Case Study 6.3 tells of Keigo, her language problem, and what her teacher might do to help her.

Not only must educators in multicultural settings understand (and be understood in) verbal interactions with Asian Americans, they must also make an equal effort to understand nonverbal communication. Several examples of nonverbal behavior that adolescents learn show the distinctive differences among cultures. First, the forward and backward leaning of the body indicates feelings: A backward lean indicates a withdrawal

■ ■ ■ ■ ■ ▬▬▬▬▬▬▬▬▬▬▬▬▬▬▬▬▬▬▬▬▬▬▬▬▬▬▬▬▬▬▬▬▬▬▬▬▬▬▬

CASE STUDY 6.3
THE LANGUAGE PROBLEM

Keigo, an Asian American fourth-grader, has a language problem that interferes with several aspects of her life. She often cannot understand her teachers, and she has a hard time making friends. Her language at home and in her community does not pose a problem. Her parents and neighbors speak either their native language or a form of English. At school, Keigo's language deficiency results in her having to study harder and having few friends.

Keigo's teacher can take several approaches to helping her improve her language, make better use of her study time, and improve her friendships. It is important at the outset to avoid a "blame the victim" perspective, in which Keigo would be at fault for her lack of fluency in English. The teacher and the school as a whole should understand Keigo's situation and try to help her overcome the language barriers. First, the teacher should make arrangements with the school's language specialist to meet with Keigo and determine the extent of her problem and possible remediation efforts. Second, Keigo's teacher might consider placing her in a cooperative learning team in which other students can help her understand. Third, the teacher might place Keigo and other children with language difficulties in a group that receives extra attention.

Whatever means the teacher uses to help Keigo, it is important that the teacher understand Keigo and her problem rather than simply hope that the problem will disappear on its own.

■ ■ ■ ■ ■

FOLLOW THROUGH 6.5

IDENTIFYING ASIAN AMERICAN LANGUAGE PROBLEMS

Discuss with a group of Asian American learners how language affects their lives and progress in school. What language problems exist? What are their opinions about forsaking their native languages and adopting English? How can educators and language specialists assist these learners?

from a conversation or topic, and a forward lean lets the speaker know that the listener is polite, concerned, and flexible. Other notable differences include Japanese American females expressing anxiety through hurried speaking and Japanese American males expressing anxiety though silence (Bond & Shiraishi, 1974). For educational efforts to be most effective, educators and Asian American learners should work actively to understand each others' verbal and nonverbal behaviors.

ACHIEVEMENT LEVELS

Although Asian Americans undoubtedly have attained enviable accomplishment in U.S. schools, it is unrealistic to expect all Asian Americans to attain such achievement levels. Not all Asian immigrant children are superior students who have no problems at school. Some have learning problems; some lack motivation, proficiency in English, and financial resources; and some have parents who do not understand the U.S. school system because of cultural or language barriers (Yao, 1988).

■ ■ ■ ■ ■

FOR ADDITIONAL INFORMATION
INTERNET ADDRESSES

NAAAP National Home Page
www.naaap.org/ Provides a look at the National Association of Asian American Professionals (NAAAP), an all-volunteer organization that promotes the personal and professional development of the Asian American community.

Korea WebWeekly
www.kimsoft.com/korea.htm Provides information on many Korean aspects such as history, culture, economy, and politics.

Asian Americans
www.va.gov/womencon/one-VA/asian.htm Provides a look at Asian Americans who have won the

Congressional Medal of Honor and other Asian American men and women who have served the nation.

Perceptions: Asian Americans
www.askasian.org/frclasrm/lessplan/1000074.htm Provides information adapted from Chinese Communities in America.

Asian Americans—Tables, Figures, Boxes
www.prb.org./pubs/bulletin/bu53-2/tfb.htm Provides a summary of Asian Americans' diversity and increasing numbers.

■ ■ ■ ■ ■

FOLLOW THROUGH 6.6
ADDRESSING ASIAN AMERICAN LANGUAGE PROBLEMS

Suggest several ways educators can address Asian Americans' language problems. What language programs will most effectively help Asian Americans? What other efforts might educators implement to help Asian Americans overcome language obstacles?

Lee and Rong (1988) sought to determine whether the reasons for Asian American successes included superior intelligence, concentration, or hard work. They concluded that Asian American children have an ability to hold a particular problem in mind until they reach a solution. In fact, they believe that Asian American children are not far above their peers in native abilities, but that concentration and hard work make up for any deficiencies (Lee & Rong, 1988).

When they first enter the United States, children often experience a clash between their cultures and the expectations of their new homes and schools. Several distinct differences exist between Asian and European American expectations and attitudes toward schools and teachers.

First, teachers in Asia are accorded a higher status than teachers in the United States. The informality between American teachers and students may seem confusing to Southeast Asian children and appalling to their families. Second, their cultural backgrounds and values cause Asian children to expect considerable structure and organization.

Obvious differences in values may include: (1) the high value of self-effacement and saving face; students wait to be answered or to participate unless the teacher requests otherwise. Having attention drawn to oneself—the teacher putting a child's name on the board for misbehaving, for example—can bring considerable distress. (2) Asian social values call for children to listen more than they speak and to speak in a soft, well-modulated voice. In the United States this characteristic is often perceived as shyness. Asian adults teach children to be modest in dress, manner, and behavior (Feng, 1994).

The European American emphasis on individualism may present challenges for Asian American learners who seek to satisfy the demands of contemporary society while feeling loyalty to Asian American family traditions. Educators need to understand the Asian American's strong regard for the father as head of the family, the value placed on sons rather than daughters, and the respect for the older family members. Maintaining loyalty to family tradition while building an identity and life in a European American society that emphasizes individuality may prove troublesome for Asian American children and adolescents.

It is important that educators understand Asian American parents' perceptions of school behavior and achievement. Asian Americans come from cultures that often view children's behavior as the result of a lack of will or attributable to supernatural causes. Cases of school failure have resulted in parents' complaining that children are lazy and lack character.

Rather than looking for educational reasons, parents often believe that the solution lies in increasing parental restrictions, more homework, and other negative sanctions designed to promote character development. Asian parents consider hard work, effort, and developing character the best avenues to improving behavior or school work. As educators quickly realize, such beliefs can be particularly acute for Asian American children with limited intellectual (or other) abilities (Kitano, 1989).

Trying to meet the high expectations of parents and educators can result in considerable frustration. Although successful Asian American students credit their families for making sacrifices for their futures, others feel resentment (Divoky, 1988): "My parents will not let me stay after school to play soccer," a tenth-grade Cambodian immigrant stated. "They say I have to study. I study and I study and I study.... If I don't have homework, still I study. They make me do it over and over again. They really want me to do well, but they don't understand about schools here" (p. 221).

Lee and Manning, in Implementing Research 6.3, offer several suggestions for working effectively with Asian parents.

■ ■ ■ ■ ■

IMPLEMENTING RESEARCH 6.3
WORKING WITH ASIAN PARENTS AND FAMILIES

Lee and Manning maintain that educators increasingly will be called on to work with Asian students and families. They also remind educators to remember the tremendous diversity among Asian Americans and to avoid stereotypes and generalizations. Whether through parent conferences, parent-involvement programs, or parent-education programs, Lee and Manning suggest that teachers and administrators must have knowledge of Asian cultures, have positive attitudes toward Asian people, and have skills to conduct successful conferences as well as involve and educate Asian parents and families.

Educators' openness to Asian cultures and commitment to working with Asian parents will contribute to teachers and parents developing a collaborative partnership that improves academic achievement and provides a more equitable learning environment for Asian students.

IMPLEMENTING THE RESEARCH
1. Respect both immediate and extended-family members; consider Asian parents' English proficiency and their nonverbal communication; and prepare education programs for Asian parents.
2. Understand diversity within Asian ethnic groups.
3. Recognize Asian traditions of respect toward teachers.
4. Encourage children to be bi-cultural.
5. Eliminate the stereotype that all Asians are automatically smart in academics.

Source: Lee, G. L., & Manning, M. L. (2001). Working with Asian parents and families. *Multicultural Education, 9,* 23–25.

LEARNING STYLES: CULTURAL CONSIDERATIONS

The adjustment of the Asian American learner's cognitive learning styles to the U.S. school system deserves attention. Asian children tend to need reinforcement from teachers, and they work efficiently in a well-structured, quiet learning environment in which there are definite goals. Asian learners seldom reveal their opinions or their abilities voluntarily or dare to challenge their teachers.

Even when they know an answer to a teacher's question, they may choose to sit quietly as though they do not know. Older children may perform well in rote memorization and mathematics operations but may do poorly in creative writing or analytical commentary. Asian children tend to seek teachers' approval and to make their decisions based on what teachers think is best, thus becoming more dependent on teachers for help with schoolwork and guidance in classroom behavior (Yao, 1985).

Some factors are clear concerning Japanese learners: Their mothers are intensely involved in the children's learning, families celebrate the starting of school, and parents introduce children to mathematics concepts earlier in life. In Japan, children must learn a great deal of material quickly, learners must pass strict examinations, teachers teach moral values and character, schools set curfews and dress codes, and children spend more time in school. Although these factors do not represent learning styles per se, they do show how Japanese regard school, and they show that learners work conscientiously and diligently to achieve.

SCHOOL PRACTICES IMPEDING ASIAN AMERICANS' PROGRESS

Educators who fail to understand Asian Americans' cultural backgrounds and their school-related problems may actually contribute to their difficulties in U.S. schools. Looking at Asian Americans from a European American perspective may promote learning experiences and expectations that are not compatible with Asian American expectations.

What school practices might interfere with the Asian American academic achievement or psychosocial development?

1. Providing predominantly verbal teaching and learning experiences that place Asian American learners at a disadvantage.
2. Failing to make school expectations clear to learners and their parents.
3. Expecting Asian American learners to participate in discussion and sharing times, which may jeopardize their (as in their family's) name or reputation.
4. Basing academic and behavioral expectations on stereotypical images of Asian American learners as "model" learners.

Understanding Asian American learners and their cultural backgrounds and diversity places these practices in proper perspective. Although educators should recognize and appreciate their accomplishments, Asian Americans deserve individual consideration of their differences, abilities, motivation, and attitudes.

Case Study 6.4 shows that Mrs. Bush does not understand her Asian American students and what she might do to improve her cultural understanding.

Suggestions for understanding and teaching Asian American learners include:

1. Avoid reprimanding or disciplining the Asian American learner in front of peers. Having one's name written on the blackboard or on other public displays may be far more damaging to the Asian child than to the European American child (West, 1983).
2. Avoid thinking that all Asian Americans are high achievers who reach excellence in all academic areas and who model impeccable behavior.
3. Help the Asian American family to understand the U.S. school system and its expectations of learners and their families. Also, try to understand how the Asian family perceives teachers, that is, with high respect. As the teacher earns the family's respect, the teacher gains its assistance and support.
4. Understand that behavior (at least to European American teachers) that may seem to indicate indifference or lack of interest (for example, looking the other way or not volunteering to answer) is appropriate for Asian learners. For example, Asian culture teaches learners to listen more than they speak and to speak in a well-modulated voice.
5. Other culturally specific traits that a teacher should understand include: Asian American learners may be modest in dress; girls might be quieter than boys; girls might not want to reveal their legs during physical education activities; and problems might result when assigning girls and boys as cooperative learning partners (West, 1983).

■ ■ ■ ■ ■ ■

CASE STUDY 6.4
"SHE WILL NOT VOLUNTEER!"

Mrs. Bush complains, "I do not know what to do. Those Asian Americans just will not volunteer or show any interest at all. I asked for volunteers to participate in a group discussion and not a hand was raised. Are they totally uninterested? I am at my wit's end. I just don't know how to motivate these students."

This perception of Asian Americans may be all too common in American schools. This problem results, however, more from the teacher's lack of understanding than from Asian Americans being noncommittal toward their education.

The teacher needs to understand that Asian Americans, because of their cultural backgrounds, are reluctant to bring attention to themselves or to stand out among peers. Although the teacher might want to talk with an Asian American student (alone, rather than in front of the class, where the conversation might seem like a reprimand) about class participation, the teacher should not force or coerce the student into participating in an activity that may be culturally or personally threatening.

■ ■ ■ ■ ■ ▬▬▬▬▬▬▬

IMPLEMENTING RESEARCH 6.4
TEACHING ASIAN AMERICAN STUDENTS

Chiang (2000) maintains that the increasing numbers of Asian immigrant children suggest educators need to recognize Asian students' cultural characteristics as well as learn to work with them effectively. In her article, Chiang looks at the history of Asian American immigrants, family and community influences on their learning, and suggestions for working with these students.

In her article, she looks specifically at the relationship between teaching styles and Asian cultures, communication patterns, cognitive activities, and social support. Overall, she finds that Asian American students adjust well to U.S. schools academically. Still, some might need psychological support and understanding from teachers and administrators— for example, they might need more assistance and encouragement and less pressure from teachers and schools.

IMPLEMENTING THE RESEARCH
1. Help Asian American students by giving clear directions, allowing choices of projects and peers, communicating on an individual basis, and providing peer tutoring.
2. Help parents of Asian students by developing an understanding of commonly accepted gender roles in the United States, an understanding of school systems and how they function, and being involved in their children's education.
3. Help policy makers assist Asian American students by recruiting Asian American teachers, revising the curriculum to reflect more positive images of Asian people, and providing in-service training for teachers to better acquaint them with school structures and family expectations.

Teachers and administrators should find Chiang's article helpful, especially as the numbers of Asian American students increase.

Source: Chiang, L. H. (2000). Teaching Asian American students. *Teacher Educator, 36*(1), 58–69.

Implementing Research 6.4 offers suggestions for helping and teaching Asian American students.

PROMOTING SELF-ESTEEM AND CULTURAL IDENTITIES

Asian American children have special needs that responsive educators should address. In a school system that might seem different, and perhaps even oblivious to their needs, these learners need teaching and learning experiences that reflect their cultural and social experience. Learners in formative developmental stages may begin to question their self-worth and their cultural worth. Responsive multicultural educators need to focus their efforts in several directions that will improve the self-esteem of Asian American learners.

First, the actual effect of the school experience on the Asian American learner deserves consideration. Attending a school that appears to direct attention toward the

■ ■ ■ ■ ■

FOLLOW THROUGH 6.7

DETERMINING DIFFERENCES IN ASIAN AMERICAN LEARNERS

Observe a group of Asian American learners doing schoolwork to determine their learning habits, such as time on a given task, individual versus cooperative work, and reliance on bilingual dictionaries. How do they differ from European American learners? What could you, as an educator in a multicultural setting, do to help these learners?

majority culture can cause Asian Americans to question their place in the school. Educators can focus attention in several directions: recognizing Asian Americans as integral and worthy learners in the school system; recognizing the Asian culture as worthy; and directly addressing the concerns of Asian Americans, for example, teachers who often have high expectations based on the model minority stereotype.

Second, educators can respond by understanding the cultural differences that affect Asian Americans and their academic and social progress in U.S. schools. For example, Asian Americans strive toward the accomplishment that brings pride to the family, in contrast to European Americans, who work for individual acclaim. The custom of many European Americans is to question the teacher, volunteer for an academic activity, or assertively raise their hands to answer a teacher's question. Such traits are in opposition to Asian beliefs. Teachers need to understand these cultural differences and then respond with appropriate teaching behaviors, rather than expect learners of all cultures to respond in a similar fashion.

Specifically, educators can:

1. Read aloud culturally appropriate children's books about Asian Americans.
2. Convey a sense of welcome that makes children feel wanted, a part of the class, and an integral presence in the classroom.
3. Encourage them to make a "Me" collage that demonstrates both the individual and the Asian culture.
4. Encourage learners to engage in "open-ended writing" in which they can probe their feelings and express them without fear of sharing.
5. Teach learners to write about "What I Like about My Life" (and perhaps culture) or "Ten Things about Me," in which learners can feel free to express opinions and emotions (Tiedt & Tiedt, 1999).

Third, responsive multicultural educators need to engage in direct activities to improve the self-esteem of Asian American learners. Such activities include specifically addressing their needs, asking about their families (using extreme caution not to make the learner feel uncomfortable or think that the teacher is prying), genuinely and truthfully conveying to the learner that other students would benefit from knowing more about the Asian culture, and letting the students know that their presence is understood, accepted, and appreciated by both school personnel and other children and adolescents.

CULTURAL PORTRAIT
MINA—AN ASIAN AMERICAN LEARNER

Mina, a ten-year-old Asian American girl, attends a large urban elementary school whose population is approximately half Caucasian, one-fourth African, and one-fourth Asian and Hispanic. Mina makes about average grades but does not make the high grades that her family and teachers expect. Her problem with the English language is probably the major factor for her grades not being among the highest, but other factors also contribute: Her family and teachers have expectations that are unrealistically high; she does not to want to volunteer for special assignments; she does not want to raise her hand to answer; and she does not always understand the European American learner's attitude toward school, teachers, and people. Mina feels a little lost. Her teachers are either European or African American. They are friendly and appear to want to help her, but they do not seem to understand her and the way she believes children should act around adults, especially teachers. She perceives the school as being oriented toward European American expectations, and perhaps a little toward the African perspective, yet very little toward the Asian or the Hispanic expectations. While she feels somewhat frustrated with this arrangement, she also realizes that she has to do her best schoolwork and that her behavior must be exemplary. Otherwise her family might feel shame or disappointment.

HOW MINA'S TEACHER CAN RESPOND
Responding to Mina's psychosocial and intellectual needs first requires understanding her as an individual learner and then as a member of the Asian American culture. After a determination of her strengths and weaknesses, her teacher should focus attention in several directions.

1. Help Mina to understand both the Asian culture and the American culture.
2. Maintain high (but not unrealistic) expectations for Mina, and avoid relying on cultural stereotypes.
3. Understand that Mina's reluctance to volunteer or raise her hand during class is a reflection of her cultural background and that it does not indicate indifference.
4. Provide appropriate multicultural experiences that teach learners of all cultures about the Asian culture, its diverse characteristics, and its many contributions.
5. Assign a professional in the school to be an adviser or mentor who will help Mina deal with daily school routines.
6. Meet with Mina's family to explain the philosophy and expectations of American school systems, and work to gain the understanding, respect, and support of Mina's family.
7. Decide how special service personnel, that is, guidance counselors, speech and language specialists, and other school support personnel, can assist Mina.

FOLLOW THROUGH 6.8
PROMOTING SELF-ESTEEM AND CULTURAL IDENTITY

Asian Americans' different cultural traditions, language difficulties, and different family values can result in lower self-esteem and negative cultural identity. What signs of lower self-esteems or confused or negative cultural identities might educators look for? Name several ways educators can help Asian Americans develop positive self-esteems and cultural identities.

Educators should remember the importance of the family in efforts to improve self-esteem. Asians generally have close-knit families, and Asian people's feelings about themselves usually include a consideration of their feelings about the family (and vice versa).

SUMMING UP

Educators planning educational experiences for Asian American learners should:

1. Reflect on both historical and contemporary Asian cultural experiences and plan teaching and learning experiences accordingly.
2. Undertake objective assessments, rather than believing all learners are members of a "model minority."
3. Understand that language warrants understanding because of its cultural basis (and its cultural value) and because of the problems many Asian Americans have with the English language.
4. Understand that positive self-esteem and cultural identities are crucial to Asian learners' psychosocial development and general outlook on life. Plan appropriate activities.
5. Recognize that students have their distinct culture with its unique cultural characteristics, rather than grouping all Asian American learners into one "Asian" culture.
6. Consider the tremendous diversity among learners—individual, generational, socioeconomic, urban, and rural—rather than categorizing all Asian American learners into one homogeneous group.
7. Exercise extreme caution by not expecting all Asian American learners to be high achievers.
8. Recognize the family and its powerful influence (e.g., the injunction against bringing shame and embarrassment on the family) on children and adolescents.

SUGGESTED LEARNING ACTIVITIES

1. Select an Asian American learner and evaluate his or her language problem. Specifically, (a) diagnose the exact problem, (b) list several educational areas on which the problem might have an effect, and (c) devise a remediation plan.

2. Complete a case study of a high-achieving Asian American student. Specifically, (a) outline outstanding accomplishments, (b) address how the family has contributed to successes, (c) describe any problems or frustrations the student may experience, (d) explain how one can account for outstanding achievements, even though language problems exist, and (e) ask how schools can address the student's problems. Show why it is imperative that educators not base teaching and learning experiences on the "model minority" stereotype.

3. Survey several educators who have taught Asian American students. Develop a survey designed to determine the strengths and weaknesses of Asian American learners, the ed-

ucators' opinions of Asian American attitudes and achievements, and how schools respond to meet the individual needs of Asian American learners. What efforts can be made to educate parents and gain their support? Generally speaking, what approaches can you suggest to educators who work with Asian American learners of varying cultural backgrounds and individual differences?

SUGGESTIONS FOR COLLABORATIVE EFFORTS

Form groups of three or four that, if possible, represent our nation's cultural and gender diversity. Working collaboratively, focus your group's attention toward the following efforts.

1. Have each member of your group select an Asian American learner: a Japanese American, a Chinese American, a Filipino American, and a Korean American. After getting to know these learners and their families, show similarities and differences among the four cultures. Specifically consider cultural characteristics, families, academic achievement, socioeconomic accomplishments, and any other area in which similarities and differences are evident.

2. Choose two to three learners of similar cultural backgrounds but of differing generational or socioeconomic status. Compare the similarities and differences that reflect the effects of socioeconomic class or generational differences. How does your group think educators can most effectively determine and address generational differences?

3. Educators often experience difficulties locating children's books that focus on Asian American learners and themes. Consult recent publishers' catalogs and make a list of current children's books that appear to provide accurate descriptions of the Asian American culture. Check with textbook publishers to determine what efforts are being made to make textbooks more reflective of our increasingly multicultural society.

EXPANDING YOUR HORIZONS: ADDITIONAL
JOURNAL READINGS AND BOOKS

Hamm, J. V. (2000). Do birds of a feather flock together? The variable bases for African American, Asian American, and European American adolescents' selection of similar friends. *Developmental Psychology, 36*(2), 209–219.
Hamm finds greater similarity in friendship selection among Asian and European Americans than with African Americans. Still, adolescents do not choose friends with identical orientations.

Lee, G. L., & Manning, M. L. (2001). Working with Asian parents and families. *Multicultural Education, 9*, 23–25.
Lee and Manning offer practical suggestions for working with and helping Asian American parents and families.

Mathews, R. (2000). Cultural patterns of South Asian and Southeast Asian Americans. *Intervention in School and Clinic, 36*(2), 101–104.
In this excellent article, Mathews provides an overview of South Asian and Southeast Asian Americans, especially the family values that many of them hold.

Tamura, E. H. (2001). Asian Americans in the history of education: An historical essay. *History of Education Quarterly, 41*(1), 58–71.
Tamura provides an succinct view of Asian American history and offers an excellent description of books on this culture's history.

Tsai, J. L., Mortensen, H., & Wong, Y. (2002). What does "being American" mean? A comparison of Asian American and European American young adults. *Cultural Diversity and Ethnic Minority Psychology, 8*(3), 257–273.

Tsai, Mortensen, and Wong find that Asian Americans and European Americans have different perspectives of what it means to "be American."

Wolfe, M. M., Tang, P. H., & Wong, E. C. (2001). Design and development of the European American values scale for Asian Americans. *Cultural Diversity and Ethnic Minority Psychology, 7*(3), 274–283.

These authors developed an instrument to determine the rate at which Asian Americans adopt European American values and found that the two cultural groups shared cultural values to some extent rather than having exclusive values.

EXPANDING YOUR STUDENTS' HORIZONS: APPROPRIATE ASIAN AMERICAN BOOKS FOR CHILDREN AND ADOLESCENTS

Bell, William. *Forbidden City: A Novel of Modern China.* Bantam, 1990.
Betancourt, Jeanne. *More than Meets the Eye.* Bantam, 1990.
Chang, Margaret, and Raymond Chang. *In the Eye of War.* Macmillan, 1990.
Chandler, David P. *The Land and People of Cambodia.* HarperCollins, 1991.
Demi. *The Empty Pot.* Henry Holt, 1990.
Demi. *The Stonecutter.* Crown, 1995.
Edmonds, I. G. *Ooka the Wise: Tales of Old Japan.* Linnet Books, 1994.
Garland, Sherry. *Vietnam: Rebuilding a Nation.* Dillon, 1990.
Haugaard, Erik Christian. *The Boy and the Samurai.* Houghton Mifflin, 1991.
Heo, Yumi. *One Afternoon.* Orchard, 1994.
Ho, Minfong. *Rice without Rain.* Lothrop, Lee and Shepard, 1990.
Hong, Maria. *Growing Up Asian.* Tupelo, 1993.
Jaffe, Nina (retold by). *Older Brother, Younger Brother.* Viking, 1995.
Johnston, Tony. *The Badger and the Magic Fan: A Japanese Folk Tale.* Putnam, 1990.
Kline, Suzy. *Horrible Harry's Secret.* Viking, 1990.
Lee, C. Y. *The Second Son of Heaven: A Novel of Nineteenth Century China.* William Morrow, 1990.
Mahy, Margaret. *The Seven Chinese Brothers.* Scholastic, 1990.
Major, John S. *The Land and People of Mongolia.* HarperCollins, 1990.
Mayberry, Jodine. *Filipinos.* Franklin Watts, 1990.
Okimoto, Jean Davis. *Molly by Any Other Name.* Scholastic, 1990.
Patent, Gregory. *Shanghai Passage.* Clarion, 1990.
Pitkanen, Matti A., and Reijo Harkonen. *The Children of China.* Lerner/Carolrhoda, 1990.
Say, Allen. *The Inn-Keeper's Apprentice.* Puffin, 1996.
Scarboro, Elizabeth. *The Secret Language of the SB.* Viking, 1990.
Schlein, Mariam. *The Year of the Panda.* HarperCollins, 1990.
Stamm, Claus. *Three Strong Women: A Tall Tale from Japan.* Viking, 1990.
Tan, Amy. *The Hundred Secret Senses.* Putnam, 1995.
Tompert, Ann. *Grandfather Tang's Story.* Crown, 1990.
Turner, Ann. *Through Moon and Stars and Night Skies.* HarperCollins, 1990.
Waters, Kate, and Madeline Slovenz-Low. *Lion Dancer: Ernie War's Chinese New Year.* Scholastic, 1990.
Wong, Janet S. *Good Luck Gold and Other Poems.* McElderry, 1994.
Yep, Laurence. *The Rainbow People.* Harper & Row, 1989.
Yep, Laurence. *Hiroshima.* Scholastic, 1995.

......

CHAPTER SEVEN

UNDERSTANDING EUROPEAN AMERICAN CHILDREN AND ADOLESCENTS

Understanding the materials and activities in this chapter will help the reader to

- Describe European Americans, their origins, and who they are today
- Identify several stereotypes of European American learners and how these stereotypes adversely affect peers' opinions as well as educators' perceptions of their propensity toward academic success and behavior
- Describe European Americans' cultural, gender, socioeconomic, family, religious, and language diversity
- Describe European American learners and show how teaching and learning practices can reflect knowledge of cultural differences and learning styles
- Suggest appropriate readings, activities, and collaborative activities for gaining a better understanding of European Americans

OVERVIEW

The African, American Indian, Arab, Asian, European, and Hispanic cultural groups make up a sizable percentage of our nation's diversity. Likewise, their differences, traditions, customs, language, and dialects enrich the United States in many ways. Another cultural group, however, also contributes to the nation's diversity. The various European American cultures bring a plethora of differences that perceptive educators will want their students to understand and appreciate. Just as Asian and Hispanic Americans originate from many places, European Americans originate from scores of locations, such as France, Germany, Greece, Hungary, Ireland, Italy, Poland, and Portugal, as Chapter 1 indicated. This chapter focuses on European Americans and their cultural, gender, socioeconomic, family, religious, and language diversity. To avoid overgeneralizing, we will discuss specific cultural groups whenever possible.

ORIGINS

The hundred-year period from 1830 to 1930 was a century of mass immigration in the history of the United States. Many millions of people uprooted themselves, primarily

157

from crowded places of Europe, and flowed outward to less crowded areas such as the United States. About 32 million left Europe for the United States, contributing enormously to the nation's expansion and industrial growth. The primary reason for this massive transfer of people from the Old World to the New World was the social and economic strain on the rural systems of Europe. More specific causes included large populations; the lack of farming land for all people; and the abolition of feudalism, which ended peasant privileges (Alba, 1985).

In the colonial days, most of America's immigrants came from Great Britain and Ireland, and a few from Germany, France, the Netherlands, Belgium, and Luxembourg. During the early nineteenth century, Germans (mainly tradesmen, farmers, weavers, tailors, shoemakers, and carpenters) began coming in ever-increasing numbers. French, Norwegians, and Swedes also began moving to the United States, feeling the push of economic pressures at home and the pull of prospective free land and good wages in the New World. Italians began arriving in 1890, and from 1900 until the start of World War I, about a quarter of all immigrants were Italians. After World War II, many Germans arrived in the United States (U.S. Bureau of the Census, 1993d).

The United States in the last thirty years has experienced a surge of immigration unseen since the turn of the century. The foreign-born population of this nation reached a record high of 19.9 million in 1990. The proportion of immigrants from Europe—more than 80 percent in 1900—was only 22 percent in 1990. Two-thirds of present-day foreign-born Americans were born in Latin American and Asia, coming from countries as diverse as Mexico, China, El Salvador, Korea, and the Philippines (Fuligni, 1997).

As Chapter 2 indicated, the European American people came from a wide array of places—western and southern portions of Europe as well as the eastern portion and the Soviet Union. Greeks, Italians, Poles, Irish, French, and Germans are well known in the United States, but other people from the Netherlands, Portugal, Spain, and Switzerland are less known. Each cultural group brought its own cultural characteristics, language, traditions, and customs, which contributed to the already rich diversity of this nation. They came to the United States for a number of different reasons: Some planned to earn money and return to their home country, whereas others planned to make the United States their home.

Although the number of European cultures makes it impossible to discuss them all, it is interesting to examine a few cultures and immigrants' reasons for coming to the United States. Such a discussion is limited to Census information and recent books written on the European people; the same information is not available for all cultural groups.

Greek immigration began in the 1880s, when the Greek economy failed to show signs of improvement. These early immigrants came from the Peloponnesus and Tripoli, both agricultural and pastoral regions that were economically depressed. In fact, the Greek government actually encouraged young men to emigrate so they could send money back to Greece (Scourby, 1984).

The majority of Poles came to the United States as a result of mass migration during World War II. The immigrating Poles were a diverse group. Some were women and children without an occupational designation; others were blacksmiths, carpenters, locksmiths, miners, dressmakers, shoemakers, and tailors. There was concern about how Polish immigrants would sustain themselves in their new land. Three percent entered with fifty dollars in their possession, having spent most of their money on transportation. Only about one-fourth had others, usually relatives, to cover the cost. Another problem, language, confronted Poles as they entered the English-speaking nation (Lopata, 1994). They worked in the steel mills and coal mines of Pennsylvania, Ohio, and Indiana; in the automobile factories of Detroit; and in the stockyards of Chicago. Many changed their names to survive and hide their native origins.

FOR ADDITIONAL INFORMATION
ASSOCIATIONS

European American Chamber of Commerce, 801 Pennsylvania Ave., NW, Washington, DC 20004.
This association works to promote U.S. and European trade by conducting seminars, studies, and educational programs.

Society for the Preservation of the Greek Heritage, 5125 MacArthur Blvd., NW, Washington, DC 20016.
As the name suggests, the association works to preserve the natural and cultural heritage of Greece. It consists of professional, business, and academic groups and publishes a quarterly newsletter.

American Hungarian Library and Historical Society (AHLHS), 213 E. 82nd St., New York, NY 10021.
The AHLHS maintains a collection of Hungariana and sponsors a library. It is affiliated with the American Hungarian Foundation and holds an annual meeting.

Irish Heritage Foundation (IHF), 2123 Market St., San Francisco, CA 94114.
The IHF includes individuals interested in Irish culture, history, and education. It maintains a library and publishes a monthly newsletter.

American Institute of Polish Culture (AIPC), 1440 79th St. Causeway, Suite 117, Miami, FL 33141.
The AIPC includes professionals, students, artists, and writers. It works to further knowledge and appreciation of the history, science, art, and culture of Poland.

French-American Foundation (FAF), 41 E. 72nd St., New York, NY 10021.
The FAF works to strengthen relations between the United States and France by promoting exchange of specialists, internships, study tours, and conferences.

American Academy for Jewish Research (AAJR), 3080 Broadway, New York, NY 10027.
Founded in 1919, the AAJR consists of scholars, rabbis, and learned laymen interested in promoting Jewish learning and research. The association publishes an annual journal, which contains articles on Judaica and related subjects.

American Jewish Historical Society (AJHS), 2 Thornton Rd., Waltham, MA 02154.
The AJHS comprises individuals and institutions interested in American Jewish history. The association maintains a reference library, gives various awards, and publishes a quarterly journal.

■ ■ ■ ■ ■

FOLLOW THROUGH 7.1
WILL WHITES BECOME A MINORITY?

In a group of three or four, discuss Warren and Twine's question: Are whites really becoming a minority because whiteness is not a fixed racial category? A number of demographic studies suggest that whites will become a minority—what does your group think?

More than 5 million immigrants from Italy arrived in the United States between 1820 and 1870, and more than 4.5 million came during the century of mass immigration, 1830–1930. Only the number of arrivals from Germany was larger. The Italian immigration was concentrated tightly into a small period of time—more than 4 million arrived between 1890 and 1921, and in fact, 2 million arrived during a single decade, 1901–1910. The peak year of Italian immigration was 1907, when nearly 300,000 came to the United States. Although it is difficult to pinpoint exact regions from which they came, many Italian immigrants came from Mezzogiorno. Between 1899 and 1910, when more than 2,200,000 immigrants came, perhaps as many as 80 percent came from the Mezzogiorno region (Alba, 1985).

Abrams (1993) reported that significant numbers of Jews migrated to Israel and to the United States from the former Soviet Union. With the crumbling of the Soviet economic system came a resurgence of anti-Semitism. Although the majority of Jewish people are choosing Israel as their new home, 40,000 immigrated to the United States in 1989.

These Jewish people, however, are not the first to arrive in the United States from the former Soviet Union. In the 1970s, some Jewish people arrived in the United States from the Soviet Union after the Six Day War and the Leningrad Trial. At first, nearly all left for Israel; but after 1972, a rising proportion chose other countries. The majority of the 90,000 Soviet Jews who chose the United States came from Russia, Byelorussia, and Ukraine, those republics most heavily under the rule of the Soviet

■ ■ ■ ■ ■

USING CHILDREN'S LITERATURE
THE EUROPEAN AMERICAN EXPERIENCE

Zheleznikov, Vladimir. *The Rainbow People.* HarperCollins, 1990.
A young girl comes to live with her grandfather in Russia. This is a powerful story of an individual against a group.

Lingard, Joan. *Tug of War.* Dutton/Lodestar, 1990.
The Germans are retreating from Russia, and the Petersons are on the enemy list.

Pettepice, Thomas, and Aleksin, Anatoly (Eds.), *Face to Face.* Putnam/Philomel, 1990.
This is the first collection of American and Russian short stories published simultaneously in both countries.

regime. These Jews had had their Jewish heritage systemically denied through the closing of synagogues, the banning of the study of Hebrew and Yiddish, and the virulent anti-Israel, anti-Zionist propaganda of the Soviet regime (Abrams, 1993).

EUROPEAN AMERICANS TODAY

European Americans today live in many geographic areas of the United States. Available data from the U.S. Census Bureau do not indicate the cities where European Americans have selected to live. Some evidence, however, suggests that immigrants to the United States tend to settle near their port of entry. More than two-thirds of those who came from Italy, for example, live in the northeastern part of the country, where they arrived.

Table 7.1 shows selected cultural groups and their immigration numbers in 1980 and 1995. Table 7.2 shows the immigrant numbers of the top five European cultural groups in 1995. Of the forty groups with more than 100,000 foreign-born persons in 1990, fourteen declined in size from the previous census. Italians, followed by Scottish, Hungarians, Germans, and Greeks, had the largest declines (U.S. Bureau of the Census, 1993d).

TABLE 7.1   Numbers of German, British, and Italian Immigrants to the United States, 1980 and 1995

	1980[1]	1995[2]
Germany	849,000	620,000
United Kingdom	669,000	1,200,000
Italy	832,000	220,000

[1]From U.S. Bureau of the Census. (1993d). *We the American . . . foreign born.* Washington, DC, p. 3.

[2]U.S. Bureau of the Census. (1997a). *Statistical abstracts of the United States,* 117th edition. Washington, DC.

TABLE 7.2   The Five European Cultural Groups with the Largest Numbers of Immigrants to the United States, 1995

Soviet Union (former)	54,500
Poland	13,800
Germany	6,200
Ireland	5,300
Romania	4,900

Source: U.S. Bureau of the Census. (1997a). *Statistical abstracts of the United States,* 117th edition. Washington, DC.

■ ■ ■ ■ ■

CASE STUDY 7.1
SCHOOL OF MANY CULTURES

Eastside Elementary School is in an urban area of California. Its diversity reflects many different cultures, each with its own traditions and customs and many with their own languages. Many students are first- and second-generation Americans who live in cultural enclaves or areas where they feel comfortable with others who share their culture and language.

Teachers and administrators at Eastside Elementary School have had many challenges. First, about half the teachers had taught only middle-class (mostly white) children before coming to Eastside. Not only did they experience culture shock, they also had to change their teaching styles. Second, language has posed a problem. One administrator commented that twelve different languages are spoken in the school. Various school committees work diligently to find ways to foster language diversity in the schools *and* provide English as a second language.

Third, they have had to address communicating with parents, many of whom have considerable difficulty with English. Fourth, Eastside implemented curricular experiences and teaching strategies to reflect cultural diversity. This planning required special training, which the teachers gained through contract courses with the nearby university and through in-service courses at the school.

The educators at Eastside have met these and other challenges with varying degrees of success. The important point is that they have realized that the changing cultural composition of the student body requires them to change the school; no longer can educational experiences reflect only the learning needs and styles of 15 percent of the student population. Likewise, the effort involves all those associated with the school—students, educators, parents, and other community members. Eastside's educators are taking a comprehensive approach, one that requires deliberate effort and dedication. The result is an excellent example of a school addressing our nation's multicultural population.

Case Study 7.1 acknowledges the tremendous cultural diversity of our nation and shows how one school offered a response.

STEREOTYPING OF EUROPEAN AMERICAN CHILDREN AND ADOLESCENTS

European cultures are not immune to the stereotyping that has dogged American Indian, African, Asian, Arab, and Hispanic cultures. Alba (1985) writes of the the stereotyping of Italian Americans and suggests that all European groups have been considered in terms of undesirable characteristics. Italians have been stereotyped as being swarthy, bearing signs of physical degradation (such as low foreheads), having criminal tendencies, and being prone to passion and violence. Jews are stereotyped as stingy, shrewd, and intellectual (Atkinson, Morten, & Sue, 1998). Germans are often characterized as evil, incompetent, or mad (Winawer-Steiner & Wetzel, 1996). Readers know that this unfair and dangerous list could continue.

Stereotyping, racism, and discrimination can affect European Americans, just as they affect all cultures. Plus, the basis for these insidious acts or feelings can result from reasons other than the color of peoples' skin or the language they speak. Weeber (2000), in Implementing Research 7.1, explains how some people might consider disabling conditions as a basis for stereotyping and as a reason for discrimination.

CULTURAL CHARACTERISTICS

What constitutes the cultural characteristics of European Americans? European Americans comprise numerous subcultures that vary by country and language, economic

■ ■ ■ ■ ■ ▬▬▬▬▬▬▬▬▬▬▬▬▬▬▬▬

IMPLEMENTING RESEARCH 7.1
ABLEISM

Joy E. Weeber (2000), a Dutch American, tells of the pain and discrimination she has endured due to her disability resulting from having had polio as an infant. She describes the pain as similar to that caused by racism. It is the pain caused by the unconscious beliefs of a society that assumes everyone is, or should be, "normal" (Weeber, 2000, p. 21) and able-bodied. It is the belief in the superiority of being nondisabled, which assumes that everyone who is disabled wishes he or she could be nondisabled. In the disability community, this is called "ableism" (p. 21) or a form or prejudice and bigotry that marks people less than those who are nondisabled. Weeber tells of how she spent her entire life trying to prove how she had overcome her polio, which she claims is no more possible than overcoming being female or African American. She also tells of her childhood, when religious strangers urged her to get "healed" (p. 21), and how at the age of ten she was marked as "other" (p. 21) when she was given a diagnosis of scoliosis and found to be "defective" (p. 21), with a curving spine and weak legs. She also told of the pain inflicted on her to make her more normal and her inner devastation after seven surgeries. In summary, she tells of her painful journey and experiences with ableism to a time where she is "proud to have found a way home to the disability community" (Weeber, 2000, p. 23).

IMPLEMENTING THE RESEARCH
1. Prejudice and discrimination can result from disabling conditions, just as they can from racism and other forms of diversity.
2. Educators should recognize that some disabled people have accepted (and, in fact, some have overcome) their disabling conditions and do not wish they could be nondisabled.
3. Educators should look for people's strengths rather than looking only at disabling conditions to determine what people can and cannot do.

Source: Weeber, J. E. (2000). What could I know of racism? *Journal of Counseling and Development, 77,* 20–23.

status, generation in the United States, religious affiliation, and a host of other factors. Still, Kitano and Perkins (2000) suggest several common European American cultural values, such as beliefs, interaction and communication patterns, and behavioral expectations. Values include an emphasis on the individual, personal achievement, independence, and control over one's environment. European Americans can best be described as holding firm beliefs in support of inalienable rights (e.g, privacy), free enterprise, and private property. Interaction patterns are characterized by role specialization, self-sufficiency (as opposed to teamwork), competition, and communication that is direct, informal, and assertive. Overall, European Americans place importance on time, cleanliness, hard work, material comforts and material wealth, and an orientation toward work and the future (Kitano & Perkins, 2000). The most valid cultural descriptions of European Americans come from considering individual cultures.

In general, Greek Americans are confident that they alone know the causes of their problems and how best to solve them. If they feel powerless, they are likely to either overdo attempts to control their families or sink into fatalistic resignation. If misfortune comes their way, they assume that the causes of the problems come not from themselves but from somewhere outside the family, such as the malice of neighbors or the envy of competitors.

Greek Americans take tremendous pride in individual achievement and consider themselves as individuals (Welts, 1982). Welts believes that Greek Americans may have difficulty cooperating with others, especially in business deals. They prefer a competitive atmosphere and are usually unwilling to put aside their individual interests for the sake of the group.

Case Study 7.2 looks at Helen, a Greek American girl, and the concerns she faced.

Italian Americans have a strong allegiance to family, and tend to live where they grew up. They believe that young people should learn from their elders and have an allegiance to a church. They are suspicious of strangers and expect filial obedience (Alba, 1985). Alba comments that some of these tendencies (e.g., suspiciousness of strangers) decrease with education and advancing occupational position.

Greek Americans value frugality, careful saving, and wise use of financial resources; they often work two jobs. Scourby (1984) describes Greek Americans in several ways: They have clearly defined status and roles in work situations; they practice patriarchal

■ ■ ■ ■ ■

FOLLOW THROUGH 7.2
CLARIFYING STEREOTYPES AND THEIR HARMFUL EFFECTS

Stereotypes, as harmful as they are to interpersonal relationships and to decisions about educational practice, persist. Name some of the more common stereotypes about the various European cultures. How might these stereotypes affect teaching and learning decisions? How might educators educate themselves and others about stereotypes?

■ ■ ■ ■ ■

CASE STUDY 7.2
HELEN—A GREEK AMERICAN GIRL

Helen, an eleventh-grader, was a second-generation Greek American. She was personable, intelligent, spoke excellent English, and was an all-around good student. She spoke of wanting to teach in an elementary school when she finished college. While Helen was sociable and others liked her, she did not have any close friends. In fact, she perceived several of her teachers as friends and spoke with them at length whenever she could.

While Helen was Americanized in many ways, her parents and extended family members held onto Greek values, customs, and traditions. They continued to speak Greek in their home on many occasions. Once the teacher telephoned Helen's home and asked to speak with her. The father spoke English with such an accent and with such difficulty that the teacher could not understand why Helen could not come to the phone. The next day, Helen asked the teacher whether she had called and explained that she had not been at home. The teacher perceived that Helen was uncomfortable that she had called and did not call Helen at home again.

The family owned a fast-food restaurant, which had been in business for nearly twenty-five years, since the father had brought his family from Greece. All family members worked at some time; Helen probably worked the least because she committed so much of her time to schoolwork.

The teacher had a genuine respect for Helen's Greek background, but she wondered how Helen considered her diversity. Did she feel accepted? Did her parents and family members' continuing to speak Greek bother her? Did she intentionally avoid working in the restaurant? The teacher did not take any specific action, but she wondered about Helen's feelings and wondered about her own decision not to discuss Helen's diversity with her.

■ ■ ■ ■ ■

USING CHILDREN'S LITERATURE
THE EUROPEAN AMERICAN EXPERIENCE

Hollinger, Peggy. *Greece*. Franklin Watts, 1990.
    This book looks at Greece and the Greek people—their education, religion, and family life.

Rosen, Billi. *Andi's War*. Dutton, 1991.
    Hostility between countrymen remains in Greece even after World War II.

Ian, James. *The Netherlands*. Franklin Watts, 1990.
    This book looks at the history, art, food, and other topics of the Netherlands.

Roberts, Elizabeth. *Europe 1992: The United States of Europe*. Franklin Watts, 1990.
    Roberts looks at the Single European Act, which proposes that twelve countries establish an area without internal frontiers.

control and have deeply binding extended kinship networks; they value interdependence among people (rather than individualism); and they demonstrate a strong need to defend family honor and, generally speaking, have a love of *philotimo* or honor.

Gender

Although it is not an area of extensive research, gender differences exist in European American males and females, just as they do in all cultures. Girls and boys have different learning styles, worldviews, perceptions of motivation and school success, and learning strategies. For example, an educator cannot conclude that a cooperative, seemingly passive female is not motivated, because boys show different signs of motivation and competitive behaviors. The educator's challenge is to recognize that girls and boys are different, make an attempt to know individual females, and plan strategies to which females can relate.

Kitano and Perkins (2000) maintain that whereas European American parents value independence, achievement, and individualism, and hard work in boys, the same is not always true with daughters. Parents' actions sometimes teach daughters to be dependent on others (perhaps a man) and to lack confidence in their abilities. For example, some daughters learn that they should not outperform men in academic or physical skills or they will end up isolated and unloved. Instead, daughters should channel their work into relationships and toward home-centered, family-oriented achievement. In Gender Perspectives 7.1, Kitano and Perkins (2000) look at fifteen gifted European American women.

Socioeconomic Status

Describing the socioeconomic status of the many European cultures is nearly impossible. Just as with other cultures we discuss in this book, many variations exist among European cultures. There are both wealthy and poor European Americans, just as among all cultures. Many criteria determine a person's socioeconomic status: Is the husband or father present? Does the wife work? How many children are in the family? Are the people living in a part of the country where the cost of living is high or low? How well does the family manage its money?

Families

An educator should approach any discussion of family characteristics with considerable caution. Family patterns differ according to time of immigration, region of origin, economic class, and religious background. Many factors influence how a family lives, the roles of the husband and wife, perspectives on and treatment of children, and the importance of extended-family members. Although preservice and in-service teachers need information about European families, providing a description of these families risks stereotyping. To avoid stereotyping, we attempt to use only the most objective information and the most widely accepted resources.

Parents and families are expected to be involved in their children's education and to work as partners with teachers. Education is highly regarded at all levels. Cultural

■ ■ ■ ■ ■

GENDER PERSPECTIVES 7.1
GIFTED EUROPEAN AMERICAN WOMEN

Kitano and Perkins (2000) describe factors affecting achievement of fifteen highly accomplished European American women. Although they focused their study on adult women, their findings definitely have implications for elementary and secondary students and educators.

Data were collected on childhood characteristics, contributions of major socializing agents, roles of social or institutional factors, and achievement strategies. They also questioned potential barriers and strategies that women used to overcome the barriers

As children and adolescents, most of the gifted European American participants read fervently, achieved in school, and lacked confidence about their popularity with peers. Consistent with the literature on Europan American culture, their communities valued hard work, achievement, and self-reliance and sometimes communicated confusing messages to women. Despite the group's high academic performance, half of the participants remembered K–12 schools as unchallenging, neglectful of their needs, and as providing poor or inadequate counseling. Still, many recalled individual teachers who encouraged and inspired them.

Implications for elementary and secondary schools include:

- Provide a more challenging curriculum, one that meets the academic needs of both girls and boys
- Provide systematic and developmentally appropriate educational and career counseling
- Provide constructivist coping strategies that have the potential to prepare gifted young women for success in a gendered and heterosexist society

Source: Kitano, M. K., & Perkins, C. O. (2000). Gifted European American women. *Journal of the Education of the Gifted, 23*(3), 287–313.

■ ■ ■ ■ ■

FOLLOW THROUGH 7.3
HELPING LEARNERS FROM LOWER SOCIOECONOMIC GROUPS

List ways that coming from a lower socioeconomic group might influence a learner's motivation, perceptions of school success, or value placed on education. Do schools genuinely address the learning needs of the poor? What steps do you or your group recommend for schools to better meet the needs of learners from lower socioeconomic groups?

emphasis on independence and achievement become manifested in parents' expectations for self-reliance on the part of children. In European American families, offspring frequently participate in decision making at early ages; have designated chores within the household; and, as adolescents, hold part-time jobs. Families expect youth

■ ■ ■ ■ ■ ■

FOR ADDITIONAL INFORMATION

For additional information on children's books, we refer readers to *Our Family, Our Friends, Our World: An Annotated Guide to Significant Multicultural Books for Children and Teenagers,* by Lyn Miller-Lachmann (Providence, NJ: R. R. Bowker, 1992). This bibliography comprehensively explores multicultural books from all over the world, divides books into age groups, and provides a brief summary of each.

to establish their own identities, leave the family home, and create their own families (Kitano & Perkins, 2000).

In the German American family, the husband or father is the head of the household and leader of the family. Traditionally the father, although sometimes sentimental, has a stern side. He is usually self-controlled, reserved, strict, and stubborn. Somewhat distant, the husband or father is often less emotionally available to the children than their mother. The German American woman, regarded as hard-working, dutiful, and subservient, adopts her husband's family and friends and gains his social status. Her contributions center mainly around household and family duties. Today the wife's main tasks continue to focus on the house and the family. In fact, how her husband and children look can be a source of pride to her (Winawer-Steiner & Wetzel, 1996).

The Greek American family maintains strict sex roles. Men provide economic necessities, and women cater to men's desires and wish to be good wives. Men are authoritarian fathers and husbands. Often appearing emotionally distant, they are parsimonious with praise and generous with criticism. They often tease their children (some say to toughen them), and children learn that teasing is part of being loved. Other male characteristics include revering their mothers, valuing the family honor, and believing the women's place is in the home. Women expect to comply with tradition and view motherhood as a fulfillment. They prefer male children over female, even in urban areas of the United States. Having a son is a mother's main source of prestige. Parents feel that some emotions, such as uncertainty, anxiety, and fear, are weaknesses that should be hidden from their children (Welts, 1982).

Irish American women have traditionally dominated family life and primarily found their social life through the church. They have enjoyed a greater amount of independence relative to women in other cultures. More Irish women have immigrated to the United Stated than Irish men. Irish families often pay as much attention to the education of their daughters as of their sons. Traditionally, fathers have been shadowy or absent figures, and husbands dealt with wives primarily by avoidance.

Discipline is maintained by ridicule, belittling, and shaming. Children are generally raised to be polite, respectful, obedient, and well behaved. Parents rarely praise or center attention on their children (McGoldrick, 1982).

For Italians, the family is the training ground for learning to cope with a difficult world. The father has traditionally been the family's undisputed head, often authoritarian in his rule and guidelines for behavior. He usually takes his responsibilities to

■ ■ ■ ■ ■

FOLLOW THROUGH 7.4

UNDERSTANDING FAMILIES FROM CULTURALLY DIFFERENT BACKGROUNDS

Use considerable caution when making generalizations about families from culturally different backgrounds. For example, although we might be able to say that Greek American families share similar cultural characteristics, we certainly cannot say that all Greek American families are alike. What factors determine what a family is like? How do factors such as generational status and socioeconomic background affect what families are like?

provide for his family very seriously. As the ultimate authority on living, he offers advice on major issues.

The mother provides the emotional sustenance. While yielding authority to the father, she traditionally assumes responsibility for the emotional aspects of the family. Her life centers around domestic duties, and she is expected to receive her primary pleasure from nurturing and servicing her family. Concerning children, there is marked difference between sons and daughters. Sons are given much more latitude in what they do. The family expects a daughter, rather than a son, to assume major responsibility for an aging or sick parent. The extended family plays a central role in all aspects of Italian family life, including decision making (Rotunno & McGoldrick, 1982).

A major characteristic of the Polish American family is its respect for individual family members. The father and husband is the acknowledged leader of the household. The family is to respect and obey his wishes. Children are raised in a strict tradition of discipline, and they are to give their fathers unquestioned obedience. They are disciplined physically, sometimes harshly. Second-generation children have become acculturated, but the practice of physical discipline continues (Mondykowski, 1982). Case Study 7.3 describes a Polish American elementary school girl and her parents' wishes to teach her the Catholic faith.

In the Portuguese American family, the man maintains great physical and emotional strength to combat life's difficulties. Family members tend to keep feelings to themselves to avoid the loss of respect or power. The father expects to receive respect and obedience from his children. Virtue and purity are desirable feminine qualities for the Portuguese woman. Her role includes loving, honoring, and obeying her husband and caring for her family's many needs. Children are to be seen and not heard. They receive most physical and emotional attention from their parents from infancy to about school age. Girls tend to receive overt displays of affection from both parents; the parents, especially the father, often don't give to boys in the same way (Moitoza, 1982).

Religion

As with other descriptors, European Americans' religion deserves careful consideration. A culture's religion often depends on its specific geographical origin and degree of acculturation.

■ ■ ■ ■ ■ ▬▬

CASE STUDY 7.3
A POLISH AMERICAN ELEMENTARY SCHOOL GIRL

Linnet was a Polish American sixth-grader who attended an all-Catholic elementary school in the North. Her parents worked in factories and had saved diligently to send Linnet to the parochial school. They did not have any quarrel with or criticism of the public school, but they wanted their daughter to have religious training in a strict Catholic environment.

Linnet's grandfather had come to the United States and worked at any job he could find to survive. His language and his lack of knowledge of U.S. customs posed major problems. He thought several times of returning to Poland but did not have the money for the return trip. Finally, despite the reluctance of employers to employ a Polish man, he landed a job and worked for many years. Linnet's father had been luckier. When he finished the tenth grade, he took a job in a factory and worked there for many years. Even though Linnet was only in the sixth grade, her parents and she planned for her to go to college when she completed high school.

Linnet studied diligently, learned the Catholic faith, and lived a strict life, both at home and at school. Her parents had high expectations for her academic achievement and behavior. Likewise, the nuns at school required strict obedience and hard work. Her school was predominantly Polish, but there were some Italians and a mixture of other cultures. In her school, Linnet learned to respect her cultural background and religion as well as to respect the cultural differences of others. She was growing up with an understanding of her Polish heritage, a solid grasp of Catholicism, and a fairly clear (especially for a sixth-grader) understanding of the value of education.

Italian Americans are predominantly Catholic. One survey showed that 90 percent of the respondents had been raised as Catholics, and 80 percent called themselves Catholic at the time of the survey. Because the church has stood for tradition, family, and community, Italians continue to offer their support to the church (Alba, 1985). Similarly, Polish Americans have a powerful allegiance to the Catholic church (Lopata, 1994).

By 1923, there were about 140 Greek churches in the United States. Each community of Greeks formed a board of directors whose function was to build a Greek Orthodox church. Some attempts were made to unite the Greek church with other Eastern churches into an American Orthodoxy, but this consolidation did not materialize. The church seems inextricably intertwined with its role as transmitter of the Greek heritage (Scourby, 1984).

For most newcomer Jews, their primary motivation in leaving the Soviet Union was fear of anti-Semitism rather than the desire for religious freedom. Most Soviet Jews view themselves as culturally Jewish. They are interested in the Jewish past expressed in history and literature, but they are not sure which religious practices have meaning (Abrams, 1993).

Language

As Table 7.3 indicates, considerable variation exists in European Americans' ability to speak English. For example, Census information suggests most learners from

TABLE 7.3   **English Proficiency among Non-Native Speakers**

CULTURAL GROUP	DO NOT SPEAK ENGLISH "VERY WELL"	SPEAK ENGLISH "VERY WELL"
Germans	22.6%	77.4%
United Kingdom	15.7%	84.3%
Italians	53.5%	46.5%

Adapted from: U.S. Bureau of the Census. (1993d). *We the American . . . foreign born.* Washington, DC, p. 6.

■ ■ ■ ■ ■

FOLLOW THROUGH 7.5
HELPING LEARNERS WITH LANGUAGE CHALLENGES

Consider Table 7.3, English Proficiency among Non-Native Speakers. Educators can expect to experience problems when considering the following cultures not speaking English "very well": Germans 22.6 percent, United Kingdom 15.7 percent, and Italians 53.5 percent. While the language barrier might not be as serious for them as it is for some of the Asian and Hispanic groups, it nonetheless presents a challenge to educators. How might language problems be addressed? How can we help the children and adolescents? What can be done to help educators?

■ ■ ■ ■ ■

FOR ADDITIONAL INFORMATION
INTERNET ADDRESSES

Teacher Talk Home Page
http://education.indiana.edu/cas/tt/tthmpg.html Provides information from the Center for Adolescent Studies at the School of Education, Bloomington, Indiana.

Immigration
www.colorado.edu/libraries/govpubs/colonumb/immdef.htm Provides a look at the Statistical Yearbook of the Immigration and Naturalization Service.

Immigration Basics
http://ilw.com/thal/immigrat.htm Provides information that explains the three ways foreign-born individuals can come to the United States legally.

Welcome to America Immigration Report
www.uslawyer.com Provides periodic updates on immigration reports.

Germany and the United Kingdom have little difficulty with the English language. On the other hand, over half of the Italians living in this country experience difficulty with the language. (Census documents do not provide information on language for the other European groups.) Without doubt, considerable diversity exists within the three groups. Several factors influence learners' ability to speak

English—for example, whether their parents and families live in "language en-claves" where people speak native languages, whether the parents speak the native language in the home, whether parents are trying to learn to speak English, and the school's efforts to provide programs in English as a second language (and show ap-preciation for native languages). Table 7.3 looks at selected cultural groups and their ability to speak English.

Ariza (2000) maintains that most teachers come from the majority culture, are native English speakers, and are usually female. This majority culture has its own set of cultural values concerning behaviors (just as do other cultures), yet these cultural ex-pectations affect immigrant students and their parents. Ariza's work is discussed in Im-plementing Research 7.2.

■ ■ ■ ■ ■ ▬▬▬▬▬▬▬▬▬▬▬▬▬▬▬▬▬▬▬▬▬▬▬▬▬▬▬▬▬▬▬▬

IMPLEMENTING RESEARCH 7.2
THE MYTH OF APATHETIC IMMIGRANT PARENTS

Ariza (2000) does an excellent job of describing how cultural differences affect student be-havior. She tells of the Puerto Rican boy who looks downward when the teacher repri-mands him and how the teacher interprets his looking away as disrespectful. She also tells of a Latin American girl who placed her toilet tissue in the trash can rather than in the toi-let, thinking the tissue would clog the plumbing. Also, she tells of two Korean children who worked together on a project and submitted identical papers. Ariza continues with her interesting and thought-provoking stories of cultural behaviors and how they are often misinterpreted.

She also explains that a common problem is teachers who assume that immigrant parents are not interested in their children's school or their progress. Since immigrant par-ents often do not attend school functions and conferences, teachers assume they are disin-terested. Ariza explains that immigrant parents often think they are neither wanted nor needed in schools unless there is a problem with their child. Second, some immigrant par-ents do not speak English well enough to communicate effectively with teachers. Third, some cultures place teachers in very high regard, considering them all-knowing and de-serving of unquestioned respect. Ariza offers several other reasons for immigrants' seem-ing lack of interest. Maintaining that actions speak louder than words, she offers some excellent suggestions, as listed below.

IMPLEMENTING THE RESEARCH
1. Educators can demonstrate pride by displaying a celebration of diversity at all school events.
2. Educators can create a carpool system that offers transportation to school confer-ences, meetings, and functions.
3. Educators can offer family literacy, ESOL (English to Speakers of Other Languages), ABE (Adult Basic Education), and GED (adult high school equivalency) classes.

Source: Ariza, E. N. (2000). Actions speak louder than words—Or do they? Debunking the myth of ap-athetic immigrant parents in education. *Contemporary Education, 71*(3), 36–38.

■ ■ ■ ■ ■ ▬▬▬▬▬▬▬▬▬▬▬▬▬▬▬▬▬▬▬▬▬▬▬

FOLLOW THROUGH 7.6
HELPING IMMIGRANT LEARNERS SUCCEED ACADEMICALLY

While educators must avoid assuming that all immigrant children and adolescents experience lower academic achievement, programs should be carefully designed and implemented to help those who do. Name four or five specific directions they can take to address
immigrants' learning (and social) needs as well as increase their academic achievement.

LEARNING STYLES: CULTURAL
CONSIDERATIONS

Very little research has focused on learning styles of European American learners. One
study (Dunn, Gemake, Jalali, Zenhausern, Quinn, & Spiridakis, 1990) included a European American group in an examination of the learning styles of four cultural
groups—Chinese, Mexican, African, and Greek—in the fourth, fifth, and sixth grades.
Researchers' suggestions included providing all groups with quiet areas and student interaction areas, providing conventional and informal seating arrangements, and allowing learners to work alone.

Contemporary educators need to remember that students from European American cultures (as well as from other cultures) may:

1. Perceive educational situations (e.g., competition and demonstration of motivation) differently
2. Perceive the world differently, such as focusing on the whole rather than the
   parts
3. Prefer to learn using visual, perceptual, and spatial modes rather than words

Directions for educators in pluralistic schools include:

1. Accept professional responsibility to recognize that students learn in different
   ways
2. Plan culturally appropriate learning experiences
3. Provide classroom environments that reflect culturally diverse learners' needs
   and expectations, such as cooperativeness over competition

■ ■ ■ ■ ■ ▬▬▬▬▬▬▬▬▬▬▬▬▬▬▬▬▬▬▬▬▬▬▬

FOLLOW THROUGH 7.7
DETERMINING AND ADDRESSING LEARNING STYLES

From a number of sources, such as journals and testing manuals, determine how educators
can most effectively determine students' learning styles. What tests or inventories can be
used? What are some ways to address students' differing learning styles?

4. Provide bias-free curricular materials that allow students to learn using visual, perceptual, and spatial styles

5. Maintain familiarity with the research and scholarly writing about learning styles among learners from culturally different backgrounds

SCHOOL PRACTICES IMPEDING EUROPEAN AMERICANS' PROGRESS

What school practices might impede European American learners' progress? It sounds ironic to even suggest that school practices would interfere with students' learning and overall school progress, especially because a major goal of schools is to teach. Schools, however, often have practices that do not contribute to the academic achievement and overall development of all learners.

First, policies toward language might be a detrimental factor. Some schools forbid learners to speak their native languages. For example, the school might not allow one Greek American child to teach another Greek American child their native language. Also, some schools fail to provide adequate English as a second language programs. As a result learners are taught in a language that they do not fully understand.

Second, perhaps because of language difficulties or teachers' perceptions, the school sometimes places European Americans in a group that is academically too high or too low for their abilities. Third, teachers sometimes fail to realize that learners in various cultures have differing learning styles and perspectives of motivation and school success.

Case Study 7.4 examines a school that was reluctant to change and the problems that resulted for both students and educators.

PROMOTING SELF-ESTEEM AND CULTURAL IDENTITY

As other chapters on the various cultures have indicated, perceptive educators, especially those teaching in multicultural settings, need to be aware of the importance to children and adolescents of the formation of self-esteem and positive cultural identities. Cultural differences play significant roles in a young person's degree of self-worth and self-image. For example, a student from a culture different from the teacher's and from a lower socioeconomic level may, indeed, consider his or her differences as inferior or wrong. Perceptive educators recognize the disastrous consequences such feelings can have on children's and adolescents' sense of personal worth.

Scholars can take special steps such as the following two to promote positive self-esteem and cultural identities:

1. Educators, perhaps through academic and extracurricular programs, can help European American children and adolescents understand "culture," recognize

■ ■ ■ ■ ■ ▬▬▬▬▬▬▬▬▬▬▬▬▬▬▬▬▬▬▬▬▬▬▬

CASE STUDY 7.4
A SCHOOL RELUCTANT TO CHANGE

The high school was located in an aging part of town, a section that had at one time been a prosperous middle-class neighborhood. Over the previous ten to twelve years, several demographic changes occurred: Many people moved out of the neighborhood, several businesses closed, and large numbers of first- and second-generation immigrants moved into the neighborhood. In other words, the neighborhood and school's student population changed, yet the school remained the same.

A number of factors could be cited for the school's lack of response: poor leadership, failure to recognize the changing demographics, and an outright refusal to change. Regardless of the reason, the school's efforts did not reflect the cultural diversity of the student population. The school failed to make its curriculum multicultural, failed to realize that learning styles could change over ten to twelve years, failed to provide an appropriate classroom management system reflective of learners' expectations, and failed to try to involve parents and families.

In essence, the school was stuck in the mid-twentieth century. The educators knew the student population had changed, but they did not try to meet the needs of a different population. Students and educators both struggled with the situation, often to the point of extreme frustration.

■ ■ ■ ■ ■ ▬▬▬▬▬▬▬▬▬▬▬▬▬▬▬▬▬▬▬▬▬▬▬

FOLLOW THROUGH 7.8
DETERMINING A SCHOOL'S RESPONSE
TO CULTURAL DIVERSITY

Design a survey to determine a school's response to cultural diversity. What aspects do you want to consider? You might list six to eight broad categories (such as Curriculum Efforts) and then add subcategories (such as Library Materials and Textbooks). Remember, efforts to instill multiculturalism should be comprehensive rather than changing just two or three aspects of the school.

how culture affects peoples' lives, and understand that they cannot place values on culture.
2. Educators can work toward providing all children and adolescents with accurate and objective materials and lead discussions about culture and cultural differences that dispel as many myths, distortions, and stereotypes as possible.

■ ■ ■ ■ ■

CULTURAL PORTRAIT
ANNA—AN ITALIAN AMERICAN GIRL

Anna is a nine-year-old, second-generation Italian American girl living in a large urban area. She lives with her father, mother, and grandmother (her father's mother). Anna attends an overcrowded city school, which has a cultural composition fairly representative of that of the nation. A number of European American cultures are represented, and there are significant numbers of African and Hispanic American students as well. Anna feels fairly safe in her school except when fights break out. The school's security guards have done a good job of curtailing fights.

Anna's teacher, Ms. Taylor, is a white American who has tried to understand Anna and her family traditions. Anna and Ms. Taylor get along, but Anna does not want her teacher to meet her parents unless absolutely necessary. Anna has a problem or conflict between her family and her school; her parents do not understand what the school is trying to do. Their English is not very good; in fact, they continue to speak Italian at home. Sometimes, Anna's schoolwork makes little sense to them, and they usually do not understand written correspondence from the school. Anna tries to interpret the English and explains the meaning of the correspondence to her parents.

Anna's schoolwork is usually pretty good. She does all right in reading (in fact, she works diligently) and other school subjects. Her weakest subject is mathematics, and although she studies daily, her grades in math are not as high as her other grades. She wants to improve, to satisfy both her teacher and her parents.

Anna has one or two friends but no one she can really call a best friend. She is sociable with people once she gets to know them, but she is a little quiet (perhaps a little suspicious) at first around strangers.

HOW ANNA'S TEACHER CAN RESPOND
Ms. Taylor can respond to Anna's learning and individual needs in several ways. She can:

1. Arrange for important school correspondence to be translated into Italian, so Anna's parents will have a better understanding of the school's roles and objectives.
2. Speak with Anna's parents if they attend a parents' meeting, make them feel comfortable, accept the fact that they might view her with suspicion, and let them know that she wants to help Anna.
3. Arrange for Anna to have tutoring or additional assistance in mathematics—Anna wants to do better, and she deserves the opportunity.
4. Help or at least provide opportunities (e.g., cooperative learning) for Anna to make closer friends with whom she can speak and socialize.

SUMMING UP

Educators planning educational experiences for European American learners should:

1. Perceive European American learners as an integral part of our nation's diversity even though little attention and research has been focused toward this group.
2. Recognize the futility of past educational practices, in which language programs were inadequate and cultural differences in motivation and learning went unrecognized.
3. Recognize that girls and boys have different perceptions of motivation and school success and perceptions of learning strategies.

4. Realize that cultural characteristics vary among European Americans and that people also differ according to generational status and age, social class, and gender.
5. Understand that European Americans vary widely in their ability to speak English and that the need is strong for methodically planned language programs.
6. Consider European American language differences, learning styles, perceptions of motivation and school success, cooperation versus competition, and differences in behavior expectation and management.
7. Be aware how important it is for European American children to develop positive self-esteem and cultural identities.

SUGGESTED LEARNING ACTIVITIES

1. Interview a first- or second-generation Greek, French, or German American student to determine the problems or special challenges he or she faces in school. If possible, meet with the family as well to learn what problems they experience with the schools. Then, list problems on the left side of your paper and possible solutions on the right.

2. Read a book such as H. Z. Lopata's *Polish Americans* (1994) or A. Scourby's *The Greek Americans* (1984) to learn of the hardships and discrimination that many European Americans have experienced. In many cases, the hardships of the past are no more; however, different forms of hardships and discrimination exist. Read several current periodicals (e.g., newspapers, popular magazines) and make a list of difficulties many European Americans are experiencing today. How might schools help remedy these situations?

3. Language problems continue to plague many European American learners: They cannot speak the language of the school but are forbidden to speak their native languages in school. Their parents cannot understand the school's language, and the school might show little appreciation for native languages. Yet, in all candor, educators feel they should use the language of the nation or the language most students speak. The dilemma challenges many schools in our nation. Think about and write a brief proposal (no matter how radical and forward-looking!) to address this challenge.

SUGGESTIONS FOR COLLABORATIVE EFFORTS

Form groups of three or four that, if possible, represent our nation's cultural and gender diversity. Work collaboratively, and focus your group's attention on the following efforts:

1. Have each member of your group interview four or five students from different European cultures, preferably first- and second-generation. As a group project, design an interview to learn about differences in cultural characteristics, language, family (be careful, some cultures may feel you are prying), social class, and gender. What differences do you find among cultures? Did you find intracultural differences? Were there significant gender differences? What role does social class play in determining what a person is like? Last, what differences did you find between first- and second-generation European Americans?

2. We hear that people from different cultures are "lazy," others "dumb," some "swarthy," and others "stingy." Some are "model minorities," and others are prone to passion and violence. Being careful to respect class members' feelings and cultures, make a list of stereotypes (perhaps on the board as a class project). To show stereotypes are myths and often the result of hate mongering, hypothesize how these stereotypes might have begun. How can stereotypes affect the person being stereotyped and the person harboring the stereotype? How should we as educators respond when we hear someone describe another person in stereotypical terms?

3. Assign individual members of your group to review catalogs of children's books (check with your children's literature professor or the college or school library) to learn titles of new books by European American authors or about European American children and adolescents. Before beginning, decide on certain criteria: whether your group wants lists for elementary-, middle-, or high-school-age youngsters; books published in the last three years or older; and other criteria your group considers important. Have each member prepare a bibliography, and compile your efforts.

EXPANDING YOUR HORIZONS: ADDITIONAL JOURNAL READINGS AND BOOKS

Chang, M. T. (2001). Is it more than about getting along? The broader educational relevance of reducing students' racial biases. *Journal of College Student Development, 42*(2), 93–105.
　Although published in a college student development journal, Chang's article is informative for elementary and secondary educators because it looks at the relationships between racial biases and commonly accepted educational experiences.

Lefkowitz, E. S., Romo, L. P., & Corona, R. (2002). How Latino American and European American adolescents discuss conflicts, sexuality, and AIDS with their mothers. *Developmental Psychology, 36*(3), 315–325.
　The authors examined how mother–daughter conversations differ by ethnic groups and found definite differences between ethnic groups as well as the mother's and daughter's ages.

Ruiz, S. Y., & Roosa, M. W., Gonzales, N. A. (2002). Predictors of self-esteem for Mexican American and European American youths: A reexamination of the influence of parenting. *Journal of Family Psychology, 16*(1), 70–80.
　These authors found that parenting behaviors of low-income Mexican American parents had less influence on children's self-esteem than did parenting behaviors of middle-class or European American parents.

Sanders, G. L., & Kroll, I. T. (2000). Generating stories of resilience: Helping gay and lesbian youth and their families. *Journal of Marital and Family Therapy, 26*(4), 433–442.
　Sanders and Kroll maintain that gay and lesbian youth need assistance, both from caring adults as well as from their families.

Warren, J. W., & Twine, F. W. (1997). White Americans: The new minority? Non-blacks and the ever expanding boundaries of whiteness. *Journal of Black Studies, 28*(2), 200–218.
　The authors pose the question of whether whites are really becoming a minority because whiteness is not a fixed racial category.

Weeber, J. E. (2000). What could I know of racism? *Journal of Counseling and Development, 77*, 20–23.
　Weeber describes the discrimination she received as a result of her disabling condition and how she became a member of the disability community.

EXPANDING YOUR STUDENTS' HORIZONS: APPROPRIATE EUROPEAN AMERICAN BOOKS FOR CHILDREN AND ADOLESCENTS

FRANCE
Harris, Jonathan. *The Land and People of France*. HarperCollins, 1989.
Roth-Hano, René. *Touch Wood: A Girlhood in Occupied France*. Penguin, 1989.
Sullam, Joanna. *Villages of France*. Rizzoli International, 1988.

GERMANY
Hartling, Peter. *Old John*. Lothrop, Lee & Shepard, 1990.
Matas, Carol. *Lisa's War*. Scribner, 1989.
Watkins, Paul. *Night over Day over Night*. Knopf, 1988.

IRELAND
MacDonald, Michael. *Children of Wrath: Political Violence in Northern Ireland*. Basil Blackwell, 1986.
Meyer, Carolyn. *Voices of Northern Ireland: Growing Up in a Troubled Land*. Harcourt Brace Jovanovich, 1987.
Moran, Tom. *A Family in Ireland*. Lerner, 1986.

PORTUGAL
DeSkalon, A., and Stadtler, Christina. *We Live in Portugal*. Franklin Watts, 1987.
Lye, Keith. *Take a Trip to Portugal*. Franklin Watts, 1986.
Wain, John. *The Free Zone Stops Here*. Delacorte, 1984.

SPAIN
Miller, Arthur. *Spain*. Chelsea House, 1989.
Woods, Geraldine. *Spain: A Shining New Democracy*. Dillon, 1987.
Wuorio, Eva-Lis. *Detour to Danger*. Delacorte, 1981.

SWEDEN
Cohen, Peter. *Olson's Meat Pies*. Farrar, Straus, & Giroux, 1989.
Lindgren, Astrid. *Lotta's Bike*. Lerner/Carolrhoda, 1990.
Peterson, Hans. *Erik Has a Squirrel*. Farrar, Straus, & Giroux, 1989.

UNITED KINGDOM
Bawden, Nina. *The Finding*. Lothrop, Lee & Shepherd, 1985.
Cross, Gillian. *Chartbreaker*. Holiday House, 1987.
Foreman, Michael. *War Boy: A Country Childhood*. Brown/Arcade, 1990.

EUROPEANS IN GENERAL
Ayer, Eleanor. *Parallel Journeys*. Athenum, 1995.
Banks, L. R. *One More River*. Morrow, 1992.
Bitton-Jackson, Livia. *I Have Lived a Thousand Years: Growing Up in the Holocaust*. Simon & Schuster, 1997.
Dalokay, Veda. *Sister Shako and Kolo the Goat*. Lothrop, Lee & Shepard, 1994.
Heese, Karen. *Letters from Rifka*. Holt, 1993.
Karas, Phyllis. *The Hate Crime*. Avon, 1995.
Laird, Elizabeth. *Kiss the Dust*. Dutton, 1993.
Morpurgo, Michael. *The Ghost of Grania O'Malley*. Viking, 1996.

CHAPTER EIGHT

UNDERSTANDING HISPANIC AMERICAN CHILDREN AND ADOLESCENTS

Understanding the material and activities in this chapter will help the reader to:

- Describe the cultural, gender, socioeconomic, familial, and language characteristics of Hispanic American children and adolescents

- Understand the dangers of stereotyping Hispanic American learners and know how to respond appropriately in teaching and learning situations

- List and describe the educational characteristics and problems of Hispanic American learners

- Name several practices that impede the educational process of Hispanic American children and adolescents

- List several points that educators of Hispanic American children and adolescents should remember

- Incorporate practical activities, suggest appropriate children's literature, implement research findings, and respond appropriately to school situations involving Hispanic American learners

OVERVIEW

Understanding Hispanic American children and adolescents requires knowledge of their families, their religion, their language, and their culture's contributions. "Knowing, understanding, and appreciating" Spanish-speaking learners are prerequisites, yet not enough: Educators must also understand the relationship of the cultural characteristics of Hispanic learners, their differences as learners, and their school-related problems. Educators' emphasis should be on understanding cultural diversity and demonstrating genuine appreciation of and respect for Hispanic cultures.

ORIGINS

Hispanic Americans as a group include people who are Mexican Americans, Central and South Americans, Chicanos, Spanish Americans, Latin Americans, Puerto Ricans,

Cubans, Guatemalans, and Salvadorans. All these Hispanics share many values and goals but are different in many aspects. In some ways, Hispanics are a single cultural group with a fairly common history and the sharing of language, values, and customs, but in other ways are a significant heterogeneous population that is an aggregate of distinct subcultures.

Tremendous cultural diversity exists among Hispanic Americans, such as the differences between Mexican Americans and Cuban Americans, among generations, and among people living in different geographic locations in the United States. Although this section examines only several Hispanic cultural characteristics, educators should learn about individual students and their respective cultural characteristics.

HISPANIC AMERICANS TODAY

No other ethnic or racial group will do more to change the makeup of U.S. schools over the next quarter-century than Hispanics. They are already the nations's largest minority group among children under eighteen. In fact, projections suggest that in twenty-five years, one in every four elementary students will be Hispanic (Zehr, 2000). With their growth occurring faster than demographers had predicted, Hispanics now rival African Americans as the nation's largest racial minority.

Olsen (1988) describes the effects of today's unprecedented racial and ethnic diversity in California classrooms. Referring to both Southeast Asian and Hispanic learners, Olsen reports issues affecting California learners as being demographic changes, changes resulting from war, "undocumented children," cultural changes, language and academic needs, and the problems of coping with a strange educational system.

As children learn about Hispanic culture and people, teachers can suggest developmentally appropriate children's informational books and biographies.

■ ■ ■ ■ ■ ▬▬▬▬▬

USING CHILDREN'S LITERATURE
INFORMATIONAL BOOKS AND BIOGRAPHIES

Hewitt, Joan. *Getting Elected: The Diary of a Campaign*. Dutton/Lodestar, 1989.
Written for students in grades 4 to 6, this book features Gloria Molina, the first Latina elected to the California Assembly.

Morey, Janet, and Wendy Dunn. *Famous Mexican Americans*. Dutton/Cobblehill, 1989.
Probably best for grades 7 through 9, this book focuses on the lives and contributions of fourteen noted Mexican Americans.

Sumption, Christine, and Kathleen Thompson. *Carlos Finlay*. Raintree, 1990.
Written for students in grades 4 to 6, this story tells of a Cuban-born scientist, a medical doctor, who developed the theory for the cure of yellow fever.

Munson, Sammye. *Our Tejano Heroes: Outstanding Mexican-Americans in Texas*. Eakin, 1989.
Students in grades 4 to 6 will benefit from this book of biographies, husband and wife teams, and families.

Garza, Carmen Lomas, and Harriet Rohmer. *Family Pictures/Cuadros de familia*. Children's Book Press, 1990.
For grades kindergarten through 3, this book introduces readers to one of the country's finest artists of Mexican American heritage.

STEREOTYPING OF HISPANIC AMERICAN CHILDREN AND ADOLESCENTS

As with other learners, Hispanic American children and adolescents may experience "double jeopardy" if educators label learners and base teaching and learning decisions on cultural stereotypes. In essence, teachers may perceive children and adolescents erroneously as exhibiting undesirable behavior, while feeling Hispanic Americans have tendencies toward emotional and violent behavior.

Educators do learners a terrible injustice when educational decisions are based on such stereotypes as the Hispanic American learner is not as "well-behaved" as the Asian American learner, is not as "intelligent" as the European American, and is not as "docile or peaceful" as the American Indian learner. In fact, such stereotypes become self-fulfilling prophecies; Hispanic learners may achieve and behave in accordance with the educator's stereotyped academic and behavior expectations.

What action should educators take? All school personnel should seriously examine the validity of their cultural "baggage" and work toward an objective understanding of Hispanic American children and adolescents. Educators can acquire a more enlightened picture of Hispanic American learners by meeting Hispanic Americans first-hand, learning their proud and diverse history, becoming acquainted with their parents and extended families, understanding the culture's contributions, and understanding their allegiance to the Spanish language. It is also helpful to understand what being a Hispanic American child or adolescent is really like and to realize the poten-

■ ■ ■ ■ ■ ▬▬▬▬▬▬▬▬▬▬▬▬▬▬▬▬▬▬▬▬▬▬▬▬▬▬▬▬▬▬▬▬▬▬▬▬▬▬

CASE STUDY 8.1
NAME-CALLING

Nine-year-old Juan wonders what his second day at his new school will be like. He quickly recognizes that most children are either white or black. During the first classes of the day, Juan notices that no one seems to want to be his friend, but he thinks things will improve during recess. At recess, however, the other children still do not pick him when choosing teams for kickball. Finally, he hears three children laughing, and although he could not hear exactly what they said, he did hear "wetback." Juan is angered and hurt; he feels like crying, but wonders whether he should fight. The teacher sees and hears the entire episode.

Juan's teacher recognizes how damaging such a situation could be for Juan's self-esteem and Mexican American identity. Although she does not want to call a great deal of attention to the situation, she does want to respond appropriately. She feels that several steps are in order.

1. She will have a class discussion on name-calling; she will show how name-calling labels or stereotypes children and how derogatory names can hurt.
2. She will plan activities to involve Juan so that students can know him as an individual and learn about the contributions he can offer the class.
3. She will integrate multiculturalism into her curriculum so that all students can understand and value each others' cultural heritages.

tially disastrous consequences of basing educational programs on cultural misperceptions. As Case Study 8.1 indicates, teachers also must accept the often difficult responsibility for changing other children's cultural attitudes.

Resiliency theory identifies factors present in the families, schools, and communities of successful youth that are missing in the lives of troubled youth. Four common attributes of resilient children include: social competence, problem-solving skills, autonomy, and sense of purpose and future. When at least some of these factors are present, researchers report the successes of many resilient youth (Chavkin & Gonzalez, 2000). Implementing Research 8.1 looks at resiliency among Mexican immigrant youth.

■ ■ ■ ■ ■ ▬▬

IMPLEMENTING RESEARCH 8.1
MEXICAN IMMIGRANT YOUTH AND RESILIENCY

The preponderance of data paints a gloomy picture of the status of Mexican immigrant youth, but at the same time, researchers report the successes of many resilient youth who have overcome tough odds to succeed. The literature on resiliency identifies five key protective factors of families, schools, and communities:

1. Supportive relationships, particularly encouragement from school personnel and other adults
2. Student characteristics, such as self-esteem, motivation, and accepting responsibility
3. Family factors such as parental support/concern and school involvement
4. Community factors such as community youth programs
5. School factors such as academic success and prosocial skills training

Chavkin and Gonzalez (2000) offered several promising programs:

1. Advancement Via Individual Determination (AVID) (San Diego, CA)   Places students from low-income and minority backgrounds in college-preparatory classes.
2. Graduation Really Achieves Dreams (GRAD) (Houston, TX)   Targets high schools with high dropout rates and provides support and scholarships.
3. *Mujeres y Hombres Nobles* (Spanish for honorable men and women) (East Los Angeles, CA)   Program for school dropouts with the primary emphasis of instilling self-pride and appreciation for the Hispanic culture and Spanish language.

IMPLEMENTING THE RESEARCH
1. Educators should understand and take advantage of resiliency factors in an effort to best address the problems of Hispanic youth.
2. Educators and program designers need to provide programs that promote self-esteem and instill pride in the Hispanic culture and Spanish language.
3. Educators should identify and use Mexican youths' strengths to foster caring relationships, active participation, increased parent-child interactions, and high expectations.

Source: Chavkin, N. F., & Gonzalez, J. (2000). Mexican immigrant youth and resiliency: Research and promising programs. Charleston, WV: ERIC Clearinghouse on Rural Education and Small Schools. ERIC Document Reproduction Service No. ED 447990.

CULTURAL CHARACTERISTICS

Educators who plan and implement a multicultural curriculum can benefit from knowledge, understanding, and appreciation of Hispanic learners and their culture. Studies of Hispanic youngsters do not differentiate sufficiently among the different Spanish-speaking ethnic groups. Differing cultures, generational, socioeconomic, and acculturation factors exist that educators must consider to understand Hispanic American learners.

The United States now has slightly more Hispanic children than African American children. There are 10.5 million Hispanic children under age eighteen; in contrast, there are 10.4 million non-Hispanic black children. Hispanic children are the fastest-growing youth population, and this increase should continue well into the next century. As a result, by 2020, projections show that more than one in five children will be of Hispanic origin (Hispanic youth edging past blacks in number, 1998).

A cultural description of Spanish-speaking peoples should include an understanding of certain values and traits (Gonzalez, 1989; Christensen, 1989). Educators can gain considerable insight into the culture by understanding several unique characteristics (see Table 8.1). Hispanic Americans tend to avoid any competition or activity that will set them apart from their own group. To stand out among one's peers is to place oneself in great jeopardy and is to be avoided at all costs.

Machismo plays a significant role in the Puerto Rican culture and significantly influences the behavior and attitudes of adolescent males during this time of identity formation. It suggests a clear-cut distinction between the sexes: Males can enjoy rights and privileges denied to females.

Used as a flattering term among Hispanic Americans, Hispanic American boys and girls learn that *machismo* refers to the male's manhood, to the courage to fight, to the many traits of honor and dignity, to keeping one's word, and to protecting one's name. On a more subtle level of analysis, *machismo* also includes dignity in personal conduct, respect for others, love for the family, and affection for children. Many chil-

TABLE 8.1   Selected Characteristics of Hispanic American Children and Adolescents

CATEGORY	CHARACTERISTICS
Behavioral/emotional expressiveness	Restraint of feelings, particularly anger and frustration
Verbal	Limited verbal expressions toward authority figures
Nonverbal	Preference for closer personal space; avoidance of eye contact when listening or speaking to authority figures
Concept of time	Present time perspective; relaxed about time and punctuality; and immediate short-term goals
Social orientation	Collective, group identity; interdependence; cooperative rather than competitive; emphasis on interpersonal relations

Developed from: Rivera, B. D., & Rogers-Adkinson, D. (1997). Culturally sensitive interventions: Social skills training with children and parents from culturally and linguistically diverse backgrounds. *Intervention in School and Clinic, 33*(2), 75–80.

■ ■ ■ ■ ■

FOLLOW THROUGH 8.1
UNDERSTANDING THE HISPANIC CULTURE

It is important that educators of Hispanic children and adolescents understand and appreciate important concepts of the Hispanic culture. On understanding these cultural characteristics, try to identify related behaviors in Hispanic learners.

corazon: heart
sensibilidad: sensitivity
afecto: warmth and demonstrativeness
dignidad: dignity
respecto: respect
machismo: biological superiority of the male

dren are taught early that European Americans are not trustworthy. Mexican Americans, for example, often teach their children to look toward European Americans with fear and hostility (Fitzpatrick, 1987).

In general, group-oriented Mexican American children are likely to change their own behavior to adapt to an interpersonal challenge rather than try to change situations. They are less assertive in expressing themselves to peers and adults and rely on authority figures to resolve interpersonal problems (Rotheram-Borus & Phinney, 1990).

Readers who want a better understanding of Hispanic children and adolescents and the contributions of the Hispanic cultures may want to write to the listed organizations.

■ ■ ■ ■ ■

FOLLOW THROUGH 8.2
DETERMINING LEARNING OPPORTUNITIES
ABOUT HISPANIC LEARNERS

Educators have realized for many years the advantages of knowing as much as possible about learners. When teaching students from culturally different backgrounds, however, educators must understand learners' cultural backgrounds so as to make the most of learners' opportunities to improve learning experiences and self-esteem. What can educators do to learn about Hispanic learners' cultural backgrounds?

1. Read objective literature about the Hispanic culture to learn about its historical background.
2. Understand Hispanic peoples' contributions and cherished cultural traits and how they are different from and similar to the majority culture and other minority populations.
3. Learn about Hispanic families—both immediate and extended—and understand the value Hispanic people place on the family.
4. Get to know individual Hispanic learners. Don't just generalize about them.
5. Visit Hispanic learners in their homes to learn first-hand about their home lives.

■ ■ ■ ■ ■

FOR ADDITIONAL INFORMATION

Association of Hispanic Arts (AHA),
200 E. 87th Street,
New York, NY 10028.
Founded in 1975, AHA promotes the general concept of Hispanic arts, specifically dance, music, art, and theatrical performances.

Hispanic Institute for the Performing Arts
(HIFPA), P. O. Box 32249, Calvert Station,
Washington, DC 20007.
Begun in 1981, HIFPA seeks to promote a better understanding of Hispanics by conducting educational and cultural activities.

Gender

In Hispanic American culture, just as in other cultures, females differ from their male counterparts. Although males and females both experience similar frustrations, such as discrimination and prejudice and sometimes poverty and lower standards of living, Hispanic American females are different from males in other ways. For example, Hispanic American females usually prefer cooperative learning environments over competitive classrooms in which many boys learn best. Likewise, Hispanic American females, because of their families' adherence to strict gender roles, are often less vocal and take less assertive stands than males do (Grossman & Grossman, 1994).

It is important to note, however, that because of acculturation and females taking steps to improve themselves economically and socially, some Hispanic American females are adhering less and less to traditional gender expectations. In any event, perceptive educators who work with Hispanic American females will want to bear in mind the gender-role differences among Hispanic cultures and among individual females.

Gender differences also exist in language acquisition and development. Gender Perspectives 8.1 looks at English language anxiety in Mexican girls.

Socioeconomic Status

Over 1 million Hispanic American families live in poverty—just over two of every ten Hispanic families, compared with less than one of every ten non-Hispanic families. About 30 percent of Puerto Rican families, 33 percent of families from the Dominican Republic, about 10 percent of families from Spain, 11 percent of Cuban families,

■ ■ ■ ■ ■

FOR ADDITIONAL INFORMATION

The Hispanic Policy Development Project,
Suite 310, 1001 Connecticut Avenue,
NW, Washington, DC 20036.
This organization examines the problems of Hispanic youth living in the United States today and

suggests public and private strategies for helping these youth.

■ ■ ■ ■ ■ ▬▬▬▬▬

GENDER PERSPECTIVES 8.1
ENGLISH LANGUAGE ANXIETY IN MEXICAN GIRLS

The process of moving from an English as a second language (ESL) class to a mainstream class with no supplementary English support can be very traumatic for many ESL students. This article describes the results of a study that shows how Mexican adolescent girls often experience more anxiety in the mainstream classroom than boys, due to differing types of English language anxiety associated with the two differing learning environments.

Suggesting classroom implications, Pappamihiel suggests that educators can take several directions:

1. Adolescent girls need more help developing affective strategies to deal with social interactions with other students. Females often mentioned they feared speaking English with native English speakers because they were afraid of being laughed at or socially rejected.
2. Teachers can incorporate more cooperative learning groups, in which students will have more opportunities to interact positively with each other and reduce anxiety.
3. Mexican females often withdraw from social interaction and allow more vocal speakers to speak. Teachers can battle this avoidance by ensuring that all female students interact in safe groups in which they feel comfortable.

Pappamihiel concludes that her work and the work of others suggest affective evaluations must be taken into consideration when mainstreaming ESL students, especially when dealing with female students. Teachers should consider social competence along with academic and linguistic competence in order to best meet Mexican girls' needs.

Source: Pappamihiel, N. E. (2001). Moving from the ESL classroom into the mainstream: An investigation of English language anxiety in Mexican girls. *Bilingual Research Journal, 25*(1 & 2), 1–8.

---

23 percent of Mexican families, and 21 percent of Central American families were below the poverty level in the United States in 1990. Poverty rates are also disturbing for Hispanic children and adolescents. About 18 percent of Hispanic children under eighteen years of age lived in poverty, compared with 17 percent of non-Hispanic children (U.S. Bureau of the Census, 1993e). Two interrelated factors contribute to this cycle of poverty among Hispanic Americans: The unemployment rate among Puerto Rican males is twice that of European Americans, and the number of female-headed households continues to increase.

Hispanic children were more likely than other children to live in very poor neighborhoods. The percentage of Hispanic children at or below 100 percent of the poverty line declined between 1996 and 1999, but Hispanic children are still twice as likely as European American children to live in poverty. Plus, Hispanic children are less likely to have health insurance than either African or European American children (Williams, 2001).

Hispanic-Americans', just as other cultures', socioeconomic status is a result of their educational attainment. Fewer Hispanics age twenty-five or older have completed high school than have African Americans and European Americans. Latinos with a median family income of $28,000 lag behind the $39,000 income of the population as a whole. While 36 percent of Latino children live in poverty, only 26 percent attend Head Start programs, which are designed to remedy the effects of poverty on academic achievement (Latinos in school: Some facts and findings, 2001).

Are there indications that the socioeconomic status of Hispanic American children and adolescents will improve? One could provide an affirmative answer to this question if Hispanics work to improve their educational levels and English skills. These improvements will allow them to venture from Spanish-speaking communities into mainstream U.S. society. Although educators should recognize (and respond appropriately to) the effects poverty often has on academic achievement, it would also be a serious mistake to categorize all lower-socioeconomic Hispanics into unmotivated or underachieving academic groups.

Families

A basic feature of the Hispanic American family is the extended family, which plays a major role in each family member's life. These are families with strong bonds and frequent interaction among a wide range of kin. Grandparents, parents, and children may live in the same household or nearby in separate households and visit one another frequently. A second feature is the emphasis on cooperativeness and on placing the needs of the family ahead of individual concerns. This aspect of Hispanic family life has led to the erroneous conclusion that the family impedes individual achievement and advancement. Generally speaking, Hispanic American children and adolescents learn to show respect for authority, the patriarchal family structure, and extended family members (Rivera & Rogers-Adkinson, 1997).

During the last several decades, the number of Hispanic children living in two-parent homes has decreased, although this is also true of all cultural groups (Williams, 2001). More than one-third (36 percent) of Hispanic households were married couples with children in 1997; only a quarter of non-Hispanic households were married couples with children. Children lived in more than half (52 percent) of the 8.2 million Hispanic households. Only about one-third (33 percent) of the 9.3 million non-Hispanic households included children ("Married with children": More likely to describe Hispanic households, 1998).

Hispanic American children learn early the importance of (1) a deep sense of family responsibility, (2) rigid definitions of sex roles, (3) respectful and reverent treatment of the elderly, and (4) the male's position of respect and authority in the family. Although some of the male's authority appears to be relaxing as the woman's role is redefined, women in the Hispanic American culture continue to occupy a subordinate position. Fathers have prestige and authority, and sons have more and earlier independence than do daughters (Lum, 1986).

Latino and Chicano families value the extended family structure and interaction in their daily lives. Parents often arrange for godparents or "companion parents" for the child, thus demonstrating the value Hispanics place on adults other than the immediate parents. These *compadres* also have a right to give advice and correction and should be responsive to the child's needs (Fitzpatrick, 1987).

■ ■ ■ ■ ■ ▬▬

FOLLOW THROUGH 8.3
GETTING TO KNOW HISPANIC FAMILIES

Learning about the Hispanic learner's family may be one of the best ways to improve the child's academic achievement and self-esteem. Educators can do several things to learn about Hispanic families.

1. Invite families to school on special occasions just to visit. While the family learns about the school and its policies and expectations, teachers can become acquainted with the families.
2. Request that students write a story or essay about their families. Be sure to emphasize including parents, grandparents, brothers and sisters, cousins, and other relatives living in the home. Keep an open mind, and remember the importance of the extended family. Tell students before they write the story whether or not their stories or essays will be shared with the class.
3. Educators who teach in areas with great numbers of Hispanics may want to schedule a day for only Hispanic families to visit. Have individual meetings to determine how the family influences school achievement and attitudes toward school. (If possible, speak Spanish to families with limited English-speaking skills.)
4. Schedule individual meetings with Hispanic students to discuss their families, but be careful that students understand the purpose of these discussions. Allow and respect a learner's privacy.

Schwartz (2001) maintains that educators need to understand and work closely with Latino families. For example, educators need to understand that while Latino families want their daughters to have a good education, many have personal problems with which to deal. Plus, they should work to increase parental involvement in children's education, for example, invite them to school functions, asking for their input on curricular and instructional activities, and suggesting specific ways they can promote their children's education.

■ ■ ■ ■ ■ ▬▬

FOR ADDITIONAL INFORMATION

Puerto Rican Family Institute (PRFI), 116 W. 14th Street, New York, NY 10011.
This organization was established in 1960 for the preservation of the health, well-being, and integrity of Puerto Ricans and other Hispanic families in the United States.

Chicano Family Center (CFC), 7145 Avenue H, Houston, TX 77011.
Founded in 1971, the CFC seeks to enhance understanding and appreciation of the Chicano culture.

Religion

Religion plays a central role in the lives of Hispanic Americans. The Spanish colonial experience brought about a distinct culture of which the Catholic faith was an important part. Catholicism was brought by the Spanish to the United States. The first mass on what is now U.S. soil was celebrated at Saint Augustine, Florida, in 1565. Spanish missionaries were active in the Southwest as early as 1539, and California missions were founded between 1770 and 1782 (Fitzpatrick, 1987).

Fitzpatrick (1987) believes that Hispanics make up 40 percent of the current Catholic membership. Numbers from *The Gallup Report* substantiate the belief that Hispanics adhere predominantly to the Catholic faith: Protestants account for 18 percent; Catholics, 70 percent; others and those not claiming a religious preference, 12 percent (*Religion in America*, 1985).

Language

Hispanic people in the United States speak many Spanish dialects, depending on where the speakers live, how long they have lived in this country, and where they came from originally. Spanish in the Southwest is different from Spanish in the Midwest, the Northeast, and Florida. Even in New York City, there are important cultural and linguistic differences between speakers from Puerto Rico, Cuba, the Dominican Republic, Colombia, Ecuador, Peru, Mexico, Venezuela, Bolivia, and other South American areas (Tiedt & Tiedt, 1999).

Some Hispanic American learners' language poses a problem outside the immediate neighborhood, because they tend to retain the native tongue rather than make a cultural transition to English. Instead of making an attempt to learn English, many do not perceive a need to develop proficiency in English and continue to risk survival in a predominantly English-speaking country. Language difficulties that learners experience may have a major impact on self-esteem and the developing identity.

■ ■ ■ ■ ■ ▬▬▬▬▬▬▬▬▬▬▬▬▬▬▬▬▬▬▬▬▬▬▬▬▬▬▬▬▬▬▬

FOR ADDITIONAL INFORMATION
INTERNET ADDRESSES

Hispanic Americans Denied Equal Educational Opportunity
www.gseis.ucla.edu/courses/ed191/assignment1/1996hispanic.html   Provides a report entitled "Our Nation on the Fault Line: Hispanic American Education."

Background—Hispanic Americans and the Business Community
www.aspeninst.org/dir/Polpro/HABC/Hispanicbkgd.html   Provides a summary of the Aspen Forum to discuss issues involving Hispanic Americans and society.

Association of NIST Hispanic Americans
www.nist.gov/director/groups/anha.htm   Provides a look at the work of the National Institute of Standards and Technology.

Hispanic Americans
http://libby.rbls.lib.il.us/dpl/hispanic.htm   Provides an examination of Hispanic Americans who have made valuable contributions.

Nonverbal language, as in other cultures, also plays a major factor in the Hispanic American culture, and professionals of other cultures must recognize and understand this. Although a complete list of nonverbal behaviors is impossible and would deny individual and intracultural differences, several examples will serve to indicate their significance. Many Hispanic Americans stand close together while communicating, touch to communicate, and often avoid eye contact.

Undoubtedly, many of the problems Hispanic American learners experience stem from their difficulties with English. Hearing Spanish spoken at home, yet feeling pressure to communicate in English at school, often results in academic and behavioral problems, lower self-esteem, negative cultural identities, and a general pessimism toward teachers and schools.

The number of school-age children who speak a language other than English at home and have difficulty speaking English has increased from 1.3 million in 1979 to 2.4 million in 1995, about 5 percent of all children in those age groups (Hispanic youth edging past blacks in number, 1998).

Case Study 8.2 shows the importance of being understood and what Mr. Donaldson did to help Maria.

Latinos comprise three-quarters of all students enrolled in Limited English Proficient (LEP) programs, although not all Latino students have limited English proficiency (Latinos in school: Some facts and findings, 2001). Implementing Research 8.2 suggests some new trends in language education for Hispanic students.

■ ■ ■ ■ ■ ▬▬▬▬▬▬▬▬▬▬▬▬▬▬▬▬▬▬▬▬▬▬▬▬▬▬

CASE STUDY 8.2

THE IMPORTANCE OF UNDERSTANDING

Mr. Donaldson, an elementary-school teacher, had a fourth-grade child whose lack of proficiency in English left her virtually unable to learn. Rather than being a meaningful learning experience, the school day became a time of boredom and frustration. Devastating consequences awaited Maria (and other, similar learners with culturally diverse backgrounds), who felt "stupid" or that teachers forgot she was there or else wished she were not. Even though language proficiency takes time and effort, Maria needed to feel that teachers and other school personnel cared and wanted to help her. Mr. Donaldson decided to take several steps to help Maria have meaningful school experiences:

1. Request that the bilingual (or other) language specialist meet with Maria to determine an immediate plan of action
2. Arrange for a professional, perhaps an aide, to work closely with Maria to show a sense of caring and concern
3. Call on or talk to Maria about anything: school, the Hispanic culture, or activities in the playground
4. Administer an "interest inventory" to learn about Maria's interests, likes, and dislikes, then plan instruction and communication accordingly

■ ■ ■ ■ ■

IMPLEMENTING RESEARCH 8.2

NEW TRENDS IN LANGUAGE EDUCATION FOR HISPANIC STUDENTS

One especially important factor is the failure of some public schools to provide a mean-ingful education that builds on students' native language and culture while also helping them to develop good English language skills. In this ERIC Digest, Schwartz summarizes effective bilingual strategies for Hispanic students, although most strategies are appropri-ate for the education of all students with immigrant and limited English-speaking back-grounds. The author focuses attention toward several directions: educational policy; teacher training and performance; effective elementary, middle, and secondary bilingual programs; instructional strategies, and effective tutoring.

IMPLEMENTING THE RESEARCH

1. Schools continually revise their approaches as new strategies are proven effective and new student needs are identified.
2. Schools embrace the philosophy that true bilingualism means proficiency in both Spanish and English, and they include Hispanic culture in the curriculum.
3. Schools offer individualized instruction and other aids to ensure that students learn English and other subjects that will enable future career fulfillment.
4. Schools, with the full participation of their teachers and staff, maintain an atmo-sphere that supports the beliefs that all students are equally valuable and bring to the school equally valuable cultures, and the expectation that all will succeed.

Source: Schwartz, W. (2000). *New trends in language education for Hispanic students.* New York, NY: ERIC Clearinghouse on Urban Education. ERIC Documentation Reproduction Service No. 442913.

■ ■ ■ ■ ■

FOLLOW THROUGH 8.4

ENHANCING HISPANIC AMERICAN LEARNERS' ACADEMIC RECORDS

It is time for school systems to do their part to enhance the Hispanic learner's academic record by:

1. Considering the Hispanic learner objectively and avoiding labels
2. Developing a more individualized instructional program that recognizes Hispanic learning styles
3. Implementing a curriculum that recognizes, respects, and builds on Hispanic learn-ers' cultural diversity
4. Involving parents by explaining the role and purposes of schooling and by showing what they can do to help their children in school

Children who feel pressure to speak Spanish at home and English at school may develop problems in both languages, may become bilingual, or may avoid English-speaking situations. Such a situation can result in dual cultural identification, additional language conflicts, and chronic anxiety. In the Southwestern United States, many Hispanic American people live in Spanish-speaking communities isolated from English-speaking communities. In fact, children often enter the English-speaking world for the first time when they begin their public school education. Then, to make matters worse, these children are often threatened with punishment in school environments for speaking Spanish.

ACHIEVEMENT LEVELS

The news media periodically raise several issues concerning the level of educational achievement of Hispanic American students, such as the relatively low number of Hispanic American students eligible for college. By the senior year, only 31 percent of Hispanic American high school students are enrolled in college-preparatory courses. Of the Hispanic students graduating from high school, only about 10 to 15 percent are academically qualified to enter state universities in California (*Closing the Educational Gap for Hispanics*, 1987). Goldenberg (1987) described Hispanic Americans' academic achievement this way:

> Hispanic students score lower than do their white, middle-class counterparts on tests of academic achievement. They are more likely to fail one or more grades in school, be placed in special education, and drop out altogether. Attitudes toward school are negative, with Hispanic students reporting a higher degree of alienation and disenchantment with school and school personnel. (p. 149)

On reaching an understanding of the social and cultural characteristics of Hispanic American children and adolescents, educators can proceed with understanding the learner in the Hispanic culture. Santiestevan (1986) maintains that "Nationwide, United States Hispanics agree that the single most crucial problem they face today is education" (p. 396).

■ ■ ■ ■ ■ ▬▬▬

FOLLOW THROUGH 8.5
APPRECIATING HISPANIC NAMES

Names and their meanings are special to learners of all cultures and ages. Teachers, other school personnel, and students should understand the special meaning and value Hispanic cultures place on names.

Soledad (solitude)	Dolores (sorrows)
Concepcion (conception)	Mercedes (mercies)
Salvador (savior)	Jesus (Jesus)

Source: Tiedt, P. L., & Tiedt, I. M. *Multicultural teaching: A handbook of activities, information, and resources.* Boston: Allyn & Bacon, 1999.

This section considers Hispanic American learners and looks for answers to several questions related to their educational progress. What special school-related problems do Hispanic learners experience? Do European American expectations and stereotypes penalize Hispanic learners? Are Hispanic learners labeled? How do learning styles of Hispanics differ? What school practices might impede Hispanics' progress? As we explore these and other questions, we caution readers to consider the intracultural, generational, and socioeconomic differences between individual learners when reaching educational decisions.

Hispanics have had much lower high school completion rates than African and European Americans, which leaves many Hispanic youth less prepared. Plus, Hispanic youth are more likely than European American youth to neither attend school nor work (Williams, 2001). The dropout rate among Hispanic youth is unacceptably high; nearly one in three students fail to graduate from high school. There are a number of reasons why Hispanic students drop out. Many youth attend overcrowded, instructionally inferior, and inadequately staffed schools that do not meet their educational needs and are breeding grounds for antisocial activities. Many also live in the most economically distressed areas of the United States; they witness their elders' limited employment opportunities; and they experience debilitating stereotyping, prejudice, and bias. In essence, Hispanic youth do not believe that remaining in school will materially improve their lives (School practices to promote the achievement of Hispanic students, 2000). The dropout rate for Hispanic Americans is partially attributed to the relatively

■ ■ ■ ■ ■ ▬▬▬▬▬▬▬▬▬▬▬

RECOMMENDATIONS FOR PROMOTING THE ACHIEVEMENT OF HISPANIC AMERICAN STUDENTS

- Each Hispanic student should have an adult in the school committed to nurturing a personal sense of self-worth and supporting the student's efforts to succeed in school.
- Schools should be safe and inviting places that personalize programs and services that succeed with Hispanic students.
- All students should have access to high-quality, relevant, and interesting curricular experiences that treat their culture and language as resources, conveys high expectations, and demands student investment in learning.
- Schools should replicate effective programs and continually try to improve programs with more reliable strategies.
- Schools should emphasize the prevention of problems, and be aggressive in responding to early warning signs that a student is disengaging from school.
- Schools and alternative programs should be coordinated.
- Teachers should teach content so that it interests and challenges Hispanic students—they should understand the roles language, race, culture, and gender play in the educational process.
- Schools should recruit Hispanic parents and extended families into a partnership of equals for educating Hispanic students.

Developed from: School Practices to Promote the Achievement of Hispanic Students (2000). New York. NY: ERIC Clearinghouse on Urban Education. ERIC Document No. ED 439186 (no author given).

■ ■ ■ ■ ■ ▬

FOLLOW THROUGH 8.6
TEACHING HISPANIC AMERICAN LEARNERS

1. Meet the learner's family, both immediate and extended, if possible.
2. Administer an "interest inventory" to determine the areas in which learners might have the most motivation.
3. Administer appropriate diagnostic instruments to determine learners' strengths and weaknesses. Be sure instruments take into account Hispanic learning styles.
4. Talk with Hispanic children or adolescents to learn more about the Hispanic culture, the family, areas of interest or confusion, fears, expectations, and any other factors that might help in planning culturally and developmentally appropriate instructions.
5. Seek the advice and input of other professionals in the school (speech correctionists, guidance counselors, and remedial, resource, and gifted teachers) who have knowledge of the Hispanic learner.

greater dropout rate for Hispanic immigrants: 44 percent, as compared with 21 percent for the U.S.-born. The high school completion rate for Hispanic Americans is increasing, but continues to be low (Latinos in school: Some facts and findings, 2001).

Only about 4 percent of public school teachers are Latinos, whereas Latinos constitute 15 percent of the student body (Latinos in school: Some facts and findings, 2001). Still, teachers should not let stereotypes and erroneous conclusion interfere with their academic and behavior expectations of Latino learners.

Case Study 8.3 underscores the necessity of perceiving Hispanic American learners objectively and as individuals.

■ ■ ■ ■ ■ ▬

CASE STUDY 8.3
BASING SCHOOL EXPECTATIONS ON LONG-HELD BELIEFS

"Hispanic students always experience learning problems in American schools," Mrs. Miller was saying in the teachers' workroom. "They have so many problems—language, poverty, and those big families! What more can you expect? It has always been that way."

One of the professionals in the workroom should explain to Mrs. Miller the danger and futility of such statements. Expecting poor academic achievement as a result of language problems and poverty may set the stage for students' failure. Without doubt, Mrs. Miller needs a better understanding of Hispanic cultural heritages, more recognition of the differences within the Hispanic cultural heritages, more recognition of the differences within the Hispanic culture, and more objectivity with regard to Hispanic students. Mrs. Miller should also understand individual differences resulting from generational factors, geographic origins, and socioeconomic factors.

In general, Mrs. Miller continues to perpetuate a European American-oriented philosophy in an increasingly multicultural society. Though unfortunate, far more serious consequences exist for learners from different cultural backgrounds, in this case, the Hispanic American learners in the school.

Disproportionately fewer Hispanic American students than European American students take challenging academic courses. Some schools rigidly track students into such courses, using test scores or previous grades to weed out those considered less able. Other schools might open their tough academic courses to anyone, but minority students choose not to enroll (Viadero, 2000).

Scribner and Scribner (2001), in Implementing Research 8.3, tell how high performing schools can best serve Mexican students.

LEARNING STYLES: CULTURAL CONSIDERATIONS

As we mentioned in the previous chapters on children and adolescents of various cultures, educators can determine learning styles by observing learners' overt behavior. What cultural or sociological elements should educators consider in the Hispanic American learner? Learners can provide clues while demonstrating any number of behaviors. Some learners work and achieve when left alone; distractions such as the presence of other people, movements, or sounds create disturbances. Other children learn best when among peers working on case studies, small-group activities, or team learnings.

Determining the most appropriate learning styles for Hispanic Americans requires that educators, whether regular classroom teachers or remedial and resource teachers, observe both individual and cultural differences that may affect learning styles.

Effective multicultural educators should look at specific Hispanic cultural characteristics to determine their potential effects on learning. Case Study 8.4 looks at several cultural characteristics that may affect learning styles. As in other chapters on cultural diversity among learners, we urge educators to use caution by considering both the culture and the individual within the culture.

■ ■ ■ ■ ■

FOLLOW THROUGH 8.7

HELPING SECOND-LANGUAGE LEARNERS

Educators can help second-language learners through bilingual programs, English as a second language (ESL) programs, English remediation classes, and instruction in Spanish for at least part of the day. Other suggestions include:

1. Read aloud to students.
2. Respect students' efforts.
3. Provide opportunities for oral communication.
4. Provide opportunities for students to speak and write.
5. Use a variety of methods and materials, such as small-group speaking situations, tapes, choral speaking, and records.
6. Respect the student's native language.

■ ■ ■ ■ ■ ▬▬▬▬▬

IMPLEMENTING RESEARCH 8.3
HIGH PERFORMING SCHOOLS AND MEXICAN STUDENTS

Scribner and Scribner, in this ERIC digest, explain what research tells educators about creating schools that better support the success of Mexican American students. They investigated three elementary schools, three middle schools, and three secondary schools. All schools had enrollment of 66.6 percent or more Mexican American students. A pilot study was conducted and data analysis and interpretation were conducted by research teams trained in multicultural research, qualitative analysis, and interpretation techniques.

IMPLEMENTING THE RESEARCH
Scribner and Scribner offer suggestions in four areas.

1. Collabarative relationships with parents and communities:
   Building on cultural values of Mexican American parents
   Stressing personal contact with parents
   Fostering communication with parents
   Creating a warm environment for parents
   Facilitating structural accommodations for parent involvement
2. Collaborative governance and leadership:
   A clear, cohesive vision and mission shared by the school community
   Humanistic leadership philosophies
   Current and appropriate professional development
   An ethic of caring
   The belief that all students can succeed
   A culture of innovation
3. Student-centered classroom environments:
   Consistent, productive, and intensive collaboration among teachers
   The encouragement of collaborative learning
   Student access to a wide variety of learning materials
   Utilization of both Spanish and English, as needed, to enhance learning
4. Advocacy-oriented assessment practices:
   Efforts to avoid premature referrals for special services, especially for students whose first language is not English
   Intensive language development, team planning/teaching, and coordination of instruction
   A philosophy that stresses collaboration and familiarity with ESL student needs, which resulted in an advocacy-oriented approach to assessment

Teaching practices alone do not make effective schools—recent research confirms the importance of inclusive leadership that creates a sense of community, drawing everyone into the learning process and preventing alienation of faculty, students, parents, and the larger Mexican American community.

Source: Scribner, A. P., & Scribner, J. D. (2001). *High-performing schools serving Mexican American students: What they can teach us.* Charleston, WV: ERIC Clearinghouse on Rural and Small Schools. ERIC Documentation Reproduction Service No. 459048.

■ ■ ■ ■ ■

CASE STUDY 8.4
CULTURAL CHARACTERISTICS AND LEARNING

Mr. Smith, an Anglo teacher in his fourth year of teaching, received his class roll for the upcoming school year and learned that nearly half his class was Hispanic. Although he had some background in providing educational experiences in multicultural situations, he was unsure how to relate Hispanic cultural characteristics to learners' teaching/learning experiences. Mr. Smith met with colleagues to discuss the challenge and received the following suggestions:

Cultural Characteristic	*Implications for Learning*
Does not want to be set apart as excelling	Provide opportunities for group work so group will excel, not individual
"Personalism"—wanting personal contact	Learner needs opportunities to have first-hand contact with teacher and others in school
"Machismo"—biological superiority of the male	Sexes may feel uncomfortable working with each other; may feel that the male must lead and reach decisions

These characteristics and implications are only representative, but Mr. Smith saw that learning could and should be based on the cultural characteristics of learners.

■ ■ ■ ■ ■

FOLLOW THROUGH 8.8
IMPROVING PERFORMANCE THROUGH UNDERSTANDING LEARNING STYLES

Give Hispanic students better understanding of their personal learning styles and you provide them an excellent means of improving their learning performance. As learners better understand how they learn, perceptive educators can also gain insight into how they should plan and implement learning experiences. Learners can ask themselves several questions:

1. Do you prefer to (a) think through a learning experience to reach a conclusion or (b) be told the conclusion and then think out how the conclusion was reached?
2. Do you think your most effective learning experiences are in the morning, the afternoon, or at night?
3. Do you prefer a quiet learning environment, or can you learn better when there is background noise?
4. Do you prefer teaching and learning experiences that require you to see, listen, or feel?
5. Do you prefer to study and learn alone or with a friend?

These represent only a few determinants of learning styles. "For Additional Information" lists sources for learning more about learning styles.

SCHOOL PRACTICES IMPEDING HISPANIC AMERICANS' PROGRESS

Is it possible that well-meaning teachers, either European American or of another culture, actually encourage school practices that may prove detrimental to Hispanic students? A look at many U.S. schools causes one to answer in the affirmative. The already somewhat overwhelmed Hispanic child or adolescent may be even more startled at the verbal emphasis in U.S schools. The extreme verbalism that characterizes U.S. schools can have profound consequences for learners with limited English-language skills.

A second, related detrimental practice is well-meaning teachers' forbidding Hispanic students to speak Spanish and actually punishing them for it. Understanding such a situation is difficult for learners who are proficient in Spanish but are experiencing considerable difficulty with their second language.

A third practice involves an entanglement of values and cultural orientations. Believing in the American cultural tradition of excelling among one's peers, teachers often motivate learners by encouraging Hispanic learners to excel above others in the class. Causing oneself to stand out among one's peers goes against Hispanic cultural traditions and expectations.

Another problem results when teachers from European American and other cultural groups have stereotypical beliefs of Hispanic learners. How many educators believe that Hispanic learners are slow, violent, prone to emotional, erratic behavior, and generally speaking, unable to perform academically in American schools? So (1987) concluded that European American teachers assigned a good or bad label to students and then gave different treatment to some students. The students began to accept the teacher's label and responded appropriately. Such practices can also affect students' motivation and academic achievement.

■ ■ ■ ■ ■ ▬▬▬

FOR ADDITIONAL INFORMATION

Learning styles, especially with multicultural learners, have considerable potential for teachers and learners. The following resources are recommended for teachers who wish to match teaching and learning activities with the students' learning styles.

Dunn, R., Beaudry, J. S., & Klavas, A. (1989). Survey of research on learning styles. *Educational Leadership, 46*(6), 50–58.
   In this theme issue dealing with diversity, Dunn, Beaudry, and Klavas comprehensively survey the research on learning styles.

Keefe, J. W. (1987). *Learning Style: Theory and Practice*. Reston, VA: National Association of Secondary School Principals.
   This succinct forty-eight-page monograph provides an overview of learning styles and focuses on assessment and application.

Theory into Practice, 23 (Winter, 1984).
   This entire issue deals with learning styles and provides twelve excellent readings, which range from the theoretical to practical application.

In Implementing Research 8.4, Schwartz (2001) prefers to use the term Latinas as she explains ways to improve the educational outcomes.

■　■　■　■　■　▬▬▬▬▬▬▬▬▬▬▬▬▬▬▬▬▬▬

IMPLEMENTING RESEARCH 8.4
IMPROVING EDUCATIONAL OUTCOMES FOR LATINAS

The educational challenges of Latinas are challenged by the high rate of poverty in their communities, the learning problems caused by a lack of English language proficiency, racism, and sexual harassment. Schwartz (2001) presents a range of strategies that serve Latinas and promote their academic achievement. These strategies will likely be most relevant for Latinas whose families have been in the United States for only a few generations, are poor, less fluent in English, and are more culturally isolated, although all Latinas can benefit from them. Some challenges facing Latinas are common to all students from poor and/or immigrant backgrounds. These families may lack communication skills, knowledge, and experiences to take advantage of educational, cultural, and social opportunities; and they may not have school readiness skills. Additional challenges to Latinas' education ironically relate to their strong and rich Hispanic culture. The belief that the welfare of the family and community supersedes individual aspirations is fairly fixed in the various Hispanic communities. For example, it can be strong enough to convince an adolescent to drop out of school to make money for the family, or it can hamper efforts to succeed if achievement requires competition rather than cooperation with other students. Also, Latina adolescents often assume adult roles in the home, for example, taking caring of younger children as well as elders. In general, Schwartz maintains that schools need to individually tailor supports they offer to Latinas and their families to accommodate their diverse needs and perspectives.

IMPLEMENTING THE RESEARCH
1. Educators need to convey the message that all students are expected to graduate and to succeed academically.
2. Educators can help Latinas understand how it is possible to value familial independence without subverting personal goals, because individual achievement reflects well on their community.
3. Schools can help Latinas develop the contacts and access to the community resources that will increase their opportunities for future fulfillment and are readily available to their more advantaged peers.
4. Schools can facilitate Latinas' learning and increase their feelings of attachment to the school community by providing the educational services needed to ensure their educational preparedness and by developing a fully multicultural curriculum.
5. Schools can create an environment in which students believe that their requests for help will receive a positive response.

Source: Schwartz, W. (2001). *Strategies for improving the educational outcomes for Latinas.* New York, NY: ERIC Clearinghouse on Urban Education. ERIC Document Reproduction Service No. ED 458344.

PROMOTING SELF-ESTEEM AND POSITIVE CULTURAL IDENTITIES

The educator's role in promoting self-esteem and positive cultural identities among learners will always be of paramount importance. Purkey and Novak (1984) have clearly demonstrated the relationship between self-esteem and school achievement. Emphatically stated, a student who feels "worthless," "not so good," and "inferior" will experience academic difficulties despite the teacher's most conscientious efforts. Drill,

■ ■ ■ ■ ■ ▬▬▬▬▬▬▬▬▬▬▬▬▬▬▬▬▬▬▬▬▬

FOLLOW THROUGH 8.9
RESPECTING HISPANIC CULTURES

Answer these questions about your school.

1. Is genuine respect shown for Hispanic learners and their culture?
2. Are efforts made to understand the cultural assets and contributions of Hispanic learners?
3. Are Hispanic people employed by the school and in what positions? Do Hispanics serve on committees and in decision-making capacities?
4. Are efforts under way to teach cultural understanding and acceptance?
5. Do teachers provide learners with chances to feel that the school appreciates their culture and individuality?
6. Do any policies (either overt or covert) limit opportunities to participate, for example, in extracurricular activities?
7. Are there efforts to diagnose and remediate specific learning problems of Hispanic learners?

Try these exercises.

Choosing Names: Ask children how they got their names—from a relative or more than one relative?

Surnames: What are they? Where do they come from? Discuss the origins of Castaneda, Chavez, Feliciano, and Vasquez.

Family Roots: Students can ask their families about family history and write information on a chart.

Name	Mother	Brothers
Birthplace	Father	Sisters
Date		

Family Tree: Have children construct a family tree using the information they collected under "Family Roots." Learning more about one's self and family has the potential for allowing learners to see the uniqueness or special qualities of all people and families.

Source: Tiedt, P. L. & Tiedt, I. M. (1995). *Multicultural Teaching,* 56, 60, 83. Boston: Allyn & Bacon.

memorization, and worksheets cannot overcome learners' feeling that they (or their culture) are inferior.

Although the problems associated with speaking one's mother tongue in a predominantly English-speaking environment deserves consideration, allowing (or even encouraging) Hispanic children to read appropriate children's literature written in Spanish might enhance their self-esteem and cultural identities.

Specifically, what can educators do to promote positive feelings of self-worth and cultural identity? First, all efforts should be genuine and honest; learners will detect hypocrisy if teachers say one thing but demonstrate another. Second, educators should plan programs that teach about the Hispanic culture and the proud history and accomplishments of the Spanish-speaking people. Third, rather than having "Spanish Art, Music, and Foods Week," educators must develop a curriculum that shows an appreciation for cultural diversity and that fully incorporates the Hispanic culture into all areas of the school curriculum. Last, educators can use literature and any other method

■ ■ ■ ■ ■

CULTURAL PORTRAIT
CARLOS—A HISPANIC AMERICAN LEARNER

Carlos S., a twelve-year-old boy of Spanish origin, is one grade level behind in his public elementary school, which is composed predominantly of black and Hispanic American children. A small percentage of Anglo students attend Carlos's school; while the majority of the teachers are Anglo, a few are black, and one is Hispanic. Carlos lives in a lower-socioeconomic Spanish-speaking neighborhood near the school. Carlos has several problems: His family speaks Spanish at home, but he is forbidden to speak Spanish at school. His difficulty with the English language has resulted in lower reading grades and achievement test scores (hence, the grade level behind), and he sees older boys dropping out of school and wonders when he can end his frustrations with school.

Carlos admits his frustrations to his best friend, another Hispanic American boy: Why does the teacher keep asking him to excel? Why does she say ignore blacks and Anglos when they pick on Hispanic children? Why doesn't she allow him to speak Spanish when his family (including his grandparents, aunts and uncles, and cousins) continues to speak Spanish? Carlos knows he has problems, and he thinks his teachers have almost given up on him.

WHAT CARLOS'S TEACHER CAN DO

Carlos's situation calls for immediate attention. First, whenever possible, Carlos needs to be allowed to speak Spanish. This is the language in which he is most proficient, and he cannot understand the reason for not being allowed to speak a language that both his family and his friends speak. Second, Carlos needs English-language instruction from qualified professionals who understand second-language instruction and who understand the problems Hispanic learners face. Third, Carlos needs appropriate diagnostic testing to determine his strengths and weaknesses, and carefully planned remediation to address his weaknesses.

Equally important is that the teachers in Carlos's school understand the Hispanic culture and situations of students like Carlos. Additionally, because the cultural diversity of the school population is not reflected in the teaching staff, the curriculum and learning environment probably reflects an Anglo perspective. More effort should be directed toward making Carlos's school more multicultural in nature and, in this case, more understanding and accepting of Hispanic American learners.

or activity that improves learner self-esteem, enhances cultural identities, and increases the appreciation of cultural differences.

SUMMING UP

Educators who plan teaching and learning experiences for Hispanic American children and adolescents should

1. Provide an educational environment in which Hispanic American children and adolescents feel that educators and other significant adults and peers respect their Spanish culture and background.
2. Allow Spanish to be spoken in schools, because it is the language spoken at home and in the neighborhoods, although learners should be taught to speak English.
3. Understand that language problems and differences are partly responsible for most academic problems.
4. Consider differences in learning styles when planning and implementing education programs.
5. Promote positive feelings toward learners' selves and their culture, because learners' self-esteem and cultural identities influence school achievement and social development.
6. Understand and appreciate cultural diversity to the degree that Hispanic learners do not feel their culture, socioeconomic class, families, religion, and language are wrong or inferior.
7. Use utmost caution not to label Hispanic learners on a basis of myth, stereotypes, prejudices, racism, or any other form of discrimination.
8. Use test data carefully, and remember that achievement tests, intelligence tests, and other measurement instruments might have a cultural bias toward European American standards and cultural expectations.

SUGGESTED LEARNING ACTIVITIES

1. Choose a typical Spanish-speaking student (from any of the Spanish-speaking cultures) and write a case study that explores individual and cultural characteristics. Consult with the school guidance counselor to better understand the child and his or her culture. After listing specific individual and cultural characteristics, plan an educational program that will meet the needs of this child.

2. Observe the overt learning behaviors of a Hispanic child to determine learning style. Consult with a remedial or resource teacher for help in interpreting the behaviors. After specifically determining the child's learning styles, tell how educators can plan appropriate learning opportunities based on these styles.

3. Choose a low-achieving Hispanic American student and assess his or her language proficiency. To what extent is the student's lower academic achievement a product of poor English skills? Interview the student to determine whether the immediate

and extended families speak Spanish or English. In what ways can the school's speech correctionist (working with language development specialists) assist this child? Plan an instructional program that addresses the student's problems with language and academic achievement.

SUGGESTIONS FOR COLLABORATIVE EFFORTS

Form groups of three or four that, if possible, represent our nation's cultural and gender diversity. Working collaboratively, focus your group's attention toward the following efforts:

1. Survey a group of Puerto Rican American and Mexican American children. Have each member of your group focus on a specific difference—cultural, language, religion, or familial. What similarities and differences exist? Also suggest ways educators can address intracultural differences within varying Spanish-speaking cultures.

2. With the increasing Spanish-speaking populations, it is becoming easier for Hispanic people to live in sections in which Spanish continues to be the mother tongue. Have each member of your group examine a specific language aspect. What language is spoken during recess, lunch times, or other breaks during the school day? Do teachers allow Spanish to be spoken in the classroom? Do teachers see the advantages of having one learner help another while speaking in Spanish? What language is spoken in the home? When parents and guardians speak to children in school, what language is spoken? Does the learner live in a predominantly Spanish-speaking neighborhood? What attempts have you made to understand the beauty of the Spanish language and to realize the language problems some students might experience?

3. Increasingly, the Spanish language will be spoken in the United States, especially because all demographic predictions suggest the Hispanic population will continue to increase. Some people feel that the United States should accept Spanish as the official second language; other people argue that English should be the only official language of the nation. In your group, discuss issues related to Spanish being increasingly spoken in the United States: whether Spanish should be accepted in an English-speaking country; whether schools should teach Spanish as well as English; whether instruction should occasionally be in Spanish; the implications for our society and schools; and other issues that your group feels are significant.

EXPANDING YOUR HORIZONS: ADDITIONAL
JOURNAL READINGS AND BOOKS

Cline, Z., & Necochea, J. (2001). Latino parents fighting entrenched racism. *Bilingual Research Journal, 25,* 1–26.
These authors tell about efforts to guarantee educational equity for their children.

Epstein, J. A., Botvin, G. J., & Diaz, T. (2000). Alcohol use among Hispanic adolescents: Role of linguistic acculturation and gender. *Journal of Alcohol and Drug Education, 45*(3), 18–32.
These authors conclude that a greater proportion of bilingual adolescents engage in drinking than more acculturated adolescents.

Erkut, S., Szalacha, L. A., Coll, C. G., & Alarcon, O. (2000). Puerto Rican early adolescents' self-esteem patterns. *Journal of Research on Adolescence, 10*(3), 339–364.

These researchers examined self-esteem in Puerto Rican early adolescents—gender differences were similar to those among European American youth.

Menchaca, V. D. (2001). Providing a culturally relevant curriculum for Hispanic children. *Multicultural Education, 8*(3), 18–20.

Menchaca maintains that a culturally relevant curriculum lets Hispanic students learn from a familiar cultural base and connect new knowledge to their own experiences.

Schwartz, W. (2000). New trends in language education for Hispanic students. New York, NY: ERIC Clearinghouse on Urban Education. (ERIC Documentation Reproduction Service No. 442913).

Schwartz focuses attention toward several directions: educational policy; teacher training and performance; effective elementary, middle, and secondary bilingual programs; instructional strategies, and effective tutoring.

Thompson, G. L. (2000). What students say about bilingual education. *Journal of At-Risk Issues, 6*(2), 24–32.

Thompson investigated what language minority and language majority high school students believe about various issues related to bilingual education programs.

EXPANDING YOUR STUDENTS' HORIZONS: APPROPRIATE HISPANIC AMERICAN BOOKS FOR CHILDREN AND ADOLESCENTS

Bachelis, Faren. *The Central Americans.* Chelsea House, 1990.
Becerra de Jenkins, Lyll. *So Loud a Silence.* Lodestar, 1996.
Bvelpre, Pura. *Firefly Summer.* Arte Publico, 1996.
Bierhorst, John. *The Mythology of Mexico and Central America.* Morrow, 1990.
Cisneros, Sandra. *The House on Mango Street.* Random House, 1991.
Codye, Corinn. *Vilma Martinez.* Raintree, 1990.
Cofer, J. O. *An Island Like You: Stories from the Barrio.* Orchard, 1995.
Cullison, Alan. *The South Americans.* Chelsea House, 1991.
Delacre, Lulu. *Arroz Con Leche* Scholastic, 1990.
Delacre, Lulu. *Las Navidades.* Scholastic, 1990.
De La Garza, Phyliss. *Chacho.* New Readers, 1990.
Dwyer, Christopher. *The Dominican Americans.* Chelsea House, 1991.
Fernandez, Roberta. *Intaglio: A Novel in Six Stories.* Arte Publico Press, 1990.
Gleiter, Jan, and Kathleen Thompson. *Jose Marti.* Raintree, 1990.
Hargrove, Jim. *Diego Rivera: Mexican Muralist.* Children's Press, 1990.
Hewitt, Joan. *Hector Lives in the United States Now: The Story of a Mexican American Child.* Harper-Collins, 1990.
Hurwitz, Johanna. *Class President.* William Morrow, 1990.
Lynn, Joseph. *Coconut Kind of Day: Island Poems.* Lothrop, Lee & Shepard, 1990.
Lopez, Tiffany Ana. *Growing Up Chicana/o.* Tupelo, 1993.
Lynn, Joseph. *A Wave in Her Pocket: Stories from Trinidad.* Clarion, 1991.
Myers, Walter Dean. *Toussaint L'Ouverture: The Fight for Haiti's Freedom.* Simon and Schuster, 1996.
Orr, Katherine. *My Grandpa and the Sea.* Lerner/Carolrhoda, 1990.
Paulsen, Gary. *The Crossing.* Dell, 1990.
Paredes, Americo. *George Washington Gomez.* Arte Publico Press, 1990.
Roe, Eileen. *Con Mi Hermano/With My Brother.* Bradbury, 1991.
Shute, Linda. *Rabbit Wishes.* Lothrop, 1995.
Soto, Gary. *Baseball in April and Other Stories.* Harcourt Brace Jovanovich, 1990.
Soto, Gary. *Local News: A Collection of Short Stories.* Harcourt Brace Jovanvich, 1993.

Sumption, Christine, and Kathleen Thompson. *Carlos Finlay*. Raintree, 1990.
Talbert, Marc. *Heart of a Jaguar*. Simon and Schuster, 1995.
Temple, Frances. *Tonight, by Sea*. Orchard, 1995.
Thompson, Kathleen. *Sor Juana Ines de la Cruz*. Raintree, 1990.
Velasquez, G. *Juanita Fights the School Board*. Piñata, 1994.
Velasquez, G. *Maya's Divided World*. Piñata, 1995.
Velasquez, G. *Tommy Stands Alone*. Piñata, 1995.

TEACHING AND LEARNING IN A DIVERSE SOCIETY

Part III focuses on what educators should consider when planning and implementing programs that teach acceptance and respect for cultural diversity. Chapters 9, 10, 11, 12, and 13 focus on curriculum, instruction, parents and families, and administrators and special school personnel, respectively. The emphasis continues to be on promoting multiculturalism and implementing effective multicultural education programs.

CHAPTER NINE

CURRICULAR EFFORTS

Understanding the material and activities in this chapter will help the reader to:

- Distinguish between the purported changes and the actual progress people from culturally different backgrounds have achieved in U.S. society
- Prepare a multicultural teaching unit that addresses the needs of learners from culturally different backgrounds and teaches European American learners about diversity
- State several reasons a school needs a multicultural education program that emphasizes an "across-the-curriculum" approach and encompasses the total school environment
- List and describe several methods for extending the multicultural education curriculum to the community and having it pervade extracurricular activities
- Understand the importance of having school administrators, faculty, and staff reflect the cultural diversity of the student body

OVERVIEW

The tremendous cultural diversity that characterizes U.S. school systems sends a strong message to educators and curriculum developers at both elementary and secondary levels. They must develop a curriculum that addresses the needs of learners and creates a school environment that reflects cultural diversity. To implement such an across-the-curriculum approach, they must carefully select bias-free teaching materials, choose evaluation instruments that take into account cultural differences, encourage appropriate community involvement, and provide extracurricular activities that involve all learners. The fundamental aim of culturally responsive pedagogy is to *empower* ethnically diverse students through academic success, cultural affiliation, and personal efficacy. Knowledge in the form of curriculum content is central to this empowerment. To be effective, this knowledge must be accessible to students and connected to their lives and experiences outside of school (Gay, 2000).

In Implementing Research 9.1, Sleeter (2000) suggests that children and adolescents need an empowering multicultural curriculum.

Five key observations provide the conceptual contours and organizational direction:

1. Curriculum content is crucial to academic performance and is an essential component of culturally responsive pedagogy.
2. The most common source of curriculum content used in classrooms is textbooks. Therefore, the quality of textbooks is an important factor in student achievement and culturally responsive teaching.

■ ■ ■ ■ ■ ■

IMPLEMENTING RESEARCH 9.1
CREATING A MULTICULTURAL CURRICULUM

Sleeter (2000) explains that a good multicultural curriculum is an ongoing process. Educators and multiculturalists are never finished with the multicultural curriculum, because they continually learn as they deal with various issues. In fact, the curriculum that educators teach is only as good as their understanding of the content and issues being taught, about diverse people, about the society in which we live, and about knowledge of the various academic disciplines.

In her article, Sleeter focuses on knowledge in a multicultural society being a political issue, how people center on their own cultural perspectives, social construction of theories, subjugation and liberation (e.g., women, people with disabilities, and people with different sexual orientations). She also explains that oppressed groups are durable, strong, and active. To support her assertion, she offers the example of slavery, under which some slaves worked for their freedom rather than being passive and powerless. One strength of Sleeter's article is its comprehensiveness—she addresses a great number of points and issues, often in thought-provoking ways.

IMPLEMENTING THE RESEARCH
1. Educators should remember that the multicultural curriculum is an ongoing process, a work in progress.
2. Educators who are most effective realize that a multicultural curriculum is more than learning superficialities about holidays and historical events—students need to learn about the racism and oppression that affect oppressed cultural groups.
3. The multicultural curriculum should work with children and adolescents to address the issues of race, gender, and class, rather trying to focus on only one entity.

Source: Sleeter, C. E. (2000). Creating an empowering multicultural curriculum. *Race, Gender, and Class,* 7(3), 178–196.

3. Curriculum content that is meaningful to students improves their learning.
4. Relevant curriculum content for teaching African American, Latino, Asian American, and American Indian students includes information about the histories, cultures, contributions, experiences, perspectives, and issues of their respective ethnic groups.
5. Curriculum content is derived from various sources, many of which exist outside the formal boundaries of schooling (Gay, 2000).

TOWARD CULTURAL DIVERSITY

Overall school curriculum and teaching and learning situations should reflect the cultural diversity of our nation. Although the *Brown* desegregation case and the civil rights legislation (Ornstein & Levine, 1993) of a number of years ago contributed to better

■ ■ ■ ■ ■

IMPLEMENTING RESEARCH 9.2

GIFTED EDUCATION AND CULTURALLY DIVERSE STUDENTS

Ford and Harmon (2001) explain that a debate centers on the issue of excellence and equity in gifted educational programs, namely that students of diverse cultural backgrounds are often under-represented. They maintain that the problem is fueled by the "deficit perspective," or the idea that populations of culturally different backgrounds have deficits rather than differences. Such thinking hinders educators from recognizing the gifts and talents of all students.

Hindrances to progress include:

- Deficit ideologies that limit access and opportunity
- Testing and assessment issues, for example, extensive reliance on tests
- IQ-based definitions and theories
- Achievement-based definitions and theories
- Inadequate policies and practices

Ford and Harmon (2001) offer several recommendations for change.

IMPLEMENTING THE RESEARCH

1. Educators can adopt contemporary theories and definitions of intelligence and giftedness, for example, theories of multiple intelligences
2. Educators can adopt culturally sensitive assessment and testing instruments.
3. Educators can identify and serve underachievers and students of low socioeconomic status.
4. Educators can gain multicultural preparation that better prepares them to assess and teach gifted students from varying cultural backgrounds.
5. Educators can develop effective home–school partnerships.

Source: Ford, D. Y., & Harmon, D. A. (2001). Equity and excellence: Providing access to gifted education for culturally diverse students. *The Journal of Secondary Gifted Education, 12*(3), 141–147.

treatment and acceptance of groups from culturally different backgrounds, there is much room for improvement. Educators should place change and progress in proper perspective. In Implementing Research 9.2, Ford and Harmon (2001) maintain that African and Hispanic American and American Indian students are often underrepresented in gifted programs.

THE ILLUSION OF CHANGE AND PROGRESS

Without doubt, U.S. education is making progress toward better relations between groups of people. The accomplishments of people of differing cultures and of women are recognized; many educators welcome youngsters with disabilities into their classrooms;

■ ■ ■ ■ ■

FOLLOW THROUGH 9.1
DETERMINING "SIGNIFICANT" CHANGE

Undoubtedly, the U.S. education system has made progress toward providing a culturally relevant curriculum—more materials reflect diversity and provide objective portrayals of females, people from culturally different backgrounds, and people with disabilities. Visit several schools to determine the extent of the changes—how far have we come? What still needs to be done? Are changes superficial or do they show genuine commitment?

most teachers work to reduce racist and sexist behavior in their classrooms; and many work to develop or obtain curricular materials free from bias and prejudice.

Consider, however, the racism and nonacceptance that continue to plague society—the growing popularity of "skinheads" and neo-Nazi groups, for instance. In addition, school practices often document either a lack of understanding of learners from culturally different backgrounds or a lack of acceptance and respect for their cultural differences.

The Continuing Need for Change in Educational Practices

Consider these observations from a number of education researchers.

- African American students suffer academically because their learning styles tend to be oriented toward cooperation, content about people, discussion and hands-on work, and whole-to-part learning (Shade, 1982).
- Young Navajo learners sometimes interpret tests as games (in contrast to Anglo students, who approach them with a more serious attitude). This "games" approach is a result of home socialization (Deyhle, 1985).
- Bilingual education teachers often find themselves in conflict with regular classroom teachers over the specific needs of students with limited English proficiency (Sleeter & Grant, 1999).
- Educators interact with, call on, and praise students who are Anglo, male, and middle-class more often than they do other students in the same classroom (Sadker & Sadker, 1982).
- Although curricular materials and textbooks reflect cultural diversity more accurately than they have in the past, Indian, Asian, and Hispanic Americans are still barely visible in the curriculum (Sleeter & Grant, 1999).
- Because students are often grouped homogeneously, there is a tendency to segregate learners by culture and by socioeconomic group.

There continues to be much room for genuine change in teaching and learning situations, compatible treatment of people who are disabled or from culturally diverse backgrounds, improvement of the cultural and ethnic compositions of school faculty and staff, and equitable representation of all people, regardless of culture, in textbooks and other curricular materials. This discussion and the accompanying recommendations do not downplay the significant progress that our society and schools have already made. It is necessary, however, to perceive society and schools objectively and to plan an appropriate agenda for positively reconstructing society and schools during the twenty-first century.

Garcia (1984) contends that schools should accept responsibility for translating illusion into reality and that they can serve as a significant force in countering discrimination and the various "-isms" that affect people from culturally diverse backgrounds, women, and the disabled.

FROM ILLUSION TO REALITY: RESPONDING TO RACISM, DISCRIMINATION, ETHNOCENTRISM, AND STEREOTYPES

Racism has many damaging and long-lasting effects on the lives of children and adolescents, the character of society, the quality of our civilization, and peoples' prospects for the future. Before an illusion of racial harmony and justice for all can become a reality, schools must take a powerful and pivotal role in teaching about racism and in working toward acceptance and respect for all people, regardless of racial and cultural background. Schools can play a powerful role in combating racism and educational inequities by confronting and challenging racism, hiring teachers from diverse cultures, developing and implementing a genuine multicultural curriculum, improving pedagogical practices that address the needs of all learners, and teaching character development and improvement of self-esteem (Pine & Hilliard, 1990).

Garcia refers to ethnocentrism as the notion some people hold that their group is better than other groups. Ethnocentrism can extend from mild group pride to extreme arrogance. The response to ethnocentrism is complex; some ethnocentrism is good, but too much group pride can result in a negative force—for example, the claims that the Aryan race is superior to all others. A society and its schools must seek to understand the many forms of ethnocentrism and work toward keeping ethnocentrism under control among individuals and student groups (Garcia, 1984).

Schools' responsibilities in our multicultural society extend to countering the dangers of stereotyping, from which even educators are not exempt. What steps can educators take to transform illusions of equality and justice into reality?

First, teachers should be aware of their own biases and stereotypes. Through self-examination or through cultural awareness workshops, educators can gain a better understanding of their attitudes toward people who are culturally different, women, and people with disabilities. Second, as cultural understandings clarify stereotypical beliefs, educators see the need for expecting as much from learners of differing cultural backgrounds as they do from other students. Too often, teachers tend to "make it easy for the downtrodden" (Garcia, 1984, p. 107). Although educators should recognize the plight of minorities, they must encourage minority students to excel in all areas of academic pursuit. Third, educators should examine curricular materials for evidence of stereotyping. Specifically, does the material present females and minorities in a realistic, nonstereotypical manner? Does the material accurately reflect a holistic view of the past in terms of the contributions of females and people of differing cultural backgrounds in U.S. history (Garcia, 1984)? Fourth, educators should strive to diversify classes of homogeneous ability levels, which have the potential for segregating students by race or socioeconomic group. Heterogeneous classes and cooperative learning activities are very important.

Because of landmark court decisions, civil rights legislation, and overall improved race relations, U.S. society is not as divided racially and culturally as it was several decades ago. We must not, however, allow illusions of grandeur to overshadow reality. Racism, discrimination, and stereotypes continue to exist and to take a heavy toll on people of differing cultural background, women, and the people with disabilities. Rather than accepting the status quo as the most equitable we can achieve, school curricula should deliberately instill in children and adolescents a sense of respect and acceptance for all people, regardless of their cultural and individual differences.

PLANNING AND IMPLEMENTING A MULTICULTURAL EDUCATION CURRICULUM

The Total School Environment

Multiculturalism should extend to and permeate all aspects of the school. In fact, multiculturalism should be such a basic part of the school that it becomes a natural and accepted aspect of the daily routine.

One way that multiculturalism can permeate the curriculum is through an approach that incorporates literature that is culturally appropriate for children and adolescents in teaching the various areas of the curriculum. Norton (1999) recommends a multicultural reading and literature program that crosses curriculum areas. Multicultural literature is essential to all areas of the curriculum to help students grow in understanding themselves and others. Through careful selection and sharing of multicultural reading materials, educators help students learn to identify with the people who created the stories, whether of the past or present. Folk tales, myths, and legends clarify the values and beliefs of people. By reading the great stories on which cultures have been founded, learners can discover the threads that weave the past with the present and the themes and values that interconnect people of all cultures.

Reform Efforts

As stated earlier, teaching units are an appropriate and viable means of reaching specific objectives. Serious reform efforts toward a more realistic portrayal of all people, however, will require a major overhaul of elementary and secondary school curricula. What steps can educators take to ensure that elementary and secondary school curricula reflect the cultural diversity of U.S. society?

Proposals for improving the achievement of students of color are often doomed to failure, largely due to their allegiance to a deficit orientation—that is, concentrating on what ethnically, racially, and linguistically different students do not have and cannot do.

■ ■ ■ ■ ■ ▬▬▬▬▬▬

FOLLOW THROUGH 9.2
RESEARCHING CULTURAL DIVERSITY

Separate into small groups that each selects a different cultural group to research. The following questions may serve as guidelines:

1. Where did the racial, religious, or ethnic group you are studying originate?
2. Why did they leave their homeland?
3. Where in the United States did they originally settle?
4. What kind of work did they do when they first came here?
5. What was their native language?
6. What was their dominant religion?
7. What is a popular myth or legend from their culture?
8. What are three notable themes from their literature?
9. Who are three notable authors from this group?

Source: Minderman, L. (1990). Literature and multicultural education. *Instructor, 99*(7), 22–23.

High-profile innovations of this kind that appear to be having some significant positive effects on the achievement of students of color include Reading Recovery, DISTAR, and Accelerated Schools. However, their effects may not stand the test of time or be as comprehensive as they claim. They may inadvertently cause students to compromise their ethnic and cultural identity to attain academic achievement. These programs attempt to deal with academic performance by divorcing it from other factors that affect achievement, such as culture, ethnicity, and personal experience (Gay, 2000).

Much more cultural content is needed in all school curricula about all ethnic groups of color. The need is especially apparent in math and science for ethnic groups other than African Americans. This is true for those subjects in which some initiatives are already underway as well as those that have not changed at all. This means designing more multicultural literacy programs in secondary schools and more math and science programs at all grade levels; teaching explicit information about gender contributions, issues, experiences, and achievement effects *within ethnic groups;* and pursuing more sustained efforts to incorporate content about ethnic and cultural diversity in regular school subjects and skills taught on a routine basis (Gay, 2000).

Guidelines for Developing Multicultural Curricula*

1. Reform the curriculum in such a way that it regularly presents diverse perspectives, experiences, and contributions. Similarly, present and teach concepts that represent diverse cultural groups and both sexes.

Source: Sleeter, C. E., & Grant, C. A. (1999). *Making choices for multicultural education: Five approaches to race, class, and gender.* 2nd ed. Columbus, OH: Merrill, 153–155.

2. Include materials and visual displays that are free of race, gender, and disability stereotypes, and that include members of all cultural groups in a positive manner.
3. Embrace concepts, rather than fragments of information, related to diverse groups.
4. Emphasize contemporary culture as much as historical culture, and represent groups as active and dynamic. The curriculum, for example, should include not only the women's suffrage movement but also more contemporary problems confronting women.
5. Strive to make the curriculum a "total effort," with multicultural aspects permeating all subject areas and all phases of the school day.
6. Make sure the curriculum uses nonsexist language.
7. Support a curriculum that endorses bilingual education and the vision of a multilingual society.
8. Draw on children's experiential background in teaching and learning. Base community and curricular concepts on children's daily life and experiences.
9. Insist on a curriculum that allows equal access for all students. All students, for example, should have the freedom to enroll in college-preparatory courses and other special curricular activities.

Diversity comes in many forms, all of which need to be addressed in the curriculum. We maintain that sexual orientation should be included in a definition of multicultural education as well as reflected in curricular efforts. Gay and lesbian adolescents confront many of the same biological, cognitive, and social developmental changes as their heterosexual counterparts. Fear of and misunderstandings about homosexuality can result in negative consequences for adolescents struggling with identity formation that differs from that of the majority of their peers.

By learning about the concerns of gay and lesbian youth, middle and secondary educators can break the barrier of silence that contributes to the difficulties and hurt these teens face. Gay and lesbian adolescents bear a double burden: They experience harassment, violence, and suicidal tendencies because of their age and their sexual preference. They sometimes feel fearful, withdrawn, depressed, and full of despair. Curricular efforts should address the needs of gay and lesbian adolescents by including

■ ■ ■ ■ ■ ■

FOLLOW THROUGH 9.3

**IDENTIFYING PRACTICAL APPROACHES TO
A CULTURALLY RELEVANT CURRICULUM**

Many preservice readers of this book have had field experience in schools; in-service teachers already have teaching experience in schools. Working in groups of three or four, prepare a list of practical approaches that could be used to make the curriculum more representative of diversity in the United States and its schools. Include such tools as curricular materials showing diversity and the provision of bilingual language programs on your list.

age-appropriate literature to explain sexual orientation as well as others' experiences with being gay or lesbian. Such books help readers develop self-understanding and gain insight into the special developmental needs of gay and lesbian youth (Vare & Norton, 1998).

The Hidden Curriculum

Although some aspects of the curriculum are readily discernible to children and adolescents attending a school, other aspects are more subtle and may be equally influential. For example, we have little difficulty determining whether people of differing backgrounds are represented honestly and adequately in textbooks and other curricular materials. We can also ascertain with relative ease whether tracking and ability grouping have resulted in the segregation and relegation to second-class status of all people from different cultural backgrounds and lower-class students. There is, however, another equally important curriculum, one that has a powerful influence on children and adolescents. This very subtle "hidden curriculum" affects learners of all races and cultures. Mrs. Brunson, in Case Study 9.1, takes a stand against the hidden curriculum in her school.

■ ■ ■ ■ ■

CASE STUDY 9.1
THE "HIDDEN CURRICULUM"

Mrs. Brunson, a teacher at Calhoun Middle School, knows she will have to take a stand at the faculty meeting. No longer can she let injustice prevail. Her only decision is how to make her point in such a way that positive action will result.

"We have a hidden curriculum," she says calmly and matter-of-factly. Although the school's philosophy purports to promote equality and equitable treatment for all, it does not act on that belief. Young adolescents learn from a hidden curriculum that teaches as much as or more than the planned curriculum.

Mrs. Brunson has numerous examples to substantiate her point: school policies that recognize only middle-class European American expectations; a media center that is oriented predominantly toward European Americans; instructional practices and academic expectations that address European American learning styles; and participants in extracurricular activities are mostly European American. What message is the school sending to learners of diverse cultural backgrounds? While the curriculum seeks to show acceptance and respect for diversity, the hidden curriculum conveys an almost totally opposite picture. Learners from different cultural backgrounds often feel unaccepted and perceive that they must adjust to middle-class, white values and customs.

Although the faculty expresses some skepticism, it is apparent that they have not considered the impact of the hidden curriculum. In fact the school is not as multicultural as some believe.

Mrs. Brunson feels better for having expressed herself. Genuine change will be slow, and supporters of the status quo will challenge efforts, but at least the faculty recognizes the problem. This is a first and significant step.

■ ■ ■ ■ ■ ▬▬▬▬

FOLLOW THROUGH 9.4
IDENTIFYING THE HIDDEN CURRICULUM

Visit an elementary or secondary school (or consider your own if you already teach) to determine the "hidden curriculum." Try to identify three curricular aspects that might be described as "hidden" and offer possible actions for addressing the problem.

Problem
Sports teams are segregated by culture: African Americans play basketball; European Americans play tennis.

Possible Action
1. Have orientation sessions for sports teams, making clear that equal access is the policy.
2. Speak with individual students and encourage their participation.
3. Teach during physical education classes that students are not limited to specific sports by cultural background.

What specific aspects might be included in a hidden curriculum? It might comprise any number of events, behavior expectations, and attitudes that might appear relatively unobtrusive to white, middle-class learners, but might appear out of character or context to learners of culturally different backgrounds. Representative examples might include teacher behaviors and expectations conveyed both verbally and nonverbally; textbooks and other curricular materials that portray white, middle-class values and orientations; segregation due to tracking or ability-grouping policies; educators' and other students' degrees of acceptance and attitudes toward learners from different cultural backgrounds; and the degree of acceptance of language differences. In other words, middle- or upper-class European American students might expect their teacher to encourage them to compete and excel above others in the class; this same teacher expectation, however, might be anathema to American Indian learners. Educators must make a deliberate effort to examine all their behaviors (both conscious and unconscious) to determine what hidden messages they are conveying and to assess carefully every aspect of the curriculum and the total school environment to determine whether learners from different cultural backgrounds are being given a different message from that sent to white students.

GUIDELINES FOR A MULTICULTURAL CURRICULUM

As with all curricular efforts, a multicultural curriculum should be carefully matched with goals and objectives and use established guidelines. Although each program should reflect the needs and goals of the respective school, the following guidelines can serve as a basis for multicultural curricular development (Hernandez, 1989).

1. Emphasize the interrelationship of multiple groups (i.e., ethnic, religious, regional, socioeconomic, language), rather than treating individual groups separately or in isolation. Such multiple-group emphasis diminishes the likelihood of stereotyping and facilitates integration of multicultural content into the overall curriculum.
2. Integrate multicultural perspectives, as appropriate, in all content areas. Although most frequently associated with the social sciences, language, literature, art, and music, multicultural perspectives are valid and applicable in areas such as mathematics, science, home economics, and physical education.
3. Use a variety of instructional approaches and materials appropriate to the students' maturity level. In particular, teacher strategies should aim to accommodate differences in learning styles and to maximize academic achievement.
4. Focus on the development of cognitive as well as affective skills. Assess learning outcomes in terms of knowledge, attitudes, and skills.
5. Emphasize school and area populations, locally oriented activities, and community resources (Hernandez, 1989, pp. 176–177).

Several other important implications for culturally responsive pedagogical practices are embedded in the nature and effects of culturally diverse curriculum content examined thus far. One is the need to *regularly* provide students with more accurate cultural information about groups of color, in order to fill knowledge voids and correct existing distortions. This information needs to be capable of facilitating many different kinds of learning—cognitive, affective, social, political, personal, and moral. It should be multiethnic, cover a wide range of perspectives and experiences, and encompass both tangible (artifacts) and intangible (values, beliefs) aspects of culture. No single content source is capable of doing all of this alone. Therefore, curriculum designers should always use a variety of content sources from different genres and disciplines, including textbooks, literature, mass media, music, personal experiences, and social science research. Information derived from new and emerging ethnic-centered and feminist literary and social science scholarship should also be included (Gay, 2000).

Assessing the Need for Curricular Change

Before planning to adopt a multicultural curriculum, the school must assess its needs to determine the direction and extent of the change. Curricular assessment should also be an ongoing and integral part of curriculum development (Ramsey, 1987). Here are some questions a school should consider in a needs assessment.

1. Do multicultural perspectives permeate the entire school curriculum and environment?
2. Do the attitudes of teachers, administrators, and staff members indicate a willingness to accept and respect cultural diversity?
3. Do textbooks and other curricular materials recognize the value of cultural diversity and gender and social class differences?
4. Do curricular activities and methods provide learners with opportunities to collaborate and cooperate?

5. Do extracurricular activities reflect cultural diversity?
6. Do curricular planning efforts reflect the views and opinions of parents and other community people?
7. Do curricular efforts include bilingual perspectives or provide assistance for students with limited English-speaking skills?

Case Study 9.2 shows how the educators at Lockhaven Elementary decided to assess the need for change in their school.

Selecting Bias-Free Curricular and Teaching and Learning Materials

Over the years a great deal of research has been done to determine if textbooks are dealing adequately with groups of color and cultural diversity issues. The variables studied include narrative text, visuals, language, and overall tone. These have been filtered through different assessment criteria such as quantitative inclusion, accuracy of

■ ■ ■ ■ ■

CASE STUDY 9.2
ASSESSING THE NEED FOR CHANGE

The educators at Lockhaven Elementary knew their school was experiencing demographic changes. Many of the European American families had moved to the suburbs, the African American population had grown to some extent, and there had been an influx of Asian and Hispanic American students. The curriculum and educational practices, however, had stayed basically the same.

The school counselor was the first to mention a need for change, but others had also begun to recognize that the school was no longer meeting the needs of the current student population. That the school should assess the need for change became clear, but the questions remained of where to begin and what to assess. Suggestions poured in as the counselor took notes:

- The actual cultural composition of the school and the community
- The cultural composition of the administration, faculty, and staff
- The curriculum and the extent to which it addresses cultural diversity
- The instructional practices and the extent to which they meet the learning styles of learners from differing cultural backgrounds
- The school policies and expectations of students
- The extracurricular program and its accessibility to all learners
- The attitudes (recognition, respect, acceptance) of the educators
- The media center and the extent to which its holdings demonstrate a respect for diversity of all types

The list could go on and on, the counselor thought, but the school had made the initial effort. They had recognized the need for change, and the needs assessment was under way.

information, placement of diversity features, authenticity, and significance (Gay, 2000).

Textbooks give little attention to different groups of color interacting with each other. Typically these groups are presented interacting only with European Americans and various segments of mainstream society. Textbooks continue to be flawed with respect to their treatment of ethnic and cultural diversity for several reasons. First, there is an imbalance across ethnic groups of color, with most attention given to African Americans and their experiences. This disparity is consistent across types of instructional materials, subjects, and grade levels. Second, the content included about ethnic issues is rather bland, conservative, conformist, and "safe." It tends to emphasize harmonious relations among racial groups. Contentious issues and individuals are avoided, and the unpleasant side of society and cultural diversity is either sanitized or bypassed entirely. Third, gender and social-class disparities prevail within the representations of ethnic groups, with preference given to males, the middle class, and events and experiences that are closely aligned with mainstream European American values, beliefs, and standard of behavior. Fourth, textbook discussions about ethnic groups and their concerns are not consistent across time, with contemporary issues being overshadowed by historical ones (Gay, 2000).

The inadequacies of textbook coverage of cultural diversity can be avoided by including accurate, wide-ranging, and appropriately contextualized content about different ethnic groups' histories, cultures, and experiences in classroom instruction on a regular basis. The efforts need not be constrained by lack of information and materials. Plenty of resources exist about most ethnic groups, and in such variety that all subjects and grades taught in schools can be served adequately. Since this information is not always in textbooks, teachers need to develop the habit of using other resources to complement or even replace them. Students also should be taught how to critique textbooks for the accuracy of their multicultural content and how to compensate.

Other equally important concerns related to bias in textbooks are omissions and distortions. Omission refers to information left out of a textbook, and a distortion is a lack of balance or systematic omission. Because of omissions, members of some cultural and ethnic groups are virtually unrepresented in textbooks. Hispanic Americans, Asian Americans, American Indians, and women continue to be underrepresented in educational materials (Hernandez, 1989). The "invisibility" of a group implies that it has less value or significance in U.S. society than others. "Invisibility" applies most often to women, culturally diverse people, people with disabilities, and the elderly (Gollnick & Chinn, 2002).

Distortions result from inaccurate or unbalanced impressions. History and reading materials too often ignore the presence and realities of certain groups in contemporary society, or they confine treatment to negative experiences. In some cases, they provide a single point of view about events that may be technically correct but is nevertheless misleading (Hernandez, 1989).

Sexism and sexist language are other factors to consider when selecting textbooks and other teaching materials. Gollnick and Chinn (2002) have called attention to the sexism that often occurs in children's and adolescents' textbooks, especially at the elementary school level. Children who were asked to draw an early caveman drew only pictures of cavemen. In contrast, when instructed to draw "cave people," the children generate drawings of men, women, and children. In classrooms, teachers can point out sexist language to students. When words appear to exclude women as full participants in society or limit their occupational options, teachers can provide alternatives—for example, mail carrier and police officer as alternatives to mailman and policeman (Gollnick & Chinn, 2002).

The challenge facing multicultural educators is to select textbooks and other materials that objectively represent various groups and people who have been traditionally either ignored or misrepresented. Table 9.1 provides educators with a means of evaluating written material to determine its suitability in our increasingly multicultural schools.

Evaluating Curricular Efforts

Evaluating the multicultural curriculum to determine overall program strengths and weaknesses and to assess how well it meets individual learner needs is as important as the actual content and teaching methods the teacher uses. One basic criterion is to determine whether teaching and learning situations reflect multiculturalism (Sleeter & Grant, 1999).

Other measures of program effectiveness include oral and written tests (teacher-made and standardized), sociograms, questionnaires, surveys, student projects, interviews, anecdotal information, and discussion groups. Indicators such as attendance records, class participation, and incidence of disruptive behavior also provide clues about student acceptance of and interest in the program. Many of these procedures are conducive to staff, parent, and student involvement. Whatever evaluation is used, the information collected should be well documented, relevant, and useful. The validity of evaluation depends on the questions asked, behaviors observed, and efforts made to sample randomly and to apply common standards.

Lee and Johnson (2000) maintain that the number of interracial families in the United States has tripled over the past thirty years. The proportion of mixed-raced births is increasing twenty-six times as fast as that of any other group in the United States. Lee and Johnson (2000), in Implementing Research 9.3, explain that the increased number of mixed-race births calls for interracial storybooks.

■ ■ ■ ■ ■ ▬▬

FOLLOW THROUGH 9.5
EVALUATING THE CURRICULUM

Evaluating the curriculum for cultural relevance, objectivity, and accuracy should be a major part of any multicultural education program. Suggest eight to ten criteria for evaluating the curriculum to determine whether it recognizes and shows respect for cultural diversity.

TABLE 9.1 How to Analyze Books for Racism and Sexism

These guidelines are a starting point and are designed to help educators detect racist and sexist bias in children's story books, picture books, primers, and fiction.

1. *Check the illustrations.* Look for stereotypes, oversimplified generalizations about a particular group, race, or sex that generally carry derogatory implications. Look for variations that in any way demean or ridicule characters because of their race or sex.

   Look for tokenism. If there are culturally diverse characters, are they just like Anglo Americans, but tinted or colored? Do all culturally diverse faces look stereotypically alike, or are they depicted as genuine individuals?

   Look at the lifestyles of the people in the book. Are culturally diverse characters and their settings depicted in such a way that they contrast unfavorably with an unstated norm of Anglo American middle-class suburbia? For example, culturally diverse people are often associated with the ghetto, migrant labor, or "primitive" living. If the story does attempt to depict another culture, does it go beyond oversimplifications of reality to offer genuine insights into another lifestyle?

2. *Check the story line.* Civil rights legislation has led publishers to weed out many insulting passages and illustrations, particularly in stories with black themes, but the attitudes still find expression in less obvious ways. The following checklist suggests some of the various subtle forms of bias to watch for:

   Relationships: Do Anglo Americans in the story have the power and make the decisions? Do culturally diverse people function in essentially subservient roles?

   Standard for success: What does it take for a character to succeed? To gain acceptance, do culturally diverse characters have to exhibit superior qualities—excel in sports, get A's, and so forth?

   Viewpoint: How are "problems" presented, conceived, and resolved in the story? Are culturally diverse people themselves considered to be "the problem"? Do solutions ultimately depend on the benevolence of an Anglo American?

   Sexism: Are the achievements of girls and women based on their own initiative and intelligence, or is their success due to their good looks or to their relationships with boys?

Are sex roles incidental or paramount to characterization and plot? Could the same story be told if the sex roles were reversed?

3. *Consider the effects of the book on the child's self-image and self-esteem.* Are norms established that limit the child's aspirations and self-esteem? What does it do to African American children to be continuously bombarded with images of white as beautiful, clean, and virtuous, and black as evil, dirty, and menacing? What happens to a girl's aspirations when she reads that boys perform all the brave and important deeds? What about a girl's self-esteem if she is not fair of skin and slim of body?

4. *Consider the authors' or illustrators' qualifications.* Read the biographical material on the jacket flap or on the back cover. If a story deals with a culturally diverse theme, what qualifies the authors or illustrators to deal with this topic? If they are not members of the culturally diverse group being written about, is there anything in the authors' or illustrators' backgrounds that would specifically recommend them for this book?

   Similarly, a book that has to do with the feelings and insights of women should be more carefully examined if it is written by a man, unless the book's avowed purpose is to present a male viewpoint.

   These observations do not deny the ability of writers to empathize with experiences other than those of their own sex or race, but the chances of their writing as honestly and as authentically about the experiences of other genders and races are not as good.

5. *Look at the copyright date.* Books on culturally diverse themes—usually hastily conceived—suddenly began appearing in the mid-1960s. There followed a growing number of "culturally diverse experience" books to meet the new market demand, but they were still written by Anglo American authors and reflected an Anglo point of view. Only in the late 1960s and early 1970s did the children's book world begin even to remotely reflect the realities of a multiracial society, and it has only just begun to reflect feminist concerns.

Adapted from: www.osi.hu/iep/Workshops/anti_bias/ten_ways.html, www.birchlane.davis.ca.us/library/10quick.html, and www.misf.org/educatorstoolkit/mce/evaluatingbooks.html. Retrieved October 17, 2002.

IMPLEMENTING RESEARCH 9.3
INTERRACIAL STORYBOOKS

Lee and Johnson (2000) propose that effective multicultural education programs require well-written multicultural literature and curricular materials that represent all students, including interracial children. To accept and affirm the pluralism in our schools, educators should recognize interracial children and integrate interracial literature in the school curriculum.

The benefits of using interracial literature include:

- Interracial literature, both fiction and nonfiction, can help build a sound personal identity in interracial children.
- Interracial literature changes the way children look at their world, by offering different perspectives of people and events.
- Interracial literature shows people who traditionally have been denied realistic images of themselves, their families, community, and culture.

IMPLEMENTING THE RESEARCH

1. Educators need to recognize interracial children and the unique challenges these students might face.
2. Educators need to identify accurate and high-quality fiction and nonfiction and curricular materials that are free from stereotypes.
3. Educators and researchers need to conduct studies of the impact of interracial literature and its use in classrooms with interracial students.

Source: Lee, G. L., & Johnson, W. (2000). The need for interracial storybooks in effective multicultural classrooms. *Multicultural Education, 8*(2), 28–30.

FOR ADDITIONAL INFORMATION
INTERNET ADDRESSES

Multiculture Nonsexist Education Home Page
www.ops.org/mne/multi.home.html Provides a look at the Omaha Public Schools' efforts to address equity issues and to respect individual differences of all students.

LSU: Multicultural Resources
http://lasalle.edu/services/mcis/multi_a.htm Provides a wealth of multicultural resources for elementary and secondary schools.

MilbankWeb: Research Resources: Pathfinders: Multicultural Education
http://lweb.tc.columbia.edu/rr/mc/ Provides access to the Milbank Memorial Library of Teach-

ers College, Columbia University, which contains the world's largest collection of materials on the educating professions

Multicultural Literature—Secondary Classroom
www.indiana.edu/~eric_rec/ieo/bibs/multisec.html Provides information on multicultural literature in secondary classrooms.

Multicultural Education—Guide
www.lps.org.instruction/guide/multiguide.html Provides a description of multicultural education in the Lincoln Public Schools and the identification, selection, and infusion of specific knowledge, attitudes, and skills.

A MULTICULTURAL EDUCATION UNIT

Our premise in this book is that multicultural education should be a total school curriculum and environmental approach rather than an occasional unit. We do, however, recognize that the situation should not be "either/or," nor should it become a battle of multicultural education curriculum versus the unit approach. We firmly believe, however, that a once-a-year (or even an every-semester) effort in the form of a multicultural week or perhaps a two- or three-week unit is insufficient to teach knowledge of and respect for cultural diversity. We remind readers, therefore, to consider units as a part of a total curriculum effort, perhaps as a means of addressing one or more specific objectives.

Considerations

Before examining a unit designed to convey knowledge and understanding of cultural diversity, it is important to define the unit approach and to look briefly at what units usually include. First, units (sometimes called modules) are designed to teach a specific body of information over a time lasting more than a class meeting or two. For example, might the unit last one, two, or three days or weeks or years or longer in some instances? Second, units contain goals, objectives, content, activities, materials, enrichment resources, and evaluational instruments. Although educators may differ about what the unit should include, generally speaking, it is a comprehensive guide that differs from the one-day lesson plan.

Example

The next several pages provide an example of an instructional unit. It is important to remember that this unit serves only as an illustration. Educators should assess their students' developmental needs, levels of knowledge, and attitudes and assess the planned instruction accordingly.

THE UNIT: UNJUST TREATMENT OF PEOPLE OF CULTURALLY DIVERSE BACKGROUNDS

Rationale

African Americans were brought to the United States to be sold into slavery. American Indians were forced off their lands. Asian Americans, especially Chinese Americans, worked on the railroad linking the Missouri River to the Pacific Coast in 1862. Hispanic Americans worked in "sweat factories" or as migrant workers. Japanese Americans were relocated to internment camps after the bombing of Pearl Harbor.

Objectives and Activities

1. Have students define the terms *racism*, *discrimination*, and *injustice*, and identify examples of each that have harmed several groups from culturally different backgrounds.

2. Have students identify three books or songs that describe the injustices that groups from different cultural backgrounds experienced.
3. Have students develop a time line showing culturally diverse people's responses to unjust treatment—for example, African Americans' march on Washington in 1963.
4. Have students identify three examples of contemporary racism, discrimination, or injustice and list possible solutions for each.

Individuals, cooperative learning groups, or interest-established pairs or triads may work on these activities.

Language Arts

- Read *The Drinking Gourd* and *Sing Down the Moon* and have students write a review of each.
- Have students prepare short stories, poems, skits, and plays on the unjust treatment many people received.
- Ask students to write and give a speech that an American Indian might have given regarding land being taken away.
- Keep a class scrapbook of unjust practices that currently exist in the United States.
- Help students write a letter to the editor of a newspaper proposing a solution to an injustice people suffer today.

Mathematics

- Compile a "numbers" list with students: acres of land taken away from American Indians, numbers of African Americans brought to the United States to work as slaves, numbers of Asian Americans who worked on the railroad, and numbers of Hispanic Americans who worked as migrant workers. Compute estimates of money saved by having workers work in low-paying jobs in poor working conditions.
- On a bar or pie graph, ask students to show numbers of workers from culturally different backgrounds in minimum-wage jobs.
- Have students estimate the value of land taken from American Indians, and compare the estimate with the amount received (if any money was actually paid).

Science

- Study terrain as part of your lesson plan—for example, land taken away from American Indians and farming land on which migrant workers grow produce.
- Have students examine climate conditions necessary for growing various types of produce and determine the effects these conditions have on people.
- Study with students the climatic conditions (e.g., temperature, humidity, heat index) of many "sweat shops" and the effect these conditions have on people.

Social Studies

- Examine with students the concepts of racism, injustice, and discrimination, and pinpoint historical and contemporary examples.
- Ask students to gather information on immigration patterns by decade or some other time frame.
- Review with students Americans' resistance to immigrants entering the United States. (For examples of resistance in the past decade, see *Newsweek*'s "Immigration backlash" [Thomas & Murr, August 9, 1993], in which a poll indicates that 60 percent of Americans thought immigration was bad for the nation, and other news magazines' reports on the Haitian and Cuban refugees who sought to come to the United States in 1994.)
- Have students prepare an essay explaining the melting pot concept and its limitations and how we currently support the salad bowl concept.
- Ask students to write a position paper for or against the resistance or unjust treatment people received on arrival to the United States.
- Develop a time line with students showing each cultural group's important dates or events—the Emancipation Proclamation, for example.
- Ask students to develop a chart listing injustices and offer possible solutions.

Art

- Introduce students to works of art depicting injustices people have suffered and struggled to overcome.
- Assign students to create collages, dioramas, and mobiles showing injustices: the bonds of slavery, the plight of American Indians, and the menial jobs many Asian and Hispanic Americans have been forced to accept.
- Study art of various cultures and ask students to look for common themes and areas. Resources include *Our Hispanic heritage* (1989), Raintree Publishing; Hargrove, J. (1990), *Diego Rivera: Mexican muralist*, Children's Press; and Sills, Leslie (1989), *Inspirations: Stories about women artists*, Albert Whitman.
- Examine American Indian art with students and the relationship between the art and the history of American Indians. Resource: Highwater, Jamake. [1978]. *Many smokes, many moons: A chronology of American Indian history through Indian art*. HarperCollins.

Music

- Listen to songs of various cultures that have helped people to survive, provided a ray of hope, and communicated pain and suffering.
- Ask students to write lyrics for a familiar melody that deal with a contemporary injustice and offer hope.
- Research musical instruments that slaves and other people in bondage used.
- Develop teaching and learning experiences from using such resources as Haskins, James (1987), *Black music in America: A history through its people*, HarperCollins; or Mattox, Cheryl Warren (Ed.) (1990), *Shake it to the one that you love the best: Play songs and lullabies from black musical traditions*. Warren-Mattox Productions.

Other Resources

Selected books appropriate for ten- to fifteen-year-olds that can complement this unit on unjust treatment of people of culturally diverse backgrounds include the following.

AFRICAN AMERICANS

Adler, David A. *Jackie Robinson: He was the first*. Holiday House, 1989, 48 pp.
> Nonfiction. This is an accurate and informative account about Jackie Robinson and the time in which he lived.

Burns, Anthony. *The defeat and triumph of a fugitive slave*. Knopf, 1988, 192 pp.
> Nonfiction. Burns, a runaway slave, was jailed in Boston and lost his legal case under the Fugitive Slave Act of 1850.

Humphrey, Kathryn Long. *Satchel Paige*. Watts, 1988, 128 pp.
> Nonfiction. The story of the most famous of the African Americans who played on the segregated teams of the Negro Baseball League.

Katz, William Loren. *Breaking the chains: African American slave resistance*. Atheneum, 1990, 208 pp.
> Nonfiction. This excellent book confutes the often-held belief that many slaves accepted servitude as a way of life.

Kosof, Anna. *The civil rights movement and its legacy*. Watts, 1989, 112 pp.
> Nonfiction. Kosof recounts her own experiences during the civil rights movement.

Lester, Julius. *This strange new feeling*. Dutton/Dial, 1982, 160 pp.
> Fiction. This story tells about Ras and the challenges he faced living in slavery.

Rummell, Jack. *Langston Hughes*. Chelsea House, 1988, 111 pp.
> Nonfiction. Middle-level students will appreciate Hughes's determination to leave home and pursue his desire to become a poet.

ASIAN AMERICANS

Batancourt, Jeanne. *More than meets the eye*. Bantam, 1990, 166 pp.
> Fiction. This book describes the variety of problems Asian Americans face in today's schools.

Bode, Janet. *New kids on the block: Oral histories of immigrant teens*. Watts, 1989, 126 pp.
> Nonfiction. Eleven teenagers relate their experiences about leaving their homelands and adjusting to their new life in the United States.

Brown, Dee Alexander, and Proctor, Linda. *Lonesome whistle: The story of the first transcontinental railroad*. Holt, Rinehart and Winston, 1980, 144 pp.
> Nonfiction. This book, adapted for young readers, describes the building of the transcontinental railroad and how the railroad selected the Chinese for the work.

Miklowitz, Gloria D. *The war between the classes*. Delacorte, 1985, 158 pp. Fiction.
> Nonfiction. This book focuses on the injustices resulting from social class structures.

Winter, Frank H. *The Filipinos in America*. Lerner, 1988, 71 pp.
> Nonfiction. This readable and balanced book provides an introduction to the fastest-growing Asian immigrant group in the United States.

AMERICAN INDIANS

Ashabranner, Brent. *Morning star, black sun: The northern Cheyenne Indians and America's energy crisis*. Putnam, 1982, 154 pp.
> Nonfiction. Ashabranner examines American Indians' reverence for the land and how their land was taken away.

Ashabranner, Brent. *To live in two worlds: American Indian youth today*. Dodd, Mead, 1984, 149 pp.
> Nonfiction. Ashabranner examines the contemporary lives of a number of American Indian teenagers and young adults.

Brown, Dee. *Wounded Knee: An Indian history of the American West*. Dell, 1975, 202 pp.
> Nonfiction. Brown's book corrects the white expansionist view of U.S. history, which Hollywood has reinforced with stereotypes of the American Indians.

Cannon, A. E. *The shadow brothers.* Delacorte, 1990, 180 pp.
   Fiction. Cannon shows that American Indians differ as individuals just as individuals do in all cultures.
Gregory, Kristiana. *Jenny of the Tetons.* Harcourt Brace Jovanovich, 1989, 119 pp.
   Fiction. A raid has left eleven-year-old Carrie orphaned and wounded and her two younger brothers kidnapped.

HISPANIC AMERICANS
Beltran Hernandez, Irene. *Across the great river.* Arte Publico, 1989, 136 pp.
   Fiction. Economic hardships force a family to cross the Rio Grande in search of a better life.
Cullison, Alan. *The South Americans.* Chelsea House, 1991, 112 pp.
   Nonfiction. Recent economic and political problems have driven increasing numbers of South Americans north.
Meltzer, Milton. *The Hispanic Americans.* HarperCollins, 1982, 149 pp.
   Nonfiction. Meltzer examines the Hispanic population from both a historical and a sociological perspective.
Mills, Claudia. *Luisa's American Dream.* Four Winds, 1981, 155 pp.
   Fiction. Luisa, a fourteen-year-old girl, hides her Cuban American background and her nationality.
Pinchot, Jane. *The Mexicans in America.* Lerner, 1989, 94 pp.
   Nonfiction. Pinchot examines issues of importance to Mexican Americans: education, immigration, and civil rights.

This partial unit could serve as a beginning point or a skeletal outline. Teachers working in interdisciplinary teams can tap their professional expertise in particular content areas and offer many exciting and productive activities and ideas within this topic.

Other Topics for Multicultural Units

- Contributions of people from culturally different groups (or a specific cultural group)
- Cultural traditions: family and society (in general or for a specific cultural group)
- Books, poems, and short stories (or music or art) by writers from culturally different backgrounds

   GEOGRAPHY AND LOCATIONS: PINPOINTING LOCATIONS OF ORIGIN*
- Native People of the Southwest (from *A Multicultural Inservice Resource Handbook,* Arizona Department of Education, 1535 W. Jefferson St., Phoenix, AZ 85007)
- *African American Scholars: Leaders, Activists, and Writers* (from NAACP, 4805 Mount Hope Dr., Baltimore, MD 21215)
- *Martin Luther King: A Lifetime of Action* (from Martin Luther King, Jr., Resource Guide, the State Education Department of New York, Long Island Field Services, #1 Regional Field Services, Room 973 EBA, Albany, NY 12234)

*Source: Manning, M. L. (1994) *Celebrating diversity: Multicultural education in middle levels schools.* Columbus, OH: National Middle School Association, 98–103.

- Contemporary contributors from culturally different backgrounds: civil rights activists
- Influential women and their contributions (women in general or women in a specific cultural group)
- Coming to the United States: immigration in the 1990s. Books we especially suggest for fifth and sixth graders include *If you were there in 1492* (Brenner, Barbara. MacMillan, 1991), *Ajeemah and his son* (Berry, James. HarperCollins, 1992), and *The Chinese American family album* (Hoobler, Dorothy, and Thomas Hoobler. Oxford University Press, 1994) (Fagella, 1994).

EXTENDING THE MULTICULTURAL EDUCATION CURRICULUM

Parental and Community Involvement

Efforts to provide multicultural education curricula and environments must extend beyond the confines of the school. Children and adolescents need to perceive evidence of recognition and respect for cultural diversity in the home and in the community. The home and the community can serve as powerful and positive forces to help reinforce the efforts of the school. Parents and other community members and organizations are valuable resources to help support the school's efforts to promote respect for cultural diversity. They should be made aware of school efforts and should feel that the school seeks and respects their advice and opinions. These two entities can also provide considerable financial and volunteer support for the multicultural education program.

As parents become involved in their children's education and learn more about the school's goals (especially in relation to the goals and materials of the multicultural education curricula), they are more likely to give overall support for school programs. Parents in all likelihood will become more interested in their children's school success and be better able to assist the school in its efforts.

Parents and educators should ask whether the community supports the school and its academic and social tasks. Is the leadership of the community concerned with school effectiveness? Does the community support efforts toward school improvement? Are the achievements of all students and teachers celebrated in the community at public occasions? Are the role models in the community educated people? If the community is not strongly positive, bring the matter to the attention of progressive community leaders with the suggestion that they sponsor a determined effort to improve the community environment (Tyler, 1989).

Case Study 9.3 suggests that involving the community can be a task of some magnitude but one that offers many rewards.

Educators often think mathematics is neutral, objective, and immune to discussions of multicultural education. Wiest (2001), in Implementing Research 9.4, disagrees and proposes educators should teach mathematics from a multicultural perspective.

CASE STUDY 9.3
COMMUNITY INVOLVEMENT

The school personnel at HS 170, an urban secondary school, had reached basic agreement on their multicultural education program. They established specific objectives for the program, one of which was to involve the community. Extending the program outside the school would show their genuine commitment. Also it would give parents, families, and other community members a chance to provide input and to offer their involvement.

The group decided on several approaches: They sent notices home with the students explaining the basic premises of the program and how parents, families, and the community could respond. They asked radio and television stations to donate brief airtime to inform the community of the effort. They placed posters the students had designed in businesses and other public places.

The group, recognizing the varying work schedules of community members, called meetings at different times and locations. The purposes of the meetings were to:

1. Explain the purposes of the program and how it would fit in with the existing academic program
2. Explain the phases of implementation and the rationale and objectives for each phase
3. Explain that all aspects of the program would be subject to evaluation and review for changes and revisions
4. Form a committee to review library and media acquisitions
5. Explain that the program would be interdisciplinary and would permeate all areas of the school: curriculum, instruction, materials, teaching and learning environment, and teacher attitudes and behaviors

Perhaps of greatest importance during the meetings, the group demonstrated the objectives of the program itself: recognition, acceptance, appreciation, and respect for all people regardless of differences.

FOLLOW THROUGH 9.6
INVOLVING PARENTS AND EXTENDED FAMILY MEMBERS

Name several ways to involve parents and extended family members of culturally different backgrounds in the curricular efforts of the school. Perhaps it would be best to divide the list into two groups, one for classes and one for the overall school programs. Include ways in which special school personnel (e.g., counselor, communications specialists) can most effectively involve parents and extended family members.

■ ■ ■ ■ ■ ▬▬▬▬

IMPLEMENTING RESEARCH 9.4
TEACHING MATHEMATICS FROM
A MULTICULTURAL PERSPECTIVE

Wiest (2001) describes principles and instructional strategies for teaching mathematics from a multicultural perspective. In her examination of mathematics and multiculturalism, she examines "what culture is" and "what culture is not." She reports that mathematics is often taught superficially; educators use irrelevant content and contexts; and stereotypes are often re-created in different ways. Then, she proposes four approaches to multicultural mathematics instruction: portrayal of cultural groups in instructional materials; historical perspectives in mathematics concepts; formal and informal mathematics of various cultures; and study of sociocultural phenomena through mathematics. Wiest (2001) offers several excellent suggestions, although educators should remember that generalizations can be dangerous because students differ in many ways.

IMPLEMENTING THE RESEARCH

1. Minority students tend to have a global orientation to learning and thus are particularly receptive to learning that is relational and holistic.
2. Minority students tend to use visual and tactile modes for the most effective learning.
3. Language issues are vitally important to consider in classes with limited-English-proficient students.
4. Open-ended and investigative cooperative work in small, heterogeneous groups is particularly important for minority students.

Source: Wiest, L. R. (2001). Teaching mathematics from a multicultural perspective. *Equity & Excellence in Education, 34*(1), 16–25.

In Implementing Research 9.5, Lutz and Kuhlman (2000) explain how teachers can integrate dance in the curriculum in order to teach children about culture.

EXTRACURRICULAR ACTIVITIES

Perceptive educators readily recognize the need for equitable representation of all races and ethnic groups in extracurricular activities.

1. Athletic programs should include minority students and women, and cheerleading teams should include both sexes as well as students of culturally different backgrounds.
2. Clubs and organizations should not perpetuate racial or gender segregation, and one group should not dominate positions of student leadership.
3. Females should participate in all sports and there should be special arrangements for students who are unable to participate for financial or other reasons (Gollnick & Chinn, 2002).

■ ■ ■ ■ ■

IMPLEMENTING RESEARCH 9.5

LEARNING ABOUT CULTURE THROUGH DANCE

Lutz and Kuhlman (2000) suggest that students can learn about culture through dance. Dance is common to all humankind, regardless of culture. Thus, the marriage of dance and cultural teaching is natural, especially for young children, who learn best through participation, movement, and constructive practices. Educators promote dance as a means to support children's positive physiological, psychological, and academic growth. Teaching children about cultures other than their own leads to greater self-esteem, especially among minority children. Plus, movement is one of the first means of expression and of learning about the world. From infancy, each new movement gives children more information about the capabilities of their bodies.

When educators integrate dance into the curriculum, particularly while studying other cultures, children benefit in many ways: body awareness and control, personal confidence and esteem, and cultural understanding and respect.

IMPLEMENTING THE RESEARCH

1. Educators should remember the physical and mental development of young children when beginning a dance project, that is, children need to feel comfortable moving expressively.
2. Educators should emphasize how dance reflects culture (and vice versa) and also emphasize the positive aspects of the culture.

Source: Lutz, T., & Kuhlman, W. D. (2000). Learning about culture through dance in kindergarten classrooms. *Early Childhood Education Journal, 28*(1), 35–40.

■ ■ ■ ■ ■

EXTRACURRICULAR ACTIVITY CHECKLIST

1. Do all the school's racial and ethnic groups participate in extracurricular activities?
2. Are financial resources equitably distributed among extracurricular activities?
3. Are extracurricular activities segregated along racial lines?
4. Do sponsors or advisers of extracurricular activities encourage learners from culturally different backgrounds to participate in the activities they sponsor?
5. Are arrangements available to support students who lack the financial or other (e.g., travel) resources to participate in extracurricular activities?
6. Are conscious efforts made to include students of differing socioeconomic groups and to involve both boys and girls in the school's extracurricular program?
7. Do the efforts to involve all children and adolescents in extracurricular activities receive the wholehearted support (not just token support) of all administrators, teachers, special service personnel, and staff members?

■ ■ ■ ■ ■ ▬▬▬▬

FOLLOW THROUGH 9.7
EVALUATING EXTRACURRICULAR ACTIVITIES

Extracurricular activities can be an important part of the total school day, especially when educators provide culturally relevant curricular activities and involve students from various cultural backgrounds. Evaluate a school's extracurricular activities to determine their cultural relevance and the school's commitment to inclusiveness. What suggestions might you offer the school for improving its extracurricular activities, especially as they relate to students from culturally different backgrounds?

SUMMING UP

Multicultural educators planning and implementing culturally responsive curricula should:

1. Reflect and recognize that the United States has experienced considerable progress toward acceptance of cultural diversity; that racism, discrimination, and prejudice continue to exist in the United States; and that curricular efforts and overall school environment should demonstrate an emphatic respect for cultural diversity.
2. Place reform efforts on an across-the-curriculum approach and on the overall school environment, rather than on a once-a-year or unit approach.
3. Have a sound multicultural basis: a careful assessment of overall needs, established guidelines, the selection of bias-free curricular materials, and the provision of evaluative procedures for both learners and curricular efforts.
4. Include extensive involvement of community resources, and permeate extracurricular activities as well as the academic curricular aspects.
5. Respect and build on, as much as possible, individual learners' native language.

SUGGESTED LEARNING ACTIVITIES

1. Visit a school with considerable cultural diversity and evaluate how well cultural diversity is reflected in the textbooks and workbooks. Answer the following questions to determine whether the school includes appropriate cultural perspectives (feel free to include your own questions):
   a. Does the text portray students from diverse backgrounds in a meaningful, non-stereotypical manner?
   b. Does the text portray various social classes?
   c. Does the text portray women and disabled people in meaningful roles?
   d. Does the text portray American Indians, Asian, Hispanic, and European Americans as well as African Americans?
   e. Does the text make provisions for learners with limited English-speaking skills?

2. Interview a curriculum coordinator of a large school (or school district) with a large percentage of students from culturally different backgrounds. What approach is the school taking to implement a multicultural education program? What mechanism is in place to ensure that all levels of educators are involved in the program? After the interview, carefully consider your findings, and write a brief paper that summarizes your findings and offers what you think are appropriate suggestions.

3. Prepare a multicultural unit (designed for perhaps two or three weeks) that a school could integrate into an overall multicultural education program. In this unit, be sure to include goals, objectives, activities, curricular materials, provisions for evaluation (of both students and the unit itself), and provisions for children and adolescents with limited English-speaking abilities.

SUGGESTIONS FOR COLLABORATIVE EFFORTS

Form groups of three or four that, if possible, represent our nation's cultural and gender diversity. Working collaboratively, focus your group's attention toward the following efforts:

1. Have each member of your group select a type of curricular material, for example, textbooks, workbooks, worksheets, audiovisuals, and any other curricular materials that elementary or secondary schools commonly use. Prepare an evaluation form (on textbooks as an example here) to answer such questions as: Is the portrayal of children and adolescents of culturally different backgrounds filled with stereotypes and myths? Of the materials on your list, consider the actual numbers of learners of culturally different backgrounds in the school, the accuracy and objectivity of their portrayal, and whether the material addresses differences among people within cultural groups (e.g., Are all Asian Americans alike? Are all Spanish-speaking people alike?).

2. Think about the curriculum when you were in elementary or secondary school. Did you study people of various cultures? Were the roles and contributions of women portrayed? Did you ever wonder why curricular materials failed to include all people? What effects can the omission of groups have on learners? If you did study people from various cultural groups and women, whom did you study? While some progress has been made in portraying the contributions of all people, progress continues to be necessary. What steps do you suggest for ensuring that all people are represented in curricular materials?

3. As a group, visit a school to determine its efforts to help children of limited English-speaking capability. What special considerations are made for these learners? What language programs are in place? What professional staff is available to offer help? What remedial programs are available? Are learners allowed to speak their native languages in schools?

EXPANDING YOUR HORIZONS: ADDITIONAL JOURNAL READINGS AND BOOKS

Binder, A. J. (2000). Why do some curricular challenges work while others do not? The case of three Afrocentric challenges. *Sociology of Education, 73,* 69–91.
   The author compares three cases in which advocates fought to have an Afrocentric curriculum developed in social studies and history classes.

Black, S., Wright, T., & Erickson, L. (2001). Polynesian folklore: An alternative to plastic toys. *Children's Literature in Education, 32*(2), 125–137.
Suggesting that folklore has the capability to teach and preserve thoughts and beliefs, these authors review specific stories and offer classroom activities.

Clawson, R. A. (2002). Poor people, Black faces: The portrayal of poverty in economics textbooks. *Journal of Black Studies, 32*(3), 352–361.
Clawson examined poor blacks in economics books. She maintains that blacks are overwhelmingly portrayed among the contemporary poor, yet are not portrayed as poor among the Great Depression poor.

Iseke-Barnes, J. M. (2000). Ethnomathematics and language in decolonizing mathematics. *Race, Gender, & Class, 7*(3), 133–149.
Iseke-Barnes examines mathematics and mathematics education, drawing upon antiracist and critical race theorizing in her discussion of mathematics and language.

Mendoza, J., & Reese, D. (2001). Examining multicultural picture books for the early childhood classroom: Possibilities and pitfalls. *Early Childhood Research and Practice, 3*(2), 1–30.
As the title suggests, Mendoza and Reese discuss the possibilities and pitfalls of using multicultural literature with young children.

Stormont, M., Stebbins, M. S., & Holliday, G. (2001). Characteristics and educational support needs of underrepresented gifted adolescents. *Psychology in the Schools, 38*(5), 413–423.
These authors describe the characteristics of underrepresented gifted adolescents and call for the development of more sensitive identification and outreach programs.

Taylor, S. V. (2000). Multicultural is who we are: Literature as a reflection of ourselves. *Teaching Exceptional Children, 32*(3), 24–29.
Taylor discusses multicultural literature, the need for teachers to include multicultural literature in their teaching, how teachers can evaluate pluralism, and evaluating and selecting multicultural literature titles.

CHAPTER TEN

INSTRUCTIONAL PRACTICES

Understanding the material and activities in this chapter will help the reader to:

- State the importance of individual and cultural differences among learners, and explain how these differences affect the teaching and learning process
- Explain the classroom teacher's role in providing teaching and learning situations that are beneficial to culturally diverse learners
- State how socioeconomic conditions, social class, and parents and families affect culturally diverse learners
- List the factors educators should consider in evaluating culturally diverse learners
- List the items educators should consider during self-evaluation to determine teaching effectiveness in multicultural situations
- Explain special considerations educators should address when planning teaching and learning experiences with African, American Indian, Arab, Asian, European, and Hispanic American children and adolescents
- List the characteristics of teachers who are effective in multicultural situations
- Explain the importance and necessity of ensuring that multicultural education permeates the total school environment, provides educational experiences that demonstrate acceptance of culturally diverse learners, and promotes positive self-concepts and cultural identities

OVERVIEW

Learners at both the elementary and secondary levels deserve the most effective educational experiences possible. In the past, however, educational experiences have all too often emphasized predominantly European American perspectives and neglected or minimized the importance of minority viewpoints and issues. Cultural diversity has been an obstacle for learners to "overcome" or for teachers to "remediate." Either consciously or unconsciously using this philosophy, educators have planned and implemented experiences for European American learners. If teachers are to provide effective culturally responsive teaching, they need to understand how ethnically diverse students learn. This is necessary because the process of learning—not the intellectual capability to do so—used by students from differing ethnic groups is influenced by their cultural socialization (Gay, 2000).

Viadero and Johnston (2000) noted an academic achievement gap that separates African and Hispanic American students from their European and Asian American counterparts in schools nationwide. On the average, these minority students start school trailing behind European and Asian children and never catch up, lagging on national tests in every subject—sometimes by as much as four grade levels. A new sense of urgency about the problem is prompting educators and policy makers around that nation to try a variety of tactics to narrow the academic disparities dividing racial and ethnic groups. In some cases, class sizes are being trimmed, teachers are receiving special training, and preschool programs for minority children are being expanded. Schools are opening access to high-level classes and encouraging minority children to enroll. Districts are looking for schoolwide-improvement models, and policy makers are raising the academic bar for students and teachers.

This chapter explores several teaching and learning contexts: learners' individual and cultural differences, characteristics of educators, organization and instruction, the teaching and learning environment, and cultural perspectives that influence the teaching and learning process in multicultural settings.

VALUING INDIVIDUAL AND CULTURAL DIFFERENCES

It is important that teachers perceive elementary and secondary learners objectively, regardless of cultural, ethnic, racial, social class, or religious differences. Learners need the psychological security of feeling valued and accepted; therefore, all educational decisions should be based on objective evidence and should be made with the individual's welfare in mind. Because of the tremendous diversity (cultural, racial, ethnic, social class, ability/disability, or combinations thereof) among contemporary learners, educators cannot consider an entire class as a homogeneous group of learners who need the same educational experiences. Just as European American students differ significantly in social class, geographic location, and family background, learners of other cultures also differ in these characteristics and in values, traditions, and customs. It is the school's responsibility to develop an understanding of each learner and to base teaching and learning experiences on reliable and objective information.

Recognizing and Accepting Diversity

It is an understatement to suggest that teaching and learning situations must demonstrate an emphatic acceptance of learners in all their cultural, ethnic, socioeconomic, and religious diversity. An environment that promotes acceptance of diversity does more than pay lip service to the concept or have goal statements that are merely rhetorical.

For culturally diverse learners to feel genuine acceptance, the teaching and learning process must concretely demonstrate respect for cultural and ethnic differences (Are all cultures and ethnic groups represented in the curriculum?); it must recognize social class (Do children come in contact with children from other socioeconomic levels? Do textbooks portray the various social classes of U.S. society?); and it must accept all religious groups (Do children feel their religious views are accepted?).

Sapon-Shevin (2000/2001), in Implementing Research 10.1, maintains that the diversity of our nation calls for schools for all students. For example, Sapon-Shevin

FOLLOW THROUGH 10.1
VALUING DIFFERENCES AMONG LEARNERS

Learners have many differences—many that educators can see, and others more subtle. Also, as we have repeatedly stated, no one can consider an individual to be like others in his or her culture. Yet some educators consider all students of one race, for example, to be the same and fail to consider their many differences. Make a list of ways educators can learn about students and their differences (e.g., get to know individual students, meet their immediate parents and extended family members, and study the respective cultures).

IMPLEMENTING RESEARCH 10.1
SCHOOLS FOR ALL STUDENTS

Sapon-Shevin (2000/2001) looks at topics such as heterogeneous classrooms (although classrooms never were homogeneous), curriculum issues, pedagogy, and school organization and climate. While Sapon-Shevin focuses on a number of issues, this Implementing Research looks primarily at instruction and various instructional strategies.

Referring to instruction, Sapon-Shevin looks at cooperative learning, peer tutoring, and multilevel teaching. First, she maintains that cooperative learning is an optimal way to teach students with different abilities in the same classroom. Research suggests that cooperative learning validates the importance of heterogeneous grouping as well as demonstrates that cooperative learning groups work best when they address differences in student status related to gender, race, and ethnicity. Second, peer tutoring allows teachers to address different skill levels and to respect differences. Still, teachers should use caution to avoid a situation in which a student is always being tutored and never has the opportunity to serve in a teacher or leader role. Third, multilevel teaching can be used to teach a wide range of students in one classroom. Teachers need to organize classroom learning activities so that all students can participate successfully.

IMPLEMENTING THE RESEARCH
1. Many forms of diversity (e.g., culture, ethnicity, gender, social class, special needs, and sexual orientation) challenge contemporary educators, yet schools should strive to meet students' diverse needs.
2. Teachers need to implement new instructional methods, ones that address students' diverse needs rather than trying to change students to fit the instructional approach
3. School organization and school climate relate to instruction and instructional methods and should receive major consideration when planning pedagogical techniques.

Source: Sapon-Shevin, M. (2000/2001). Schools fit for all. *Educational Leadership, 58*(4), 34–39.

lists growing signs of our schools' diversity: school-aged students who speak a language other than English; growing numbers of migrant families whose children attend schools intermittently; and inclusion, which brings increasing numbers of students with disabilities into mainstream classrooms.

EFFECTIVE EDUCATORS IN MULTICULTURAL SETTINGS

Educators who seek a comprehensive understanding of cultural diversity and expertise in multicultural education should direct attention to both cognitive and affective factors. It will not suffice for educators to have knowledge of culturally diverse learners and yet be unable to recognize learners' individual and cultural needs and the complex relationship between culture and learning. Educators also need to develop appropriate attitudes that show genuine concern and caring, as well as skills to plan and implement instruction that addresses cultural and individual diversity.

This section looks briefly at the knowledge, attitudes, and skills teachers need in multicultural settings. It is important to emphasize that these three attributes do not work in isolation. Teachers who work in multicultural situations are responsible for developing expertise in all three areas so they can provide learners with the most effective learning environment.

Knowledge

Teachers may lack factual information about ethnic, racial, and cultural differences; teacher education programs traditionally have not provided appropriate experiences to prepare teachers to teach in an increasingly multicultural classroom. A teacher's diversity knowledge base should include culture, race, ethnicity, and social class, and the teacher should comprehend the implications for the teaching and learning process. Similarly, teachers must know and understand the ramifications of racism, discrimination, prejudice, and injustice and what it means to be a culturally different learner in a predominantly European American school and world. Teachers need sufficient knowledge to be able to understand culturally different learners and to plan both developmentally and culturally appropriate instruction.

In Case Study 10.1, several educators discuss the importance of knowledge, attitudes, and skills.

Attitudes

Both elementary and secondary teachers need to acquire specific attitudes that will contribute to their ability to teach in contemporary multicultural classrooms: (1) a sense of democracy, in which differences are respected as well as students rights are respected; (2) an educational philosophy that includes recognition and respect for all types of di-

■ ■ ■ ■ ■ ▬▬▬▬▬▬▬▬▬▬▬▬▬▬▬▬▬▬▬▬▬▬▬▬▬▬▬▬▬▬▬

CASE STUDY 10.1

KNOWLEDGE, ATTITUDES, AND SKILLS

The discussion continues in the teachers' lounge at Ocean View Middle School. When working in multicultural situations, which characteristics does a teacher need the most: knowledge, attitudes, or skills? Although the discussion is professional in nature, it is growing increasingly intense.

"Knowledge is what it takes," says one person. "If we know about diversity and the cultural characteristics of learners, we can plan appropriate teaching and learning activities. Also, we will better understand how others' characteristics differ from our own."

"True," another person responds, "but knowledge is not enough. You need proper attitudes; you need to examine your attitudes toward diversity, and you need to respond to culturally diverse students and their needs. History is full of instances in which people had cultural knowledge yet failed to respond when injustices occurred."

"Your arguments are missing a vital point," states a person from another group. "Even with knowledge and attitudes, you will still fail to provide the most effective educational experiences for culturally diverse learners unless you have skills."

They consider the issue and decide that perhaps, it takes all three—knowledge, attitudes, and skills—to provide an effective multicultural education. Some recognize the shortcomings of their positions. Whereas some had tried to improve their knowledge, others had worked to develop more humane attitudes. One had even taken a "skills course" to improve his ability to work with students of varying cultures.

The effective teacher in multicultural education settings, however, needs knowledge, attitudes, and skills. As the educators file back to their classes, someone says, "Quite a challenge, but just think of the benefits for culturally diverse learners; in fact, for all learners."

versity; (3) the ability to perceive events and situations from other cultural perspectives; (4) an understanding of the complexities of culture and ethnicity in U.S. society; and (5) the desire and willingness to work on a daily basis with people who are different.

In Implementing Research 10.2, Allen and Labbo (2001) maintain that teaching and instructional practices should be culturally engaging.

Teachers, for the most part unknowingly, have long transmitted biased messages to students. Whether lining up students for lunch by sex or allowing ability grouping to result in racial segregation, teachers often send messages to students that one sex or race is entitled to preferential treatment. Most educators do not consciously or intentionally stereotype students or discriminate against them; they usually try to treat all students fairly and equitably. Nevertheless, teachers, like others in U.S. society, have learned attitudes and behaviors that are ageist, disability-biased, racist, sexist, and enthnocentric. Some biases are so deeply internalized that individuals do not realize they hold them. Only when teachers can (and are willing to) recognize the subtle and unintentional biases of their behavior can they make positive changes in the classroom (Gollnick & Chinn, 2002).

■ ■ ■ ■ ■

IMPLEMENTING RESEARCH 10.2
CULTURALLY ENGAGING TEACHING

Teacher educators are increasingly aware of the importance of preparing teachers to teach in a multiethnic, multilingual, economically stratified society. To better prepare teachers for these challenges, Allen and Labbo (2001) explored how inquiry into teachers' own cultural influences shaped their interactions with and reflections on students of diverse cultural backgrounds. If teachers begin to see cultures—their own and their students'—in complex, shifting terms, they might begin to apply their understandings to making their teaching culturally engaging.

Allen and Labbo explored practices with their teacher education students that had the potential for building a self-reflective, culturally conscious community that maintains a balance between comfort in who we are and confrontation of ourselves as cultural beings in a multicultural society. Through building cultural memoirs, the teachers in this study gained a better understanding of their cultural backgrounds, and in essence gave their cultural backgrounds and lives a second thought.

IMPLEMENTING THE RESEARCH

1. We agree with Allen and Labbo (2001) that teachers, both preservice and inservice, need to give their culture and cultural characteristics serious and deliberate consideration.
2. Cultural memoirs or almost any method of getting teachers to think and write about their cultural heritage (as well as their assumptions about themselves and others) will benefit teachers in gaining a better understanding of their culture, others' culture, and the effects of culture on learning and socialization.

Source: Allen, J., & Labbo, L. (2001). Giving it a second thought: Making culturally engaged teaching culturally engaging. *Language Arts, 79*(1), 40–52.

Referring primarily to young children, Huber (2000), in Implementing Research 10.3, suggests promoting multicultural awareness through dramatic play.

Skills

Daily, teachers must understand many complicated areas: learning styles, the dangers of ability grouping, the benefits of cooperative learning, culturally different perceptions of motivation and competition, learners who may not want to excel at the expense of their peers, and stereotypical beliefs about a culture's ability to learn or not to learn. Generally speaking, teachers need the skills to teach children and adolescents in the various cultural groups and the ability to convey that teachers genuinely want what is best for learners, both as students and as people.

Teachers, working in a position to speak for change, have a responsibility to do whatever is possible to reduce racism, prejudice, and injustice among children and adolescents and to instill attitudes of equality and democratic values, which may continue for life. Teachers, indeed, should be significant influences on the values, hopes, and

■ ■ ■ ■ ■ ▬▬▬▬▬▬▬▬▬▬▬▬▬▬▬▬▬▬▬▬▬▬

IMPLEMENTING RESEARCH 10.3

PROMOTING MULTICULTURAL AWARENESS THROUGH DRAMATIC PLAY

Huber (2000) explains how teachers can promote multicultural awareness through dramatic play centers. She begins her article by stating that teachers need to do several things. First, they need to examine their own biases and beliefs. People might not like to admit their biases, but most people harbor biases of some type. Second, teachers may not feel they know enough about another culture to feel comfortable providing materials and answering children's questions. Third, teachers may feel that they are already incorporating some multicultural materials in their classrooms. Fourth, a teacher may not know what props or materials would be appropriate for the classroom.

One answer, Huber thinks, is promoting multicultural awareness through dramatic play. The dramatic play center is useful because children and learn about themselves and their world. Selecting materials for dramatic play centers requires both incorporating multicultural awareness and examining materials currently available in the center. Reflecting on the center's goals is another worthwhile goal.

Teachers can take several directions: respond accurately and appropriately to students' questions, observe and listen to children's conversations, participate in children's play, allow students time to interact with multicultural materials, and provide learners with concrete experiences.

IMPLEMENTING THE RESEARCH

1. Teachers need to learn about their and others' cultures as well as consider and address any biases and prejudices.
2. Teachers in their efforts to promote multicultural awareness can use other learning centers that require learners to cooperate and collaborate.
3. Teachers' efforts should be more than superficial—they should strive to provide culturally relevant curricular materials and instructional practices.

Source: Huber, L. K. (2000). Promoting multicultural awareness through dramatic play centers. *Early Childhood Education Journal, 27*(4), 235–238.

■ ■ ■ ■ ■ ▬▬▬▬▬▬▬▬▬▬▬▬▬▬▬▬▬▬▬▬▬▬

FOLLOW THROUGH 10.2

GAINING KNOWLEDGE, ATTITUDES, AND SKILLS TO WORK IN MULTICULTURAL SETTINGS

Culturally appropriate knowledge, attitudes, and skills are essential for educators who deal with students of culturally differing backgrounds on a daily basis. But how can the knowledge, attitudes, and skills be acquired? List ways (such as reading, in-service workshops, college coursework) you can use to become an effective educator in multicultural situations.

dreams of their students. In a democratic classroom, teachers and students who are committed to human freedom should have the liberty to express their views, values, and beliefs with regard to democratic ideals such as human dignity, justice, and equality.

Behaviors Essential in Multicultural Classrooms

1. Provide learning experiences that reflect individual cultures' learning styles and perceptions of competition, group welfare, sharing, motivation, and success. For example, some American Indian learners may prefer sharing and helping peers to competitive learning activities, and Puerto Ricans may not wish to excel or be set apart from the group as being different or excelling.

2. Provide learning experiences that reflect gender differences. To confront gender bias in curricular materials, encourage gender integration through peer tutoring and other small learning groups. Encourage open dialogue and collaboration (Butler & Manning, 1998).

3. Encourage and support the development of bilingual programs (Crawford, 1993).

4. Immerse students in a variety of written and oral language activities that are meaningful, relevant, and functional in a pluralistic society (Crawford, 1993).

5. Treat all students fairly and establish a democratic classroom in which all students give and receive equal treatment.

6. Expect the best from *all* students. Encourage all of them to succeed academically; don't automatically assume that minority students will perform less well (Garcia, 1984).

7. Group heterogeneously whenever possible, to enhance self-esteem and promote ethnic interaction (Gollnick & Chinn, 2002).

8. Demonstrate daily the necessity of democratic values and attitudes, a multicultural education philosophy, and an ability to view events and situations from diverse ethnic perspectives and points of view.

9. Recognize as a myth the belief that culturally diverse parents and families do not care about their children's education. This myth has serious consequences (Chavkin, 1989).

10. Encourage cross-cultural friendships and social interaction, cooperation, and socialization among boys and girls in the classroom, on the playground, and in the community.

■ ■ ■ ■ ■ ▬▬▬

FOLLOW THROUGH 10.3

DETERMINING OTHER NEEDED CHARACTERISTICS AND BEHAVIORS

Work in groups of three or four to identify *other* characteristics or behaviors that educators need to address in multicultural settings. Consider this task from several perspectives: What type of teacher do you want to be? What might parents from a culturally different background want for their child? How might a child or adolescent want his or her teacher to be?

11. Address the special problems that culturally diverse parents and families may face, such as language difficulties and misunderstanding the U.S. school system.
12. Acquire factual knowledge about learner differences such as culture, race, ethnicity, social class, and gender and commit to having educational experiences reflect these differences.
13. Arrange your classroom so that it reflects cultural diversity in bulletin boards and on the walls, and in selection of artwork and artifacts on display.

EDUCATOR SELF-EVALUATION

Educators of all grade levels and all cultures probably agree that some type of evaluation is necessary periodically to determine whether the school is meeting goals and objectives. Whether of an informal or formal nature, the evaluation instrument should focus on teachers' ability to plan and implement appropriate teaching and learning activities for children and adolescents.

Ketter and Lewis (2001) maintain that white people often do not see themselves as having a race, but instead accept whiteness as the norm and see anyone nonwhite as different or exceptional. In this manner, people other than white European Americans are seen as "foreign" (p. 176). White teachers who have not been taught to examine their cultural backgrounds often feel raceless and apolitical. In Implementing Research 10.4, Ketter and Lewis (2001) explain how teachers can use multicultural literature in a predominantly white rural schools.

Teachers should also use a self-evaluation instrument designed to measure their ability to provide the environment and learning activities that are responsive to culturally diverse learners. Such a self-evaluation should include several questions designed to provide insight into the teacher's knowledge, attitudes, and skills:

1. Have there been efforts to understand and respect cultural diversity among learners, not as a problem to solve but as a challenging opportunity and a rich gift?
2. Have there been efforts to provide a classroom in which learners feel free to speak and express diverse opinions? Are students free to express opinions contrary to middle-class European American beliefs? Does the teacher repress them or allow other students to stifle diverse opinion?
3. Have there been efforts to have the classroom reflect cultural diversity? Do the walls, bulletin boards, and artwork in the classroom demonstrate respect for cultural diversity, or do the contents of the classroom indicate an appreciation or valuing of only one culture?
4. Have there been efforts to provide organizational patterns that do not result in segregation of some learners according to race, culture, ethnicity, or social class?
5. Have there been efforts to understand language differences and differing learning styles? Has the school developed organizational patterns and instructional methodologies that might be helpful to culturally diverse learners?
6. Have there been efforts to understand culturally different learners' perspectives toward motivation, excelling among one's peers, competition, group welfare, and sharing?

IMPLEMENTING RESEARCH 10.4
MULTICULTURAL LITERATURE IN A PREDOMINANTLY WHITE RURAL COMMUNITY

Ketter and Lewis (2001) explain a long-term research project that aimed at better understanding the conditions that shape how new teachers select and use multicultural literature teach and how they use texts in their classrooms. Teachers in the study (as well as other classroom teachers) often feel frustrated when confronted with the purposes of teaching multicultural literature that conflicts with their beliefs about how to teach multicultural literature sensitively and positively.

In their article, Ketter and Lewis examine topics and issues such as the local politics of multicultural literature, purposes of teaching multicultural literature, teaching universal themes, teaching cultural criticism, and teaching a message in context.

The article also explores books such as *Sounder, Journey to Topaz, The Cay,* and *The Watsons Go to Birmingham.* In using these books, teachers explored their assumptions about events and people as well as had an opportunity to confront biases.

IMPLEMENTING THE RESEARCH
1. Multicultural literature should be carefully selected in an effort to avoid stereotypical images and prejudicial views.
2. Teachers often face challenges as they teach multicultural literature, especially in communities where diversity is not the norm.
3. Multicultural books, previously accepted as classics, might need to be reexamined using contemporary literary evaluative standards to determine the extent that a person in one culture is represented as the whole culture.

Source: Ketter, J., & Lewis, C. (2001). Already reading texts and contexts: Multicultural literature in a predominantly white rural community. *Theory into Practice, 40*(3), 175–183.

7. Have there been efforts to understand culturally diverse parents and extended families and to ensure their participation in learners' academic and social life at school?
8. Have there been efforts to treat each learner with respect, to consider each learner as equal to other students, and to treat each learner as a valued and worthwhile member of the class? Are all learners accorded similar academic assistance? Do all learners receive help from the school's special service personnel?
9. Have there been efforts to allow (and indeed encourage) all students to work in cross-cultural groups, to carry on conversation and meaningful dialogue, and to feel they are valued members of the group?
10. Have there been efforts to instill multiculturalism as a genuine part of the teaching and learning process and overall school environment?

Case Study 10.2 suggests that teacher self-evaluation can be one of the most effective means of evaluating one's performance.

■ ■ ■ ■ ■

CASE STUDY 10.2
TEACHER SELF-EVALUATION

The faculty at PS High School 93 was accustomed to being evaluated by the principal, a central office evaluational specialist, and occasionally peer teachers. The teachers were beginning to realize, however, that something was missing. Evaluation forms indicated the degree of success, yet a teacher basically knew, better than the instrument could suggest, whether he or she had met the school's expectations and whether he or she was working to maximum potential. There was yet another issue: While the existing instruments evaluated overall performance, they did little to determine the educator's efforts to address the needs of culturally diverse learners.

In keeping with the research on evaluation, the counselor suggested a self-evaluation form for educators. Interested faculty members decided to work as a committee to develop a self-evaluation scale—a measure that each teacher might share with peers or administrators (the decision to share was one they could make at a later date).

While the evaluation committee would study the various possibilities and make final recommendations, broad categories for evaluation might include (with the specifics to be added later):

- The teacher's knowledge, attitudes, and skills
- The teacher's classroom environment
- The teacher's instructional process
- The teacher's curricular materials
- The teacher's management system
- The teacher's evaluation process

The specifics to be added later would provide a base for individual educators to evaluate their efforts and commitment to the multicultural education program.

■ ■ ■ ■ ■

FOLLOW THROUGH 10.4
EVALUATING EDUCATORS' EFFORTS

List ten to twelve criteria by which to evaluate a teacher's (or any school professional's) performance working with students of culturally different backgrounds. Perhaps you will want to separate your list into three categories: knowledge, attitudes, and skills. Or you might just want to write a list of characteristics or behaviors. Consider the perspectives of the educator, the parent, and the learner as you make your list.

ORGANIZATION AND INSTRUCTION— CULTURAL CONSIDERATIONS

Students are often organized for instructional purposes on the basis of test scores, previous grades, teacher recommendations, and other supposedly objective information.

▪ ▪ ▪ ▪ ▪ ▬▬▬▬▬▬▬▬▬▬▬▬▬▬▬▬▬▬▬▬▬▬▬▬

FOLLOW THROUGH 10.5
HETEROGENEOUS EDUCATION

Many teachers complain that teaching heterogeneous groups can be difficult because of the wide array of academic abilities and levels. Name four or five ways educators can teach effectively in heterogenous classrooms (in which students are randomly assigned to classes without consideration of their ability levels).

The basic rationale for grouping students is to narrow the abilities range and thus provide teachers with a homogeneous group that is supposedly easier to teach. Two dangers inherent in any grouping process are (1) placing students in the wrong group and (2) having an organization pattern that segregates students by race. Whether considering race, social class, or gender, organizational patterns should not result in segregation, whereby inferior teachers teach some students or teach in inferior schools, and other students receive preferential treatment. Organizational patterns should result in a student population that is as representative as possible of the entire school population and, if possible, the composition of the community at large.

Ability Grouping

Ability grouping may result in a form of segregation. Ability-grouping patterns often parallel students' nonacademic characteristics, such as race or ethnic background, socioeconomic class, or personal appearance. Learners of low socioeconomic status and minority groups often find themselves in lower-ability groups. Such practices may be discriminatory, because the segregation of students is along ethnic and social-class lines. These patterns of grouping appear to be related to ethnicity and socioeconomic standing, rather than purely academic abilities and achievement levels. Case Study 10.3 shows how ability grouping can result in a form of segregation.

Cooperative Learning

People who help one another by joining forces to achieve a common goal generally feel more positively about each other and are willing to interact more positively when performing collective tasks. Rather than treating academic learning and social or intergroup relations as two distinct entities, cooperative learning has contributed positively to overall intergroup relations and particularly to improving relations with multicultural and multiethnic students (Sharan, 1985). Cooperative learning procedures can reinforce the efforts of culturally diverse children to continue their schoolwork successfully. Children who work cooperatively in groups, rather than in isolation, are usually motivated to help each other carry out the assigned or chosen project.

Research on cooperative learning and intergroup relationships has concluded that students in cooperative learning situations had a greater appreciation for cooperative-learning classmates. Specifically, cooperative learning increases contact between stu-

■ ■ ■ ■ ■

CASE STUDY 10.3
CULTURALLY DIVERSE GROUPS AND ABILITY GROUPING

In a meeting with all the fifth-grade teachers, Dr. Mallory, the principal at Southside Elementary School, voiced a concern that some classes consisted almost entirely of culturally diverse students. "How did this happen?" she questioned. While two classes were almost all minority, the other two classes were almost all white.

One teacher explained that the students were in ability groups, based on their achievement test scores, reading grades, and the recommendations of their previous teachers. "The groups just worked out that way," he explained.

The principal pointed out that a form of segregation was occurring and that students did not have adequate opportunities for social interaction. As professional educators they had a responsibility to address the situation. Dr. Mallory explained that evidence shows clearly that ability grouping does not improve student achievement in the elementary school; ability grouping may seriously impair self-concepts of low-ability learners; teachers interact differently with students from various ability groups; and ability groups too often parallel students' nonacademic characteristics, such as race, ethnicity, and social class. Because they had to change the existing segregation, Dr. Mallory asked for specific suggestions to remediate the situation.

The fifth-grade teachers brainstormed and came up with possibilities: heterogeneous grouping, individualized instruction, mastery learning, and cooperative learning. The teachers decided that because the principal had mandated change (and that she was correct about students being segregated), they would group heterogeneously and then try other means of providing appropriate instruction.

dents, provides a feeling of group membership, engages learners in pleasant activities, and requires that team members work toward a common goal (Slavin, 1996).

Several research studies have indicated that students' working cooperatively can contribute positively to specific multiethnic populations. Aronson, Blaney, Stephan, Sikes, and Snapp (1978) concluded that both black and white students working in cooperative learning situations liked school better than those of the same ethnic groups working in competitive classrooms. Other research suggests that working cooperatively seems to have particularly strong effects on Hispanic and black students, regardless of achievement levels (Slavin, 1987). One study indicates that European and Asian Americans, in a learning situation similar to the Jigsaw method in Table 10.1, had more positive attitudes toward Mexican Americans than learners in competitive classes. A study of Jigsaw II-related classes that included recent European and West Indian immigrants and white Canadians documented substantially more cross-ethnic friendships than in the control groups (Slavin, 1983).

Cooperation, collaborating, and community are prominent themes, techniques, and goals in educating African, Arab, and Hispanic American as well as American Indian students. Two major reasons help to explain these pedagogical trends. First, underlying values of human connectedness and collaborative problem solving are high priorities in the cultures of most groups of color in the United States. Second, cooperation plays a central role in these groups' learning styles, especially the communicative, procedural, motivational, and relational dimensions. Therefore, they should be key pillars of culturally responsive teaching. Research projects and instructional programs can demonstrate a sense of community, collaboration, and cooperation for improving the achievement (Gay, 2000).

Concerning specific cooperative learning methods, there have been positive effects with Student Teams–Achievement Divisions (STAD), Teams-Games-Tournament (TGT), Team-Assisted Individualization (TAI), and Jigsaw II (Slavin, 1996). Studies also found that improved student attitudes and behaviors toward classmates of different ethnic backgrounds were extended to classmates of different groups (Sharan & Sharan, 1989/1990). In conclusion, Slavin (1987) summarized by saying that cooperative learning strategies apparently contribute to students' seeing each other in a positive light and forming friendships based on human qualities. Table 10.1 summarizes some cooperative learning methods.

Language Differences

Language diversity is so great in some parts of the United States that sometimes classroom communication is virtually impossible. In addition, many schools are unable to provide appropriate learning experiences for children whose native language is not English. As a result, language-minority children do not learn the essential lessons of school and do not participate fully in the economic, social, and political life of the United States (Bowman, 1989). As they decide on organizing students for instruction, culturally sensitive educators recognize the dilemma that learners with limited English skills often face.

Maintaining that language differences pose a major stumbling block for American Indian students, Little Soldier (1989) offers several precepts for educators:

1. Implement cooperative learning techniques. American Indians, reared to value cooperation and sharing, are not accustomed culturally to working alone or to competing for grades and teacher approval. Cooperative learning situations in which warm personal relationships develop have contributed to the language development of American Indian pupils.
2. Avoid large-group, formal lessons in the lecture–recitation mode. American Indian students tend to withdraw during formal patterns. These learners perceive more opportunity in student-to-student dialogues and group problem-solving efforts.
3. Liberally give encouragement and positive reinforcement. Include language-lifting techniques and modeling of correct language patterns. Avoid correcting pupils' oral language errors except during formal language lessons (Little Soldier, 1989).

Bowman (1989) offers several suggestions for educators working with language-minority learners:

1. The use of formal language, teacher leadership and control of verbal exchanges, question-and-answer formats, and references to increasingly abstract ideas often characterize a classroom environment with which many minority children are

TABLE 10.1 Overview of Selected Cooperative Learning Methods

METHOD/PROPONENT	BRIEF DESCRIPTION/COMMENTS
Learning Together (Johnson & Johnson, 1987, 1989/1990)	Emphasizing cooperative effort, *Learning Together* has five basic elements: positive interdependence (students believe that they are responsible for both their learning and the team's); face-to-face interaction (students explain their learning and help others with assignments); individual accountability (students demonstrate mastery of material); social skills (students communicate effectively, build and maintain trust, and resolve conflicts); group processing (groups periodically assess their progress and ways to improve effectiveness). Uses four- or five-member heterogeneous teams.
Student Teams–Achievement Divisions (STAD; Slavin, 1978)	Four-student learning teams (mixed in performance levels, sex, and ethnicity); teacher presents lesson, students work in teams and help others master material. Students take quizzes; cooperative efforts are not allowed on quizzes; teams earn reward. Application to most grades and subjects.
Teams-Games-Tournament (TGT; Devries & Slavin, 1978)	Using the same teacher presentation and teamwork as STAD, TGT replaces the quizzes with weekly tournaments in which students compete with members of other teams to contribute points to team scores. Competition occurs at "tournament tables" against others with similar academic records. The winner of each tournament brings six points to her or his team. Low achievers compete with low achievers (a similar arrangement exists for high achievers), a system that provides all students with equal opportunity for success. As with STAD, teams earn rewards. Applicable to most grades and subjects.
Jigsaw (Aronson, Blaney, Stephan, Sikes, & Snapp, 1978)	Teachers assign students to six-member teams to work on academic material divided into sections. Each member reads a section; then, members of different teams meet to become experts. Students return to groups and teach other members about the sections. Students must listen to their teammates to learn other sections.
Jigsaw II (Slavin, 1987)	Students work in four- or five-member teams as in TGT or STAD. Rather than being assigned specific parts, students read a common narrative (e.g., a chapter). Students also receive a topic on which to become an expert. Learners with same topics meet together as in Jigsaw, then teach the material to their original group. Students take individual quizzes.
Team-Assisted Individualization (TAI) (Slavin, Leavey, & Madden, 1989)	Uses four-member mixed-ability groups (as with STAD and TGT); differs from STAD and TGT in that it combines cooperative learning and individualized instruction and is applicable only to mathematics in grades three through six. Learners take a placement test, then proceed at their own pace. Team members check one another's work and help with problems. Without help, students take unit tests that student monitors score. Each week the teacher evaluates and gives team rewards.
Cooperative Integrated Reading and Composition (CIRC, Madden, Slavin, & Stevens, 1986)	Designed to teach reading and writing in the upper elementary grades, CIRC assigns students to different reading teams. Teacher works with one team, while other teams engage in cognitive activities: reading, predicting story endings, summarizing stories, writing responses, practicing decoding, and learning vocabulary. Teams follow sequence of teacher instruction, team practice, team preassessments, and quizzes. A team does not take a quiz until the team feels each student is ready. Teams receive rewards.
Group Investigation (Sharan & Sharan, 1989/1990)	Groups form according to common interest in a topic. Students plan research, divide learning assignments among members, synthesize and summarize feelings, and present the findings to the entire class.

Source: Manning, M. L., & Lucking, R. *The Clearing House, 64,* p. 153. Reprinted with permission of the Helen Dwight Reid Educational Foundation. Published by Heldref Publications, 1319 Eighteenth St., NW, Washington, DC 20036-1802. Copyright © 1991.

unfamiliar. Whenever possible, communication is made easier if these ideas overlap with those the learners already know.

2. Language-minority learners should experience familiar communication styles to establish a basis for communication. This basis may include speaking in the child's primary language, using culturally appropriate styles of address, and relying on management patterns that are familiar to and comfortable for children.

3. The meanings of words, gestures, and actions may be quite different from culture to culture. As Little Soldier (1989) suggests, educators should carefully consider language differences and developmental levels for all decisions concerning organizing for instruction.

THE SCHOOL ENVIRONMENT

The school environment includes all experiences with which learners come in contact: content, instructional methods, the actual teaching and learning process and environment, the professional staff and other staff members, as well as the actions and attitudes of other students. This definition of environment is synonymous with curriculum itself.

Working toward a Multicultural School Environment

It is important that the multicultural environment demonstrate genuine respect and concern for all learners, regardless of their racial, cultural, or ethnic backgrounds. With a supportive school environment, culturally different children, along with other learners, can learn to take an active role in a democratic society, guided by relevant understanding, and develop skills in communication and computation, social attitudes and interests, and human appreciation. The school environment should support school learning and socialization for all students. A supportive school environment is one in which the morale of both teachers and students is high. Teachers believe in their mission to help guide and stimulate the learning activities of their students and are pleased with their students' responsive behavior.

Although it is impossible to describe in detail all the factors that make a school environment responsive to cultural diversity, briefly discussing several areas illustrates the environment in its broadest sense: the unconditional acceptance of diversity, the promotion of positive self-concepts and cultural identities, and a faculty and staff

■ ■ ■ ■ ■

FOLLOW THROUGH 10.6
MAKING CLASSROOMS REFLECT DIVERSITY

Ask your students to suggest ways to make the classroom better reflect the cultural diversity of the learners. Consider things like artwork, displays showing contributions of various cultures, and holiday displays, just to name a few. Ask students how school rules, policies, and expectations could better reflect the needs of culturally diverse learners.

FOLLOW THROUGH 10.7
ADDRESSING DIVERSITY IN ITS MANY FORMS

1. Check district and school policies, procedures, practices, curriculum guides, lesson plans, and instructional materials to be sure they are free of bias toward race, gender, religion, culture, and disabilities.
2. Make newcomers feel welcome through a formal program.
3. Be sure that assignments are not offensive or frustrating to students of cultural minorities. For example, asking students to discuss or write about their Christmas experiences is inappropriate for non-Christian students. Let students discuss their similar holidays.
4. Form a schoolwide planning committee to address the implementation of multicultural education.
5. Contact your district curriculum coordinators for ideas and assistance.
6. Let faculty knowledgeable about multicultural topics provide in-service for others or guest-teach their classes.
7. Take a cultural census of the class or school to find out what cultures are represented; let students be the ethnographers.
8. Form a multicultural club.
9. Select a theme to tie various multicultural activities together; hold school programs with art, music, and dramatic presentations; hold a multicultural fair or festival featuring music, art, dance, dress, and so on; adopt a multicultural theme for existing activities.
10. Hold a school cross-cultural food festival.
11. Have multicultural celebrations and teach-ins with schoolwide activities in all classes.
12. Decorate classrooms, hallways, and the library media center with murals, bulletin boards, posters, artifacts, and other materials representative of the students in the class or school or other cultures the class is studying. Posters and other information are available from foreign government travel bureaus and education agencies, private travel agencies, consulates, the United Nations, and ethnic and cultural organizations.
13. Designate a permanent bulletin board for multicultural news and displays.
14. Help students develop the skills necessary to locate and organize information about cultures from the library media center, the mass media, people, and personal observations.
15. Have students write to foreign consulates, tourist bureaus, minority organizations, and others, for information and decorative materials.
16. Supplement textbooks with authentic materials on different cultures from newspapers, magazines, and other media of the culture. Such materials are available from the Department of Education Foreign Language Documentation Center.
17. Take advantage of community resources. Have representatives of various cultures talk to classes; actors portray characters or events; and musicians and dance groups, such as salsa bands or bagpipe units, perform.
18. Work with the library media center on special bibliographies, collections, displays, and audiovisuals.
19. Hold a mock legislature to debate current or historical issues affecting minorities and cultural groups.
20. Hold oratorical, debate, essay, poster, art, brain brawl, or other competitions with a multicultural focus.

(continued)

FOLLOW THROUGH 10.7   CONTINUED

21. Feature stories in the school newspaper on multicultural topics; publish a multi-cultural newspaper or newsletter.
22. Make reminders during daily announcements about multicultural activities.
23. Use your Newspapers-in-Education program.
24. Develop a radio or television program with a multicultural theme for the educational or local community access channel.
25. Study works in science, art, music, and literature of various cultures, focusing on the contributions of minority individuals.
26. Have students write short stories or essays on multicultural topics.
27. Have student debates, speeches, skits, and so forth on multicultural topics and present them to classes, parent–teacher organizations (PTOs), nursing homes, and other community groups.
28. Study the provisions and freedoms of the Constitution as they relate to minorities.
29. Compare and contrast other cultures with that of U.S. mainstream culture.
30. Discuss the issues and personalities involved in various cultures from historical, political, and literary standpoints.
31. Use skills and information from various disciplines (math, social studies, geography, language arts) to compare population, economy, politics, lifestyle, culture, and other aspects of different culture groups in the United States during different historical periods and as they are today. Discuss the meaning of the differences.
32. Discuss the relevance of the Constitution and government in dealing with today's problems that relate to minorities and cultural diversity.
33. Hold mock campaigns and elections based on multicultural issues.
34. Hold a video film festival dealing with various cultures and multicultural issues.
35. Have children of other cultures and their parents share native songs with classmates; have students share instruments or recordings of their native cultures.
36. Take field trips to local multicultural sites, such as a neighborhood, ethnic recreation or social center, workplace, historical site, museum, restaurant, and grocery.
37. Focus on geography skills and knowledge in geography courses as part of related courses.
38. Establish pen-pal or video exchange programs with students from other cultures.
39. Discuss the importance of international trade and the skills necessary for employment in that area.
40. Focus on the everyday artifacts of cultures that differentiate the way people behave in different cultures, such as greetings, friendly exchanges, farewells, expressions of respect, verbal taboos, ways of using numbers, body language, and gestures. Also consider gender roles, folklore, childhood literature, discipline, festivals, holidays, religious practices, games, music, pets, personal possessions, keeping warm and cool, cosmetics, fashions, and health and hygiene practices. Competitions, dating and courtship, transportation and traffic, sports, radio and television programs, hobbies, foods, family mealtimes, snacking, and cafes and restaurants provide further aspects of culture to compare. Also yards and sidewalks, parks and playgrounds, flowers and gardens, movies and theaters, circuses, museums, vacations and resort areas, careers are rich sources.
41. Discuss what it means to be a member of a minority or different cultural group.
42. Discuss what it means to be a responsible U.S. citizen.

Source: Multicultural teaching strategies. (1990). (Technical Assistance. Paper No. 9). Tallahassee: Florida State Department of Education.

composition that represents the cultural diversity of the school population. The school environment is by no means limited to these three aspects. These three, however, have a powerful influence on how learners perceive others' opinions of cultural diversity.

Recommendations for creating a teaching and learning environment that reflects the cultural diversity of the school include:

- As a part of the daily learning environment, provide and consistently update a variety of multiethnic, multicultural, and self-awareness materials.
- Plan learning experiences that are flexible, unbiased, and inclusive of contributions from diverse cultures.
- Find good people to serve as role models and material resources that focus on problems in a pluralistic society.
- Adopt instructional strategies relevant to the physical, emotional, social, and intellectual development of children of multiethnic heritage.
- Use instructional material that shows individuals from diverse cultural groups working in different occupational and social roles. Make sure all materials are free of bias, omissions, and stereotypes.
- Adopt flexible scheduling that provides ample time and space for children to share their uniqueness through role-play, art, conversation, and games.
- Continuously use ideas and materials that represent cultures throughout the year, not just during special holidays such as Black History Week, Christmas, Thanksgiving, Hanukkah, or Chinese New Year (Southern Association for Children under Six, 1988).

Banks (1988), believing that an educational setting should allow children to feel accepted, encouraged, and respected, offers several insights into creating appropriate school environments in our culturally pluralistic society:

1. The total school environment should undergo reform, not just the courses and programs. The school's informal "hidden curriculum" is as important as, or perhaps more important than, the formal course of study.
2. Ethnic content should be part of all subject areas from preschool through grade twelve and beyond.
3. Learning centers, libraries, and resource centers should include resources for history, literature, music, folklore, views of life, and the arts of the various groups of people.
4. Ethnic diversity should be reflected in assembly programs; classroom, hallway, and entrance decorations; cafeteria menus; counseling interactions; and, as we previously discussed, extracurricular activities.
5. School-sponsored dances and other such activities should reflect a respect for a culturally pluralistic society.

Service learning should accompany multicultural education courses, so preservice and in-service teachers can better relate to the content examined in multicultural education courses. Multicultural service learning, examined in Implementing Research 10.5, is best achieved through shared control.

■ ■ ■ ■ ■

IMPLEMENTING RESEARCH 10.5
MULTICULTURAL SERVICE LEARNING

The authors explain a one-hour university field experience that is linked to a three-hour multicultural education course. Preservice teachers offered twenty hours of their time and service to churches and community organizations in a culturally diverse, low-income area.

In the article, the authors looked at the meaning of community, the actual project, partnership and shared control, putting community into service learning research, and the spirit of shared control. They maintained that most research focuses on the potential benefits of service learning for service learners. Their study suggested that community learning motivated, engaged, and gratified community leaders, tapping into resources of local community associations. The principles of true partnership—reciprocity, mutuality, and empowerment—are illustrated.

An essential key to the success of their project was that shared control demonstrated resolute commitment to collective endeavor and unyielding faith in the value of diverse perspectives. The spirit of shared control recognized the strength of a pluralistic university–community teaching coalition for multicultural education. It engendered genuine feelings of teamwork, community, and partnership.

IMPLEMENTING THE RESEARCH

1. A field experience in a diverse setting will complement a multicultural education course preservice and in-service teachers can get first-hand looks and experiences with the diverse populations discussed in multicultural education books.
2. Field experiences should include more than simply placing students in diverse settings—there should be a sense of shared control whereby all stakeholders participate to provide the best possible field experience.

Source: Boyle-Baise, M., Epler, B., McCoy, W., Paulk, G,. Clark, J., Slough, N., & Truelock, C. (2001). Shared control: Community voices in multicultural learning. *The Educational Forum, 65,* 344–353.

PROMOTING SELF-ESTEEM AND
POSITIVE CULTURAL IDENTITIES

It is imperative that educators understand the school environment's influence (perhaps an unconscious or unrecognized influence) on a child's self-concept and cultural identity. Without doubt, the school environment affects both the manner in which children perceive themselves and their cultural images.

Self-concept, or self-image, is a complex set of beliefs that an individual holds about himself or herself. A person may have more than one self-image and actually hold positive feelings in some areas and negative images in others. For example, a person might have a positive self-image in intellectual pursuits while harboring negative feelings toward his or her athletic abilities. The actions of others or the way in which learners think others perceive and treat them significantly influences their self-concepts. A person's self-concept affects behavior, school achievement, and social development.

The environment should allow culturally diverse people to feel a sense of being able to cope or to feel that they can control their lives at least to some extent. Youngsters who feel torn between two cultures may have a low self-image because they assume they cannot be successful in either society (Ramsey, 1987).

Self-concepts of learners relate not only to their race, culture, and social class but also to their feelings of power in the school environment. The task facing educators is to help students build positive perceptions about their reference groups and to develop confidence in actively participating in social discussion and change (Ramsey, 1987).

The educators' goal should be to provide a school environment that either raises or contributes positively to the self-concepts and the racial and cultural pride of all people. Students should not feel like intruders in a school that emphasizes middle-class European American values, expectations, and perspectives.

■ ■ ■ ■ ■ ▬▬▬▬

FOLLOW THROUGH 10.8
TEACHING STUDENTS TO UNDERSTAND
AND APPRECIATE THEIR DIVERSITY

Have students clip from magazines and prepare a collage that reveals things about their lives. Talk about the things they might include: birthplace—picture, part of a map; baby pictures; things they like—food, sports; their families—people, pets; or where they have lived or traveled. Have the students write brief biographical descriptions that they can attach to the collage or read to the class.

Source: Tiedt, P. L., & Tiedt, I. M. (1999). *Multicultural teaching: A handbook of activities, information, and resources,* 2d ed. Boston: Allyn & Bacon, 45–46.

■ ■ ■ ■ ■ ▬▬▬▬

FOR ADDITIONAL INFORMATION
INTERNET ADDRESSES

**Multicultural Resources from
James Madison University**
http://falcon.jmu.edu/~ramseyil/multipub.htm
Provides a wealth of resources for the design and implementation of multicultural education programs.

Schedule
www.potter.flint.k12.mi.us/schedule.htm
Provides information on Potter Multicultural Global Elementary School

**A Multicultural Curriculum and
Standardized Testing Program**
http://multicultural.mining.co.com/library/weekly/aa100498.htm Provides a look at both curriculum and standardized testing from multicultural perspectives.

KCRPDC Educational Equity
http://oseda.missouri.edu/rpdc/umkc/equity.html
Provides a wealth of multicultural education resources such as lesson plans, suggested reading lists, mailing lists, multicultural literature, and instructional activities.

DIVERSITY AMONG FACULTY AND STAFF

Members of different ethnic groups must be an integral part of the school's instructional, administrative, and supportive staffs. School personnel—teachers, principals, cooks, custodians, secretaries, students, and counselors—make contributions as important to multicultural environments as do the courses of study and instructional materials. Students learn important lessons about culture and cultural diversity by observing interactions among different racial, ethnic, and cultural groups in their school; hearing verbal exchanges between the professional and support staffs; and observing the extent to which the staff is culturally representative of the student population. It is imperative that schools establish and implement policies to recruit and maintain a totally multicultural school staff (Banks, 1988).

CULTURAL PERSPECTIVES

Socioeconomic and Class Differences

The student's socioeconomic level and social class deserve consideration as elementary and secondary educators plan teaching and learning experiences. If a group of individuals has particular characteristics that are valued by a society, the group so identified will enjoy high status. The reverse is also true. Thus, when speaking of upper and lower classes, we are referring to groups of individuals who either have or do not have qualities in common that are prized by a larger society.

In the United States, upper classes are those groups that have wealth, advanced education, professional occupations, and relative freedom from concern about their material needs. Conversely, lower classes are those groups that live in or on the edge of poverty, have poor education, are irregularly employed or employed in jobs requiring little or no training, often require assistance from government welfare agencies, and are constantly concerned with meeting the basic needs of life.

At least two perspectives stand out as being important for educators to consider: (1) some social classes may be able to provide their children with additional experiences that may be conducive to education and academic achievement, and (2) the belief that determination, hard work, and middle-class values pay rich dividends. The problem with the former is that many students do not bring to school experiential backgrounds that contribute to their education. The latter often causes poor people to be perceived as and feel like failures who lack the ambition or determination to pursue long-term goals.

Realistically, culturally diverse students often come from poorer financial backgrounds and homes in which language differences impede communication and upward social mobility. Such obstacles, however, do not mean that these social classes value education and school achievement any less. It is educators' responsibility to provide teaching and learning experiences that build on the strengths and backgrounds of all children and adolescents.

It is important to emphasize the economic advances and achievements of culturally diverse learners and their families during the past decade or two. Educators should objectively consider each learner to determine individual strengths and weaknesses. To equate poverty with a particular culture, race, or ethnic group is a serious mistake and can jeopardize a learner's educational future.

What are the implications for educators working with children and adolescents from lower socioeconomic and social classes?

1. Teachers, counselors, and administrators should recognize the dangers of associating negative and harmful expectations with culturally diverse groups and lower classes. In fact, educators should periodically review their beliefs about children and adolescents as well as their behavioral and academic expectations (Gollnick & Chinn, 2002).

2. Educators should examine curricular and instructional efforts to determine whether they reflect only middle-class European American perspectives. Culturally diverse learners and students from low socioeconomic backgrounds need to see a reflection of their values and lifestyles in the educational content and in the instructional methods (Gollnick & Chinn, 2002).

3. Educators should be on a constant lookout for grouping patterns that segregate students along cultural, racial, or ethnic lines. Teachers often place students from lower socioeconomic classes or who are culturally diverse in lower ability groups. Such practices may be discriminatory, because students are segregated along ethnic and social class lines.

The Role of Parents and Families

Research (Simich-Dudgeon, 1987) supports the importance of parent involvement and cooperative relationships between parents and schools. First, parental interest and participation in schools and classrooms has a positive influence on academic achievement. Second, parents involved in academic activities with their children gain knowledge that helps them to assess their children's education. They can help their children with areas of education in which they need assistance. Third, the results of parental involvement in tutoring limited English–proficient students are consistent with those for native English-speaking students and their families. To be effective as home tutors, all parents need school support and direct teacher involvement (Simich-Dudgeon, 1987).

Educators must employ special strategies to accommodate the unique cultural characteristics of Asian immigrant parents. Their agenda should include: (1) educators asking themselves some difficult questions about their prejudices and stereotypical beliefs about Asian Americans, (2) understanding Asian beliefs about education, and (3) providing opportunities for Asian American parents to participate in school activities, to communicate through newsletters, and to serve on advisory committees (Yao, 1988).

Educators working with European Americans usually work only with the mother and the father. Culturally diverse children and adolescents, however, often perceive the roles of grandparents, aunts, and uncles as similar to those of the mother and the father. For this reason, educators should welcome extended families who are interested in the learner's educational progress. Culturally diverse parents and families may not understand the U.S. school system and its emphasis on competition and individual welfare and achievement over group accomplishments. Teachers may offer suggestions and directions to parents and families who are able to assist their children and adolescents. Teachers need a better understanding of culturally diverse families and their values, customs, traditions, and expectations. All too often, teachers view the benefits of parent involvement too narrowly. Not only do children benefit, but parents and teachers as well.

LEARNER EVALUATION

The evaluation of learners should include a consideration of individual and cultural differences, variations in learning and testing styles, and differences in motivation. Rather than evaluating only what paper and pencil can measure, evaluation efforts should also focus on student behaviors, attitudes, and everyday actions. For example, a student might be able to list examples of racist behavior and offer several valid reasons on paper why racism should be reduced. The evaluation process, however, should also include a consideration of actions. Do students make racist remarks? Do students demonstrate racial harmony? Do students engage in segregationist activities? Generally speaking, have students developed respect and acceptance for, as well as knowledge of, our increasingly culturally diverse world?

Evaluating Learners' Progress

Sleeter and Grant (1999) offer several recommendations for educators planning and implementing programs that evaluate learners:

1. Evaluation procedures should not include standardized achievement tests that are monocultural in nature and that sort students into different groups that result in different and unequal opportunities.
2. Evaluation procedures should not penalize students by requiring skills that are extraneous to what is being evaluated. For example, a science teacher assessing science concepts should not require students to read and write about their skill level.
3. Evaluation procedures designed to assess students' English proficiency levels should take into account the different contexts in which school communication takes place and the different factors involved.
4. Evaluation procedures should be free of sexist or racist stereotypes.

As we can see, decisions concerning evaluation include both what should be evaluated and a determination of the evaluation methods. As with all curricular efforts, educators should closely match the evaluation with goals and objectives, should measure what was taught, and should measure attitudes and behaviors as well as cognitive knowledge.

SUMMING UP

Educators who plan teaching, learning, and classroom environments in multicultural settings should remember to

1. Recognize and respect learner diversity: culture, race, ethnicity, individuality, gender, social class, and religion.
2. Develop the knowledge, attitudes, and skills to teach and relate to culturally diverse children and adolescents.
3. Recognize that some organizational practices contribute to exclusivity and segregation and that, therefore, educators should provide instructional methods to which culturally diverse children and adolescents can most effectively relate.
4. Plan a school curriculum and environment that reflect respect for all cultural, ethnic, social class, and religious differences among people and that promote learners' self-concepts and cultural identities.
5. Recognize and respond appropriately to cultural perspectives that influence the academic achievement and overall school progress of culturally diverse learners; for example, socioeconomic class and social class, parents and families, and learner evaluation.
6. Implement a teaching and learning environment that affects positively how children and adolescents feel about school, about being culturally different in a predominantly European American school, and about feeling genuinely accepted and cared about.
7. Provide culturally diverse learners with an administration, faculty, and staff that reflects the cultural diversity of the overall school population.

SUGGESTED LEARNING ACTIVITIES

1. Design a plan for involving culturally diverse parents and immediate families in the teaching and learning process. Explain specifically how you would address the following points: language barriers between culturally diverse parents and you; explaining school expectations to parents and families who might not understand how U.S. schools function; and ways you might involve parents and families.

2. Use a case-study approach to study a culturally diverse learner and to pinpoint cultural differences in the ways the student learns, perceives events, and behaves. In a paper summarizing your observations and reflections, state how the student's behavior and attitudes might affect school achievement and how the school might provide more appropriate teaching and learning experiences for this learner.

3. Observe a teaching demonstration to determine a teacher's "unintended bias." Did the teacher call on more girls than boys or more European Americans than Hispanic Americans, expect Asian Americans to answer more difficult questions, or tend to ignore students from lower socioeconomic groups? How might you help this teacher recognize bias? What items would you include on a teacher self-evaluation scale designed to help teachers recognize unintended bias?

SUGGESTIONS FOR COLLABORATIVE EFFORTS

Form groups of three or four that, if possible, represent U.S. cultural and gender diversity. Working collaboratively, focus your group's attention toward the following efforts:

1. Have each member of your group survey elementary and secondary school teachers to determine their efforts to include multicultural perspectives in their teaching and learning activities. Look specifically at items such as curriculum content, teacher expectations for achievement and behavior, grouping strategies, testing and evaluation, and involvement of parents and extended family members. How does your group believe teachers could improve their efforts?

2. Devise a checklist to evaluate the degree to which the overall school environment reflects multicultural perspectives. Although your group should include perspectives it feels are important, the basic underlying question should be: Does the overall school environment portray multicultural perspectives? Other questions might be: Is there evidence that cultural, ethnic, social class, and religious diversity is accepted? Are there deliberate attempts to promote positive self-concepts and cultural identities? Is cultural diversity represented among faculty and staff and at all levels of administration?

EXPANDING YOUR HORIZONS: ADDITIONAL JOURNAL READINGS AND BOOKS

Lee, J. (2002). Racial and ethnic achievement gap trends: Reversing the progress toward equity? *Educational Researcher, 31*(1), 3–12.
Believing that achievement gaps widened during the 1990s, which resulted in setbacks for some ethnic groups, Lee identifies key factors that contributed to the bifurcated patterns.

McCarthey, S. J., Dressman, M., Smolkin, L., McGill-Franzen, A., & Harris, V. J. (2000). How will diversity affect literacy in the next millennium? *Reading Research Quarterly, 35*(4), 548–552.
These authors discuss literacy during the next twenty-five years and focus on the tensions in teaching and learning that accompany diversity and literacy.

Montgomery, W. (2001). Creating culturally responsive, inclusive classrooms. *Teaching Exceptional Children, 33*(4), 4–9.
Montgomery offers guidelines for creating culturally responsive, inclusive classrooms and suggests a range of culturally sensitive methods and materials.

Powell, R., Cantrell, S. C., & Adams, S. (2001). Saving Black Mountain: The promise of critical literacy in a multicultural democracy. *Reading Teacher, 54*(8), 772–781.
These authors explore the concept of democracy and what it means in a multicultural society.

Sianjina, R. R. (2000). Educational technology and the diverse classroom. *Kappa Delta Pi Record, 37*(1), 26–29.
Sianjina describes how thoughtful, creative technology use in the classroom can encourage development in diverse students, explaining that the key to effective computer use within culturally diverse classrooms is the teacher.

Svennbeck, M. (2001). Rethinking the discussion about science education in a multicultural world: Some alternative questions as a new point of departure. *Science and Education, 85*(1), 80–81.
Svennbeck discusses universalists and multiculturalists with regard to science and science curriculum.

.... ▪ ▪ ▪ ▪ ▪ ▪

CHAPTER ELEVEN

INDIVIDUAL AND CULTURAL DIFFERENCES

Understanding the material and activities in this chapter will help the reader to:

- List individual and cultural differences and similarities, and explain their influence on learning and achievement
- Develop positive orientations toward "cultural deficiencies" and "cultural differences" perspectives, and understand the importance of providing educational experiences based on the "differences" perspective
- List at least six individual differences (e.g., self-esteem, gender, development, motivation, social class, exceptionalities) that affect learning and achievement
- List several dangers associated with labeling exceptional learners (and, in fact, all children and adolescents), and demonstrate how their exceptionalities affect learning and achievement
- Describe an educational program (e.g., bilingual education, teaching English as a second language [ESL]) that effectively addresses the needs of language-minority learners
- Define learning styles, explain the complex relationship between culture and learning styles, and suggest inventories designed to assess learners' styles
- Recognize the need for a celebration of cultural diversity and how diversity among learners can enrich elementary and secondary school programs
- Understand the importance of positive cultural identities, and suggest methods to build positive identities among learners

OVERVIEW

Educators' positive responses to elementary and secondary learners' differences are crucial to celebrating cultural, ethnic, and racial diversity among African, Arab, Asian, European, and Hispanic Americans as well as American Indians. Cultural diversity is a strength—a persistent, vitalizing force in our lives. It is a useful resource for improving educational effectiveness for all students. Just as European American, middle-class heritage contributes to the achievement of white students, using the cultures and experiences of African, Arab, Asian, and Hispanic American students as well as American Indians facilitates their school success. Learning experiences and achievement outcomes for ethnically diverse students should include more than cognitive performances in academic subjects and standardized test scores. Moral, social, cultural, personal, and political developments are also important. All of these are essential to the healthy and complete functioning of human beings and societies. If education is, as it should be, devoted to teaching the whole child, then this comprehensive focus should be evident throughout curriculum, instruction, and assessment (Gay, 2000).

No ethnic group is ethnically or intellectually monolithic. For instance, African Americans include people who are descendants of Africans enslaved in the United States, others whose origins are in the Caribbean, and recent immigrants from various African nations. Some are native speakers of English, some are dialect speakers, and others speak English as a second language. Some African Americans are academically gifted, some are average students, and some are failing in school. This kind of variability exists in all ethnic groups, and it affects the achievement of students in different ways. What these differences are must be more clearly defined if teachers are to further encourage those students who are already performing well and remediate those who are not. Thus, effective teaching and learning for diverse students are contingent upon the thorough disaggregation of achievement data by student demographics and types of academic skills (Gay, 2000).

Individual and cultural differences can provide an effective framework for teaching and learning experiences and can enrich and contribute to individual teaching and learning situations and to the total school program. This chapter looks at individual and cultural diversities and examines their influence on student learning and overall development.

THE REALITY OF INDIVIDUAL AND CULTURAL DIVERSITY

All too often classroom teachers, special services personnel, and administrators assume too much homogeneity among learners' abilities, backgrounds, and interests. Some educators still subscribe to the belief that a purpose of the school is to homogenize students (along the lines of the melting pot idea) and to eradicate or "remediate" differences. The reality is that learners' many differences affect their perceptions of learning and achievement, their ways of learning and knowing, and their overall learning and school achievement.

Educational institutions, regardless of grade or academic level, have the responsibility for recognizing individual and cultural differences and planning appropriate educational experiences for all learners. Differences such as poverty, home and family conditions, and some exceptionalities may appear difficult to overcome; nevertheless, students deserve an affirmative response to their differences and learning needs. It no longer suffices to plan educational experiences only for middle- or upper-class white learners and then expect students of other social classes and cultures to change perspectives on motivation and competition, learning styles, and attitudes and values that their homes and families have instilled in them.

Today, society increasingly considers differences among children and adolescents as entities to be appreciated and on which educational experiences can be built. Teachers should recognize and respect children's and adolescents' attitudes, customs, and sacred values. A positive perspective toward these differences must inform curricular decisions and instructional practices.

DIFFERENCES AND THEIR INFLUENCE ON LEARNING

Children's and adolescents' every difference, whether of intellectual, developmental, or gender origin, affects their academic achievement and overall school success. For too many years, educators have planned for the "learner in the middle" (e.g., white, middle-class, nondisabled, male, normally developing) and have expected other learners to conform and to use "middle" cognitive strategies to process information. Schools are challenged to take a more enlightened or multicultural approach and to recognize the multitude of differences among learners.

Perez (1994) maintains that U.S. public schools have never offered an enthusiastic welcome to student differences. In fact, educators sometimes have attempted to remove student differences that they deemed "barriers" to more equal access to opportunities in the larger society.

Perez challenges educators to offer an appropriate response to the increasing diversity in cultures and languages. Schools should reflect the perspective that diversity is not the problem but rather an opportunity for every American to experience other peoples and cultures. Perez offers several ways to seize that opportunity: respect students' names, language, and cultures (Perez, 1994).

Achievement, Intelligence, and Cognitive Processes

A definition of a *learner's achievement level* is previously acquired knowledge that relates to what is being taught. Most educators believe that what students already know affects their present and future achievement. The question the educator should always ask is, "To what extent and how can previous learning contribute to new learning?" The learner who already knows numbers, who is fascinated with science, or who is interested in geography will have a head start over learners without special areas of expertise or interests.

The educational systems from which immigrant students come rarely match U.S. school systems, since culture determines the content of school curricula, assumptions about background knowledge, teaching approaches, classroom interaction, classroom routines, and parental participation (Quinn, 2001). Also, a school environment that takes multiculturalism to a level of quality and makes it a perspective rather than a once-a-month assembly demonstrates respect for different cultures in the life of the school.

Quinn (2001), in Implementing Research 11.1, looks at cultural differences in classrooms and tells educators that no generalizations can be stated as true for all members of a nationality. Still, most members of cultural groups are united by customs, language, and values that differ from those of other groups.

IMPLEMENTING RESEARCH 11.1
CULTURAL DIFFERENCES IN CLASSROOMS

Quinn (2001) maintains that most teachers of Hispanic students in rural areas are white American women from middle-class backgrounds. Therefore, most teachers are unfamiliar with Mexican traditions and lifestyles. Plus, some of these teachers graduated from institutions that rarely offer teacher candidates courses in teaching linguistically and culturally diverse students.

Often, when teachers are asked to educate non-native-English speakers, they believe that if the students acquire the language of the majority culture, the students' problems will be solved. Still, Quinn maintains that students who are living on the margins of school life cannot succeed academically and socially. In order to facilitate language learning, which begins with accepting the language and the need for literacy in a new language, teachers must bring the students who are different into the classroom community.

Quinn focuses on a number of interesting topics, such as migration, diversity among diverse groups, family hierarchy, the need for high expectations, and appropriate responses. Teachers will find Quinn's excellent description of the Mexican culture beneficial.

IMPLEMENTING THE RESEARCH

1. Teachers of Hispanic Americans (and, in fact, students of all cultures) should work to understand intracultural differences—generalizations cannot be made after learning about only a few people of a specific cultural group.
2. Teachers should hold high expectations for Hispanic students and for other students—in terms of both academic achievement and behavior.
3. Teachers need to understand that parents and families might be unfamiliar with the U.S. school system and might benefit from parent education programs designed specifically for their native culture.

Source: Quinn, A. E. (2001). Moving marginalized students inside the lines: Cultural differences in classrooms. *English Journal, 90*(4), 44–50.

FOLLOW THROUGH 11.1
DEALING WITH UNFAMILIAR BEHAVIORS AND CUSTOMS

Name a number of ways in which educators can deal effectively with unfamiliar behaviors and customs in our schools. For example, using White's (1998) example of "personal space," what activities can you suggest for teaching students that "how far people stand apart" is a cultural mannerism. It is not a matter of right and wrong, and people are not necessarily being rude or overly presumptuous. Name several activities that might engage students that would teach them the concept of and acceptance of "personal space."

A learner's overall intelligence, abilities, or special expertise contributes to the degree to which he or she processes information. Learners organize their perceptions and experiences of the school and physical world into cognitive structures. Much is still to be learned about cognition, but it is known that cognitive development is an active process in which learners assimilate information into cognitive categories and adapt their previous categories to accommodate new information. These functions of assimilation and accommodation cause the change and growth in learners' thinking that constitutes cognitive development. Educators who work with students from differing cultural backgrounds should plan educational experiences that recognize the developmental capabilities of children as well as their cultural perspectives.

The learners' cognitive development is of particular importance in multicultural situations, because teachers cannot assume that all learners process information in the same manner. Children's language, thinking strategies, ability to make comparisons and hypotheses, and skill at applying concepts and information depend on their overall cognitive development, which is grounded in their cultural backgrounds. Rather than assuming too much homogeneity among learners, educators have to consider cultural orientations toward achievement, cultural diversity among learning styles, and the learner's degree of active participation.

Self-Esteem

We have mentioned repeatedly throughout this text the importance of the learner's self-esteem and its effects on academic achievement. How learners perceive themselves is especially significant for those of differing cultural backgrounds. The learner who feels that others perceive him or her as inferior, deficient in some manner, or in stereotypical terms may begin to feel less than adequate or unable to cope with the U.S. school system. A child's self-esteem and the value he or she places on cultural heritage and background can plummet to a point where success in school and in other areas of life is in jeopardy.

Implementing Research 11.2 looks at cross-cultural studies, child development, and Asian cultures.

■ ■ ■ ■ ■ ▬▬▬▬▬▬▬▬▬▬▬▬▬▬▬▬▬▬

FOLLOW THROUGH 11.2
PROMOTING SELF-ESTEEM

Perceptive educators realize the importance of self-esteem and the relationship between learning and students' feelings about themselves. A powerful need exists for all students to have strong self-esteem; however, learners from culturally different backgrounds might experience more challenges developing self-esteem. Name several ways in which educators might promote self-esteem (and cultural identities). For example, your list might include having students make a personal collage that shows "who I am" or the positive contributions of another person of the same cultural background.

■ ■ ■ ■ ■

IMPLEMENTING RESEARCH 11.2

CROSS-CULTURAL STUDIES, CHILD DEVELOPMENT, AND ASIAN CULTURES

Keats (2000) reported on her cross-cultural research with Asian (mainly Malaysia, Thailand, and Indonesia) and Australian children. In each of these countries, far-reaching changes challenge traditional cultural values in family relationships and child-rearing practices. The author examined aspects such as the role of communication, development of values, and culturally related differences. Keats maintains that there is a great need for cross-cultural research in multicultural contexts of these Asian countries. Western ideas of desirable practices in the development of children often conflict with an Asian culture's traditional views and more recent ideologies. Examples of conflicts include Islamic views of child development and the attitudes of many Westerners to China's one-child policy. Also, Asian countries have all been undergoing massive lifestyle changes, including economic, social, and psychological changes, that threaten many traditional child-rearing practices and values. Keats maintains that cross-cultural developmental psychology challenges researchers to continue working with each other within multicultural contexts.

IMPLEMENTING THE RESEARCH

1. Generalizations should be reached with considerable caution, because of the far-reaching changes that have challenged traditional cultural values.
2. Teachers should avoid assuming that Asian parents and families will be receptive to Western ideas of desirable child-rearing practices.

Source: Keats, D. M. (2000). Cross-cultural studies in child development in Asian cultures. *Cross-Cultural Research, 34*(3), 339–350.

Gender

Gender determines masculine and feminine differences—the thoughts, feelings, and behaviors one identifies as being either male or female. Culturally determined masculine and feminine behavior can differ significantly. For example, a boy demonstrating feminine traits might be called a "sissy" in one culture but be accepted in another (Gollnick & Chinn, 2002).

Educational experiences and outcomes differ for males and females:

■ Lundeberg, Fox, and Puncochar (1994) reported that, as early as the sixth grade, girls have less self-confidence than boys, and the differences increase with age. Both boys and girls lose self-esteem as they grow older, but girls show a far greater loss. For example, girls in elementary, middle, and secondary schools experience continuous decreases in self-esteem of 60, 37, and 29 percent, respectively (*Education and gender*, 1994).

■ *Everybody Counts: A Report to the Nation on the Future of Mathematics Education* (National Research Council, 1989) indicates that girls and boys progress through the mathematics curriculum and in fact show little difference in ability, effort, or

■ ■ ■ ■ ■ ▬▬▬▬

FOLLOW THROUGH 11.3
COUNTERACTING GENDER BIAS

Interview six or eight girls at the middle or secondary school level. In an effort to determine their perceptions of schools' efforts to counteract gender bias, focus your questions around areas such as curricular materials, school environment, interpersonal relationships, and instructional methods. Also ask about overall school philosophy, such as individualism versus group welfare and collaboration versus competition.

interest until the adolescent years. Then, as social pressures increase, girls' decisions to reduce effort in the study of mathematics progressively limit their future education and eventually their career choices.

■ Focusing on risk taking and mathematics achievement, Ramos and Lambating (1996) examined females' reluctance to be risk takers and males' tendency to be greater risk takers. Females' reluctance to guess on multiple-choice tests and their tendency to leave more questions unanswered (true–false, multiple choice, and relationship analysis) contributes to their lower achievement.

■ Male and female students in grades 4 and 8 have similar science achievement scores; however, by grade 12, male students have higher scores than females (National Assessment of Educational Progress, 1997).

How can educators address gender differences? How can educators provide females with an education that adopts feminine perspectives? First, women's studies should include consciousness-raising efforts and attempt to create a more enlightened view of women and their unique individual perspectives. Second, education should be as nonsexist as possible. Teachers should scrutinize all instructional materials and seek to eliminate sexist connotations and promote feminine learning styles. Teachers should understand and consider cognitive strategies whenever possible. Third, Title IX of the 1972 Educational Amendment addresses the discriminatory treatment of students based on their sex. Title IX (Gollnick & Chin, 2002) states that "no person shall, on the basis of sex, be excluded from participation in, be denied the benefits of, or be subjected to, discrimination under any education program or activity receiving federal financial assistance."

DEVELOPMENTAL LEVELS
AND COGNITIVE READINESS

The learner's developmental stage is perhaps the most significant individual difference affecting learning. Learners functioning at one developmental level simply cannot comprehend material that requires the thinking and cognitive skills of the next higher developmental level. Rather than assuming that learners can succeed by trying hard or doing more homework, educators should understand that development and readiness, not effort alone, affect what youngsters can learn.

A youngster at the concrete-operations stage cannot master intellectual challenges that demand formal, abstract thinking abilities. Although some memorization might occur, learners will be unable to learn information that is beyond their cognitive ability at any given age. To assume that all learners can perform functions and master content at a level that a few precocious and intellectually advanced students attain ignores individual differences and what is known about cognitive readiness (Manning, 2002).

The challenge for educators is to determine developmental and readiness levels and to plan and implement appropriate instruction. Educators might raise some questions about theories that proclaim growth and development as cross-culturally valid. However, development as an individual difference affects learning and crosses cultural boundaries. Regardless of cultural backgrounds and when they reach certain developmental stages, learners cannot master material they are not developmentally ready to learn. The challenge for educators is to diagnose the learner's developmental stage and then provide developmentally appropriate curricular experiences and instructional practices.

Implementing Research 11.3 examines social expectations and African American, Hispanic, and European American adolescents.

Beliefs, Attitudes, and Values

Understanding children and adolescents from culturally different backgrounds requires knowing their beliefs, attitudes, and values. These idiosyncrasies are based in each learner's culture and influence all aspects of his or her life, whether in motivation, competition, perspectives toward the family, or perceptions of racism and its effects. Numerous illustrations provide evidence of the effects of attitudes: the Asian American student who is taught to revere teachers; the African American child who can listen to someone without looking the speaker in the eye; the American Indian learner who values cooperation and sharing as being more worthy than competition; or the Hispanic American adolescent who believes he or she should not stand out among peers.

Perceptive educators recognize the cultural baggage (prejudices, myths, and stereotypes) that children and adolescents bring to school, baggage that affects attitudes toward school, other learners, and learning achievement. The educator's challenge is to understand and to respect these personal aspects and, whenever possible, to provide school experiences that are culturally compatible. Curricular practices and instructional methods that are genuinely multicultural in both theory and practice reflect the values, attitudes, and beliefs of learners of culturally different backgrounds and do not require learners to participate in actions that contradict their cultural beliefs.

Motivation

It is important for educators in multicultural situations to understand motivation. Rather than perceive motivation through middle-class, European American eyes, educators must understand the complex relationship between motivation and cultural di-

■ ■ ■ ■ ■ ▬▬▬▬▬▬▬▬▬▬▬▬▬▬▬

IMPLEMENTING RESEARCH 11.3
SOCIAL EXPECTATIONS AND ADOLESCENTS

Using sixteen brief videotaped scenes of everyday social encounters, Yager and Rotheram-Borus (2000) investigated ethnic, gender, and developmental differences in the social expectations of African American, Hispanic, and European American high school students. The four domains included group orientation, expressiveness, assertiveness, and aggressiveness. Yager and Rotheram-Borus reached several conclusions. Group-oriented responses were given significantly more often to Hispanic and European students; expressive and aggressive responses were significantly more frequent among African Americans and Hispanic students; and assertive responses were more frequent among European Americans compared to African Americans. Males' social expectations were less group-oriented and assertive and more expressive and aggressive. Females' expectations for assertiveness increased with grade level. Ethnic and gender differences were similar across youth of different ages.

IMPLEMENTING THE RESEARCH
1. Rather than basing educational expectations and decisions on generalizations, educators should get to know individual adolescents. They should not simply assume that Hispanic and European students are group-oriented; African Americans and Hispanic students are expressive and aggressive; and European Americans are assertive.
2. Females' expectations for assertiveness can be influenced by many factors (e.g., individuality and parental influences) and deserve teacher consideration prior to assuming that assertiveness increases with grade level.

Source: Yager, T. J., & Rotheram-Borus, M. J. (2000). Social expectations among African American, Hispanic, and European American adolescents. *Cross-Cultural Research, 34*(3), 283–305.

■ ■ ■ ■ ■ ▬▬▬▬▬▬▬▬▬▬▬▬▬▬▬

FOLLOW THROUGH 11.4
DETERMINING SOURCES OF MOTIVATION

In a group or individual setting (whichever will prompt students to share personal information), talk with learners to see what motivates them. Does competing with peers motivate them? Do their parents' expectations motivate them? Does the teacher play a significant role in motivation?

versity. For example, middle-class European Americans might be motivated by competition, by an outstanding achievement that sets the individual apart from peers, or by the desire to work independently. Learners from culturally different backgrounds may not hold those same values and might appear unmotivated when they do not want to stand out among their peers or to excel at the expense of others or when they choose to work in cooperative learning situations sharing expertise.

Closely related to learners' motivation and willingness to employ cognitive abilities is their expectation of success or failure. Beliefs related to the likelihood of success, to judgments about their ability, and to emotional reactions of pride and hopelessness all contribute to the extent learners are willing to use cognitive strategies. Over time, learners who believe that lack of ability causes failure are likely to feel a sense of helplessness. This theory of the relationship among motivation, feelings of self-worth, and the willingness to use cognitive strategies might be especially useful for educators who work with learners from culturally different backgrounds.

Educators should focus on the particular motivational problems of individual students. School learning requires active effort, and children are not likely to put forth the active effort if they do not see that their schoolwork helps them to achieve their own purposes or to satisfy their own interests. They may respond to their parents' or teachers' pressures, but unless students have a personal reason to complete school assignments, motivation will be difficult to maintain. Educators need to understand motivation from its cultural perspective and then attempt to help learners understand qualities in their assignments that are either interesting or useful.

Case Study 11.1 shows how thirteen-year-old Carl's motivation is misunderstood and suggests that teachers should not view children and adolescents of culturally different backgrounds from middle-class, European American perspectives.

■ ■ ■ ■ ■ ■

CASE STUDY 11.1
MOTIVATION AND CULTURAL CONSIDERATIONS

Carl, a thirteen-year-old American Indian middle-school student, shows a lack of motivation, initiative, and competitive drive. He does not demonstrate any desire to set himself apart from or to rise above others in his class. His teachers see him as "different." Whereas most of the white students in this school strive for success and good grades, Carl does his work but shows no desire to achieve more. The teachers who work together in Carl's unit wonder what to do and how to motivate him.

Although this pattern has been typical of American Indians in this school, Mrs. Westerly, the special education teacher, recognizes a crucial aspect of this situation that others either have not seen or do not want to admit. Rather than look at Carl from a European American perspective, Mrs. Westerly suggests understanding the American Indian perspective. Perhaps, from Carl's cultural perspective, he is motivated. His family has transmitted a cultural heritage that does not emphasize competition or achievement that would set him apart from his peers. He does not value competing with other learners, because it seems far more logical to share ideas and to work cooperatively and in harmony.

The teachers begin to realize that they have evaluated Carl's motivation through a middle-class, European American lens. They had in fact been expecting Carl to conform to behaviors that were completely alien to his cultural heritage and background.

Socioeconomic Class

The social class differential that exists in the United States includes the family's absolute income, educational background, occupational prestige, place of residence, lifestyle, and relative autonomy and power. It is worth remembering, however, that wealth and material success are relative concepts; one family might consider ownership of a swimming pool a sign of success, whereas another family might perceive the addition of a porch to a mobile home as an indicator of success (Ramsey, 1987). In any event, a family's socioeconomic class and income level determine children's and adolescents' experiences, as do other factors (e.g., conditions of the home, the presence of books and other reading materials and computers, trips with educational significance) that have positive effects on educational progress.

An educator must remember to consider learners and their families individually. It is a serious mistake and an injustice to learners to make assumptions of wealth and social class based on culture, race, or ethnicity. Conversely, a teacher should never predict a learner's educational potential on the basis of socioeconomic level. Just as many higher socioeconomic class learners often fail to respond to their educators' efforts, students from lower-class homes and neighborhoods have achieved extraordinary educational successes.

EXCEPTIONALITIES

The Dangers of Labeling and Erroneous Placement

Labeling learners has such potentially harmful effects that educators who assign labels may be placing children and adolescents at great risk. Although such educators probably have the learner's interest and educational welfare in mind, labeling learners as "slow" or "disabled" can sometimes cause irreparable harm, not only during school programs but throughout their lives. Educators should be cognizant of the disadvantages of labeling and should know when the practice is or is not in the learner's best interest. Disadvantages of labeling children and adolescents include:

1. Learners who are identified as disabled or exceptional may be permanently stigmatized, rejected, or denied opportunities for full development.
2. Learners labeled as *mentally retarded* (or the equivalent) may be assigned to inferior educational programs in school or illegally placed in institutions.
3. Large numbers of learners from culturally diverse backgrounds are inaccurately classified as mentally disabled on the basis of scores they earn on inappropriate tests.

Case Study 11.2 illustrates the dangers of labeling learners and shows how placing learners in categories can affect both students' and teachers' perceptions.

The disadvantages of labeling are sufficient to cause alarm, but another problem may result from labeling: the overt segregation of learners. Sendor (1988) suggests that

■ ■ ■ ■ ■ ▬▬▬▬▬▬▬▬▬▬▬▬▬▬▬

CASE STUDY 11.2

THE DANGERS OF LABELING

Dr. Strobecker, principal of Cedarwood Elementary School, was looking through students' permanent records when several labels caught her eye: "behaviorally maladjusted," "slow learner," "retarded," "below average," "gifted," "troublemaker," "unmotivated," "emotionally disturbed," and other labels that educators can imagine. She realized the dangers of labeling: Teachers sometimes expect too little, sometimes too much; learners are often in the wrong group; and labels assigned to them in the elementary school may affect learners' entire lives. Further, such labeling may be both unprofessional and unethical. She admitted to herself that, although labeling learners had the potential for helping, the practice should be limited to only those cases in which learners will clearly be helped.

Dr. Strobecker knew that, as principal, she had the professional responsibility for addressing the situation. There were several things she might do: first, she should make teachers aware of the dangers of labeling; second, she should encourage teachers to read professional articles that deal with labeling and alternatives; third, she should encourage teachers to diagnose learners by using the most objective and reliable means; and fourth, teachers should assign a label only when the diagnosis is accurate and in the learner's best interest.

grouping and placement practices have segregated learners racially. Using subjective means or teacher recommendations, labeling or placement policies can contribute (either intentionally or unintentionally) to the segregation of students along racial and ethnic lines. Such policies are both unethical and unprofessional and can condemn learners to "slow" groups or inferior materials and methods. Such situations may occur because educators want learners segregated or because educators erroneously equate race or ethnicity with achievement and ability.

When, if ever, should educators label learners? Teachers should give a learner a label when, and *only* when, it is in the student's best interest and when substantial objective data can document the learner's condition. The label should serve a meaningful purpose and provide a basis for assisting the learner's overall educational progress.

■ ■ ■ ■ ■ ▬▬▬▬▬▬▬▬▬▬▬▬▬▬▬

FOLLOW THROUGH 11.5

AVOIDING ERRONEOUS LABELING

Name five or six ways in which educators can avoid the hazards of labeling learners. Your list might include getting to know individuals, talking with parents and extended family members, conversing with others in the culture, and using culturally relevant testing devices for assessment purposes.

Even when this is the case, educators have a moral, ethical, and professional responsibility to assess learners periodically, to diagnose accurately, to follow all due-process procedures, and to ensure that learners are placed in other groups or classes if the disabling or exceptional conditions change.

Disabling Conditions

Children and adolescents from culturally different backgrounds can experience the same disabling conditions that other children or adolescents experience, such as behavior disorders, mentally disabling conditions, visual impairments, communication disorders, or hearing and visual impairments. It is crucial, however, to ascertain that diagnostic tests accurately reflect the strengths and weaknesses of disabled youngsters from culturally different backgrounds and make decisions accordingly. When working with disabled learners, educators must identify the concept of behavior and its role in determining eligibility for special programs. Most important, professionals who make eligibility decisions should be sensitive to what is educationally best for the student (Patton & Polloway, 1990).

Gifted and Talented

Some people continue to question the use of *gifted* in the same breath with *cultural diversity*. It has been difficult for some people to understand that a child or adolescent may be verbally gifted (although perhaps in a language other than English), that learners have higher-order cognitive processes in survival techniques (that do not reveal themselves on school assessments), and that the term *culturally different* does not imply that students are lacking in some areas.

Although many papers in the literature urge educators to be sensitive to the special characteristics of culturally diverse populations, most programs for gifted learners continue to use traditional methods of identification, which rely on popular notions of gifted characteristics. Identifying gifted learners from different cultural backgrounds may be difficult. Learners from culturally different backgrounds might be from a home environment that rewards certain types of behavior that are not consonant with conventional notions of giftedness. For example, some Hispanic American families may provide less reinforcement of highly verbal behavior. Children from such a family, on entering school, may be somewhat reticent and might not stand out in screening for giftedness.

Gifted children are found in every socioeconomic and cultural group. Educators have been less than successful in identifying gifted learners from culturally different backgrounds, perhaps because they are more difficult to recognize and teach. Several factors have contributed to an increased emphasis on identifying gifted learners from culturally different backgrounds: First, broader definitions of giftedness and intellectual ability are contributing to the identification of more learners; and second, there is a new willingness among educators to use a variety of screening and evaluation techniques and instruments.

What instruments and techniques do experts recommend for identifying gifted learners from culturally different backgrounds?

1. Research indicates that gifted students from culturally different backgrounds are likely to score higher on the K-ABC Instrument than on the Stanford-Binet or Wechsler scales, which depend more on verbal skills.
2. A study has attempted to identify and to test for specific types of giftedness using Guilford's Structure of Intellect Model. This is an important step because it relates traditional intelligence measures to the nontraditional structure of the intellect.
3. The subcultural Indices of Academic Potential is a test that requires students to assess their reactions to everyday situations. This test produces a profile of preferences, learning styles, and ways of approaching tasks.
4. The Kranz Talent Identification Instrument is designed to raise awareness of the multiple criteria of giftedness and to assist teachers in screening for talented learners in the classrooms (Wolf, 1990).

After educators have identified gifted learners, they must select programs that match the needs of gifted youngsters from culturally diverse backgrounds. These programs should have a design and method of implementation that considers the learner's psychological, cultural, and linguistic characteristics. Simply integrating learners into an established gifted curriculum may not be successful, because it requires learners to accommodate themselves to the school program, rather than having the program meet the needs of individual learners.

LANGUAGE

Language differences continue to challenge educators in the twenty-first century:

1. Significant numbers of groups speak a language other than English at home and do not speak English very well.
2. Linguistic diversity (both limited English proficiency and use of dialects) is controversial, dividing much of the nation.
3. Inseparable relationships exist between language and culture.
4. Effective multicultural education programs place considerable emphasis on accepting linguistic diversity and encouraging learners to be bilingual and bidialectal.
5. Teaching linguistically different students requires effective strategies.

Some suggest that linguistically different learners forsake their native languages, and others suggest learning English as a second language. A genuine multicultural education program teaches learners to hold onto their native languages so they can be bilingual and have access to two cultures (Byrnes & Cortez, 1996).

■ ■ ■ ■ ■ ▬▬▬

FOLLOW THROUGH 11.6
DETERMINING GIFTEDNESS

Identifying gifted learners from culturally different backgrounds can pose challenges for educators who might be accustomed to looking for particular traits that might relate to a specific culture. Traits suggesting giftedness in learners from differing cultural backgrounds might go undetected. Name several ways educators might determine learners' areas of giftedness, remembering that learners in some cultures might be reluctant to reveal special talents at the expense of other students.

Dialect Differences

Dialect and the issue of whether to require use of standard American English in the schools are sensitive and controversial subjects. Because there is a close relationship between groups of differing cultural backgrounds and dialects that are often nonstandard, this issue also has civil rights implications. Some consider any requirement that standard English be spoken in schools discriminatory. They think that such a requirement places an additional educational burden on the non-standard-English-speaking students. Further, the insistence on standard English may hinder the acquisition of other educational skills, making it difficult for these students to succeed. Such a practice may deny non-standard-English-speaking students the same educational opportunities as others and thus morally, if not legally, denies them their civil rights (Gollnick & Chinn, 2002).

A learner's dialect is closely related to her or his cultural identity and overall self-esteem. School programs that are effective with students of culturally different backgrounds are sufficiently flexible to accommodate the range of dialects learners bring to school. While speaking a nonstandard dialect may have detrimental economic, social, and educational consequences for students, teachers should nonetheless accept, value, and appreciate a student's language (Crawford, 1993).

Dialects also pose a challenging issue for educators, who can address them in several ways: (1) accommodate all dialects, based on the assumption that they are all equal, (2) insist on learners speaking only one dialect in school, and (3) accept dialects for

■ ■ ■ ■ ■ ▬▬▬

FOLLOW THROUGH 11.7
MAKING DECISIONS ABOUT DIALECTS

Decide how you will address dialects and dialectical differences, remembering the close relationship between language (and dialects) and cultural backgrounds. Trying to change a student's dialect can have deleterious effects on his or her self-esteem and cultural identity. Specifically, how do you plan to address dialects?

certain uses but insist on standard English in other situations. Educators should allow dialects in social and recreational situations (i.e., other than formal classroom discourse) but should encourage students in school settings to use standard English, because it is the primary written and spoken language in the United States. Such a compromise allows students to use dialects as it recognizes the social and economic implications of being able to function in standard English (Gollnick & Chinn, 2002).

Language and Culture: Inseparable Relationships

English as a second language and multicultural education are two closely related concepts. Learners acquire language through socialization, and, in turn, language shapes perception of the physical and social worlds in which they live. It is not possible to effectively address linguistic differences without acknowledging and respecting cultural differences. Likewise, it is not possible to respect cultural differences without acknowledging and respecting the importance of a person's language.

Learners think about and understand the world in their native tongue, which is intricately tied to their identity. Ignoring or devaluing learners' native language denies an important part of the rich past and present cultural experiences learners bring to school. Thus, it is critical for classroom teachers to acknowledge and respect children's home language, whether it is a completely different language or an English dialect (Byrnes & Cortez, 1996).

Multicultural Programs Emphasizing Language Diversity

Perceptive educators at all school levels understand how respect for language diversity is a prerequisite to effective multicultural programs. They support language diversity by:

1. Ensuring that linguistically different learners have teachers trained to work with second-language learners
2. Understanding that a student might have sufficient ability in English to socialize in the hallways, yet may need support to comprehend academic language usage
3. Relating learning to students' life experiences, prior knowledge, and cultural perspectives
4. Validating, respecting, and building, whenever possible, on students' native language abilities
5. Recognizing, not eliminating, and in fact valuing dialects (Crawford, 1993)

Effective Strategies for Linguistically Different Learners

Several important general lessons emerge when one considers the specific culturally responsive instructional programs and practices. When instructional processes are consistent with the cultural orientations, experiences, and learning styles of African, Hispanic, Arab, and Asian American and American Indian students, their school achievement improves significantly. This success is most evident when students learn culturally relevant curricular content, teacher attitudes and expectations, and instructional actions strategies. Students come to school having already mastered many cultural skills and ways of knowing. To the extent that teaching builds on these capabilities, academic success will result. Translating this mindset into instructional action begins with accepting the cultural knowledge and skills of ethnically diverse students as valuable teaching–learning resources and using them as scaffolds or bridges to academic achievement (Gay, 2000).

Academic performance is maximized when multiple areas of learning (e.g., academic, cultural, personal) are facilitated at once and difference teaching techniques are used, all within the cultural contexts of various cultural groups. Culturally responsive practices unveil some solutions to the seemingly unsolvable mystery of the perpetual underachievement of students who are diverse. They are not being taught in school the way they learn in their cultural communities. This discontinuity interrupts their mental schemata and makes academic learning harder to achieve. Filtering teaching through the cultural lens of African, Arab, Asian, and Hispanic American students as well as American Indians can lead to much greater school success (Gay, 2000).

O'Malley and Chamot (1990) listed techniques for learning a second language.

Sound acquisition—learners can listen carefully to language sounds on a tape or those of a teacher or other native speaker. Then, they can practice the sounds by talking aloud and role-playing verbal situations.

Grammar—learners can follow or infer language rules in textbooks, compare native languages with English, and practice grammatical structures, both written and oral.

Vocabulary—learners can prepare charts, learn words in context, learn words by association with others, use new words in phrases, and use a dictionary when necessary.

Listening comprehension—learners can listen to the radio, records, television, and movies for different accents, dialects, and registers.

Learning to talk—learners need to be open to making mistakes, make contact with native speakers, ask for corrections, and learn dialogues.

Learning to write—learners can maintain journals and write frequently to pen pals using any of the writing forms commonly accepted in schools.

Learning to read—learners can read something in English every day, read things that are familiar, read texts at the beginner's level, and look for meaning from context (O'Malley & Chamot, 1990).

Teachers can help by

1. Directing activities (a strategy that research suggests is highly effective in teaching English) during which students listen and respond to effective role models.
2. Providing classroom situations in which students follow distinct patterns every day and have the time and environment to concentrate on language and educational content.

3. Allowing students to help students—they may be more likely to ask for language clarification from another student than from the teacher, or they may be better able to communicate with another student with similar language skills

4. Asking for volunteers, then asking for group responses, and establishing a pattern of taking turns that requires all students to participate orally.

5. Taking special care to speak clearly and to use concrete references, repetitions, rephrasings, gestures, visual aids, and demonstrations.

6. Providing curricular materials on an appropriate cognitive level; for example, a teacher should not give a book written for a kindergarten student to a sixth-grader.

7. Using whole-language activities whenever possible, so students will have opportunities for rich, meaningful interactions with both written and oral language.

8. Providing opportunities for recounts (essentially extended versions of known information and answer exchanges), accounts (narratives the teller generates to provide new information), event casts (ongoing narratives interesting to both teller and listener), and stories (the telling of a narrative) in which learners practice second-language skills, both chronologically and thematically (Faltis, 1993).

9. Encouraging students to work in cooperative groups so maximum language interaction can occur; primary language speakers can assist second-language learners and provide role models.

10. Reading appropriate books aloud (actually an excellent idea for all learners), so linguistically different learners can hear pronunciations and words in context.

11. Allowing students to read books and then give oral book reports to small groups; second-language learners can have role models and can practice English skills.

12. Allowing learners to write messages, letters, cards, and notes and read them in English.

13. Including listening centers with records and tapes so second-language learners can practice listening skills and learn English simultaneously.

14. Allowing a panel of reporters or reviewers to interview a person or imaginary author in English and clarifying unclear language points.

15. Allowing students to prepare radio or television broadcasts that include book talks, advertisements for books and other products, or reading sections of books (Crawford, 1993).

Bilingual Education and English as a Second Language

The language diversity in the United States extends into the schools, and in large urban and metropolitan school districts nearly a hundred different languages may be spoken. Whereas some students are bilingual in English and their native language, others either do not speak English at all or have limited English-speaking skills. Indications are that the number of students with limited English-speaking skills will continue to increase (Gollnick & Chinn, 2002).

Some learners are competent in English; others, however, may speak only Spanish, the second most common language in the United States; one of the many Asian languages; or a less common language such as Arabic or Tongian (Haring,

■ ■ ■ ■ ■ ▬▬▬▬▬▬▬▬▬▬▬▬▬▬▬▬

FOLLOW THROUGH 11.8
SUPPORTING BILINGUAL EDUCATION

Assume that you have been asked by the school board to propose a public service announcement supporting bilingual education programs. What points do you want to address? How will you respond to critics and many communities' feeling that bilingual programs should be eliminated? What other issues need to be addressed in such a controversial program?

1990). This section looks at efforts such as bilingual education and English as a second language (ESL) programs (or the teaching of English to speakers of other languages), which attempt to address the needs of learners of culturally different backgrounds.

Some confusion exists concerning bilingual education and ESL programs, which many often assume to be synonymous. In the United States, the teaching of English is an integral aspect of bilingual programs, but the teaching of English in and by itself (ESL) does not constitute a bilingual program. Both programs promote English proficiency for students whose English is limited (Hernandez, 1989).

Bilingual education is generally defined as "the use of two languages as media of instruction" (Baca & Cervantes, 1989, p. 24). Bilingual education has received federal funds as a provision of the Bilingual Education Act of 1968, which Congress reauthorized in 1974, 1978, and 1984 (Gollnick & Chinn, 2002).

Bilingual education reinforces the student's home language and culture, and simultaneously teaches the ability to function in another language. Instruction in both skills and content is usually in the student's home language and in English. The most important legal action related to bilingual education was the 1974 *Lau v. Nichols* decision, which pointed to the need for some type of special instructional program for students with limited English-speaking ability.

ESL programs rely exclusively on English for teaching and learning. Educators use ESL programs extensively in the United States as the primary means of assimilating limited-English-speaking students into the linguistic mainstream as quickly as possible. The main feature of the program is that educators place less emphasis on the maintenance of home language and culture than on English language acquisition (Hernandez, 1989). The emphasis of the ESL program is concentrated in three major areas (TESOL, 1976):

1. *Culture:* Integrating students' cultural experiences and background into meaningful language learning
2. *Language development:* Teaching structures and vocabulary relevant to students' learning experiences
3. *Content-Area instruction:* Applying techniques from second-language learning to subject learning and to subject matter presented in English

Table 11.1 provides an overview of ESL programs.

TABLE 11.1   Questions and Answers about English as a Second Language

What Is English as a Second Language?

English as a second language (ESL) is intensive English-language instruction by teachers trained in recognizing and working with language differences. The ESL program is required by state laws in school districts with students who have limited English-language skills.

What Is an ESL Program?

- An ESL program is structured language instruction designed to teach English to students whose English-language skills are limited.
- ESL instruction considers the student's learning experiences and cultural backgrounds.
- ESL is taught through second-language methods that are applied to the teaching of mathematics, science, and social studies.

What Is the Purpose of an ESL Program?

- An ESL program develops competence in English.
- English-language skills are taught through listening, speaking, reading, writing, and grammar.
- A student's instructional program is modified to make learning English easier.

Who Should Be Enrolled in an ESL Program?

- Students in prekindergarten through grade 12 who speak or hear a language other than English in their home and who have difficulty in English are eligible.

Who Is Responsible for Teaching an ESL Program?

- Teachers who are specially trained, tested, and certified to teach ESL programs.

Source: English as a second language program: Benefits for your child. (1987). Austin, TX: Texas Education Agency.

CELEBRATING AND RESPONDING TO CULTURAL DIVERSITY

Educators usually do not question the premise that culture plays a major role in a learner's overall achievement and attitudes toward school. The ultimate challenge, however, is to recognize cultural diversity as a strength on which to build a solid education. The first step is to respond to diversity with a sense of positiveness, rather than view it as a hurdle to be overcome.

One example of diversity among groups is the variety of formal and informal rules governing interaction between individuals. When classroom interactional patterns are not consistent or compatible with those that children and adolescents experience in their homes and community, such variations may cause problems. For example,

■ ■ ■ ■ ■ ▬▬▬▬▬▬▬▬▬▬▬▬▬▬▬

FOR ADDITIONAL INFORMATION
INTERNET ADDRESSES

National Clearinghouse for Bilingual Education (NCBE)
www.ncbe.gwu.edu   Provides information and resources for educators who design and implement bilingual education programs.

Bilingual Multicultural Education Classes
www.nau.edu/nauonline/courses/edbme.html Provides information on English as a second language as well as multicultural education.

Bilingual/Multicultural Studies Major
www.umfk.maine.edu/registrar/cat94-5.majbilin. htm   Provides information on a college major

that addresses the needs of teachers of children whose home language and culture differ from the language and culture of the classroom.

Toronto District School Board
www.multi.demon.co.uk/coelho.htm   Provides practical advice and suggestions for educators in schools serving culturally and linguistically diverse communities.

Bilingual Education Resources
www.librosdericardo.com/resource.html   Provides a listing of resources for bilingual education.

variations in how and when the teacher says something (although perhaps unintentional) as well as what is said may interfere with learning and damage attitudes toward school (Gollnick & Chinn, 2002). Some differences are easily recognized, but educators sometimes overlook the less visible aspects of the culture associated with everyday etiquette and interaction, as well as with the expression of rights, obligations, values, and aspirations.

An excellent example of how cultural backgrounds affect learning is the manner in which teaching and learning environments are structured according to rules that the students and their community do not share. Several differences may surface: how students and teachers interact, how teachers control and monitor behavior, what kinds of behaviors people use to intervene, what kinds of organizational patterns exist, and whether teachers expect learners to participate by interrupting another speaker for a chance to voice an opinion.

American Indian learners, for example, might perceive instructional demands as strange or contradictory to cultural expectations. American Indian learners who should respond competitively might feel that such instructional expectations violate their desire for cooperation and group efforts (Hernandez, 1990).

Children have many diversities such as family types, ethnicities, cultures, and abilities. The challenge facing educators is to implement educational programs that address differences and create an atmosphere in which harmony and diversity reign. Winter (1994/1995) maintains that each child should be understood as an individual and that individually appropriate learning should be planned. Other directions include creating an atmosphere of acceptance, addressing personal biases, promoting attitudes of acceptance, encouraging open communication, building the competence of children, and incorporating instructional technology.

An equitable response to differences among learners includes:

1. Encouraging students to build and maintain self-esteem
2. Using the ethnic backgrounds of students to teach effectively
3. Helping students overcome their prejudices
4. Expanding the knowledge and appreciation of the historical, economic, political, and social experiences of ethnic and national groups
5. Assisting students in understanding that the world's knowledge and culture have been, and continue to be, created from the contributions of all cultural groups and nations

A response should also include the provision of environments in which students can learn to participate in the dominant society while maintaining distinct cultural differences. Educators can work toward such responses by demonstrating respect and support for differences, by reflecting diversity in the curriculum, and by using positive differences to teach and interact with learners (Hernandez, 1989).

BUILDING CULTURAL IDENTITIES

An individual's cultural identity is based on a number of traits and values that are related to national or ethnic origin, family, religion, gender, age, occupation, socioeconomic level, language, geographic region, and exceptionality (Gollnick & Chinn, 1998). The interaction of these factors and the degree to which individuals identify with different subcultures or cultural groups that share political and social institutions and other distinctive cultural elements determines the identity to a large degree (Hernandez, 1989). Rather than allowing "different is wrong" perceptions to prevail and to lower learners' opinions of cultural identities, perceptive educators recognize learners' cultural identities and assist learners in developing positive, healthy, cultural identities.

James P. Comer, a prominent African American psychiatrist and a coauthor of *Black Child Care*, proposes that children of all cultures need to establish a positive racial identity. Comer suggests that children of all racial groups should be able to develop positive feelings about themselves and their cultural group. Negative or ambivalent feelings may result in adverse social and psychological consequences (Comer, 1988).

Case Study 11.3 suggests that affirmative approaches, such as activities that promote the understanding of cultural diversity and assessment of the overall teaching and learning environment, can improve cultural identities.

Educators who celebrate the richness that cultural diversity brings to the classroom readily recognize the need to build or enhance learners' cultural identity. Family and cultural ties are so important to every learner that teachers should give these aspects prime consideration in teaching and learning experiences.

Learners' earliest experiences are of home and family, and language is an important part of this background. Teachers should remember the importance of respecting learners' cultural backgrounds, and at all times they should avoid abusing or dishonoring them. A first step in building a learner's cultural identity is for educators to understand that learner's heritage, values and traditions, and language. While efforts to

■ ■ ■ ■ ■ ▬▬▬▬▬▬▬▬▬▬▬▬▬▬▬▬▬▬▬▬▬▬▬▬▬▬▬▬▬▬▬▬▬▬▬▬▬

CASE STUDY 11.3
ENHANCING CULTURAL IDENTITIES

Ms. Stepp is a teacher well known for her plans and activities designed to enhance students' self-esteem and cultural identities. Her principal has asked her to do an in-service presentation on working with children and adolescents from culturally diverse backgrounds. The steadily increasing cultural diversity of the school has caused the administrative staff to recognize self-esteem and cultural identity as crucial to the overall success of learners.

Ms. Stepp wonders what ideas, suggestions, activities, and materials she will be able to share. As she plans a rough outline, several broad topics come to mind: student activities (especially designed for each cultural group), informal assessments, the overall teaching and learning climate, and teachers' attitudes and behaviors.

The presentation would include teaching and encouraging respect for home, family, self, traditions, heritages, customs, and anything that accentuates the positive in the learner's culture. The presentation would stress that teachers must have appropriate attitudes and must value and respect cultural diversity, if attempts to improve it are to be successful.

▬▬▬▬▬▬▬▬▬▬▬▬▬▬▬▬▬▬▬▬▬▬▬▬▬▬▬▬▬▬▬▬▬▬▬▬▬▬▬

ensure self-esteem and positive cultural identities should be an ongoing process, educators should also work toward helping learners have positive attitudes toward school.

Learning Styles

A *learning style* is the process one habitually uses for cognitive problem solving and for showing what one knows and is capable of doing. The essence of learning styles can be attained from analyzing what people do routinely when they interact with new ideas, people, situations, and information. This involves (1) cognition (ways of knowing); (2) conceptualizing (formulating ideas and thoughts); (3) affective reacting (feeling and valuing); and (4) acting (exhibiting some kind of behavior). The mere mention of ethnically specific learning styles causes contention and resistance from many, because individuals differ within a culture. There are exceptions to any cultural descriptions. Every individual in an ethnic group does not have to exhibit cultural characteristics as described for those characteristics to be valid. Characteristics of learning styles are pedagogically promising to the extent that they illuminate patterns of cultural values and behaviors that influence how children learn, and they provide functional directions for modifying instructional techniques to better meet the academic needs of ethnically diverse students. Therefore, learning styles should be seen not only as categories for labeling students but also as tools improving the school achievement of African, Arab, Asian, and Hispanic American students as well as American Indians by creating more *cultural congruity* in the teaching–learning process (Gay, 2000).

Emotionality, variability, novelty, and active participation are important aspects of the learning styles of some ethnic groups and the ways in which they demonstrate what they know. For them, teaching and learning are more than cognitive and technical tasks; they are also active and emotional processes. Consequently, all these are critical features of culturally responsive teaching (Gay, 2000).

Although the relationship between culture and learning style is not fully under-stood, it is important to the teaching and learning process. Cultural and cognitive fac-tors and socialization practices influence cognitive and affective preferences and are manifested in incentives and motivation, interpersonal relationships, and patterns of intellectual abilities (Hernandez, 1989). It is important for all educators to know how all students learn. Educators who work in multicultural situations are in a particularly challenging position. They must recognize that all students have unique learning styles, and they must determine the most appropriate instructional approaches and techniques for each.

Guild suggests that researchers agree on several findings: (1) students of any par-ticular age differ in their ways of learning; (2) learning styles are a function of both na-ture and nurture; and (3) within a group, the variations among individuals are as great as their commonalities (Guild, 1994).

Educators who recognize cultural differences should remember the dangers of generalizing group findings to individuals. The growing numbers and increased recog-nition of learners from culturally diverse backgrounds have resulted in research that focuses on the intricate relationships between cultural diversity and learning styles. The speculation surrounding the relationship of learning styles and cultural diversity notwithstanding, what does the evidence indicate or suggest? Although reliable re-search on the learning styles of all cultural groups is not available, Table 11.2 provides a cursory look at several representative findings.

TABLE 11.2 Cultural Diversity and Learning Styles: Representative Examples

Mexican Americans. In Dunn and Dunn's (1978) sample, Mexican Americans were more motivated to learn than were students in the general population. The boys were the most authority-oriented students in the group and were far more parent-motivated than were students in the general population. The students were far more peer-oriented and were more likely to succeed in small-group learning situations.

African Americans. Shade (1982) concluded that African Americans have the following tendencies: They view things in their environment in entirety, rather than in isolated parts. They prefer intuitive, rather than deductive or inductive, reasoning. They approximate concepts of space, number, and time, rather than aiming at exactness or accuracy. They rely on both nonverbal and verbal communication.

American Indians. More (1987) reports that many American Indians show strengths in visual/spatial/perceptual information, and that given a choice, they prefer these modes to verbal modes. They frequently and effectively use coding with imagery to remember concepts and words (mental associations assist in remembering). They are more reflective than impulsive and utilize watch-then-do rather than trial-and-error. They are more likely to participate in global processing for both verbal and nonverbal tasks; for example, students might process using the whole and the relationships between the parts, rather than emphasizing the parts to build the whole.

SUMMING UP

Educators who base educational experiences on the individual and cultural characteristics of children and adolescents should:

1. Recognize the various models and orientations of diversity and adopt the culturally different model (Sleeter & Grant, 1999) as the basis for instruction and personal interaction
2. Recognize that the learning styles and cognitive processes of learners from different cultural backgrounds may differ from those of the dominant population
3. Provide carefully planned experiences for children and adolescents with exceptionalities
4. Recognize the importance of self-esteem and positive cultural identities
5. Plan activities that teach learners from both culturally different and the majority population the importance of cultural diversity and the many contributions of people from different cultures
6. Plan special experiences for learners from language-minority backgrounds, and recognize the differences between bilingual education and ESL programs
7. Understand that attitudes, values, and beliefs of culturally different children and adolescents differ from those of the majority culture and not expect minority learners to forsake their cultural identities to achieve school "success"
8. Recognize gender as a variable that affects children and adolescents, and recognize the complex relationship between gender and culture

SUGGESTED LEARNING ACTIVITIES

1. Visit several schools to determine how or on what basis they group learners or place them in special classes. Does it appear that racial segregation occurs as a result of grouping or placement? To what extent are students "labeled"? What efforts are being made to reduce the negative effects of labeling?

2. List several ways to improve learners' self-esteem and cultural identities. What factors might educators consider to improve self-esteem? How might teachers determine the level of a learner's self-esteem and cultural identity?

3. Respond to the language dilemma many learners face: Many cannot speak English well enough to understand educators or to cope in a predominantly English-speaking society. What are the roles of administrators, classroom teachers, speech correctionists, and language specialists? What suggestions can you offer for helping learners with limited English-speaking skills?

SUGGESTIONS FOR COLLABORATIVE EFFORTS

Form groups of three or four that, if possible, represent U.S. cultural and gender diversity. Working collaboratively, focus your group's attention toward the following efforts.

1. Survey several programs designed to address the needs of gifted learners from different cultural backgrounds. What instruments or techniques determine eligibility? To what extent do the instruments measure the unique abilities and talents of learners from different backgrounds? Do the programs expect learners to change to meet the demands of the program, or do programs reflect knowledge of cultural diversity?

2. Make a list of commonly held stereotypical beliefs about boys and girls (e.g., boys should not cry, girls have a tendency to giggle a lot). Observe the girls and boys in your class to test the validity of your list. Next, have the boys and girls make a list, and have a discussion of the differences between girls and boys. How might an educator's expectation of girls or boys affect teaching situations? How do members of your group feel these stereotypical beliefs affected them when they were in elementary or secondary school?

3. As a group activity, draw six columns on a sheet. Label them African, American Indian, Asian, Arab, Hispanic, and European American, and list your group's beliefs, attitudes, and values about each culture. Seek your students' input. Next, list school policies, practices, and expectations that the students might want to reconsider for the sake of cultural implications.

EXPANDING YOUR HORIZONS: ADDITIONAL JOURNAL READINGS AND BOOKS

Ferdman, B. M. (2000). "Why am I who I am?" Constructing the cultural self in multicultural perspective. *Human Development, 43*, 19–23.
Ferdman asks engaging questions as he explores the construction of the cultural self.

Fish, L. S. (2000). Hierarchical relationship development: Parents and children. *Journal of Marital and Family Therapy, 26*(4), 501–510.
Fish maintains that child growth and development occur in hierarchical relationships and describes a method of child and relational growth.

Killen, M., & Stangor, C. (2001). Children's social reasoning about inclusion and exclusion in gender and race peer group contexts. *Child Development, 72*(1), 174–186.
These authors investigated whether children's and adolescents' judgments about exclusion of peers from peer-group activities—older children (aged thirteen years) were more likely to allow exclusion than younger children (aged seven to ten years).

Phinney, J. S. (2000). Identity formation across cultures: The interaction of personal, societal, and historical change. *Human Development, 43*, 27–31.
As the title implies, Phinney looks at how personal, societal, and historical change affects identity development.

Quinn, A. E. (2001). Moving marginalized students inside the lines: Cultural differences in classrooms. *English Journal, 90*(4), 44–50.
In this excellent article, Quinn provides a discussion of cultural diversity among Hispanics and especially the Mexican culture.

Shafer, G. (2001). Standard English and the migrant community. *English Journal, 90*(4), 37–43.
Shafer talks about immigrant communities in the agrarian community of Homestead, Florida, and examines how culture and language influence the teaching–learning process.

■ ■ ■ ■ ■ ■

CHAPTER TWELVE

PARENTS AND FAMILIES OF CULTURALLY DIVERSE BACKGROUNDS

Understanding the material and activities in this chapter will help the reader to:

- State several reasons for including parents and families of culturally diverse backgrounds in parent involvement programs in elementary and secondary schools
- Understand that both immediate and extended families should be included in schools, especially because African, Arab, Asian, European, and Hispanic American as well as American Indians place considerable value on the extended-family concept
- State at least five reasons that parents and families of culturally different backgrounds resist teachers' efforts
- Understand that considerable diversity (including intracultural, generational, and socioeconomic differences) results in difficulty as teachers plan for "typical" or "prototype" families
- List the essential elements of effective parent involvement programs
- Explain procedures and factors that parents and teachers should consider during conferences
- Explain the essential aspects and considerations of forming a parent advisory committee designed to address the needs and concerns of families from culturally different backgrounds
- Understand the importance of parent and family education, and explain how such programs can assist families from culturally diverse backgrounds

OVERVIEW

For years, educators have recognized the importance of involving parents in children's education. Whether through involving, conferring, or educating, efforts to include parents in the educational process have paid rich dividends. Until the past decade or so, however, educators mainly worked with middle- and upper-class European Americans and ignored other races, cultures, and ethnic groups, probably because educators lacked knowledge of unique backgrounds and special needs of culturally diverse parents and families. As schools increasingly reflect the cultural diversity that characterizes the nation, educators will be challenged to involve, educate, and confer with all parents and families. This chapter focuses attention on parent involvement and conferences and suggests that educators should implement parent education programs designed to acquaint families of culturally different backgrounds with U.S. school systems.

INVOLVING AND EDUCATING PARENTS AND FAMILIES

That parent involvement has a positive effect on student achievement and overall school progress is undeniable. An even more compelling reason to seek the involvement and participation of parents is to have them understand the U.S. school system, its expectations, and its predominantly middle-class white educators. Families from diverse cultures may feel uncomfortable conversing with educators and participating in school-sponsored events. The educator's challenge is to involve parents of all cultural, ethnic, racial, and social class groups, rather than only middle- and upper-class European American parents.

The issue for educators, however, is more complex than simply convincing parents to visit the school. It includes making conscientious efforts in several areas: explaining the school's function, making parents feel welcome and valued, educating parents about their children and adolescents, and involving parents in their children's and adolescents' education whenever possible. Only with the involvement and participation of all parents can schools genuinely reflect multiculturalism and address the needs and concerns of learners and parents from culturally different backgrounds.

Behavioral consultation is defined as a systematic form of service delivery in which two or more persons work together to identify, analyze, remediate and evaluate an individual's needs. It is characterized by a problem-solving process, adherence to behavioral assessment techniques, reliance on behavioral intervention strategies, and evaluation of outcomes (Sheridan, 2000). In Implementing Research 12.1, Sheridan (2000) explains conjoint behavioral consultation, an extension of behavioral consultation.

The Advantages of Parent Involvement and Education

The reasons for, and advantages of, parents and teachers working as partners and for teachers providing appropriate educational experiences for parents have been well documented. A strong positive correlation exists between parent involvement and pupil school achievement, increased student attendance, positive parent–child communication, improved student attitudes and behavior, and more parent–community support of the schools (Chavkin 1989; Hoover-Dempsey, Bassler, & Brissie, 1987).

Children of all backgrounds deserve the full consideration of teachers and parents; for children and parents of culturally different backgrounds, the need may be even greater. Many parents and families of culturally different backgrounds do not understand school expectations. Some expect high achievement in all areas from their children and adolescents. Many have difficulties communicating with the school (Yao, 1988). Much can be gained, in terms of improved overall school achievement and improved cultural and interpersonal relationships between parents, teachers, and students, when educators actively seek parent and family involvement.

■ ■ ■ ■ ■

IMPLEMENTING RESEARCH 12.1
MULTICULTURALISM, PARENTS, AND TEACHERS

Conjoint behavioral consultation is an extension of behavioral consultation that combines the resources of the home and school to effect positive change in children. It is an indirect model of service delivery in which parents, teachers, and a consultant work together to address the academic, social, and behavioral needs of a child. Problems are identified, defined, analyzed, and treated through mutual and collaborative interactions between parents and teachers with the guidance and assistance of a school psychologist. The model promotes a partnership model that allows opportunities for families and schools to work together for the common interest of children and build on and promote capabilities of family members and school personnel. An advantage is that conjoint behavioral consultation emphasizes the need to consider factors that might be counterproductive to relations with people from diverse backgrounds. For example, people from backgrounds other than European American might hold different orientations toward values such as social relationships, achievement, activity, and time.

IMPLEMENTING THE RESEARCH
1. Culture and cultural differences must be remembered when using this model (and other models); for example, a child who makes eye contact or speaks directly with an elder might be perceived as showing disrespect, or a child who is socially withdrawn might be perceived as lacking assertiveness.
2. Professionals who treat all children in an identical manner without considering different backgrounds, experiences, language, and dialects and perspectives on parenting and education communicate that differences are not important.

Source: Sheridan, S. M. (2000). Considerations of multiculturalism and diversity in behavioral consultation with parents and teachers. *The School Psychology Review, 29*(3), 344–353.

Understanding Both Immediate and Extended Families

Another important reason for educators to promote parent involvement is to recognize the differences between European American and other families' beliefs toward the family. Whereas European Americans focus more on the immediate family, families of most other cultures include extended-family members, such as grandparents, aunts, uncles, and cousins.

The implications of extended families are readily apparent for educators. Rather than conferring with, educating, or involving only the mother and father, educators should make conscientious attempts to recognize immediate and extended families.

Reasons Parents Might Resist Teachers' Efforts

Some parents resist teachers' efforts to involve them in the educational process, whether these efforts include conferences, involvement activities, or serving on committees. Why might parents and extended-family members from minority cultures

■ ■ ■ ■ ■

FOLLOW THROUGH 12.1

ADDRESSING LANGUAGE BARRIERS

Consult with the communication disorders specialist or ESL specialist in a school and the social service agencies in the community to learn how to work with and assist parents and family members whose language poses a barrier to effective communication. Make a list of publications, resource people, and special programs that help parents and families from culturally diverse backgrounds.

resist teachers' efforts? First, some cultures may harbor distrust and negative feelings toward professionals of other cultural backgrounds. Parents and children who harbor such attitudes have difficulty believing that professionals of differing cultural backgrounds understand them and want what is best for them. Parents with such powerful feelings of distrust will, in all likelihood, shun a teacher's efforts to build a working relationship between school and family.

Second, family members often fear disclosing personal problems or familial matters that might reflect negatively on themselves, the family, or the father's ability to manage home affairs. To reveal difficulties in the family may arouse feelings of shame in some cultures and the perception of having failed the family (Hartman & Askounis, 1989).

Third, some groups view a child's failure in school achievement or behavior to be a negative reflection on them and their parenting skills. West (1983) tells the story of a teacher who felt that she was not "reaching" a Vietnamese student. Although he was not disruptive, he was not participating fully in class. When she requested a parent–teacher conference, the father came to school full of dismay and feeling his son had done something terrible. The teacher repeatedly explained that she liked the student and was only trying to improve communication.

Fourth, home and school language differences can contribute to parents' resistance. Olsen (1988) reports several instances: immigrant children who had to translate and explain school events and bulletins sent home to parents; a Mexican mother in San Francisco who did not understand repeated notices, written in English, that her daughter was failing to attend school; and one Chinese father who understood that the grading system began with *A* and progressed downward. When the daughter received *S* for *satisfactory*, the father became confused and beat his daughter for her bad grades. To further complicate the situation, when he called the school, he could not understand the secretary and repeatedly hung up the telephone (Olsen, 1988).

Case Study 12.1 discusses how teachers might misunderstand parents and families of differing cultural backgrounds.

In effect, the teachers in Case Study 12.1 understood neither Asian American parent and family members nor their expectations of schools and teachers. A more enlightened perspective would allow those teachers to understand that all the visitors were interested, even if reticent. Such understanding might lead to more productive parent conferences in the future.

■ ■ ■ ■ ■ ▬

CASE STUDY 12.1
DIFFERING EXPECTATIONS

The teachers at Park Street Elementary School, an urban school with a significant Asian American population, did not understand what had happened. The Asian American parents and families who had come to the PTA meeting the previous night were quiet, even subdued, and offered very few comments or suggestions during the discussion times. "Why did they even come?" one teacher asked. "During individual conferences, they just sat there and listened. They were not any help."

A teacher who had more enlightened knowledge and more first-hand contact with Asian Americans overheard the conversation and recognized the need to clarify several points.

First, she explained, Asian Americans often place teachers on a pedestal and, generally speaking, consider teachers as worthy of honor and respect. Giving advice or suggestions to teachers is often considered as speaking against an authority figure. In their culture, teachers know what is best, and to question a teacher's decision can be construed as a personal attack.

Second, she explained that the Asian American concept of family causes individuals to be reluctant to reveal information; admitting problems might be considered a negative reflection on the family. Educators must remember to take care in trying to understand the source of a problem. Their efforts must not be construed as prying or as a personal criticism of the family.

Third, she explained that the extended-family concept resulted in other family members coming to the PTA meeting. Not only do the parents feel a responsibility for a learner's progress, but other relatives feel a sense of duty and take pride or shame in the learner's behavior.

Parents often do not understand the U.S. school system and its expectations. For example, major differences exist between U.S. teachers and Indochinese teachers: Indochinese teachers are accorded higher levels of respect than are teachers in the United States; they are often awarded honorific titles; they expect students to bow, avoid eye contact, and not ask questions. Because Indochinese parents in their native lands do not take active roles in schools, they have difficulty understanding PTA and other parent-involvement programs. They view the teacher as the expert and feel that making suggestions to teachers about the education of children is inappropriate. Likewise, immigrant parents are often baffled by group activities, independent projects, and library research, because in their cultures, the lecture method is considered the most effective means of teaching (West, 1983).

Parents from multicultural backgrounds have indicated that the staff and institutional structure of the school intimidate them. They may feel awkward about approaching school personnel, particularly if they have had previous negative contacts with the school (Chavkin, 1989).

Speaking only of Asian American immigrant parents, Yao (1988) maintains that Asians' great respect for teachers and the learning process can actually pose a potential barrier. These parents are often reluctant to challenge the teacher's authority, and they sometimes feel that communicating with teachers may be perceived as disrespectful. Although these parents are usually attentive listeners, they seldom initiate contact with teachers and administrators, rarely ask questions, and seldom offer comments.

Cultural conflicts over child-rearing expectations and differing value systems also disturb many Asian families. As they arrive at the need to make child-rearing decisions on such issues as diet preference, sex education, dating patterns, and obedience to parents, these families are often torn between Eastern and Western manners, expectations, moral standards, and traditions (Yao, 1988).

UNDERSTANDING CULTURAL DIVERSITY

Educators can readily see the reasons for understanding cultural diversity among families. However, they might have more difficulty reducing the myths, stereotypes, and other baggage that educators (and other professionals in U.S. society) have about parents and families from differing cultural backgrounds. Follow Through 12.2 provides a checklist by which educators can examine their beliefs and attitudes toward families from culturally different backgrounds.

When reaching decisions about families, we cannot overemphasize the need for objectivity. Educators cannot reach objective decisions concerning whether, and to what extent, to involve parents and families when they believe such statements as, "These parents just don't care," "The father is an alcoholic," "The father never lets his wife speak," or "Neither the mother nor the father has any ambition; they are satisfied to live off welfare." Educators who stereotype parents will probably do little to get to know and involve parents and families in their individual classrooms and certainly not in the overall school program.

An educator should not think he or she knows the prototypical "American Indian family," "African American family," or any other "family." For example, African American families are so diverse that some believe that there is no such thing as a "typical" African American family.

Social class differences play a significant role in determining how a person acts, lives, thinks, and relates to others. Low wages; unemployment or underemployment; lack of property, savings, and food reserves; and having to meet the most basic needs on a day-to-day basis easily lead to feelings of helplessness, dependence, and inferiority. Differences in values, attitudes, behaviors, and beliefs among the various socioeconomic groups warrant the professional's consideration, especially because some minority groups' members come from the lower socioeconomic classes (Atkinson, Morten, & Sue, 1999).

Regrettably, a person's social class is sometimes thought to indicate his or her ambitions or motivation to achieve. It is a serious mistake to stereotype people according to social class, to assume, for example, that the lower classes lack ambition, do not want to work, or do not want to improve their education status. It is not unreasonable to suggest that people of the lower socioeconomic classes, whether African, Arab, Asian, European, and Hispanic American or American Indian, want to improve their

■ ■ ■ ■ ■ ▬▬▬▬▬▬▬

FOLLOW THROUGH 12.2
EXAMINING PERCEPTIONS

Ask yourself these questions:

1. Are my opinions of parents and families based on myths and stereotypes or on accurate and objective perceptions?
2. Have my experiences included positive firsthand contact with people from culturally different backgrounds?
3. What means have I employed to learn about the customs, traditions, values, and beliefs of all people?
4. Do I understand the extended-family concept, or do I only think "too many people live in the same house because of poverty conditions"?
5. Am I prejudiced, or do I have genuine feelings of acceptance for all people, regardless of culture, ethnicity, race, and socioeconomic background?
6. Do I hold the perceptions that American Indians are alcoholics, that African American families are headed by single females, that Asian Americans are the model minority and have achieved what represents the American Dream, or that Hispanic Americans have large families and live on welfare?
7. Can I perceive that aunts, uncles, and grandparents are as important as more immediate-family members (that is, the mother and father)?
8. Do I understand the rich cultural backgrounds of families, and am I willing to base educational experiences on this diversity?
9. Do I know appropriate sources of information to learn more about parents and families from culturally diverse backgrounds?
10. Do I have the motivation, skills, and attitudes to develop close interrelationships with parents and families from culturally different backgrounds?

social status in life, but that they meet with considerable frustration when faced with low education, high unemployment, conditions associated with poverty, and the racism and discrimination still prevalent in U.S. society.

Generational differences are another reason that an educator must not assume homogeneity within a culture. Older generations may be more prone to retain Old World values and traditions, because they tend to live in close proximity to people of similar language, traditions, and customs, whereas young people are likely to move anywhere in the United States.

One generational difference involves facility with the English language. While older generations may have lived in cultural enclaves with others who speak their native languages or who speak English at similar levels of fluency, younger generations who can communicate effectively in English are better able to cope in a predominantly English-speaking society.

Implementing Research 12.2 looks at parents and culture and maintains that teachers should work to understand and improve communication and cultural differences.

■ ■ ■ ■ ■ ▬▬▬

IMPLEMENTING RESEARCH 12.2
PARENTS AND CULTURE

Trumbull, Rothstein-Fisch, and Greenfield (2001) maintain that differences in culture often block communication between teachers and parents. Teachers who teach children who are diverse know that the challenges extend beyond language. Even as educators try to help children of diverse backgrounds deal with the U.S. education system, their own teaching methods and most routine classroom expectations can result in perplexing conflicts with the children's cultural ways of knowing and behaving. The authors explain that a student may resist offering a right answer after another student has answered incorrectly, in order not to embarrass that person in front of the group. It is not only immigrant children who challenge teachers: U.S.-born students—American Indians, African Americans, and Hispanic Americans whose families have lived here for generations—may also feel alienated by common classroom practices.

Trumbull, Rothstein-Fisch, and Greenfield explain the Bridging Cultures project, which sought to improve cross-cultural communication in the classroom. The cultural framework is a tool for understanding how the expectations for a student at school may conflict with the values of the students' family. For example, European American parents often stress making their children socially and economically independent. This emphasis on self-reliance affects nearly all European American family decisions. In contrast, collectivist societies are quite hierarchical and point their children in a different direction—they encourage the children to be contributing members of a family unit. Children are expected to understand and act on a strong sense of responsibility to the group, the family, and the community. Again, in contrast, children in individualistic societies are expected to make educational and occupational decisions that develop their own potential, usually without regard for how their success may benefit their families.

IMPLEMENTING THE RESEARCH
1. Educators should consider programs that contribute to cultural understandings with parents and families—for example, language and communication, collectivist–individualistic perspectives, and succeeding at the expense of peers.
2. Educators should strive to understand concerns of cultural groups—for example, American Indians often complain that U.S. schools teach facts independent of their social and ethical implications.
3. Educators should work constantly to understand parents' ways of thinking and the norms in children's homes, thus making classrooms and schools more hospitable for students and their families.

Source: Trumbull, E., Rothstein-Fisch, C., & Greenfield, P. M. (2001). Ours and mine. *Journal of Staff Development, 22*(2), 10–14.

▬▬▬

EFFECTIVE PARENT INVOLVEMENT PROGRAMS

The Southwest Educational Development Laboratory (SEDL) has identified and described characteristics of promising parent involvement programs. Some of the selected programs are affiliated with resources such as the National Educational Association or the National School Volunteer Program, and others are the result of the efforts of local schools. The programs share seven essential elements:

1. Written policies, which legitimize the importance of parent involvement and help frame the context for program activities
2. Administrative support, including a main budget for implementing programs, material and product resources, and people with designated responsibilities
3. Promising training programs for both staff and parents
4. Programs that make the partnership approach their essence
5. Two-way communication between home and school that occurs frequently and regularly
6. Use of networking to identify additional resources and encourage people to share information, resources, and technique expertise
7. Regular evaluation, during key stages and at the end of the cycle or phase of the program, that provides indicators of progress and outcomes (Williams & Chavkin, 1989)

Most programs designed to work with families have served mainly English-speaking families who know how to benefit from parent–teacher programs. Educators need to consider cross-cultural perspectives when working with families. To lessen the problems associated with communication, both written and oral, the educators in the parent-involvement program at Emerson School in Rosemead, California, sent letters in four languages to parents and conducted meetings in six languages. The program encourages parents to offer, in their native languages, their input and opinions about school services. The school then translates their responses and reports back in the parents' native languages.

■ ■ ■ ■ ■ ▬▬▬▬▬▬▬▬▬▬▬▬▬▬▬▬▬▬▬▬▬▬▬▬▬▬▬▬▬▬▬▬▬▬▬▬

FOR ADDITIONAL INFORMATION
INTERNET ADDRESSES

Parents Involvement in Middle-School Life
http://familyeducation.com/experts/advice/0,11 83,1-1144,00.html   Focuses on communication and lack thereof between parents and teachers.

Involved Dads Get an "A"
http://familyeducation.com/article/0,1120,3-220,00.html   Provides information supporting father involvement in children's education.

Working with Families
www.speakeasy.org/~moonshyn/family.html Provides information on learning to work with families.

How to Define Parent Involvement
http://list.pta.org:8001/GMDocs/GMHtml/ EMOCJABD.html   Provides information on various definitions of parent involvement.

Annotated Bibliography Reference #20
http://scov.csos.jhu.edu/p2000/bibref20.htm Provides information from the Center on Families, Communities, Schools, and Children's Learning.

Parents and Families of Culturally Different Backgrounds

A prerequisite to understanding culturally diverse parents and families is gaining accurate and objective knowledge about expectations, needs, and challenges facing people with differing cultural backgrounds. Without doubt, educators can improve their understanding by reading books and journals, taking courses, and attending professional conferences. Although these means can provide considerable insight into cultural diversity and should be an integral part of the educator's learning agenda, first-hand contact with individuals continues to be one of the most effective means of gaining an accurate perspective of cultural diversity.

First-hand contact has an advantage that other means cannot always provide: learning directly about "people" and their individual attitudes, values, and beliefs. With understanding and knowledge, the potential exists for genuine feelings of caring and empathy to develop between people of differing races, cultures, and ethnic backgrounds.

Case Study 12.2 encourages teachers to have first-hand contact with people from culturally different backgrounds.

Although there is probably no adequate substitute for first-hand contact with parents and families, it is possible to gain information through a parent survey. Without doubt, the most effective means would be to use a parent survey in addition to first-hand contact. It is important for the educators who design the survey to remember that some questions may be culturally sensitive; for example, questions that might not be offensive to European American populations might be construed as an invasion of pri-

■ ■ ■ ■ ■ ▬▬▬▬▬▬▬▬▬▬▬▬▬▬▬▬▬▬▬▬▬▬▬▬▬▬▬▬▬▬▬▬

CASE STUDY 12.2
FIRST-HAND CONTACT

Mr. Johnson, principal at Central Middle School, encourages teachers in his school to have first-hand contact with people from various cultures. He praises teachers who take courses focusing on cultural diversity, attend seminars and conferences, and read professional books and journals. These are all excellent sources, he thinks, but he still wants teachers to have first-hand contact, which is imperative if genuine knowledge and respect are to develop.

Mr. Johnson encourages first-hand contact in several ways: First, he expects and encourages teachers to be integral members of the community and to participate in as many social and cultural activities as possible. Second, he encourages parents and families from culturally different backgrounds to visit the school any time, not just for parent conferences. During these impromptu visits, Mr. Johnson urges teachers to meet parents and families and to discuss items of interest. Third, he encourages home visits, which are scheduled at times convenient for the parents. These visits provide a means for teachers to get to know family members on a more personal basis. Although the principal requires the teachers to record their observations and perceptions, the purpose of the visits is neither to judge nor to condemn. He believes that knowledge of cultural diversity contributes to improving attitudes toward people with differences, regardless of degree or type.

vacy by many parents and families from culturally different backgrounds. Examples of culturally sensitive questions are those on child-rearing techniques, sex education, dating patterns, and parental authority.

Implementing Research 12.3 looks at diversity and families and suggests ways educators can work with parents and families of diverse backgrounds.

Although the questions in Follow Through 12.3 might be included on a parent survey, any final determination should depend on the degree of cultural diversity and the specific information sought.

Educators may decide to develop the survey in the parents' native language, rather than risk that the survey will not be completed or that problems will result from poor communication. Generally speaking, parent surveys should be clear and short, require only a brief amount of time to complete, and avoid conveying middle-class European American perspectives.

We remind readers that the questions in Follow Through 12.3 are sample questions; they are neither intended to be all-inclusive nor designed for a specific culturally diverse group. Educators with a large percentage of one culturally diverse population might want specific questions designed to pinpoint certain areas.

■ ■ ■ ■ ■ ▬▬▬▬▬▬▬▬▬▬▬▬▬▬▬▬▬▬▬▬▬▬▬▬▬▬▬▬▬▬

IMPLEMENTING RESEARCH 12.3
DIVERSITY AND FAMILIES

Parette and Petch-Hogan (2000) maintain that communication with families is increasingly important in schools today. Parents of culturally/linguistically diverse students should be involved in sharing of culture, participating as assistants on field trips, assisting in arts and crafts, assisting with music and recreational activities, and participating actively in the special-education planning process. Such involvement causes a problem for some diverse families, especially those with language differences, different cultural expectations, and mistrust of or lack of experience with U.S. education systems.

The authors focus on communication and contacts with families; location of meetings and supports; providing information training; understanding family priorities, needs, and resources; family lifespan issues; family functions; and family communication styles.

IMPLEMENTING THE RESEARCH

1. Educators should address the distrust that some parents have for school officials; mistrust can result from past negative experiences or bureaucratic problems.
2. Educators should consider interpreters who can facilitate communication between school personnel and parents who have limited English-proficiency skills.
3. Educators should realize and recognize that parent/family decision makers (e.g., grandmothers and aunts) in culturally/linguistically diverse families may assume primary responsibility for children with special needs.

Source: Parette, H. P., & Petch-Hogan, B. (2000). Approaching families. *Teaching Exceptional Children,* *33*(2), 4–10.

■ ■ ■ ■ ■ ▬▬▬▬▬▬▬▬▬▬▬▬▬▬▬▬▬▬▬▬▬▬▬▬▬▬▬▬▬▬▬▬▬▬▬▬

FOLLOW THROUGH 12.3
SELECTED PARENT SURVEY QUESTIONS

1. Do you feel that educators in your child's or adolescent's school understand and meet the overall needs and concerns of learners from different cultural backgrounds?
2. Do you feel that school policies recognize that children and adolescents of culturally different backgrounds differ from the European American population?
3. Does the media center (children's and adolescents' books, films, other visual material) reflect the cultural diversity of the school?
4. How well has the school succeeded in employing a faculty and staff (administrators, teachers, library media specialists, special personnel, speech therapists, guidance counselors, psychologies, school nurses) that reflects the cultural diversity of the student body?
5. Do you feel that school expectations (competition, motivation, achievements, aspirations) reflect the values and expectations of learners of culturally diverse backgrounds?
6. Do you feel that extracurricular activities in the school reflect the needs and interests of children and adolescents of culturally diverse backgrounds?
7. Do teaching methods and strategies (lecture format, small group, cooperative learning, ability grouping) reflect a concern for the educational well-being of all learners?
8. Has the school provided opportunities to offer opinions, input, advice, and suggestions concerning improvement of the school program or changing an aspect you would like to see changed?
9. Is your child progressing toward or succeeding at goals that you feel are important?
10. Do you feel the school provides information and assistance concerning social service organizations?
11. What comments or suggestions do you want to offer concerning your child or adolescent in school?

VISITING PARENTS AND FAMILIES IN THE HOME

Home visits may be one of the most effective ways for teachers to get to know learners, their immediate and extended families, and their home environment and culture. Families from different cultural backgrounds often perceive family roles differently, have differing expectations of the schools, and expect older family members to play significantly greater child-rearing roles than European Americans might expect. The only way to understand such differences is to get to know the families personally.

Home visits can provide valuable information about learners and their homes, but perhaps an even greater benefit is that learners and their families see that educators care and are interested in all children and adolescents. Parents from culturally different backgrounds may also feel more at ease in their own surroundings than they would in the (perhaps) strange and sterile school environment.

■ ■ ■ ■ ■

FOLLOW THROUGH 12.4
VISITING IN THE HOME

Visiting in the homes of children and adolescents can raise sensitive issues, especially with parents and families of culturally different backgrounds. Perceiving family life and parenting practices from different cultural perspectives can result in misunderstanding. For example, a middle-class African American educator might fail to understand a Hispanic or Asian American family. Make a list of "do's and don'ts"—those behaviors you should demonstrate and should not demonstrate in an effort to show understanding and respect for the parents' cultural heritage.

Before the home visit, educators should call or send a note to the parents and establish a time that is convenient for both the teacher and the parent. At the beginning of the visit, the teacher should talk informally with the parents and the child for a few minutes to establish a friendly tone and to reduce the parents' anxiety. At all times, teachers should remember that they are visitors and should avoid judging situations and conditions in the home. Parents will have greater confidence in the teacher if they think the discussion will be held in confidence (Shea & Bauer, 1985).

COMMUNICATION

Educators should be careful about how they speak to parents, especially parents and families from non-native-English-speaking backgrounds. Misunderstandings might also result not only from language differences, but also if the parent or the teacher (or both) misunderstand each others' eye contact or body posture. Believing that educators should speak so parents can and will listen, Studer (1993/1994) offers several suggestions:

1. Listen actively rather than passively.
2. Pose questions in such a way that parents and families do not feel their privacy is being invaded.
3. Listening includes attending skills, such as use of particular body postures. Other listening behaviors include squaring shoulders and looking directly at the speaker, using a posture of uncrossed arms and legs, leaning toward the speaker, and maintaining eye contact (Studer, 1993/1994).

Educators in multicultural situations must recognize that these behaviors are to be understood rather than expected. Listening behaviors that are typical and expected of middle-class white parents might be far different from those that people of other cultural backgrounds exhibit. For example, maintaining eye contact might be considered rude in some cultures. Likewise, body postures are also culturally based. Educators should not assess parents' and families' interest and commitment to children's education by using middle-class European American standards and expectations.

Humans communicate at several levels simultaneously: through verbal expression, or what they say; through body language or nonverbal expression, or how they behave; and through emotional responses, or how they show what they feel. The more congruent these levels of expression are, the more meaningful or understanding the communication becomes to others (Shea & Bauer, 1985). One can easily recognize the importance of understanding the various types of communication with families of differing cultural backgrounds.

Whether communicating through speaking directly, telephoning, or writing to parents, educators are responsible for not allowing language or communication differences, verbal or nonverbal, to interfere with overall communication. Several factors warrant consideration. First, as we mentioned previously, the parents' English skills might not allow effective communication. Second, nonverbal communication might pose a problem; for example, the European American who looks an American Indian directly in the eye while communicating might be considered rude, and the educator might think an American Indian's glancing away to indicate disinterest or irritation.

Another example of problems that can result from nonverbal communication is Asian American parents and families, who are especially sensitive to nonverbal messages and who may construe a teacher's folded arms or other casual gestures as indicative of an indifferent attitude (Chavkin, 1989). Third, educators should avoid jargon with which parents might be unfamiliar: *PET, assertive discipline, critical thinking, cooperative learning, mastery learning, percentiles*, or terms associated with computers or technology, for example.

Telephoning represents another means of communicating with parents and demonstrates the teacher's personal interest in both the learner and the parents. Positive telephone contacts can significantly affect a child's school performance; conversely, negative calls can have a negative effect. As with other forms of communication, teachers must exercise caution when using the telephone to communicate with parents.

Telephoning is a great way to encourage parents to attend meetings, conferences, and other school events (Shea & Bauer, 1985). It can be extremely threatening, however, to parents and families of culturally different backgrounds, because they have come to expect bad news whenever a representative of the school calls. Guidelines for minimizing parent and teacher misunderstanding include:

1. Address parents as Mr. or Mrs., because parents from different backgrounds often do not receive the same respect and courtesy as other people.
2. Use a tone of voice that expresses respect and courtesy, because a call from school often raises anxiety levels.
3. Discuss the child's or adolescent's positive points before discussing the problem to be solved.
4. Use language the parent understands and a tone that does not sound condescending.
5. Respond with empathy if the parent has difficulty understanding unfamiliar educational concepts.

Educators can also write notes and letters to keep parents informed of children's progress and of administrative and record-keeping problems and concerns, schedule changes, special events, holidays, workshops, field trips, and other items of interest. Effective notes are clear, concise, and positive and may speak to parents and family members in their primary language. Unless used systematically, however, notes and letters have limited value in reinforcing the child's academic performance or social and emotional behavior and are best used as one component of the overall parent and teacher communication (Shea & Bauer, 1985).

INVOLVING PARENTS AND FAMILIES AS VOLUNTEERS

Parent volunteers can contribute significantly to the quality of the services offered to learners in the school (Shea & Bauer, 1985). The National School Volunteer Program cites four reasons for using volunteers in the classroom and school:

1. Relieving the professional staff of nonteaching duties
2. Providing needed services to individual children to supplement the work of the classroom teacher
3. Enriching the experiences of children beyond those normally available in school
4. Building a better understanding among citizens of school problems, and stimulating widespread citizen support for public education

Although parents are the most frequent volunteers, siblings, relatives, older elementary and secondary students, college students, senior citizens, business and professional groups, and other members of the community can volunteer to participate in school activities (Shea & Bauer, 1985).

Although Shea and Bauer (1985) were referring to volunteers working with children who have disabilities, many of their recommendations and suggestions also apply to parents and family members of different cultural backgrounds. Volunteers should participate in a brief preservice training program and an on-the-job training program. Preservice training programs should introduce volunteers to school procedures and expectations and spell out their roles and functions. This training should emphasize the importance of confidentiality and attendance. It should offer an opportunity for parents to discuss the program with experienced volunteers and to visit with the teacher in the classroom setting. On-the-job training is a continuous process in which volunteers learn their specific activities (Shea & Bauer, 1985).

Parents and extended-family members from all cultures have numerous talents and skills to share with children and adolescents. People from differing cultural backgrounds, however, often consider educators and schools as both authoritarian and worthy of honor and praise. Therefore, some people might be hesitant to "interfere" with school routines or may feel that their talents are not worthy to be shared with the school. The administrator's and teacher's role in this situation is to encourage and convince people that schools are open to new ideas and that their talents are worth sharing. To accomplish such a goal, educators should send home, at the beginning of the school year, a parent-involvement questionnaire designed to determine skills, talents, and areas of interest.

Serving on committees is another way parents and extended-family members can become involved in classrooms and school. Through committee work, parents contribute to the classroom and school and learn about program development, operation, staffing, and evaluation. Parents also develop an appreciation for staffing concerns, curriculum development, fiscal exigencies, materials and equipment needs, and other demands of the instructional program (Shea & Bauer, 1985).

As with other forms of involvement, these parents and families might not understand the purpose of committees and how they function. Educators must work toward making the composition of the committee representative of the diversity of the student body. Guidelines for parents working on school committees include:

1. Remember the committee's purpose and objectives.
2. Be confident of the committee's ability to accomplish the assigned task.
3. Begin small, and take one step at a time.
4. Function within the school, and become an integral part of the classroom or school.
5. Seek financial, administrative, informational, and other assistance when necessary.

Parent involvement is an important factor in promoting the successful transition of youth with disabilities into adulthood. In Implementing Research 12.4, Geenen, Powers, and Lopez-Vasquez (2001) look at multicultural aspects of parent involvement in student transitioning activities.

Parents of different cultural backgrounds should not serve only on committees that deal with multicultural concerns; these parents may serve on any committee in which they have an interest. Committees might include curriculum, discipline and related problems, teacher evaluation, student–teacher relations, home study and work habits, extracurricular activities, student assessment and test results, career education, school dropouts, or any other aspect of the school (Shea & Bauer, 1985).

■ ■ ■ ■ ■ ▬

FOLLOW THROUGH 12.5
INVOLVING PARENTS AND FAMILIES IN SCHOOLS

Design a program to involve parents and families from culturally different backgrounds. Plan how you will invite and obtain their participation, help them understand that elementary and secondary schools need their participation, and teach them appropriate activities or utilize their individual expertise. Name several points that educators should consider (and propose an appropriate response) such as parents' language difficulties, lack of understanding of U.S. schools, and the immense respect that many parents and families have for educators.

■ ■ ■ ■ ■ ▬▬▬▬▬▬▬▬▬▬▬▬

IMPLEMENTING RESEARCH 12.4
MULTICULTURAL ASPECTS OF PARENT INVOLVEMENT

Geenen, Powers, and Lopez-Vasquez (2001) surveyed American Indian, African American, Hispanic American, and European American parents to assess their level of participation in their child's transitioning activities. They found that culturally and linguistically diverse groups report higher levels of participation than European American parents. Parent participation might be particularly important for culturally and linguistically diverse youth, as a strong relationship between parents and the school can promote cultural understanding and responsiveness in transition planning. Ethically diverse groups often emphasize norm-related behaviors and define adult roles differently, and parents can be a valuable resource in helping educators understand, identify, and support transition outcomes that are valued in a child's culture.

Parents of all ethnic groups are likely to encounter barriers to school participation, including parental fatigue, lack of parental knowledge regarding their rights and school procedures, logistical constraints (e.g., lack of child care), rigid or limited options for parental involvement in educational planning, and language. However, for culturally and linguistically diverse parents and families, the problems are made more formidable by racism, discrimination, insensitivity, and cultural unresponsiveness.

IMPLEMENTING THE RESEARCH

1. Professionals should work to involve all parents in children's transitioning activities; however, culturally and linguistically diverse parents and families might need additional attention and effort.
2. While all the strategies suggested by Geenen, Powers, and Lopez-Vasquez can be helpful, educators still have the responsibility to make the effort to involve culturally and linguistically diverse parents and families—diverse parents often do not know their rights and do not know how to involve themselves in the transition process.

Source: Geenen, S., Powers, L. E., & Lopez-Vasquez, A. (2001). Multicultural aspects of parent involvement in transitional planning. *Exceptional Children, 67*(1), 265–275.

PARENT–TEACHER CONFERENCES

The parent–teacher conference presents an opportunity for parents and teachers to exchange information about the child's school and home activities. It also provides an occasion to involve parents in planning and implementing their child's educational program. When teachers contact parents to schedule progress report conferences, they should explain the purpose of the conference.

To lessen the parent's anxiety about the conference, teachers might provide parents with a written agenda. Educators should also remember that the purpose of the conference is the child and school progress, not the teacher's or parent's personal, social, emotional, or marital problems. Although these issues may affect the learner's overall school progress, educators should direct the focus of the conference toward areas of school function.

■ ■ ■ ■ ■ ▬▬▬▬▬▬▬▬▬▬▬

FOLLOW THROUGH 12.6
DETERMINING CONCERNS DURING
PARENT–TEACHER CONFERENCES

Make a list of possible concerns and barriers that might interfere with the success of the parent–teacher conference. How will you motivate parents and families (who might feel that speaking forthrightly to the teacher is disrespectful) to speak, voice concerns, and make suggestions?

The agenda for the parent–teacher conference might include discussion of the learner's test scores or assessment results. Although most parents, regardless of cultural background, might benefit from an explanation of the terms normally associated with measurement and evaluation, parents might need even more detailed information. Test results are often a concern for parents and children, and parents may react strongly to results that indicate their child or adolescent is functioning at a lower level than most learners. Educators should ask parents from differing cultural backgrounds to state their understanding of the information and make sure parents understand the results and conclusions. Teachers should make a sincere effort to alleviate any anxiety that parents express over possible misuse of test results (Shea & Bauer, 1985).

Spaulding (1994) offers four suggestions for effective parent conferences. These might be even more important for educators meeting with parents and families from different cultural backgrounds:

1. Begin to work toward positive relationships with parents and families before school begins.
2. Talk regularly with students' parents; tell them of accomplishments and concerns, and ask for their advice and suggestions. Extra efforts might be necessary to convince parents to become active participants, especially because some cultures hold teachers in high regard and are reluctant to question or offer advice.
3. Ask students to join in parent conferences and to offer their opinions. Culturally diverse parents and their children might have difficulty with this suggestion, because some cultures place value on children being "seen and not heard."
4. Make the conference as comfortable as possible; reinforce students' accomplishments, avoid using confusing jargon, show parents how they can help, and end the conference on a positive note.

PARENT ADVISORY COUNCILS

A parent advisory council can be an excellent means of providing parents and families of culturally diverse backgrounds opportunities to voice opinions and generally influence the overall operation of the school. By having a council composition that reflects the cultural diversity of the student body, council representatives (or parents who make suggestions and comments through selected representatives) can offer specific suggestions for devising the school curriculum and making the teaching and learning environment more multicultural in nature. Council members might want to discuss the cultural diversity of the administrative and teaching staff, how the curriculum and teaching and learning process reflect diversity, policies that groups of differing cultural backgrounds might not understand, methods of making the school more multicultural in nature, or any topic that might seem relevant at the time.

Case Study 12.3 examines how Dr. Suarez carefully planned for cultural diversity on the parent advisory council.

An advisory council can serve as a liaison between school and classroom and between home and community, and it can function as a permanent parent-to-parent communications committee to announce meetings, special events, personnel changes, and other notices of interest. The advisory committee can also assume responsibility for organizing and directing ad hoc or temporary committees.

Orientation sessions might be in order, especially for parents and families who may not understand the purpose of the council, may feel that parents would be meddling in schools' business, or may not understand procedures by which meetings work. An orientation meeting can help council members feel better prepared and feel more

■ ■ ■ ■ ■

CASE STUDY 12.3
PARENT ADVISORY COUNCILS

Dr. Suarez, principal at Westview High School, carefully planned his parent advisory council. The composition was all-important this academic year. The state department of education had mandated increasingly stringent academic rules that would threaten the academic standards of slower students; the number of students of diverse cultural backgrounds was increasing; several acts of racism had plagued the previous school year; and his faculty was almost all white and middle-class. He thought parents could play a significant role this year, especially if he could convince leaders of the various diverse communities to participate.

He wondered what issues he might raise as the council progressed with its work. His list grew: grades, racism, evaluation, his district's inability (or lack of initiative, he thought) to employ faculty and staff members from culturally diverse backgrounds, language programs, school policies, curricular materials, instructional practices—the list seemed endless. "This will certainly be a challenging year," he thought. He wanted a council with cultural diversity proportional to that of the student body.

What problems might this diversity on the council bring? Again, his list grew: differing expectations of schools and teachers, misunderstandings about U.S. school systems, language and communication problems, reluctance to take an active role, and not understanding the role of the council. For the members with different cultural backgrounds, he planned an additional meeting to provide opportunities to answer questions, resolve concerns, and become better acquainted. Even with the pressing issues and the challenges of involving all members, regardless of culture, on the council, Dr. Suarez perceived this as a positive time—a time when his school's role in helping learners from different backgrounds could be defined more accurately and a time of enhanced acceptance and understanding.

comfortable about future meetings. Suggested topics for an orientation session include: council role and authority, purpose, district organization, value and functions of committees, decision-making procedures (perhaps including a brief session on Robert's Rules of Order), how to disagree and the value of expressing a different view, and expectations of members (Jennings, 1989).

PARENT AND FAMILY EDUCATION

The concept of parent education dates back to the 1800s and carries differing definitions and perceptions that have resulted in a variety of forms and emphases. A wide array of activities continues to be appropriate for parent education programs. These range from family and cultural transmission of childrearing values, skills, and techniques to more specific parenting behaviors. Specifically, however, we define the term *parent education* as planned activities that are designed to educate parents about their children and adolescents, goals of U.S. school systems, and ways they can help their child or adolescent experience success, both academically and behaviorally, in school.

Although schools should develop parent education programs specifically for individual learners and their parents, some programs help parents with special needs, enhance knowledge of family life, teach techniques for changing attitudes and behaviors, help parents change their own negative behaviors, provide health and sex education information, and teach parents how to help with the education process.

The need for parent education has been documented: Parents become more involved and develop more positive attitudes toward school activities; parents often dread the changes in their child's or adolescent's development; parents sometimes absolve themselves of responsibility; and parents often need assistance in understanding curricular areas. The need results from the heightened concern about pressures related to more working mothers, the effects of geographic mobility, divorce rates, and economic uncertainties as well as from parents needing relevant information for children's social, physical, emotional, and intellectual development.

The realities, however, pose a dilemma that demands educators' understanding. Although parent education programs have become routine aspects of many early childhood programs, evidence indicates that many middle- and secondary-school educators have not developed parent education programs. Early-childhood education appears to have made substantial progress in planning and implementing parent education programs and has provided the framework in both theory and practice for schools or other levels.

Rationale for Parent Education Programs

Two reasons speak to the importance of parent education: understanding the various developmental periods and responding appropriately to children's and adolescents' behavior. Although we address each reason separately, close and intricate relationships between the two areas warrant parental recognition and understanding.

Effective parent education programs provide experiences that show a developmental basis for children's and adolescents' behavior. Rather than allowing parents to assume that they have failed in parenting roles or to absolve themselves of responsibility for behavior, programs can help parents understand the developmental changes and the contemporary world of children and adolescents.

Specifically, parents need to understand the cause-and-effect relationship between development and behavior. The cause of certain behavior may result from children's and adolescents' quest for independence and from peer pressure to experiment with alcohol, drugs, sex, and other challenges to authority.

Basically, educators should provide programs that convince parents that their children are not necessarily "going bad" or "turning into hoodlums" and that, although understanding changes in behavioral patterns may be difficult for parents, children and adolescents need to feel accepted and understood. Parents need to understand that feeling guilty or absolving themselves of responsibility may result in even worse attention-getting, or even delinquent, behaviors. Parents need to understand the effects of one-parent homes on development and behavior. At the same time, educators should emphasize that not all behavior results from family disruption.

SPECIAL NEEDS OF PARENTS AND FAMILIES

Planning parent education programs for parents and families from differing cultural backgrounds requires that educators look at issues, topics, and formats from the perspective of these parents and families. Prepackaged programs, or programs that European Americans in middle- or upper-class suburban schools use might not be adequate for culturally diverse parents and families, whatever their social class.

Although special needs vary with culture, social class, and geographic area, what specific needs might parents and families have? Educators, after an objective and accurate needs assessment, might find that parents of diverse cultural backgrounds require educational assistance in understanding such areas as: school expectations, parent's roles in the school, tests and assessment scores, children's and adolescents' development, appropriate social services agencies and organizations that can provide assistance, homework and how to get help, school committees and parent advisory councils, and other involvement activities. This list provides only a few examples, but it suffices to show that parent education programs should be designed for a specific cultural group and not rely on a program that parents may not understand or feel is not culturally relevant.

Methods and activities selected for the parent education program determine the success of the effort. Programs for minority parents should not rely too heavily on reading material (unless participants are clearly proficient in English), should not expect parents to take active vocal roles in the beginning stages, and should not expect or require parents to reveal situations or information that may be personal or a negative reflection on the family or the home.

Formats of Parent Education Programs

Teachers must reach a decision about whether to employ a prepackaged parenting program that may lead to a loosely organized discussion group or to develop a program

■ ■ ■ ■ ■ ■

FOLLOW THROUGH 12.7
DESIGNING PARENT EDUCATION PROGRAMS

In all likelihood, it will be difficult to purchase a prepackaged parent education program that meets the needs of parents from a number of cultural backgrounds. For example, African American parents might not experience the same challenges as American Indians. Likewise, first-generation Asian Americans probably do not experience the same problems as third-generation Asian Americans. We think it might be more feasible to design programs with individual cultural groups in mind. Name a number of methods (such as first-hand contact and surveys, perhaps written in native languages) that will provide information on directions the parent education program should take.

that addresses parental needs for a particular school. Prepackaged programs have several advantages (e.g., they require less preparatory time and little revision), but they may not be applicable to a diverse range of cultures.

Developing a parent education program based on specific family and community needs might prove effective, and parents might receive it more enthusiastically. The format of the program can take several directions and should reflect the needs and interests of individual schools and parents.

Before scheduling planning sessions, educators should conduct an assessment or needs inventory to determine preferred methods and content. Parent education modes may include lectures, discussion groups, CD-ROMs, computer programs, videotapes, cassettes, and PowerPoint presentations. Parents may schedule appointments with available parent educators to discuss confidential and personal matters concerning their children and adolescents that they do not want revealed in large group settings.

Parent education sessions will undoubtedly stimulate questions, comments, and other discussion. Rather than relying on a lecture format with a large group, the leader of the session should allow time for parents to speak or meet in small groups. Sometimes, one of the leader's most effective approaches may be to let parents know that other parents experience similar problems.

Helping Parents Understand Their Roles and School Expectations

A major role of parent education programs should be to help parents of differing cultural groups understand the school's expectations and the parent's role in the teaching and learning process. Designing such a program requires educators to assess the needs and concerns of the specific culture. For example, although American Indian and Asian American parents might have similarities, they have substantial differences that necessitate culture-specific programs.

First, educators need to recognize that some parents and families, especially of more recent generations, might not understand U.S. school expectations and perspectives, which place emphasis on individual achievement, competition, and responsibility for one's own possessions. Parents and families of differing cultural backgrounds should

■ ■ ■ ■ ■ ■

FOLLOW THROUGH 12.8
DISCUSSING SCHOOL EXPECTATIONS

Discuss with a group of parents from differing cultural backgrounds their expectations of the U.S. school systems. After listening, begin thinking about expectations that need clarification and of ways to respond to the needs of children, adolescents, and their parents. How do their expectations differ from those of European Americans? How can educators convey school expectations to parents and families?

not encourage their children and adolescents to adopt middle- or upper-class white perspectives. Instead, educators can explain to parents the differing cultural expectations (e.g., group versus individual achievement, competition versus working together, sharing versus ownership) of various cultural groups. Educators should also explain the school's expectations in other areas, such as curricular matters, instructional strategies, classroom management and discipline, homework and extracurricular activities, and other aspects of the school that parents and families may need assistance in understanding.

Second, educators should make clear the parents' role and responsibilities in their children's or adolescents' education. Sometimes, people from different cultural backgrounds may think they do not know enough about U.S. school systems to make a contribution, or they may perceive the school as an authoritarian institution that does not appreciate input and suggestions. The educator's role is to change misconceptions of the schools and to show that learners' academic achievement and overall school progress can be enhanced when parents take an active role in the school. In meeting this goal, educators need to show all parents and families that:

1. They are responsible for encouraging and helping their children and adolescents in all phases of the teaching and learning process.
2. They are encouraged to visit the school and voice their input, recommendations, and suggestions.
3. They are encouraged to participate in conferences, involvement activities, parent education sessions, and parent advisory councils.

SUMMING UP

Educators who want to involve parents and families from culturally different backgrounds should:

1. Understand the extended-family concept, and plan educational experiences for both immediate and extended-family members.
2. Understand that parents and families may resist teachers' efforts to involve them in school activities.
3. Understand parents as individuals with intracultural, socioeconomic, and generational differences.

4. Learn as much as possible about parents and families through first-hand contact, parent surveys, and any other means that provide accurate and objective information.
5. Visit the homes of students to gain a better understanding of family backgrounds, values, customs, and traditions.
6. Ensure that communication between the school and family reflects a genuine understanding of the problems that might result from language and communication differences, both verbal and nonverbal.
7. Plan and conduct parent–teacher conferences so that parents will understand the purposes and procedures of the conference process.
8. Ensure that parent advisory councils have a composition that represents the cultural, ethnic, and racial composition of the student body, and ensure that the councils address the specific needs and concerns of parents and families from differing cultural backgrounds.
9. Understand that parent education programs are especially important for parents who might not understand the school's roles and expectations and who may need assistance with their child or adolescent in a predominantly European American school and society.

SUGGESTED LEARNING ACTIVITIES

1. Prepare a parent survey designed to obtain information from parents and families of different cultural backgrounds. List questions that will provide specific information about what parents and families expect from schools, how teachers can help children and adolescents, and how parents and families can contribute to the educational process. In preparing this survey, what are some precautions you might want to consider?

2. Design procedures for an effective parent advisory committee, with the purpose of involving parents and families. Your design should consider what means you will use to engage participants of all cultural backgrounds, the overall goals of the committee, how the committee will report to the general school population, a sample agenda (for an individual meeting and for the school year), how you will accommodate participants who are not proficient in English, and any special factors that educators should consider when dealing with minority populations.

3. Design a parent involvement program that builds on the strengths of cultural diversity. How might you capitalize on the knowledge and experiences of parents and extended-family members? Specifically, how could you determine their strengths and convince them to participate and share areas of expertise in parent involvement programs? How might you deal with problems resulting from language difficulties?

SUGGESTIONS FOR COLLABORATIVE EFFORTS

Form groups of three or four that, if possible, represent our nation's cultural and gender diversity. Working collaboratively, focus your group's attention toward the following efforts:

1. With the help of your group, prepare a survey to determine the reasons that parents might resist educators' efforts. Using the results, write a plan in which your goal is to obtain the family's participation and involvement.

2. Arrange an opportunity for each member of your group to meet with a parent or extended family member to learn what problems they experience with U.S. schools. Have as many cultural groups represented as possible. As a group, decide on a list of questions that might provide the information you want. Then, as a group, share your responses to determine whether you can establish a plan or agenda for addressing parents' and families' concerns. Caution: Remember that some cultures hold schools and educators in high regard and therefore might not want to share concerns and problems. In such cases, you should respect their privacy.

3. Prepare a list of booklets or pamphlets designed to educate parents and families from culturally different backgrounds about children and adolescents or the U.S. school system and its goals. Whenever possible, offer suggestions written in the parents' native language (unless the parent is proficient in English). Examples include: Sida o AIDs (available from Network Publications, P.O. Box 1830, Santa Cruz, CA 95061-1830) and the many fine publications in Cantonese, Korean, Spanish, and Vietnamese (catalog available) from the California State Department of Education, 721 Capitol Mall, P.O. Box 944272, Sacramento, CA 94244-2720.

EXPANDING YOUR HORIZONS: ADDITIONAL JOURNAL READINGS AND BOOKS

Barrera, R. M. (2001). Bringing home to school. *Scholastic Early Childhood Today, 16*(3), 44–56.
  Barrera maintains that diversity soon will become the norm and educators will need to be able to connect with children and families.

Carroll, M. (2001). Dim sum, bagels, and grits: A sourcebook for multicultural families. *Booklist, 97*(12), 1096.
  Carroll reviews this sourcebook that provides multicultural families with useful advice such as problems, choices, and opportunities.

High, P. C., LaGasse, L., Becker, S., Ahlgren, I., & Gardner, A. (2000). Literacy promotion in primary care pediatrics: Can we make a difference? *Pediatrics, 105*(14), 927–945.
  These authors evaluate the effects of a literacy promoting intervention as a part of well-child care on parent attitudes and behaviors.

Lie, Gwat-Yong. (2000). Multicultural perspectives in working with families. *Families in Society: The Journal of Contemporary Human Services, 81*(5), 544.
  Actually a book review, the reviewer critiques this book that addresses culturally competent strategies and challenges families encounter at different stages of the life cycle.

Midobuche, E. (2001). Building cultural bridges between home and the mathematics classroom. *Teaching Children Mathematics, 7*(9), 500–502.
  Midobuche shares a personal story of her childhood as she looks at cultural perspectives of how children learn mathematics.

Moon, T. R., & Callahan, C. M. (2001). Curricular modifications, family outreach, and a mentoring program: Impacts on achievement and gifted identification in high-risk primary students. *Journal of Education of the Gifted, 24*(4), 305–321.
  These authors describe a program that was a collaborative research effort between a university and a large urban school district to determine the efficacy of specific intervention efforts.

■ ■ ■ ■ ■

CHAPTER THIRTEEN

ADMINISTRATORS AND SPECIAL SCHOOL PERSONNEL

Understanding the material and activities in this chapter will help the reader:

- Explain why the cultural diversity of administrators, faculty, and staff should reflect that of the student population
- List several roles of administrators, special educators, library media specialists, counselors, and communications disorders specialists in a school that promotes multiculturalism at all levels
- List several ways administrators can lead school personnel in efforts to promote multiculturalism
- Explain the unique challenges that face special-education teachers in diagnosing and remediating learners from culturally different backgrounds
- Explain how the library media specialist can select appropriate print and nonprint materials that accurately portray children and adolescents from all cultural backgrounds
- Explain how the school counselor can understand culturally different children and adolescents and select culturally appropriate counseling techniques and testing instruments
- Explain how the communications disorders specialist can accurately distinguish between communications disorders and communications variations
- Explain, from the teacher's perspective, how the various professionals can work together and how the teacher can most effectively utilize the various areas of expertise for the benefit of learners of all cultural backgrounds

OVERVIEW

Genuine multicultural education efforts include more than lofty goals and school philosophies. The school's effort to recognize and celebrate cultural diversity should demonstrate total school involvement by including the efforts of all school personnel. A commitment to multicultural education also includes an administration, faculty, and staff that reflects the cultural diversity of the student body. Employing school personnel of all cultural backgrounds at all levels shows respect for diversity; however, educators still need to work together, within their individual areas of expertise, to provide learners with educational experiences that address both individual and cultural needs. This chapter shows, from the classroom teacher's perspective, how administrators and special school personnel can contribute to the overall multicultural education program.

ADMINISTRATORS, FACULTY, AND STAFF: TOWARD TOTAL SCHOOL EFFORTS

Multicultural education programs and curricula may have lofty goal statements, but perhaps the best measure of a school's commitment to cultural diversity is the actual cultural, ethnic, and racial composition of the administration, faculty, and staff. Specifically, do school personnel reflect the cultural diversity of the student population? If school personnel are predominantly from one background, one might justifiably ask whether the school administration is striving for the goals of the multicultural education program. Learners of various cultural backgrounds who hear the rhetoric of multiculturalism but see members of their cultural group represented only in custodial positions might question the school's commitment to equal opportunity.

Defending the goal of employing school personnel of varying cultural backgrounds is not difficult. First, having diverse school personnel shows students a commitment to include all people, regardless of cultural, ethnic, and racial backgrounds; second, such a policy shows a respect for the legal mandates that ensure equal opportunity for people of all cultures. Having the school staff reflect the diversity of the student body is undoubtedly a fundamental goal and a prerequisite to showing respect for cultural diversity and for equal opportunity under the law. Deliberate recruitment programs aimed at professionals of differing cultural backgrounds can contribute to employing faculty and staff more representative of our nation's diversity.

Responsive multicultural education programs include a commitment by professionals at all levels to multiculturalism and an acceptance of all learners regardless of diversity. While classroom teachers might have the most influence because of their proximity to many learners, administrators have a major responsibility for ensuring the implementation of multicultural procedures. Similarly, special educators and communication disorders specialists must project equal dedication, enthusiasm, and commitment to the overall school goals of acceptance and respect. The following sections examine the roles of administrators and special school personnel, show how classroom educators can work most effectively with these professionals for the benefit of learners, suggest a means of evaluating professional efforts, and suggest how all educators can encourage service learning.

The demographic shifts and often negative social relations in schools and communities have resulted in some educators considering the research and literature on practices in multiculturalism to promote cross-cultural understandings among students, faculty, and staff. Leistyna (2001) maintained that multicultural professional development can improve cultural relations and educational opportunities. Professional development should be a major component in any multicultural education effort because some educators can have a negative impact on students' self-image, academic achievement, and overall school relations. One example of multicultural professional development is sensitivity training that sensitizes teachers to other cultures and also affirms diversity. For multicultural professional development to be most successful, facilitators and participants must move beyond internationalizing multiculturalism and reducing issues of diversity to immigration, especially since the families of some of the most disenfranchised children have been in the United States for generations. Such a professional development effort should include the development of deeper understandings of what defines culture in order to be able to move beyond discussions of values, beliefs, group ethos, language, and practices and to understand how these elements are produced within the context of abuses of power (Leistyna, 2001).

In Implementing Research 13.1, Gay and Howard (2000) seriously doubt whether teacher education programs prepare preservice teachers to meet the instructional challenges of ethnically, racially, socially, and linguistically diverse students in

■ ■ ■ ■ ■

IMPLEMENTING RESEARCH 13.1
MULTICULTURAL TEACHER EDUCATION FOR THE TWENTY-FIRST CENTURY

Gay and Howard argue that teacher education programs should be more deliberate about preparing European American teachers to teach ethnically diverse students of color. Troubling attitudes and assumptions include fear of teaching diversity and resistance to dealing with race and racism. Gay and Howard maintain that instructors of multicultural education should engage in critical cultural consciousness and techniques for developing ethnic and cultural self-awareness.

Preparation for multicultural learning should include six major areas of competence: (1) multicultural classroom communications, (2) multicultural foundations of education, (3) multicultural pedagogical knowledge and skills, (4) multicultural performance appraisal, (5) public relations skills for culturally diverse families, groups, and communities, and (6) multicultural change agency.

Gay and Howard argued that, ideally, all of the multicultural competencies should be prominent in all aspects of the entire teacher education program, from course work to practicum, exit requirements, certification, and employment. Unfortunately, this might not happen for some time because of strong resistance to multicultural education among professors of education. Gay and Howard also ask whether professors can teach something they do not know. Still, teacher education programs should be held accountable for implementing quality multicultural education for K–12 teachers.

IMPLEMENTING THE RESEARCH
1. We cannot wait until all college of education faculties have developed the multicultural knowledge, skills, and attitudes they need. Therefore, multicultural education courses should be academically strong and be present across the teacher education program.
2. Preservice teachers need pedagogical experiences that illustrate the necessity of considering diversity in teaching–learning areas such as curriculum, instruction, learning environment, and student assessment.
3. Colleges of education should have planned professional development opportunities for instructors who lack the knowledge, skills, and attitudes to make multicultural education an integral thread throughout the teacher education program.

Source: Gay, G., & Howard, T. C. (2000). Multicultural teacher education for the 21st century. *Teacher Educator, 36*(1), 1–16.

the twenty-first century. They also explain several reasons why multicultural education preservice teacher education can be better accomplished.

THE ROLES OF ADMINISTRATORS IN MULTICULTURAL EDUCATION

The administrator's primary responsibilities include ensuring that multicultural education programs are carefully and methodically planned and that procedures are implemented to meet specific goals and objectives. Administrators require the ability and motivation to challenge and to lead school personnel toward responsive efforts. Although their participation might not include extensive first-hand efforts with youngsters of differing cultural backgrounds, their commitment and leadership remain crucial to the success of the overall school program and to generating other professionals' enthusiasm toward multicultural efforts. Administrators' efforts and the zeal they bring to this task undoubtedly determine the degree of success of the multicultural education program.

A major role of administrators is to provide learners with faculty and staff that reflect the cultural diversity of the student body and the community. The recent push for increased teacher certification standards might challenge principals who seek teachers from as many cultural backgrounds as possible. Most states have initiated minimum competency tests for all beginning teachers. Some claim that these tests measure teaching effectiveness, but an unintended result is that the number of minority teachers is rapidly declining.

A second challenge to administrators is to provide appropriate leadership efforts for an all-school approach to multicultural education. Teachers often base their dedication or enthusiasm for educational programs on the administrator's apparent commitment. Administrators should demonstrate leadership toward specific objectives, convey a genuine respect for cultural diversity, and demonstrate a willingness to be involved. These efforts may be among the most important, because the administrator is a major influence in the overall effectiveness of the programs and can lead faculty and staff members toward excellence in all professional endeavors.

A third challenge for principals is to deal affirmatively with the racial attitudes of their staffs. For many teachers and other staff members, joining the school ranks is their first sustained contact with members of another culture, and they may enter the situations not only lacking knowledge but fearful of confronting the issue of race. Such feelings can lead to an uneasiness that not only hurts work performance but can also do further harm to racial relations.

Another role in which administrators can offer significant contributions is communicating with, and involving, parents and community leaders. The administrator is in a position to assume the role of communicating the purposes of the multicultural education program to all parents.

Parents and other community members may erroneously view the multicultural education program as a "frill" or as a program that takes much-needed resources away from the curriculum or other school activities. Parents may be skeptical of programs that were not integral parts of their own educational experience and of which they might have little knowledge. Programs that are misunderstood will likely receive little support from the general public. Such a situation requires a skilled and competent administrator who is able to garner the support of parents and other community members.

Jenks, Lee, and Kanpol (2001) maintain that the primarily white and middle-class teachers in our nation's schools are ill-prepared in knowledge, skills, and attitudes to teach for equity and excellence in multicultural classrooms. In Implementing Research 13.2, these authors connect teacher education to multiple theoretical frameworks around the ongoing debate and issues of multicultural education.

■ ■ ■ ■ ■ ▬

IMPLEMENTING RESEARCH 13.2
APPROACHES TO MULTICULTURAL EDUCATION
IN PRESERVICE TEACHER EDUCATION

Jenks, Lee, and Kanpol (2001) connect conservative, liberal, and critical theories of multi-cultural education, particularly to preservice teachers, and argue for a more eclectic theo-retical means if there is to be any hope in transforming schools in urban environments. After discussing conservative, liberal, and critical theories of multicultural education, the authors examine Banks's models of multicultural curriculum and pedagogy such as contri-butions, additive, transformative, and social action. The authors argue that teachers cannot teach for cross-cultural competency when they lack it themselves.

Teacher education programs that want to prepare teachers to work in multicultural classrooms need to undergo substantive curricular and other changes to better prepare teachers to work with students who are diverse. To meet this goal, Jenks, Lee, and Kanpol recommend that the curriculum for preservice teaches include an understanding of the rel-ative strengths and weaknesses of the philosophical frameworks and specific multicultural models. Such understandings can stimulate critical reflection regarding one's own philo-sophical perspectives, moral commitment, and readiness to teach for equity and excellence, for it is only through study and self-reflection when confronted with perspectives that chal-lenge preconceived assumptions that one can effect significant changes in beliefs, attitudes, and knowledge.

IMPLEMENTING THE RESEARCH
1. Preservice teachers need to recognize the primary importance of diversity in all their educational decisions—for example, determining student readiness, designing curric-ula, selecting instructional materials, assessing performance, and developing appro-priate programs and teaching techniques.
2. Preservice teachers should have field experiences in urban settings in which they observe first-hand the need for multicultural education and pedagogy in schools with diverse populations.
3. Preservice teachers should work closely with minority students in tutorial relation-ships in order to gain a more sensitive and concrete understanding of how culture shapes learning styles.

Source: Jenks, C., Lee, J. O., & Kanpol, B. (2001). Approaches to multicultural education in preservice teacher education: Philosophical frameworks and models for teaching. *The Urban Review, 33*(2), 87–105.

Referring specifically to African Americans, Lomotey (1989) suggests that principals who work in effective schools demonstrate confidence in students' ability to learn, a commitment to ensure students' success, and an understanding of students and their communities. Lomotey's research in school climate, principal leadership, school culture, and effective schools indicates that principals should:

1. Believe that all their students can learn and reflect this belief in their goals
2. Be concerned with the least successful students in their schools, rather than being satisfied that some students are doing above-average work
3. Broaden the base of recognized achievement by acknowledging nontraditional accomplishments, particularly with minority students
4. Acknowledge students who have exceptionally good attendance or punctuality records

Principals must believe that all students can learn, have confidence in their students, involve parents in their children's education, reflect on the impact of the reform movement, and push for appropriate role models for all learners (Lomotey, 1989).

FROM THE PERSPECTIVE OF CLASSROOM EDUCATORS: WORKING WITH ADMINISTRATORS

Classroom educators need administrators' attention and support. Teachers and administrators must not work in isolation and risk the possibility that they will move toward different goals. Administrative support of teachers is imperative.

What, then, can educators do as they work with, and seek assistance from, administrators? Classroom educators who have direct contact with learners of various cultural backgrounds are in the best position to determine learner needs and convey these needs to administrators.

Educators, keeping in mind the many demands placed on administrators, must make their concerns known and insist on changes. Presenting the problem or concern is the first step. Working with the principal (suggesting, providing input, and offering

■ ■ ■ ■ ■

FOLLOW THROUGH 13.1
SEEKING INFORMATION FROM PRINCIPALS

Ask one or more principals or assistant principals to describe their multicultural education programs and their specific roles in the program. Specifically, seek information on how they have led school efforts to ensure that their school effectively reflects U.S. diversity. Ask also about school philosophy, library materials, efforts to celebrate cultural diversity, programs for students whose English proficiency is limited, and cultural diversity among their faculty and staffs.

recommendations) is the second step. Classroom educators, who have a better perspective on problems than administrators, must take responsibility for explaining the problems in accurate and objective terms. Once a problem has been explained and classified, the classroom educator's responsibility is to follow through on appropriate plans and strategies.

Case Study 13.1 looks at a teacher who seeks an administrator's support on behalf of seventh-grade students.

CASE STUDY 13.1
CULTURALLY RELEVANT EDUCATIONAL EXPERIENCES

Mrs. Miller, a seventh-grade teacher at Evergreen Middle School, had twenty-eight students in her class: twelve European Americans, eleven African Americans, two Hispanic Americans, and two Asian Americans. Mrs. Miller recognized that the school, its policies, and its teaching and learning practices were predominantly white and middle-class in perspective. Many students had to obey rules they did not understand, work toward meeting expectations and levels of motivation compatible with white perspectives, and learn to use cognitive styles similar to those of middle-class white learners. Mrs. Miller recognized the need for change but also realized she had limited time, resources, and expertise. For her students' welfare, she decided to seek the principal's assistance.

Mrs. Johnson, the principal, listened attentively to Mrs. Miller's concerns. She agreed not only that the sixteen students of culturally different backgrounds needed culturally relevant educational experiences, but also that the twelve European American students needed to acquire a better understanding of the other learners (and vice versa). Mrs. Johnson and Mrs. Miller decided to form a committee to address the learners' needs. The committee consisted of Mrs. Johnson, Mrs. Miller, another seventh-grade teacher, one European American parent who had expressed interest, and three parents from other cultural groups (one from each group represented). Mrs. Johnson made a list of her and the committee's recommendations:

1. The task called for commitment of administrators, faculty, and parents; it was not something Mrs. Miller should tackle alone.
2. All parents—majority culture and minority cultures—should be notified (and their advice sought) of the effort to meet learners' needs and to provide multicultural experiences for all learners.
3. Textbooks and other curricular materials should be examined for bias, stereotypes, and cultural relevance.
4. Teaching and learning practices and the school environment should be examined from an administrative perspective.

Mrs. Johnson thought these steps served as a good starting point and that, from an administrative perspective, it was a manageable agenda. Viewing this agenda as only a first phase, Mrs. Johnson started to consider how the efforts could become a total school effort.

EVALUATION OF ADMINISTRATORS' EFFORTS AND COMMITMENT

Administrators' effort and commitment to multicultural education should be evaluated, just as educators' teaching effectiveness and learners' academic achievement are evaluated. The Evaluation Checklist provides examples of items to assess in determining administrators' effectiveness.

EVALUATION CHECKLIST
1. The principal demonstrates and models respect for all forms of diversity among students and their parents and families.
2. The principal seeks to employ faculty and staff of as many different cultures as possible.
3. The principal seeks to provide financial resources and other less tangible forms of support for the multicultural education program.
4. The principal works cooperatively with the school faculty and staff to provide effective multicultural educational experiences.
5. The principal supports a total school program (curriculum, instruction, and environment), rather than the occasional teaching-unit approach.
6. The principal accepts responsibility for acting as a catalyst and for providing significant leadership for the multicultural education program.
7. The principal arranges for convenient sessions for parents and families of differing cultural backgrounds to voice concerns and suggestions.
8. The principal recognizes cultural differences among people as traits to be valued rather than to be eliminated or remediated.
9. The principal evaluates the efforts of faculty and staff and offers constructive criticism and positive suggestions in areas needing improvement.
10. The principal coordinates efforts of faculty and staff members toward a common goal of recognizing and building on cultural differences.

THE ROLE OF SPECIAL EDUCATION IN THE MULTICULTURAL EDUCATION PROGRAM

Special-education personnel can play significant roles in the multicultural education program. Tasks confronting them include the cultural considerations surrounding testing and assessment, the legal aspects of educating children with disabilities, the psychosocial variables affecting the teaching and learning process, and the effective coordination of efforts between special-education and regular classroom teachers.

Students of culturally different backgrounds are overrepresented in special-education classes. In the past, children who came from poor families or from homes where English was the second language or not spoken at all often ended up in special-needs classes. The role of special-education teachers includes responding to the increasing cultural diversity among learners by using culturally appropriate assessment devices and making placement decisions that reflect an understanding of cultural differences.

■ ■ ■ ■ ■

FOR ADDITONAL INFORMATION
WEBSITES FOR ADMINISTRATORS

Ohio Association of Secondary School Administrators
www.oassa.org   Provides information on a variety of topics for middle-level and secondary administrators and others.

American Association of School Administrators (AASA)
www.aasa.org   Provides information for both elementary and secondary-school administrators about effective leadership.

Principal Magazine: November 1998
www.naesp.org/comm/p1198.htm   *Principal* magazine provides elementary school principals with a wealth of information on various administrative topics.

■ ■ ■ ■ ■

FOLLOW THROUGH 13.2
SPEAKING WITH SPECIAL-EDUCATION PERSONNEL

Talk with several special-education teachers to learn how they objectively assess learners from culturally different backgrounds who have disabilities. Specifically, try to determine how they deal with the influence of culture during assessment, how they distinguish between differences and disabling conditions, and how they determine whether characteristics result from an actual disability or limited language proficiency.

TESTING AND ASSESSMENT

Special-education teachers, like all educators, should exercise extreme caution when labeling learners of different cultural backgrounds. They must carefully distinguish between disability and difference. They must not make placement decisions based on faulty evidence or culturally biased assessment instruments.

Teachers should not consider learners intellectually inferior because of poor performance on standardized tests. Scores on standardized tests too often influence teachers' expectations of learners' academic performance in the classroom. Teachers must maintain high expectations for all learners, regardless of cultural background. A standardized test score can provide an indication of a student's degree of assimilation but provide little evidence of an individual's intelligence (Gollnick & Chinn, 2002).

In developing tests, and in using the results of standardized tests, special-education teachers, and all educators, should recognize the inherent cultural bias that favors students of the majority culture. In fact, few tests have been developed from the perspective of a culturally diverse group. One such test is the Black Test of Bicultural Homogeneity (BITCH), which is based on urban African American culture and includes language and terms familiar to this culture. Although African Americans consistently score higher on this test than do members of the majority culture, it is rarely used to determine intelligence of individuals or groups (Gollnick & Chinn, 2002).

Special-education teachers should be constantly aware of the cultural biases among tests and remind themselves not to rely on test scores as the only indication of students' intelligence. Like all educators, special-education teachers should employ a number of culturally appropriate assessments and other sources of information to avoid basing placement decisions and judgments of intelligence on faulty data.

LEGAL PERSPECTIVES

Special-education teachers must understand the increasingly prominent role of the federal government in special education. The government has done more in recent years to promote the education rights of learners with disabilities than in the entire previous history of the nation. During this period, legislation has been notable for an affirmation of the education rights of students with disabilities. It addresses the problems of students who have disabilities as well as those who have limited proficiency in English. It also has provisions for nondiscriminatory assessment, parental involvement, and expanded instructional services.

From the teacher's perspective, the Education for All Handicapped Students Act of 1975 (PL 94-142) was a landmark law for students with disabilities in general and for culturally and linguistically different populations in particular. Among the most important provisions of PL 94-142 are those addressing the right to due process, protection against discriminatory testing during assessment, placement in the least restrictive education environment, and individualized education programs. In essence, PL 94-142 addresses the basic rights and equal protection issues with respect to the evaluation, identification, and placement of learners with disabilities. Under this law, assessment should serve to identify learners with disabilities and to guide instructional planning based on established educational goals (Hernandez, 1989).

Litigation, as well as PL 94-142, has also dramatically affected the educational system. Court cases have examined the legality of assessment, classification, and placement of low-achieving children (*Diana v. State Board of Education*, 1970; *Larry P. v. Wilson Riles*, 1972) and the right of learners who are severely disabled to a free and public education (*Pennsylvania Association for Retarded Children v. the Commonwealth of Pennsylvania*). These cases and other, similar litigation have led to the establishment of the following legal standards:

1. Assessment of intellectual capabilities using measures in English is inappropriate for students with limited English proficiency.
2. Identification of children as mildly mentally retarded requires consideration of factors such as adaptive behavior, sociocultural group, and motivational systems, in addition to measures of intelligence.
3. The degree to which culturally different groups have been overrepresented in special-education classes for the educably mentally retarded (EMR) is sufficient to constitute bias. Causes of the overrepresentation have included: (a) failure to consider linguistic and cultural factors, (b) failure to identify appropriately and

to determine the eligibility of disabled students, and failure to provide proper procedures and special services, and (c) excessive reliance on IQ test results as placement criteria.

4. Factors such as item bias on measure of IQ and discriminatory instruments alone does not suffice to account for misplacements and disproportionate representation of learners from culturally different groups in special-education classes (Hernandez, 1989).

In summary, from a classroom educator's perspective, the placement procedures that special-education teachers employ must be in accordance with PL 94-142 and the litigation addressing the rights of the disabled. Classroom teachers are responsible for helping special educators understand all learners and the role of psychocultural factors in learning and assessment.

From the Perspective of Classroom Educators: Working with Special-Education Teachers

From the perspective of the classroom educator, the special-education teacher should be considered a major instructional resource. Although teacher accreditation requirements mandate that all teachers have at least a basic knowledge of disabilities, most regular classroom teachers lack expertise in the techniques of working with children who have disabilities, especially those from culturally diverse backgrounds. When student needs can be addressed in the regular classroom, classroom educators should seek help from special-education teachers. Similarly, regular educators should rely on qualified special-education teachers to handle students who, by law, cannot benefit from education in a regular classroom setting.

Special-education teachers must respond to the classroom educator's request to assess students in need and provide culturally appropriate testing and assessment. They work with regular classroom teachers to provide appropriate educational experiences for all students with disabilities (regardless of cultural background). They must understand the effects of cultural factors on the teaching and learning process. The classroom teacher should perceive special-education personnel as valuable resources whose training and expertise can contribute to the education of nearly any exceptional (or so-called normal) learner.

Classroom educators must follow appropriate procedures for referring students to special-education teachers. They must help special-education teachers understand learners' cultural diversity and provide follow-up as the special-education teacher recommends. It is important that regular classroom teachers view special-education teachers as partners and not as people on whom to "dump" unwanted students. Special-education teachers can provide educational assistance to learners who have disabilities as well as those who do not. In many cases, the organization of the school and the legalities of the referral process require regular classroom teachers to take the initial steps.

Case Study 13.2 shows how a secondary social studies teacher sought the professional assistance of the special-education teacher.

■ ■ ■ ■ ■

CASE STUDY 13.2
SEEKING THE SPECIAL EDUCATOR'S HELP

Mrs. Heath, a tenth-grade social studies teacher, noticed that four or five of her American Indian students seemed uninterested. She wondered whether the students were really unmotivated, whether they had reading problems and attention deficits, or whether the curricula topics simply were uninteresting to them. Fully realizing the consequences of making judgments based on erroneous beliefs, Mrs. Heath took her concern to the special-education teacher in the school.

Mrs. Blackmon listened carefully to Mrs. Heath's concerns. Mrs. Blackmon first decided to test the students' reading abilities to determine their reading vocabulary and comprehension skills. Second, she explained to Mrs. Heath that American Indians could listen without looking a person in the eye, and that "looking interested" might be more of a "white perspective," one that might not cross cultural boundaries.

Mrs. Blackmon felt that, although the students' reading abilities were below grade level, they basically could read. She offered several suggestions to help Mrs. Heath and the students. First, she would work with the students two or three times a week to improve their reading comprehension. Second, she would help Mrs. Heath to provide some culturally relevant materials. Third, she would help Mrs. Heath to develop a better understanding of American Indian learners.

Without labeling or making unjustified placements, both teachers realized the importance of working as a team to help the American Indian learners. Each recognized that working separately would not result in the most effective educational experiences for the learners. A coordinated effort, with each teacher reinforcing and building on the effects of the other, would best address the needs of the American Indian learners.

The following checklist provides special educators with a means of self-evaluation to determine strengths, weaknesses, and overall commitment to promoting cultural diversity. Ask yourself each question and answer it in terms of your responsibilities as a special-education teacher.

A SELF-EVALUATION CHECKLIST FOR SPECIAL-EDUCATION TEACHERS

1. Do I value and respect cultural diversity in all forms and degrees?
2. Do I recognize differences between disabilities and cultural diversity, or do I perceive differences as liabilities or deficiencies in need of remediation?
3. Do I coordinate the efforts of administrators, faculty, and staff to provide the least restrictive environment for all disabled learners?
4. Do I support a racially and culturally diverse faculty and staff for all youngsters with disabilities?
5. Do I insist that screening and placement procedures recognize cultural diversity and that such procedures follow legal mandates and guidelines for special education?
6. Do I work with parents and families on a regular basis, help them understand programs for learners with disabilities, and make referrals to appropriate social service agencies?

■ ■ ■ ■ ■ ▬▬▬▬▬▬▬▬▬▬▬▬▬▬▬▬▬▬▬▬▬▬▬▬

FOLLOW THROUGH 13.3
DEVISING A PLAN TO HELP LEARNERS
WHO HAVE DISABILITIES

Work with special-education teachers to devise a plan to make learners with disabilities from culturally different backgrounds feel more a part of the whole school. List at least four or five specific ways to involve these learners in the mainstream of the school.

7. Do I use testing and assessment instruments with the least racial, cultural, and social-class bias?
8. Do I provide opportunities for youngsters with disabilities to be mainstreamed or integrated with nondisabled learners of all cultural backgrounds whenever possible?
9. Do I plan learning experiences that recognize differences in language and dialect?
10. Do I support community recognition and efforts to provide appropriate educational experiences for learners with disabilities from both majority and minority cultural backgrounds?

LIBRARY MEDIA SPECIALISTS

The library media specialist in a multicultural setting must understand the cultural diversity of his or her school and build a library and media collection that shows positive portrayals of all cultural groups. Library or media specialists also work with classroom educators in positive, constructive ways that demonstrate a respect for and commitment to providing appropriate multicultural education experiences.

■ ■ ■ ■ ■ ▬▬▬▬▬▬▬▬▬▬▬▬▬▬▬▬▬▬▬▬▬▬▬▬

FOLLOW THROUGH 13.4
DETERMINING CULTURALLY APPROPRIATE
READING MATERIALS

Work with a library media specialist as he or she engages in the book selection process. What selection criteria are used? Is a particular assessment device used? What "red flags" (e.g., stereotyped images, lack of diverse characters, insensitive use of dialects) indicate to library media specialists that reading materials might be inappropriate? Is selection done by one person or by a committee consisting of educators and parents from a number of different cultural groups?

Selecting Culturally Appropriate Print and Nonprint Media

School library media specialists, like all educators, are challenged to meet the needs of an increasingly diverse student population. Chapter 9 emphasized the importance of positive portrayals of children and adolescents from varying cultural backgrounds and the necessity of addressing problems of sexism, racism, stereotyping, and outright omissions. Libraries are responsible for ensuring that books, magazines, audiovisual materials, computer software, and all library and media materials positively and realistically represent characters of many cultural backgrounds with whom learners can relate.

One of the better and more pragmatic solutions to library media specialists' and teachers' problems has been offered by the Council on Interracial Books for Children, which regularly evaluates children's materials, trade books, textbooks, and other educational resources. This text (especially Using Children's Literature and the Suggested Children's Books in Chapters 3, 4, 5, 6, 7, and 8) provides examples of accurate literary descriptions of children and adolescents from various cultural backgrounds.

Library media specialists can refer to Table 9.1 (a checklist for determining racism and sexism in children's books).

Coordinating Efforts with Classroom Educators

Like other professionals working in elementary and secondary schools, library media specialists and classroom educators must work together for the welfare of children and adolescents. Library media specialists can be a valuable resource for regular classroom teachers. They can supplement learning experiences or provide a children's literature–based approach to instruction. Some classroom teachers received their education training before accrediting associations required experiences in multicultural education. For these teachers especially library media specialists can suggest culturally appropriate books for all children.

From the Perspective of Classroom Educators: Working with Library Media Specialists

The professional paths of classroom educators and school library media specialists should probably cross more than they do. Teachers bring or allow learners to visit the

■ ■ ■ ■ ■

FOLLOW THROUGH 13.5
COORDINATING EFFORTS OF EDUCATORS AND LIBRARY MEDIA SPECIALISTS

How might educators and library media specialists coordinate efforts to most effectively serve children and adolescents of various cultural backgrounds? Consider books, poems, speakers, films, plays, skits, computer software, and occasions to celebrate diversity.

library during a specified time, during which the library media specialist might or might not have an activity planned. Teachers sometimes remain with students during the library period and make suggestions or encourage students' interest in books and reading. In other situations, teachers leave the students and work elsewhere.

From the perspective of classroom educators, the library media specialist should be considered a prime resource professional. He or she can teach learners about the library and about books and magazines that provide positive cultural images. Teachers and library media specialists must work together.

Library media specialists' roles in supporting the multicultural education program include stocking the library and media center with books, magazines, and other materials that accurately portray children and adolescents from various cultural groups; assisting classroom educators to choose and use these books; ensuring that library collections have works by nonwhite authors and illustrators; ensuring that library holdings and materials are accessible to all students, regardless of social class and cultural background; and assisting students as they search for reading materials.

The classroom educator's responsibilities include working with the library media specialist (suggesting acquisitions and completing book request forms) to secure a multicultural library; encouraging students of all cultures to read books that provide accurate portrayals of learners from different cultural backgrounds; encouraging learners to read books by qualified authors; and working with the library media specialist to plan activities that feature well-written reading materials. Case Study 13.3 shows how one teacher improved her knowledge of multicultural books by seeking help from the school library media specialist.

The following checklist provides self-evaluation questions library media specialists can use to rate their own effectiveness.

SELF-EVALUATION FOR LIBRARY MEDIA SPECIALISTS

1. Do I acquire a collection of print and nonprint media that provides positive and accurate examples of children and adolescents from various cultural groups?
2. Do I have an overall library program that contributes to the school's multicultural education program?
3. Do I work with teachers and other educators to plan appropriate multicultural experiences for all learners?
4. Do I have a system that makes library materials accessible to all learners, regardless of cultural or socioeconomic background?
5. Do I plan developmentally and culturally appropriate teaching and learning activities for learners of all cultural groups?
6. Does the library have multicultural materials that are appropriate for varying reading, interest, and developmental levels?
7. Have I established and approved criteria for evaluating the appropriateness (cultural, gender, socioeconomic, etc.) of print and nonprint media?
8. Do I seek input and suggestions for library purchases from teachers, organizations promoting cultural diversity, and interested parents?
9. Have I acquired a professional library of print and nonprint materials for educators who want to improve their professional knowledge of cultural diversity?

■ ■ ■ ■ ■ ▬▬▬▬▬▬

CASE STUDY 13.3
IMPROVING KNOWLEDGE OF MULTICULTURAL BOOKS

Mrs. D'Micio, the sixth-grade teacher, and Mrs. Benton, the library media specialist, discussed with some intensity cultural diversity and children's books.

"Children's literature just has not kept pace with the cultural diversity in our society," Mrs. D'Micio said.

"Perhaps not to the extent it should have, but there are some very good children's and adolescents' books that do include people from many different backgrounds," Mrs. Benton responded.

Mrs. D'Micio looked at her class rolls and thought, "Well, it has been about ten years since I took a children's literature course. Maybe there are some good books around now." She asked Mrs. Benton, "Can you help me find some books for my students? They are sixth-graders, you know."

Mrs. Benton responded in the affirmative and began thinking of the sources she could consult: *Books in Print*, Charlotte Huck's *Children's Literature in the Elementary School*, Donna Norton's *Through the Eyes of a Child*, the *Hornbook Magazine*, and trade book publishers that specialize in multicultural books, such as Children's Book Press (1461 Ninth Avenue, San Francisco, CA 94122).

Mrs. Benton gave Mrs. D'Micio a great list and began collecting books that provided accurate portrayals of children and adolescents in various cultural groups. She also wondered whether other teachers in the school would like such books to supplement their instruction or to suggest to their students and decided to begin a program designed to increase the library's holdings of multicultural books. She also decided to make all teachers in the school aware of the books and appropriate uses.

COUNSELORS' ROLES IN MULTICULTURAL EDUCATION

The role of school counselors includes understanding culturally different children and adolescents, providing culturally responsive counseling, understanding testing and assessment issues, and working with classroom teachers for the welfare of all learners.

Understanding and Counseling

Cultural, intracultural, ethnic, and racial differences are important considerations in the counseling of children and adolescents in multicultural situations. Learners are not a homogeneous population. They differ widely as individuals and particularly as pertains to culture, gender, generation, and socioeconomic status.

Children are basically now oriented and view their world, their cultures, their peers, their language, and their morality from a child's perspective. Adolescents function developmentally in a stage between childhood and adulthood and are developing self-concepts and cultural identities that will affect their entire adult lives.

American Indians

Herring (1989) describes the dismal situations of many American Indian children and suggests that guidance and counseling are the best vehicles for helping these children. Herring's suggestions include:

1. Counseling intervention should be highly individualized.
2. Assessment should have minimal socioeconomic or cultural bias.
3. Counselors should recognize learning styles and life purposes.
4. The child's culture must not be devalued.
5. Methodologies should place high value on self-worth.
6. The school counselor should help the school staff become sensitive to the needs of American Indians.

African Americans

School counselors should consider African American learners' individual heritages and special needs, rather than assuming too much cultural homogeneity or approaching counseling situations from a white perspective. Specifically, school counselors can organize self-awareness groups that emphasize self-appreciation through cultural heritage; explore the nature and importance of positive interpersonal relationships; conduct social behavior guidance groups; and offer motivation sessions and guidance workshops in areas such as academic planning, study skills, and time management.

Arab Americans

Counseling Arab Americans might be a little more intimidating, since more has been written on counseling other cultural groups. Still, counselors can look at the challenges these students face and implement counseling strategies that are culturally appropriate for the Arab culture. Suggestions for counselors include:

1. Realize that Arab culture has been basically ignored—Arabs are "the lost sheep" (Wingfield & Karaman, 1995, p. 8) in the school system, and they deserve to have culturally appropriate counseling strategies.
2. Develop a genuine awareness of the Arab culture and acknowledge rather than devalue the student's culture.
3. Remember that children's and adolescents' perceptions of situations and events might differ from the perspective of middle-class European American and in fact, other cultures' perspectives.
4. Avoid making assumptions about religious beliefs—if in doubt, ask the student about his or her religious beliefs, traditions, and customs.
5. Recognize the importance of the family, both immediate and extended, and respect it being patriarchal and hierarchal with regard to age and sex.
6. Provide counseling strategies that promote self-esteem and cultural identities.
7. Consider the students' generational status and the accompanying acculturation that might have occurred and how these might affect counseling intervention.

Asian Americans

Reminding counselors of the tremendous cultural and individual diversity among Asian Americans, Hartman and Askounis (1989) suggest:

1. Determining individual strengths and weaknesses, and assessing cultural backgrounds.
2. Understanding each learner's degree of acculturation.
3. Understanding Asian Americans' difficulty in exhibiting openness. In a culture that regards restraint as a sign of emotional maturity, admitting problems is thought to reflect badly on the entire family.
4. Understanding that overly confrontational, emotional, and tense approaches may cause additional problems and turmoil for Asian American learners.
5. Learning about individuals and their respective cultures; asking about the culture, accepting the learner's world, developing cultural and ethnic sensitivity and consciousness, and avoiding stereotyping.

Hispanic Americans

For the most effective multicultural intervention, Nieves and Valle (1982) offer several counseling suggestions:

1. Use active counseling approaches that are concrete, specific, and focus on the student's behalf.
2. Develop an awareness of the individual's culture.
3. Use approaches that take the client's frame of reference as a vehicle for growth.
4. Examine prejudices and attitudes toward Hispanic Americans.
5. Make home visits if possible, and make reference to the family during sessions.
6. Call students by their correct names. In Puerto Rico and elsewhere, people have two last names: The first is that of the family, and the second is that of the mother's family. Using the wrong name is an insult and may raise identity questions.
7. Accept the role of expert, but work to relinquish the role of authority. Clients must accept responsibility for their own lives.

European Americans

Counselors working with European Americans should consider the tremendous diversity among individuals as well as individual cultures. European Americans come from many different geographic regions and cultural backgrounds. For example, children and adolescents with Hungarian backgrounds differ significantly from those with Greek backgrounds. Likewise, Polish people differ from Italians. Counselors should use extreme caution when forming decisions about cultural backgrounds, religious beliefs, and other personal characteristics. Suggestions for counseling European Americans include:

1. Understanding some cultures' (such as that of Italians) allegiance and commitment to family members and to the overall welfare of the family

2. Understanding the language problems of some children and adolescents and how these problems affect schoolwork, interpersonal relationships, and willingness to become active participants in U.S. society

3. Understanding cultural traditions that, in some cases, have been taught and emphasized for many generations, and understanding how these cultural traditions might conflict with U.S. values and expectations.

4. Understanding that considerable effort might be necessary to build trust in the counseling relationship.

5. Understanding such differences as social class and generational status (e.g., the differences in perspectives of a first- and a third-generation child or adolescent) and the effects of these differences on counseling sessions.

Testing and Assessment

The counselor's goal in assessment is to minimize ethnocentrism and to maximize culturally appropriate information. Assessment in counseling and psychotherapy includes interviewing, observing, and testing, as well as analyzing documents. To what extent does cultural diversity affect assessment? Will a characteristic indigenous to a specific culture be mistakenly perceived and assessed using European American middle-class standards?

Two important issues in multicultural assessment include whether psychological constructs or concepts are universally valid and how to counter the effects of diagnosing and placing false labels. Other questions related to multicultural assessment are:

1. What level and type of assessment are indicated?
2. Which tests are most useful and why?
3. What are the ethical and legal responsibilities associated with multicultural assessment?

Are multicultural groups being assessed with instruments actually designed for middle-class white clients? Lonner and Ibrahim (1989) maintain that without appropriate assessment strategies, counseling professionals are unable to diagnose problems, to develop appropriate goals, and to assess the outcomes of intervention. Specific as-

■ ■ ■ ■ ■ ▬▬▬▬▬

FOLLOW THROUGH 13.6

PROVIDING CULTURALLY APPROPRIATE COUNSELING INTERVENTION

Ask several school counselors about the special challenges of counseling children and adolescents from African, Arab, Asian, European, Hispanic, and American Indian backgrounds (as well as other cultures). Ask about differences in counseling intervention, differing worldviews, and different perspectives toward life and school. How do counselors adjust their strategies to reflect children's and adolescents' cultural backgrounds?

sessment issues include initial client assessment, clinical judgment, standardized and nonstandardized assessment, and the outcome of counseling evaluation (Lonner & Ibrahim, 1989).

From the Perspective of Classroom Educators: Working with Counselors

Counselors may work with individuals, small groups, and large classes. The classroom educator may initiate the first contact between a school counselor and a troubled student.

Classroom teachers, who have daily contact with learners, may be the first professionals to detect a potential problem. Individual teachers are in a prime position either to ask the counselor for direct assistance or to refer students with problems to the counselor. It is wise for teachers and counselors to determine the best means of referring students, of coordinating and scheduling large group counseling, and of determining the correct needs of learners from diverse cultural backgrounds.

Counselors may provide several forms of assistance to classroom teachers and their students. Considering the many demands on the counselor's time and expertise, however, the teacher may have to initiate contact or inform the counselor of special areas of concern. Generally speaking, counselors can:

1. Determine and facilitate joint efforts of administrators and other educators to improve an adolescent's self-concepts and cultural identity
2. Provide assistance in suggesting culturally appropriate instruments and in interpreting test scores of learners of culturally different backgrounds
3. Work with families of all cultural backgrounds (both immediate and extended) in parent education endeavors
4. Offer parents meaningful roles in school governance, and offer families opportunities to support the teaching and learning process at home and at school
5. Provide individual and small-group counseling in areas of concern to all learners, such as peer acceptance and approval
6. Provide large-group counseling sessions in areas such as involvement meetings, rules meetings, and values-clarification meetings
7. Suggest culturally relevant materials to help all children and adolescents better understand each other's cultures
8. Work with older students in career planning, and suggest appropriate subjects needed to pursue career plans
9. Help learners deal with concern over body development, the desire for social acceptance, and the conflicts between adult expectations and peer expectations of culturally appropriate behaviors
10. Design special programs for at-risk learners who are from culturally different backgrounds

Classroom educators should view their roles and those of counselors as complementary. Because classroom educators have the most daily contact with learners from various cultural backgrounds, they are usually in the best position to detect learners with problems, make referrals, and to follow up on counselors' efforts. Likewise, the

■ ■ ■ ■ ■

FOLLOW THROUGH 13.7

ADDRESSING CONCERNS OF CHILDREN
AND ADOLESCENTS OF DIFFERENT CULTURES

Through "thinking sessions" with a counselor, plan several large-group topics that address subjects of concern to children and adolescents of different cultures. Make two lists, because topics vary according to students' developmental differences.

CHILDREN
1. Making friends across cultures
2. Feeling accepted regardless of cultural diversity

ADOLESCENTS
1. Friends' versus family expectations
2. Expanding socialization in a predominantly white world

classroom teacher and the counselor should always know each other's purposes and strategies and, whenever possible, provide joint efforts for the benefit of the learners.

Case Study 13.4 looks at how a third-grade teacher sought the counselor's assistance.

■ ■ ■ ■ ■

CASE STUDY 13.4

THE IMPORTANCE OF FRIENDSHIPS

Mr. Scott, a third-grade teacher, recognized that several of his Hispanic American students appeared bothered that the white children did not ask them to play. He was unsure whether the Hispanic American children lacked the social or linguistic skills to participate or whether they felt unwanted. Mr. Scott decided to seek the counselor's help with the situation.

Mr. Scott and the counselor, Ms. Wilkie, discussed the options and decided on a joint effort with three main purposes: (1) to help the Hispanic American students feel better about themselves and their cultural heritages; (2) to help the European American students gain a better understanding of the Hispanic cultures; and (3) to develop situations in which both cultures could play or learn together.

Ms. Wilkie decided on several small-group sessions with the Hispanics and several large-group counseling sessions with the entire class. In the small-group sessions, she tried to help the Hispanic American children better understand themselves and, overall, experience feelings of acceptance about themselves and their culture. The large-group sessions with the entire class focused on accepting cultural diversity and understanding and accepting peers.

Working as an integral part of the team, Mr. Scott planned play and learning activities that required learners of both cultures to work together. With the suggestions and materials that Ms. Wilkie provided, Mr. Scott continued the effort to improve the Hispanic American learners' self-concepts and cultural identities. He also provided follow-up efforts that stressed the importance of friendships and of making all people feel comfortable and accepted in both learning and play situations.

As with all professionals, the counselor's efforts and commitment to promoting cultural diversity and to working with classroom educators should be evaluated periodically. The following checklist can serve as a means of self-evaluation.

SELF-EVALUATION FOR COUNSELORS

1. Do I recognize that all children and adolescents differ in their cultural background, perspectives, traditions, and worldviews?
2. Do I plan culturally appropriate counseling strategies that reflect learners' cultural backgrounds?
3. Do I recognize that traditional tests and assessment devices may not measure the abilities and talents of all learners because of their differing cultural backgrounds?
4. Do I recognize that families differ according to cultural backgrounds (e.g., in sex roles, expectations, and childrearing techniques)?
5. Do I work with classroom educators for the overall welfare of learners from all cultural backgrounds?
6. Do I suggest special service agencies and resources that respond to the needs of learners and their families in all cultures?
7. Do I recognize the dangers of racial bias and cultural stereotypes and work to overcome these limitations?
8. Do I recognize the richness that cultural diversity adds to both elementary and secondary schools?
9. Do I recognize the need for all students to experience appropriate multicultural education experiences?
10. Do I recognize the need to use resources (e.g., films and other materials) that portray positive images of children's and adolescents' cultural backgrounds?

COMMUNICATIONS DISORDER SPECIALISTS

Several titles designate the professional working with speech-disabled learners, including *speech-language clinician, speech correctionist, speech clinician,* and *speech therapist,* but we prefer *communications disorder specialist* because the term is sufficiently broad in nature to include communication problems of children and adolescents from various cultural groups. The communications disorder specialist who works in multicultural settings has a broad knowledge of communication and understands unique communication situations, such as dialects, bilingualism, and teaching of English as a second language (TOESL), as well as the various assessment challenges and the differences between home and school language.

Roles in Multicultural Education

Because communication is such a vital human aspect to learners of all cultural and ethnic backgrounds, communications disorder specialists play an important role in helping educators distinguish between disorders and differences. They can also help learners who are experiencing differences with communication for any reason. All communications disorder specialists need to become sensitive to cultural diversity and to develop cross-cultural communication competencies as they work with children classified as non-English-proficient (NEP) and as having limited English proficiency (LEP).

A primary role of the communications disorder specialist is to distinguish between communications disorders and communication variations and to convey to classroom educators the differences between the two. Communications disorders include speech disorders (impairment of voice, articulation, or fluency) and language disorders (the impairment or deviant development of comprehension of a spoken or written symbol system).

Communications disorder specialists in multicultural situations must distinguish between disorders and variations. Learners who use a particular dialect or regional accent should not be labeled as having a disorder in need of elimination.

A second, closely related role of the communications disorder specialist is to understand and to help classroom educators to understand the difference between school language and home language. A learner may appear so quiet and withdrawn that the educator wonders if the child or adolescent has physical or emotional problems. The same child or adolescent at home and in the community shows considerable verbal proficiency.

When substantial differences exist between conversational language use in the home and official use in the classroom, children and adolescents often appear to have low verbal ability. Despite being verbal in nonschool settings, these learners may talk very little in the classroom and, even then, use only simple words and sentences (McCormick, 1990b). In such a situation, the communications disorder specialist might have to convince the classroom educator that the child or adolescent is not speech-disabled and is not in need of remediation or therapy.

Another goal of the communications disorder specialist is to understand dialect differences—among learners from differing cultural backgrounds as well as learners of the majority culture. Understanding and responding appropriately to the dialect of the learner within a classroom can be a complex and sensitive issue.

■ ■ ■ ■ ■ ▬▬▬▬▬▬▬▬▬▬▬▬▬▬▬▬▬▬▬▬▬▬▬▬▬▬▬

FOLLOW THROUGH 13.8
DISTINGUISHING BETWEEN COMMUNICATIONS DISORDERS AND VARIATIONS

How can educators and communications disorder specialists best distinguish between communication disorders and variations? List several ways to address disorders and variations under the following headings. *Articulation* and *Dialects* serve as examples:

DISORDER	RESPONSE	VARIATION	RESPONSE
Articulation	Specific work on pronunciation of letters and patterns of letters	Dialects	To what extent does the dialect interfere with communication? Accept as part of cultural heritage.

First, the specialist and teacher should recognize that dialects are not communicative disorders and should not treat them as such. The teacher should note, however, that a dialect and a communications disorder can coexist. If, for example, a learner with a Spanish or African American dialect also has defective articulation or stutters, the classroom educator should refer the learner to the communications disorder specialist.

Teachers and communications disorder specialists should learn to distinguish accurately between linguistic diversity and disorders. Dialects should not be considered less than but merely different from that which is recognized as standard English. A teacher is in a strategic position to promote understanding and acceptance of a child who has a dialectal difference.

From the Perspective of Classroom Educators: Working with the Communications Disorder Specialist

The classroom educator should view the communications disorder specialist as a valuable resource person with a wide range of expertise. Working in a complementary fashion for the welfare of learners, the communications disorder specialist and the classroom educator can determine whether communication problems exist that need to be remediated or whether students are simply manifesting variations that should be accepted and appreciated.

Considerable interaction should occur between classroom educators and communications disorder specialists. First, the communications disorder specialist and the teacher need to consult with each other about their goals for a learner and how they expect to accomplish these goals. They should evaluate what success they achieve. Such interaction can be formal or informal, or the communications disorder specialist can provide the teacher with copies of written therapy progress reports sent home to parents.

Second, the classroom teacher has more contact with parents and spends more school hours with learners, who may talk about their feelings, wants, and life at home. Some information that a teacher receives from learners or their parents may be important to the communications disorder specialist, and the teacher should pass it on.

Third, the teacher is in an ideal position to provide the communications disorder specialist with information about a learner's speech and language function in the classroom and in informal situations, such as in the hallway or lunchroom or on the playground. The teacher may also be able to provide reminders to the child during the habit-forming stages of therapy, when the child can best produce the targeted speech behaviors but still must make them a habit in all communicative situations. Fourth, the communications disorder specialist requires the teacher's input on referrals and in establishing whether there is an adverse effect on education because of a communicative problem (Oyer, Crowe, & Haas, 1987).

The communications disorder specialist's responsibilities include appropriate assessment, therapy, scheduling, and consultation with teachers and parents (Oyer, Crowe, & Haas, 1987). Other responsibilities in multicultural situations include understanding the communication problems of children and adolescents, conveying to teachers an assessment of disorders and variations, and providing a climate of understanding and acceptance for all learners.

The classroom teacher plays a major role in the lives of learners by serving as an important role model and a major force in shaping ideas and has an influence on emotional development (McFarlane, Fujiki, & Britton, 1984). The classroom educator's responsibilities include being a good speech model; creating a classroom atmosphere conducive to communication; accepting learners, and encouraging classmates to accept learners with communications problems; consulting with the communications disorder specialist; detecting possible communications disorders and making referrals; reinforcing the goals of the communications disorder specialist; and helping the learner catch up on what he or she missed while at therapy (Oyer, Crowe, & Haas, 1987). Another responsibility is fully participating when a decision has been made to place the child in a limited- or non-English-proficient program.

Case Study 13.5 shows how disorders and variations can be confused and how the communications disorder specialist can work with classroom teachers.

The following self-evaluation checklist enables communications disorder specialists to evaluate their efforts and commitment to multicultural education.

SELF-EVALUATION CHECKLIST FOR
COMMUNICATIONS DISORDER SPECIALISTS

1. Do I recognize and accept all learners, regardless of cultural, ethnic, or social class backgrounds?

■ ■ ■ ■ ■ ▬

CASE STUDY 13.5
RESPONDING TO COMMUNICATION DIFFERENCES

Ms. Tyler, a ninth-grade reading teacher in an inner-city school, felt somewhat overwhelmed as she took her concerns to the communications disorder specialist, Mrs. Clyburn. She said, "I have four, perhaps five, African American students whom I have difficulty understanding, two Hispanic American students who have tremendous difficulty with English and intersperse Spanish with English, and one bilingual Japanese American. What do I do, Mrs. Clyburn? There is such a wide variety of communication disorders in my class."

Mrs. Clyburn said, "Let's talk about your situation first; then, I will meet with the students individually to decide whether the apparent problems really are disorders."

About a week later, after Mrs. Clyburn met with the students, she met with Ms. Tyler concerning the students. First, Mrs. Clyburn found that the African American students had dialectal differences or variations instead of outright disorders. Second, she recommended the Hispanic American students for the LEP program so they could receive individual or small-group instruction. Third, she determined that the Japanese American student could speak both Japanese and English as long as speaking two languages did not interfere with communication.

Ms. Tyler and Mrs. Clyburn agreed to meet again later in the month to see whether the classroom teacher could better understand African American dialects and to discuss the Hispanic Americans' progress in the LEP program. Ms. Tyler felt better. She understood her students better, and she knew what should be accepted and what should be remediated. I will continue working with Mrs. Clyburn, she thought.

2. Do I recognize how the increasing cultural diversity in U.S. school systems affects the roles and responsibilities of the speech professional?
3. Do I distinguish between communicative disorders and communicative variations?
4. Do I understand dialects as "differences" and not as "disorders"?
5. Do I plan appropriate communication for NEP or LEP students and seek the appropriate professionals to help these students?
6. Do I work with professionals responsible for bilingual students and assist as needed?
7. Do I work with classroom teachers and other school personnel in joint efforts to help children and adolescents of differing cultural backgrounds with communications disorders?
8. Do I understand the various speech and language disorders, and am I able to assist learners from differing cultural backgrounds who are having communications problems?

SERVICE LEARNING

Administrators, special school personnel, and classroom teachers should encourage students to become involved with multicultural communities, whether in direct learning or service opportunities. Not only does service learning address children's and adolescents' feelings of altruism and idealism, it reinforces the content that they learn in school and helps them develop the skills to be productive citizens in a multicultural society. In essence, students become involved in activities related to the needs of the community while they are advancing academic goals and acquiring essential skills in real-life contexts (Hope, 1999).

The idea behind service learning is not just to involve students in multicultural communities (which in and of itself is also a worthwhile idea) but also to *reinforce* or *refine* actual learning objectives from the classroom. Students can tutor younger children or adults, organize a clean-up effort for environmental protection, or help preserve an endangered-wildlife area. Rather than having a one-size-fits-all program, each school needs to consider its own individual student population and community to see how community learning projects can be tied into instructional objectives and the multicultural education program.

As Wade (2000) points out in Implementing Research 13.3, service learning can be beneficial in promoting multicultural teaching competency.

SUMMING UP

Educators who are working toward the involvement of the entire school professional staff in the multicultural education program should:

1. Encourage all administrators and special school personnel to offer whole-hearted commitment and support to the multicultural education program. They should not perceive the effort as someone else's responsibility.

■ ■ ■ ■ ■ ▬▬▬▬▬▬▬▬▬▬▬▬▬▬▬▬▬▬▬▬▬▬▬▬▬▬▬▬▬▬▬▬

IMPLEMENTING RESEARCH 13.3

SERVICE LEARNING FOR MULTICULTURAL TEACHING COMPETENCY

Competency Wade (2000) maintains that the growing disparity between the largely white teacher population and the increasingly diverse student body in the United States substantiates the need for preservice teachers having field experiences in diverse settings. Greater interest is being focused toward enhancing preservice teachers' multicultural competencies and also addressing teachers' low expectations for children of color. Wade states that the literature on multicultural education has clearly shown the shortcomings of using course work and didactic methods alone to achieve this goal.

Calling for community service learning, Wade provides rationales for service learning in multicultural teacher education—for example, enhanced student outcomes in both K–12 and teacher education, academic achievement and social/emotional growth, preservice teachers' enhanced reflections skills, and understanding preservice teachers' roles. Service learning in diverse communities can lead preservice teachers to increase their awareness of diversity; to learn and accept children and families of color; and to begin questioning preexisting attitudes and beliefs.

Research on service learning in multicultural teacher education programs has revealed promising findings. These findings include increased awareness of those who are culturally different from themselves; acceptance of youth of color, their lifestyles, and their communities; difficult feelings and personal satisfaction; and awareness of self and prior assumptions and beliefs.

IMPLEMENTING THE RESEARCH
1. Teacher education institutions should provide opportunities for preservice teachers to have field experiences with people in diverse settings that are representative of the students they will teach.
2. The growing disparity between the largely white teacher population and the increasingly diverse student body in the United States calls for deliberate efforts to recruit teachers of color.
3. Teacher educators should take appropriate action to address challenges such as how well dominant-culture teachers serve children of color; how to make service learning activities emphasize charity rather than social change; and how to address teachers' resilient attitudes toward children and families of color.

Source: Wade, R. C. (2000). Service learning for multicultural teaching competency: Insights from the literature for teacher educators. *Equity and Excellence in Education, 33*(1), 21–29.

2. Convey to administrators, special education teachers, counselors, library media specialists, and the communications disorder specialist the importance of a total school effort in the multicultural education program.
3. Emphasize the necessity for cultural diversity among the administration, faculty, and special school personnel that reflects the composition of the school and community.

4. Encourage administrators, special-education teachers, library media specialists, counselors, and communications disorder specialists to recognize and respond appropriately to their unique roles in the multicultural education program.
5. Encourage administrators and special school personnel to work with regular classroom educators.
6. Convey the importance of evaluating all professionals (by self, peer, or administrator) for the purpose of learning ways to contribute to the overall multicultural program.

SUGGESTED LEARNING ACTIVITIES

1. Visit an elementary or secondary school to learn how administrators and special school personnel contribute to the multicultural education program. Are roles clearly defined, or are they assumed, whereby professionals simply do whatever appears to benefit the learner? How might administrators and special school personnel better address the needs of learners of differing cultural backgrounds?

2. Some professionals and the general public feel that learners of minority cultures are over-represented in special-education classes. Meet with a special-education teacher to discuss the concern of overrepresentation. What legal mandates and placement procedures protect minorities from being placed in special-education classes simply for being different from mainstream learners?

3. Visit an elementary or secondary school counselor in a multicultural setting to determine such factors as:
   a. Differences in assessing and counseling children or adolescents from culturally different backgrounds
   b. Best methods of working and coordinating efforts with classroom teachers
   c. Interaction settings; that is, individual, small group, and large group, and which mode appears most effective with learners from culturally different backgrounds
   d. Ways counselors can best help classroom educators who work daily with learners from differing cultural backgrounds

SUGGESTIONS FOR COLLABORATIVE EFFORTS

Form groups of three or four that, if possible, represent our nation's cultural and gender diversity. Working collaboratively, focus your group's attention toward the following efforts:

1. Prepare an evaluation scale that determines how print and nonprint media portray culturally different children and adolescents. Pinpoint such factors as objectivity, accuracy, stereotyping, gender values, and actual people from the various cultural groups (and what they are doing) and their contributions to an increasingly multicultural world. With the help of a library specialist, prepare a list of print and nonprint materials that provide an honest portrayal of all people, regardless of cultural background.

2. Brainstorm in your group to list special ways that administrators and special school personnel can contribute to multicultural education programs. How does your group think

these professionals can contribute to or complement classroom teachers' efforts? What books or other materials can your group suggest to help each of these professionals?

3. Have your group members think about when they were in school or about a school they have visited during a practicum or other field experience. What evidence did they find that special school personnel and classroom educators work as a team? Considering the recent journal articles and books on teaming efforts, do you think these professionals will work in a more collaborative manner in the future? For years, professionals basically worked alone, doing their own job with little knowledge of each other's jobs. What efforts do you suggest for all educators working in collaborative teams?

EXPANDING YOUR HORIZONS: ADDITIONAL JOURNAL READINGS AND BOOKS

Dils, A. K. (2002). Service learning can narrow the potential mismatch between future teachers and their students. *ACEI Focus on Teacher Education, 3*(1), 1–3.
Dils explains the two main approaches to preparing preservice teachers to work with racially and ethnically different students, and the positive results of service learning.

McAllister, G., & Irvine, J. J. (2000). Cultural competency and multicultural teacher education. *Review of Educational Research, 70*(1), 3–24.
These authors review materials in three process-oriented models that have been used to describe and measure development of racial identity.

McFalls, E. L., & Cobb-Roberts, D. (2001). Reducing resistance to diversity through cognitive dissonance instruction: Implications for teacher education. *Journal of Teacher Education, 52*(2), 164–172.
McFalls and Cobb-Roberts apply the concept of cognitive dissonance theory to instructional strategy used to reduce resistance to the idea of white privilege.

Peterson, K. M., Cross, L. F., Johnson, E. J., & Howell, G. L. (2000). Diversity education for preservice teachers: Strategies and attitude outcomes. *Action in Teacher Education, 22*(2), 33–38.
These authors analyze the impact of emphasizing diversity in a "foundations of education" course and address several instructional strategies.

Weaver, H. N. (2000). Culture and professional education: The experiences of Native American social workers. *Journal of Social Work Education, 36*(3), 415–428.
As the title suggests, Weaver looks at the experiences of Native American social workers, especially their culture and professional education.

THE FUTURE OF MULTICULTURAL EDUCATION

Part IV examines issues that educators face, such as multicultural education as a concept; racism, discrimination, and injustice; blaming the victim; testing and assessment; language and communication; accepting professional responsibilities; and involving parents and families. They will continue to challenge educators for years to come, but deliberate action must be taken to address them now.

CHAPTER FOURTEEN

ISSUES FOR THE TWENTY-FIRST CENTURY

Understanding the material and activities in this chapter will help the reader to:

- Describe multicultural education as an issue challenging educators, its differing definitions, and the difference between ideal and practice

- Explain how racism continues to affect the United States, although conditions are better than they used to be

- Explain why people often blame victims for the conditions affecting their lives, instead of seeking more plausible causes

- List the arguments, pro and con, of standardized testing, and explain how culture affects testing

- Describe how the issue of language and communication affects individuals and social institutions

- List the responsibilities of professional educators in multicultural education programs

- Describe how various contemporary issues affect the progress and success of multicultural education programs

OVERVIEW

Multicultural education has progressed considerably as a means of explaining diversity and teaching acceptance of all people, but several issues remain unresolved. Educators should do whatever they can at least to reduce the impact of each issue; they cannot, however, solve them all. A societal response is necessary to combat racism and discrimination, the tendency to blame victims for their plights, and the issue of testing and assessing learners of culturally different backgrounds. This chapter examines some of the issues, not to make educators feel guilty or negligent, but to describe obstacles to the progress of multicultural education and to show where present and future challenges lie.

■ ■ ■ ■ ■ ▬

FOLLOW THROUGH 14.1
NARROWING THE GAP BETWEEN IDEALS AND PRACTICE

What specific directions can educators take to make multicultural education more concrete? What could we do to turn "ideals" into "practice"? In other words, what could we do to make multicultural education programs effective?

MULTICULTURAL EDUCATION AS A CONCEPT

As it progresses in its third decade, multicultural education has changed in definition and has not been wholehearted endorsed in all circles. In multicultural education, as in U.S. society as a whole, disturbing gaps exist between stated ideals and actual practice. In addition, while multicultural education appears to be the most effective means of teaching acceptance of cultural diversity, several other approaches serve to address racial, gender, and socioeconomic class differences.

Scope of Multicultural Education

Questions that linger include: Does multicultural education include only ethnic, cultural, and racial differences? Should multicultural education address gender and class differences? Should multicultural education include sexual orientation? Should multicultural educators use unit approaches or adopt total-school approaches?

As stated previously, we support a broad definition that includes all types of cultures, including ethnic, cultural, racial, gender, sexual orientation, and social class. Also, in line with our thinking, we support including European Americans in multicultural education for the effort to be truly multicultural.

Differences between Stated Ideals and Practice

Concerned educators do not have to look far for disturbing gaps between ideal and actual practice: children's language differences are not taken seriously, the only language used is English; segregation is practiced; and learners of culturally different backgrounds are labeled as inferior or culturally disadvantaged.

Case Study 14.1 looks at a situation in which a high school principal recognizes that her school is not really meeting its goals and stated philosophy.

Approaches to Race, Class, and Gender

Educators may address diversity with approaches other than multicultural education: teaching the exceptional and the culturally different, human relations, single-group studies, and education that is multicultural and social versus reconstructionist. Rather than outlining the advantages and disadvantages of each approach, we state that each has expressed purposes, goals, and directions. From an issues perspective, however,

CASE STUDY 14.1
DIFFERENCES BETWEEN GOALS AND PRACTICE

Dr. MacDonald, a high school principal, looked objectively at her school's lofty goals, objectives, and philosophical statements, which spoke eloquently of valuing, recognizing, accepting, and respecting all people, regardless of differences. She compared these statements with what was actually happening in the school. Couldn't the students see that much of what was occurring was only rhetoric with no substance? Without being overly pessimistic or cynical, Dr. MacDonald asked herself several questions concerning the extent to which educators respect and address diversity:

- Do school policies reflect an understanding of cultural diversity?
- Do instructional practices recognize the differing learning styles of learners from various cultures?
- Is there an understanding of motivation and competition in relation to learners from diverse cultural heritages?
- Are efforts made to promote social interaction between learners of all cultures?
- Is there genuine respect for all people?
- Do educators recognize and address testing and assessment differences among cultures?
- Do language programs assist students of limited English proficiency?
- Are the teachers and other school personnel professionally trained and competent to deal with and teach children and adolescents from culturally different backgrounds?

Dr. MacDonald decided that an affirmative action plan was necessary to address these and other issues and concerns. Such an effort would take a large-scale approach and would include discussion groups, committees, in-service programs and activities, speakers, and an improved professional library.

FOR ADDITIONAL INFORMATION
INTERNET ADDRESSES

Multicultural Issues Committee
www.vcn.bc.ca/scd/culture.htm   Promotes awareness and appreciation of the multicultural nature of the community.

Ten Things Men Can Do to End Sexism and Male Violence against Women.
www.cs.utk.edu/~bartley/other/10Things.html Provides articles, essays, and books about masculinity and gender inequality to give a better understanding of individual men and women.

Sexism/Sex and Gender Discrimination
www.nau.edu/wst/access/sxism/sxismsub.html

Studies of women, gender, and sexism, such as general discussions of job discrimination.

FairTest: Introduction
http://fairtest.org   Information from the nation's only nonprofit advocacy group (National Center for Fair & Open Testing) that works to prevent unfair use of standardized tests.

Racism
www.avalon.net/~foshe.racism.htm   Provides information on racism, specifically the most blatant forms centering on the actions of hate groups.

347

each in some ways takes away from or competes for resources for other programs. While we do not in any way discredit other approaches, it does appear that multicultural education is a broad and comprehensive approach to addressing diversity of all kinds and degrees.

RACISM, DISCRIMINATION, AND INJUSTICE

Without doubt, people today are more aware of racism, discrimination, and injustices. Even during times of racist acts, evidence suggests that there has been notable progress: More people from diverse cultures are joining the workforce in positions that require more than manual labor or custodianship. Opportunities in housing (although admittedly not equal) have improved, doors to higher education are open to the culturally diverse, and federal legislation guarantees equal rights for all people.

Examples of progress and the improved relationships between majority cultures and people of culturally diverse backgrounds can be looked on with pride, but educators must be careful not to assume that "all is well." There is room for improvement in reducing racism and discrimination and in providing a just and equal society for all people.

Lingering Racism and Discrimination

Although there has been progress toward reducing racism and discrimination, most would also agree that the U.S. society as a whole still has hurdles to overcome. Fifty years after *Brown v. Board of Education* and forty years after the Civil Rights Act of 1964, racism and discrimination continue to impede the progress of many people. Increasingly, we see acts of violence toward people of all races and cultures and the increasing number of skinheads or neo-Nazi groups. Racial slurs, threats, slogans, physical assaults, and conflicts occur in schools across the nation. While *Brown v. Board of Education* ruled against legal segregation, de facto segregation (or segregation by the fact) continues to exist. Similarly, even with the Civil Rights Act, notable gaps in income and level of position continue to exist among racial groups, and, in some cases, differences are becoming more acute.

Institutional racism affects many children in the United States. Although people have voiced such issues as equal opportunity, desegregation, and inequities in educational

■ ■ ■ ■ ■

FOLLOW THROUGH 14.2
KEEPING A CONSTANT VIGIL AGAINST RACISM

As stated previously, it is unlikely that racism will ever be completely eliminated. Still, racism affects and hurts all cultures and deserves to be addressed. Concerned educators and others should keep a constant lookout for racism—racist remarks, racist jokes, and racist actions. Name four or five specific steps educators can take to address racism.

achievement in recent years, few schools have developed deliberate and systematic programs to address these problems. Some believe that society has eliminated racism through legislative and special programs, but overt racism and institutional racism continue to occur. Whereas many educators are on guard against racism of all forms, institutional racism, which is less blatant and therefore more dangerous, continues to hurt the aspirations and talents of many learners.

BLAMING THE VICTIM

An issue facing some learners and their educators is where to place the blame for the minority person's plight. In essence, should the victim or the society be held accountable? For example, should lower-class African Americans blame themselves for their high unemployment rates and poverty, or should they blame a racist society that allows discrimination? Must American Indians blame themselves for their high school dropout rates and high levels of alcoholism? Should Hispanic and Asian learners get the blame for their poor English skills? Responsive educators recognize that such questions are examples of the "blaming-the-victim" issue. They realize that children and adolescents are often victims of racism and discrimination and that all too often they cannot change the conditions surrounding their lives.

As Case Study 14.2 shows, it is possible to adopt the blaming-the-victim attitude and perhaps fail to realize its dangers.

There are two orientations toward victims. First, people who hold a person-centered orientation emphasize the individual's motivation, values, feelings, and goals.

■ ■ ■ ■ ■

CASE STUDY 14.2
BLAMING THE VICTIM

Mrs. Smith said despairingly, "I don't know what to do! Why don't they try to better understand themselves, improve their grades? They just sit there all day and do nothing. They didn't know today what I taught yesterday. How do they expect to make something of their lives? I will never understand those people."

The assistant principal, Mr. Allen, overheard this classic blaming-the-victim statement and thought that this tendency failed to recognize the real problem. All too often, victims, especially people from culturally diverse groups, are blamed for being uneducated, slow learners, poor, and unable to find employment.

Mr. Allen thought of the consequences of such thinking and of considering all people from a middle-class, white perspective. He thought a serious effort must be made to look for more valid social, economic, or educational causes. The implications of blaming the victim can be widespread and can influence educational decisions such as grouping, questioning, curricular issues, and teaching and learning activities. Yet the problem extends even further: students are being blamed for not wanting to learn when they really do want to learn and are considered too unmotivated to change when, actually, significant change is extremely difficult.

■ ■ ■ ■ ■ ▬▬▬▬▬▬▬▬▬▬▬▬▬▬▬▬▬▬▬▬▬▬▬▬▬▬▬▬

FOLLOW THROUGH 14.3
AVOIDING BLAMING THE VICTIM

People sometimes find it convenient to blame the victim for such factors as language difficulties, being poor or homeless, and even for being culturally different. Working in groups of three or four, name several examples of "blaming the victim." Think of an exercise that will show middle- and secondary-school students the problems associated with blaming the victim.

A person's success or failure is attributed to individual skills or inadequacies, and many people correlate ability and effort with success in society. Second, the system-blame view holds that success or failure is generally dependent on the social and economic system rather than on personal attributes.

It is easier for some people to blame victims for their condition than to look for more specific societal and economic causes. The consequences of blaming the victim, however, often extend further than just thinking that people deserve blame for their shortcomings. Blaming learners for their conditions is a practice that excuses or justifies many unjust actions: poor-quality educational programs in areas with "victims," outdated and worn-out textbooks and curricular materials; teachers who give "victims" less wait time during questioning sessions, belief that poor or minority students cannot learn, and a plethora of other reactions.

More Humanistic Perspectives

Educators should offer a personal and professional commitment to victims of discrimination. Teachers must understand how children and adolescents become victims and the difficulty victims have in changing their lives. On a larger scale, educators should do their part in working to reduce the racism, poverty, despair, injustice, and discrimination that contribute to the victimization of people.

TESTING AND ASSESSMENT

Standardized testing dates back to the mid-1800s, and in fact, the problems associated with standardized testing have been similar over the years. The first documented use of standardized tests dates back to the period 1840–1875, when U.S. educators changed their focus from educating the elite to educating the masses. The earliest tests were intended for individual evaluation, but test results were used inappropriately to compare students and schools.

As millions of immigrants came to the United States in the nineteenth century, the standardized test became a way to ensure that all children were receiving the same standard of education. At the turn of the century, the focus of testing shifted from achievement testing to ability testing for the purpose of classifying students. Schools

▪ ▪ ▪ ▪ ▪ ▬▬▬▬▬▬▬▬▬▬▬▬▬▬▬▬▬▬▬▬▬▬▬▬▬▬▬▬▬▬▬▬▬▬▬▬▬

FOLLOW THROUGH 14.4
REDUCING THE HARMFUL EFFECTS OF TESTING

How do you or how does your group think educators might address cultural bias in assessment instruments? Suggest how a test item might be culturally biased. Testing is not likely to "go away," especially since the move toward testing appears to be growing stronger. How can educators reduce some of the more harmful effects of testing?

wanted to weed out students who were not going to succeed academically. Consequently, many ethnic groups faced new discrimination.

Educators have long known that standardized testing instruments are prepared from white, middle-class perspectives; however, they still test children and adolescents from culturally diverse backgrounds with these instruments that do not satisfactorily measure intelligence. One issue is why educators and testing specialists administer these assessment devices, especially when they have concluded that learning styles and cognitive strategies differ among cultures (Haladyna, Haas, & Allison, 1998).

Valid uses of test scores include using standardized tests to provide a national ranking, predict future achievement, provide a means of curriculum evaluation, assist with policy decisions, and serve as a device to identify weak areas of the curriculum. Invalid uses of test scores include providing financial incentives for teachers with high student test scores, graduation or certification testing, a means of evaluating teaching, and a method of evaluating and comparing schools and school districts. Several recommendations include: (1) Test score interpretation must be valid; test scores measure only a sample of a large domain of knowledge, and they should not be considered a means of evaluating the school curriculum or instructional emphasis. (2) Test score uses must be valid and educators need to examine and evaluate the consequences of standardized testing—for example, reporting test scores by racial or ethnic categories rarely serves useful purposes (Haladyna, Haas, & Allison, 1998).

Zehr (1999) maintains that Hispanic students are not being tested properly, nor are their scores on standardized tests being used for the right purposes. Calls are being made for better tests for assessing Hispanic students, particularly those with limited proficiency in English. Nearly half of the nation's Hispanic students are considered to be have limited proficiency in English, and about 75 percent of students who fall under that category are in high-poverty-area schools. In addition, test scores should be used to hold schools accountable for providing an adequate education to Hispanic students. Until that time, some question whether Hispanic's test scores should be used to keep them from being promoted or from graduating (Zehr, 1999). States are increasingly using statewide assessments to ensure that standards and learning benchmarks are being met. Plus, educators need to know if children are learning what is supposedly being taught. With this responsibility in mind, it is imperative that educators ensure the validity and reliability of assessment devices (Pappamihiel, 2002).

In Implementing Research 14.1, Pappamihiel (2002) looks at high-stakes testing and limited-English-proficient students.

■ ■ ■ ■ ■ ▬▬▬▬▬▬▬▬▬▬▬▬▬▬▬▬▬▬▬▬▬▬▬▬▬▬▬

IMPLEMENTING RESEARCH 14.1
HIGH-STAKES TESTING AND LIMITED-ENGLISH-PROFICIENT STUDENTS

One major issue related to standardized testing and limited-English-proficient (LEP) students is the fact that many times these assessments are indirect tests of English proficiency rather than content mastery. In other words, LEP students cannot accurately demonstrate their knowledge of content and skills without relatively high fluency in English. They may know the content in their native language, but not be able to express it because they lack sufficient knowledge of English.

Accommodations for these students are controversial. The most common accommodations for LEP students include flexible settings, flexible times, flexible scheduling, and the use of a translation dictionary. Still, some think these accommodations are rarely effective and can give the impression that LEP students are being given an advantage, when they are not. Also, some think LEP students lack opportunities to learn in the classroom. LEP students often face serious hurdles due to their language limitations and also when schools test information that was inappropriately taught or cannot be expressed.

IMPLEMENTING THE RESEARCH

1. Educators can gain a better understanding of the challenges faced by students who score lower on standardized tests and other accountability measures due to their limited English proficiency—they might know the content, but be unable to express themselves in English.
2. Educators should not assume that accommodations reduce or eliminate the hurdles caused by limited English proficiency.
3. Test designers and educators need to make a commitment to develop accountability measures that measure content mastery rather than only English proficiency.

Source: Pappamihiel, N. E. (2002). High stakes testing and limited English proficient (LEP) students. www.coe.fsu.edu/whitepapers/high.html. Retrieved August 22, 2002.

LANGUAGE AND COMMUNICATION

Language and communication have been sensitive and controversial issues with far-reaching implications for learners and educators. Whereas some argue that English should be the primary language for all, others feel that a person's native language is a personal and precious aspect of his or her cultural heritage. The issue extends further, however. Should students be allowed to learn in their native language? What should educators do about dialects? Should learners actually become bilingual? This section focuses on dialects, bilingual education, English as a second language, and nonverbal communication.

Dialects

Although English is the primary language of the United States, numerous English dialects are spoken throughout the country. *Dialects* are variations of a language that groups of speakers share. The language variation typically corresponds to other differ-ences among groups, such as ethnicity, religion, culture, geographic location, and so-cial class (Gollnick & Chinn, 2002). It is important to emphasize that all people speak in a dialect of their native language.

Dialect is a popular term that carries a negative connotation. It sometimes refers to a particular variety of English that may have a social or geographic basis and that dif-fers from what is usually considered "standard" English. Dialects may include such variations as black English, Hawaiian Pidgin English, and rural Appalachian English (Gollnick & Chinn, 2002).

What should multicultural educators do about dialects? One group has sug-gested that students be allowed to learn in their own dialects and that to do otherwise only further disables learners. Others have argued that schools have the responsibility for teaching each student standard English to better cope with the demands of society. There is little doubt that the inability to speak standard English can be a decided dis-advantage to an individual in certain situations, such as seeking employment (Gollnick & Chinn, 2002).

There are several alternatives for handling dialect in the educational setting: The first is the accommodation of all dialects, based on the assumption that they are all equal. The second is the insistence that only a standard dialect be allowed in the schools; this alternative allows for the position that functional ability in such a dialect is necessary for success in personal as well as vocational pursuits. A third alternative is a position between the two extremes, and it is the alternative educators most often choose. They accept native dialects for certain uses but encourage and insist on stan-dard English in other circumstances. Students in such a school setting may read and write in standard English, because this is the primary written language they will en-counter in this nation. They are not required to eliminate their natural dialect. Such a compromise allows the student to use two or more dialects in the school. This com-promise acknowledges the legitimacy of all dialects, while it recognizes the social and vocational implications of being able to function using standard English (Gollnick & Chinn, 2002).

Bilingual Education

Today, there are nearly 3 million limited-English-proficient (LEP) students in U.S. schools. According to the National Center for Education Statistics, 58 percent of all LEP students were born in the United States and 74 percent are Spanish speakers. The next largest language group is the Vietnamese, with 3.9 percent. Although "bilingual" programs for non-Spanish-languages groups can be found, few actually teach children to read and write in their native languages before teaching them these skills in English. These programs are bilingual only in the sense that they contain some measure of native-language support (Chavez & Amselle, 1997).

The theory behind bilingual education is that children must first fully develop their native language before they can achieve academic proficiency in a second language—a process that takes five to seven years, according to its proponents. In practical terms, children must be taught to read and write in their native language before they are taught those skills in English (Chavez & Amselle, 1997).

In her review of the research on bilingual education programs, Rosalie Porter (1997) summarizes the findings of a General Accounting Office report that looked at five school districts. She thinks these findings are representative of all public schools with LEP students:

- Immigrant students are almost 100 percent non-English-speaking on arriving in the United States.
- LEP students arrive at different times of the school year, which causes upheavals in classrooms and educational programs.
- Some high school students have not been schooled in their native lands and lack literacy in any language.
- There is a high level of family poverty and transiency and a low level of parental involvement in students' education.
- There is an acute shortage of bilingual teachers and of textbooks and assessment devices in the native languages. (Porter, 1997)

According to Rosalie Porter (1997), the efforts being made and the money being invested in special programs to help immigrant, migrant, and refugee schoolchildren who do not speak English when they enter schools is largely misguided. The politically righteous assumption is that these groups cannot learn English quickly and must be taught all their subjects in their native languages for three to seven years while having English introduced gradually.

Porter does not think such policy is beneficial for most LEP students. In fact, her experience and a growing body of research show no benefits from native-language teaching, either in better learning English or better learning school subjects. Further explaining the issue, Porter also discusses the difficulty of voicing criticism of bilingual education programs "without being pilloried as a hater of foreigners and foreign languages and of contributing to the anti-immigrant climate" (p. 31).

Proponents of bilingual education have recommended children learn their native language prior to introduction of English. They believe that competencies in the native language provide an important literacy foundations for second-language acquisitions as well as for academic learning. Opponents recommend introduction of the English curriculum from the very beginning of the student's schooling experience, with only a minimal use of the native language. This approach is typically combined with an English as a second language (ESL) component.

English as a Second Language

English as a second language programs are often confused with bilingual education. In the United States, the learning of English is an integral part of bilingual programs. However, the teaching of ESL, in and by itself, does not constitute a bilingual program. Both bilingual education and ESL programs promote English proficiency for limited-English-proficiency (LEP) students.

The approach to instruction distinguishes the two programs. Bilingual education accepts and develops native language and culture in the instructional process. Bilingual education may use both the native language and English as the medium of instruction.

ESL instruction, however, relies exclusively on English as the medium to assimilate LEP children into the linguistic mainstream as quickly as possible. Hence, some educators place less emphasis on the maintenance of home language and culture than on English-language acquisition, and they view ESL programs as viable means of achieving these goals (Gollnick & Chinn, 2002).

Beginning during the times of increased immigration from southern and eastern Europe at the turn of the century, there has been a concern in the U.S. about immigrants' ability to understand and embrace the principles of democracy. Language was seen as a part of the Americanization process. In recent years, English has become a central topic surrounding the education of immigrant students. Part of the difficulty is that most policy makers and members of the public have little information about what actually happens in schools. Still, far-reaching decisions are often made about immigrant children and how they should be taught English (Valdes, 1998).

Educators of all curricular areas need to develop an understanding of ESL students—their problems, strengths, challenges, and individual characteristics. They can also gain an understanding of the language dilemma—immigrant students must learn, yet considerable confusion exists in the public's mind about how students can best acquire the academic English necessary to succeed in school. Policy makers need to understand the challenges that immigrant students face—they need to realize the far-reaching consequences of their decisions. Children and adolescents need instruction in English for success (social, personal, and economic); however, it might also be necessary to provide educational experiences in their native language, at least until students develop proficiency in English (Valdes, 1998).

Nonverbal Communication

The issue of nonverbal differences and misunderstandings can be frustrating for both students and educators. To reduce the difficulty often associated with this form of communication, educators must analyze particular nonverbal behaviors when students do not respond as educators expect. Miscommunication may result from several nonverbal behaviors: A student may appear inattentive even when he or she is listening, a student may look away from the teacher when called on or addressed, or a student may interrupt at times that appear inappropriate to educators.

FOLLOW THROUGH 14.5
UNDERSTANDING NONVERBAL COMMUNICATION

Working in groups of three or four, have each person consider his or her own culture to determine nonverbal communication. Name several types of nonverbal communication from each culture, and explain how these forms of communication might be misunderstood.

It is easy to jump to the conclusion that a student is not showing respect, when actually she or he is simply not following the unwritten rules of the classroom. In most school settings, educators expect learners from culturally different backgrounds to become bicultural and to adopt the nonverbal communication of the majority culture of the school. The ill effects of the issue lessen when educators also learn to operate biculturally in the classroom (Gollnick & Chinn, 2002).

ACCEPTING THE RESPONSIBILITY TO BE PROFESSIONALLY QUALIFIED AND COMMITTED

First and foremost, educators must accept responsibility for being trained to work with students of differing cultural backgrounds. Regardless of the multicultural education program and its goals, efforts will succeed only when educators are trained in cultural diversity, understand the effects of culture on learning, and are able to convey genuine feelings of acceptance and respect for all people. Professional education for all teachers, not just those planning to teach in multicultural areas, should include content methodologies courses that show the relationship between culture and learning and how to address this relationship in teaching situations; first-hand practica and clinical experiences in working with learners from diverse cultural backgrounds and socioeconomic classes; and appropriate experiences in interpersonal skills.

We reemphasize that professional responsibilities include broad expertise in content, instructional techniques, and the ability to work with learners from differing cultural backgrounds. Responsibilities extend even further, however. Having knowledge of people, but holding on to racist attitudes and the belief that "different is wrong," will not provide responsive multicultural education. Knowing that a relationship exists between cultures and education is a prerequisite to effective teaching, but continuing to teach with styles and strategies appropriate only for one culture fails to meet the needs of children and adolescents of other cultures.

Case Study 14.3 examines Dr. Thomas's thoughts concerning professional competencies of teachers who work in multicultural situations.

■ ■ ■ ■ ■

FOLLOW THROUGH 14.6
DEVELOPING INDIVIDUAL PROFESSIONAL IMPROVEMENT PLANS

Educators often develop their own individual professional plans to develop competencies as a means to better understanding of cultural diversity and the effects of culture on learning and of providing culturally appropriate educational experiences for all students. Suggest a development plan such as college coursework, reading of professional journals, and in-service training.

■ ■ ■ ■ ■ ▬▬▬▬▬▬▬▬▬▬▬▬▬▬▬▬▬▬▬▬▬▬▬▬▬▬▬▬▬▬▬

CASE STUDY 14.3
PROFESSIONAL COMPETENCE

As Dr. Thomas, a staff development specialist, looked at his district's guidelines for determining professional competence, he wondered what specific attributes or characteristics teachers should have, especially regarding cultural diversity. Although he considered his initial efforts to be only brainstorming, he placed items into several categories:

A. Overall competencies
   1. Knowledge
   2. Attitudes
   3. Skills
B. Educational competencies
   4. Curricular practices
   5. Instructional techniques
   6. Classroom rules and policies
   7. Language considerations
   8. Testing and assessment

Dr. Thomas knew his thoughts represented only a beginning point, but he did realize that teachers working with learners of different cultures need an understanding of how culture affects learning and achievement. He also realized that in all likelihood the teachers in his district needed appropriate in-service training and activities to make them more effective with learners from different cultures.

Ensuring Cultural Diversity in All Curricular Materials

A major responsibility, and one that educators must accept, is the commitment to ensure cultural diversity in all curricular materials. Educators play a significant role as they scrutinize all print and nonprint materials for bias and racism. This issue includes omissions as well as distortions. Educators are responsible for being on the lookout for material that shows people's culture in a derogatory light or in demeaning situations or that shows minorities in stereotypical images. Only two decades ago, families were portrayed as two-parent, white, and living in white houses with picket fences. Educators in most situations can readily perceive that most learners would be unable to

■ ■ ■ ■ ■ ▬▬▬▬▬▬▬▬▬▬▬▬▬▬▬▬▬▬▬▬▬▬▬▬▬▬▬▬▬▬▬

FOLLOW THROUGH 14.7
DECIDING WHAT CURRICULAR MATERIALS SHOULD REFLECT

What should contemporary curricular materials portray to reflect our nation's diversity? We know we need to move away from an overreliance on two-parent homes and European American middle-class people, but who and what should curricular materials reflect?

understand or relate to such images in stories. While there has been considerable progress, educators continue to be responsible for insisting on materials and adopting textbooks that include culturally diverse characters and their families only in positive, fulfilling roles.

Ensuring That Multicultural Emphasis Permeates All Curricular Areas and the School Environment

Another major responsibility of educators is working toward multiculturalism in all areas of the curriculum and school environment. A basic assumption of this text is that multicultural education should be a broad-based effort that has the full cooperation and support of all school personnel, rather than a half-hearted effort.

Because they are representative of our culturally pluralistic society, schools must plan appropriate learning experiences for different children: American Indian, African, Arab, Asian, Hispanic, and European American, as well as children and adolescents from differing economic, social, and religious backgrounds. Educators must answer many questions. Which (or perhaps whose) religious holidays will be observed? How will cultural differences affect testing and assessment? What special problems will learners from diverse cultures bring to school? How will learning styles differ?

These and other questions raise the overall question of what, specifically, should educators do? A one-time multicultural week or single unit featuring African American history, tacos, and oriental dresses and customs will not suffice. Such approaches have not worked and will not work, because mere awareness of diversity does not necessarily result in acceptance and respect for individuals within the cultural group. The curriculum, learning environment, and the mindset of learners and faculty and staff must become multicultural in nature and must reflect the cultural diversity of the school.

Well-meaning multicultural education programs may serve only cosmetic purposes if students and school personnel harbor long-held cultural biases and stereotypes. Schools must not presuppose learners' abilities and behaviors based on stereotypes and myth: The school curriculum must genuinely respect cultural diversity and regard all learners objectively.

Involving Parents, Families, and the Community

Educators' recognition of the role of parents, the family, and the community in the multicultural education effort is an absolute prerequisite to the multicultural education program's success. Actually, two aspects are at stake, and both play a significant role in determining the success of the multicultural education program. First, including both immediate and extended families and community members demonstrates concretely that educators are serious about accepting and promoting multiculturalism outside the school boundaries. When educators show that their efforts do not stop at the schoolhouse gate, such a commitment adds credence to the multicultural education program's efforts.

Second, parents, families, and community members can play significant roles when they come to visit schools and offer their participation. Educators may have to deal with parents' language differences, misunderstandings associated with U.S. school systems, and the reluctance of some parents to share strengths. Although overcoming these challenges requires both time and energy, the benefits outweigh the efforts expended.

Our devoting an entire chapter (Chapter 12) to including parents and families from differing cultural backgrounds shows how important we believe the role of parents and families in education to be. The main issue is the extent to which educators genuinely want to effect multiculturalism. Children and adolescents who see only white parents in schools could easily conclude that cultural diversity is not as valuable as educators suggest. Although educators usually find it is easier to gain the attention of middle- and upper-class white parents, perceptive educators recognize the need to involve parents and families of many different cultures.

SUMMING UP

Educators who understand the issues facing multicultural education and the challenges that such programs will face in the future should:

1. Understand that several issues affect the social and educational progress of children and adolescents from different cultural backgrounds and contribute to the degree of support the multicultural education program receives.
2. Remember that although *multicultural education* may have several definitions, its overall rationale is to assist all learners to gain a better understanding and acceptance of others' cultural, ethnic, racial, and socioeconomic backgrounds.
3. Understand the futility of blaming the victim for life conditions, develop more enlightened perspectives of the reasons people become victims, and recognize the difficulty in overcoming victim status.
4. Understand that a relationship exists between culture and testing and that learners' cultural backgrounds can significantly affect standardized test scores.
5. Remember that the language issue includes dialectal differences, bilingual education, and teaching of English as a second language and that all educators need to address learners' language differences and needs.
6. Accept that educators have professional responsibilities that are prerequisite for responsive multicultural education programs to become a reality.
7. Remember that the ultimate success of any multicultural education program depends on every teacher's commitment to the program and to the acceptance of and respect for all people, regardless of differences or backgrounds.

SUGGESTED LEARNING ACTIVITIES

1. In a study of racism, look at specific examples of racist acts during the latter half of the twentieth century. Begin with the integration of America's schools during the 1950s and 1960s and the accompanying racial violence. Then, examine the more current acts of racism occurring in the United States. What programs do schools have that teach the dangers of racism and that reduce racism and its effects on children and adolescents?

2. Discuss with several educators ways in which teachers may, knowingly or unknowingly, blame the victim for learning problems, socioeconomic conditions, or language problems. List several consequences of blaming the victim. Rather than blaming victims for particular conditions, how can educators gain a better, or more objective, perspective of learners' conditions?

3. Write *your* definition of *multicultural education*. In your opinion, what differences should multicultural education include? Should it be only cultural, or should it include social class, gender, and religion? For example, do you think there is a culture of religion or a culture of social class? Does your definition include only knowledge of differences, or is appreciation of differences acknowledged or implied? Why are individual definitions of multicultural education important?

SUGGESTIONS FOR COLLABORATIVE EFFORTS

Form groups of three or four that, if possible, represent U.S. cultural and gender diversity. Working collaboratively, focus your group's attention toward the following efforts:

1. In an honest and frank discussion of racism, has any member of your group felt like a victim of racism? Remember, racism can affect all cultures, and, regrettably, there are racists in all cultures. How did the act of racism make that person feel? How do you believe racism affects teaching and learning situations? Why do you think racist acts are increasing? How can schools address racism?

2. Make a list of assessment instruments (and the addresses of publishers) that claim to reduce cultural bias in their test items. Provide two or three examples of culturally biased test items. How might educators determine cultural bias in assessment instruments?

3. Survey a number of schools in an urban area with a significant percentage of students from culturally different backgrounds. What programs do these schools have to address language differences? Do language-minority youngsters receive equal opportunities, or are learners sometimes expected to learn and deal with language problems simultaneously? Looking at your survey, what language programs or approaches appear more likely to meet the needs of language-minority learners?

EXPANDING YOUR HORIZONS: ADDITIONAL JOURNAL READINGS AND BOOKS

Gallavan, N. P. (2000). Multicultural education at the academy: Teacher educators' challenges, conflicts, and coping skills. *Equity and Excellence in Education, 33*(3), 5–12.
Gallavan explains the results of a study that examined the challenges and conflicts associated with teaching multicultural education courses.

Martin, J. N., & Davis, O. I. (2001). Conceptual foundations for teaching about whiteness in intercultural communication courses. *Communication Education, 50*(4), 298–302.
Martin and Davis address the growing interest in incorporating "whiteness" studies into the intercultural communication curriculum—for example, e.g., the historical whitening of some U.S. immigrant groups, white privilege, communication patterns of U.S. whites, and representations of whiteness in popular culture.

Paccione, A. V. (2000). Developing a commitment to multicultural education. *Teachers College Record, 102*(6), 980–1005.
Paccione looks at the types of lived experiences that contributed to commitment to multicultural education.

Sleeter, C. E. (2001). Preparing teachers for culturally diverse schools: Research and the overwhelming presence of whiteness. *Journal of Teacher Education, 52*(2), 94–106.
Sleeter reviews research studies on preservice teacher preparation for multicultural schools, particularly schools serving underserved communities.

Wallace, B. C. (2000). A call for change in multicultural training at graduate schools of education: Educating to end oppression and for social justice. *Teachers College Record, 102*(6), 1086–1111.
Wallace maintains that graduate-level multicultural training is important for preparing future teachers and should be expanded to include sexuality, disability, and spirituality.

REFERENCES

■ ■ ■ ■ ■ ▬▬▬▬▬▬▬▬▬▬▬▬▬▬▬▬▬▬▬▬▬▬▬▬▬

100 Questions and answers about Arab Americans: A journalist's guide. *Detroit Free Press* www.freep.com/jobspage/arabs.

Abrams, R. D. (1993). Meeting the educational and cultural needs of Soviet newcomers. *Religious Education, 88*(2), 315–323.

Abu-Ali, A., & Reisen, C. A. (1999). Gender role identity among adolescent Muslim girls living in the U.S. *Current Psychology, 18*, 185–192.

Abudabbeh, N. (1996). Arab families. In M. McGoldrick, J. Girodano, & J. K. Pearce (Eds.). *Ethnicity and family therapy* (2nd ed.) (pp. 333–346). New York: Guilford.

Ajrouch, K. J. (2000). Community living and ethnic identity among Lebanese American adolescents. *Small Group Research, 31*, 447–469.

Alba, R. D. (1985). *Italian Americans into the twilight of ethnicity*. Englewood Cliffs, NJ: Prentice-Hall.

Alexander, C. (1989). Gender differences in adolescent health concerns and self-assessed health. *Journal of Early Adolescence, 9*, 467–479.

Allen, J., & Labbo, L. (2001). Giving it a second thought: Making culturally engaged teaching culturally engaging. *Language Arts, 79*(1), 40–52.

Ambler, M. (1997). Without racism: Indian students could be both Indian and students. *Tribal College, 8*(4), 8–11.

American Association of University Women. (1992). *How schools shortchange girls*. Annapolis Junction, MD: AAUW.

American Speech and Hearing Association. (1983). Social dialects. *ASHA, 25*(9), 23–24.

Anokye, A. D. (1997). A case for orality in the classroom. *The Clearing House, 70*(5), 229–231.

Ames, C. A. (1990). Motivation: What teachers need to know. *Teachers College Record, 91*, 409–421.

Ariza, E. N. (2000). Actions speak louder than words—or do they? Debunking the myth of apathetic immigrant parents in education. *Contemporary Education, 71*(3), 36–38.

Aronson, E., Blaney, N., Stephan, C., Sikes, J., & Snapp, M. (1978). *The jigsaw classroom*. Beverly Hills, CA: Sage.

Asakawa, K., & Csikszentmihalyi, M. (1998). The quality of experiences of Asian American adolescents related to future goals. *Journal of Youth and Adolescence, 27*(2), 141–163.

Asher, N. (2002). Class acts: Indian American high school students negotiate professional and ethnic identities. *Urban Education, 37*(2), 267–295.

Atkinson, D. R., Morten, G., & Sue, D. W. (1999). *Counseling American minorities: A cross-cultural perspective* (5th ed.). Dubuque, IA: Wm. C. Brown.

Axelson, J. A. (1999). *Counseling and development in a multicultural society.* (2nd ed.). Monterey, CA: Brooks/Cole.

Baca, L. M., & Amato, C. (1989). Bilingual special education: Training issues. *Exceptional Children, 56*, 168–173.

Baca, L. M., & Cervantes, H. T. (1989). *The bilingual special education interface*. Columbus, OH: Merrill.

Bailey, N. J., & Phariss, T. (1996). Breaking the wall of silence: Gay, lesbian, and bisexual issues for middle level educators. *Middle School Journal, 27*(3), 38–46.

Baker, G. C. (1994). Teaching children to respect diversity. *Childhood Education, 71*, 33–35.

Banks, C. A., & Banks, J. A. (1997). Reforming schools in a democratic pluralistic society. *Educational Policy, 11*(2), 183–193.

Banks, J. A. (1981). Education in the 80's: Multiethnic education. Washington, DC: National Education Association.

Banks, J. A. (1987). *Teaching strategies for ethnic studies.* Boston: Allyn & Bacon.

Banks, J. A. (1988). Multiethnic education: Theory and practice. Boston: Allyn & Bacon.

Banks, J. A. (1993). Multicultural education: Progress and prospects. *Phi Delta Kappan, 75*, 21.

Banks, J. A. (1998). The lives and values of researchers: Implications for educating citizens in a multicultural society. *Educational Researcher, 27*(7), 4–17.

Banks, J. A., & Banks, C. A. M. (1993). *Multicultural education: Issues and perspectives* (2nd ed.). Boston: Allyn & Bacon.

Barrera, R. M. (2001). Bringing home to school. *Scholastic Early Childhood Today, 16*(3), 44–56.

Basen-Engquist, K., Tortolero, S., & Parcel, G. S. (1997). HIV risk behavior and theory-based psychosocial determinants in Hispanic and non-Hispanic white adolescents. *Journal of Health Education, 28*(4), S-44–S-50.

Baunach, D. M. (2001). Gender inequality in childhood: Toward a life course perspective. *Gender Issues, 19*(3), 61–86.

Bay, M., & Lopez-Reyna, N. (1997). Preparing bilingual special educators: The lessons we've learned. *Teacher Education and Special Education, 20*(1), 1–10.

Bell-Scott, P., & McKenry, P. C. (1986). Black adolescents and their families. In G. K. Leigh & G. W.

Peterson (Eds.), *Adolescents in families* (pp. 410–432). Cincinnati, OH: Southwestern.

Benenson, J. F. (1990). Gender differences in social networks. *Journal of Early Adolescence, 10,* 472–495.

Bennett, C. I. (1986). *Comprehensive multicultural education: Theory and practice.* Boston: Allyn & Bacon.

Biehler, R., & Snowman, J. (1990). *Psychology as applied to teaching* (6th ed.). Boston: Houghton Mifflin.

Binder, A. J. (2000). Why do some curricular challenges work while others do not? The case of three Afrocentric challenges. *Sociology of Education, 73,* 69–91.

Bing-Canar, J., & Zerkel, M. (1998). Reading the media and myself: Experiences in critical media literacy with young Arab American women. *Signs, 23*(3), 735–741.

Birkel, L. F. (2000). Multicultural education: It is education first of all. *Teacher Educator, 36*(1), 23–28.

Black, S., Wright, T., & Erickson, L. (2001). Polynesian folklore: An alternative to plastic toys. *Children's Literature in Education, 32*(2), 125–137.

Blacks are slipping through the health gap. (November 27, 1998). *The Virginia-Pilot,* pp. A1, A14.

Bond, M. H., & Shiraishi, N. (1974). The effect of body lean and status of an interviewer on the nonverbal behavior of Japanese interviewees. *International Journal of Psychology, 9*(2), 117–128.

Borden, J. F. (1998). The pitfalls and possibilities for organizing quality ESL programs. *Middle School Journal, 29*(3), 25–33.

Bowman, B. T. (1989). Educating language-minority children: Challenges and opportunities. *Phi Delta Kappan, 71,* 118–120.

Boyd, B. F. (1998). Issues in education: A guide to multicultural education. *Childhood Education, 75*(1), 33.

Boyle-Baise, M., Epler, B., McCoy, W., Paulk, G,. Clark, J., Slough, N., & Truelock, C. (2001). Shared control: Community voices in multicultural learning. *The Educational Forum, 65,* 344–353.

Buda, R., & Elsayed-Elkhouly, S. M.(1998). Cultural differences between Arabs and Americans: Individualism-collectivism revisited. *Journal of Cross-Cultural Psychology, 29*(3), 487–492.

Butler, D. A., & Manning, M. L. (1998). *Gender differences in young adolescents.* Olney, MD: Association for Childhood Education International.

Butler, D. A., & Sperry, S. (1991). Gender issues and the middle school curriculum. *Middle School Journal, 23*(2), 18–23.

Byrnes, D. A., & Cortez, D. (1996). Language diversity in the classroom. In D. A. Byrnes & G. Kiger (Eds.), *Common bonds: Anti-bias teaching in a diverse society* (pp. 65–78). Olney, MD: Association for Childhood Education International.

Byrnes, D. A., & Kiger, G. (1996). *Common bonds: Anti-bias teaching in a diverse society* (2nd ed.). Olney, MD: Association for Childhood Education International.

Calderon, M. (1997). Staff development in multilingual multicultural schools. (ERIC Document Reproduction Service No. 410 368).

CampbellJones, B., & CampbellJones, F. (2002). Educating African American children: Credibility at the crossroads. *Educational Horizons 80*(3), 133–139.

Carr, C. L. (1998). Tomboy resistance and conformity: Agency in social psychological gender theory. *Gender & Society, 12*(5), 528–553.

Carroll, M. (2001). Dim sum, bagels, and grits: A sourcebook for multicultural families. *Booklist, 97*(12), 1096.

Chang, J. I. (1997). Contexts of adolescent worries: Impacts of ethnicity, gender, family structure, and socioeconomic status. (ERIC Document Reproduction Service No. ED 417 003.)

Chang, M. T. (2001). Is it more than about getting along? The broader educational relevance of reducing students' racial biases. *Journal of College Student Development, 42*(2), 93–105.

Chavez, L., & Amselle, J. (1997). Bilingual education theory and practice: Its effectiveness and parental opinions. *NASSP Bulletin, 81*(586), 101–106.

Chavkin, N. F. (1989). Debunking the myth about minority parents. *Educational Horizons, 67*(4), 119–123.

Chavkin, N. F., & Gonzalez, J. (2000). Mexican immigrant youth and resiliency: Research and promising programs. Charleston, WV: ERIC Clearinghouse on Rural Education and Small Schools. ERIC Document Reproduction Service No. ED 447990)

Chen, S. (1987, April 6). Suicide and depression identified as serious problems for Asian youth. *East-West News, 9,* 3–4.

Cheng, L. L. (1987). Cross-cultural and linguistic considerations in working with Asian populations. *American Speech and Hearing Association, 29*(6), 33–36.

Chiang, L. H. (2000). Teaching Asian American students. *Teacher Educator, 36*(1), 58–69.

Christensen, E. W. (1989). Counseling Puerto Ricans: Some cultural considerations. In D. R. Atkinson, G. Morten, & D. W. Sue (Eds.), *Counseling American minorities: A Cross-cultural perspective* (3rd ed.) (pp. 205–212). Dubuque, IA: W. C. Brown.

Clark-Johnson, G. (1988). Black children. *Teaching Exceptional Children, 20,* 46–47.

Clawson, R. A. (2002). Poor people, black faces: The portrayal of poverty in economics textbooks. *Journal of Black Studies, 32*(3), 352–361.

Cline, Z., & Necochea, J. (2001). Latino parents fighting entrenched racism. *Bilingual Research Journal, 25*, 1–26.

Closing the educational gap for Hispanics: State aims to forestall a divided society. (1987, September 16). *The Chronicle of Higher Education,* p. 1.

Coballes-Vega, C. (1992, January). Considerations for teaching culturally diverse children. *ERIC Digest,* 1–2.

Cohen, E. G., & Lotan, R. A. (Eds.) (1997). *Working for equity in heterogeneous classrooms: Sociological theory in practice.* New York: Teachers College Press.

Coladarci, T. (1983). High-school dropout among Native Americans. *Journal of American Indian Education, 23*, 15–21.

Colburn, D., & Melillo, W. (1987, June 16). Hispanics: A forgotten help population. *Washington Post,* p. 16.

Collier, C., & Hoover, J. J., (1987). *Cognitive strategies for minority handicapped students.* Lindale, TX: Hamilton Publications.

Comer, J. P. (1988). Establishing a positive racial identity. *Parents, 63*(3), 167.

Conley, D. (2000). 40 acres and a mule. *National Forum, 80*(2), 21–24.

Constantine, M. G., & Blackmon, S. M. (2002). Black adolescents' racial socialization experiences: Their relations to home, school, and peer self-esteem. *Journal of Black Studies, 32*(3), 322–335.

Cornett, C. E. (1983). *What should you know about teaching and learning styles* (Fastback 191). Bloomington, IN: Phi Delta Kappa.

Crawford, L. W. (1993). *Language and literacy learning in multicultural classrooms.* Boston: Allyn & Bacon.

Darling-Hammond, L. (1998). New standards, old inequalities: The current challenge for African American education. In L. A. Daniels, D. McSween, & R. Jefferson-Franzier (Eds.), *The state of black America 1998* (pp. 109–171). New York: National Urban League.

Davison, D. M., & Miller, K. W. (1998). An ethnoscience approach to curriculum issues for American Indian students. *School Science and Mathematics, 95*(5), 260–264.

Dawson, M. M. (1987). Beyond ability grouping: A review of the effectiveness of ability grouping and its alternatives. *School Psychology Review, 16*, 348–369.

Derman-Sparks, L. (1993/1994). Empowering children to create a caring culture in a world of differences. *Childhood Education, 70*, 66–71.

Deyhle, D. (1985). Testing among Navajo and Anglo students: Another consideration of cultural bias. *Journal of Educational Equity and Leadership, 5*, 119–131.

Dils, A. K. (2002). Service learning can narrow the potential mismatch between future teachers and their students. *ACEI Focus on Teacher Education, 3*(1), 1–3.

Dilworth, M. E. (Ed.). (1998). *Being responsive to cultural differences: How teachers learn.* Thousand Oaks, CA: Corwin.

Dirda, M. A. (November 9, 1997). Classrooms and their discontents. *Washington Post,* p. 2.

Divoky, D. (1988). The model minority goes to school. *Phi Delta Kappan, 70*, 219–222.

Dorriss, M. A. (1981). The grass still grow, the rivers still flow: Contemporary Native Americans. *Daedalus, 110*(2), 43–69.

Draguns, J. G. (1989). Dilemmas and choices in cross-cultural counseling: The universal versus the culturally distinctive. In P. D. Pedersen, J. G. Draguns, J. Lonner, & J. E. Trimble (Eds.), *Counseling across cultures* (3rd ed.) (pp. 1–21). Honolulu: University of Hawaii Press.

Duncan, G. (1993). Racism as a developmental mediator. *The Educational Forum, 57*, 360–369.

Dunn, R., Gemake, J., Jalali, F., Zenhausern, R., Quinn, P., & Spiridakis, J. (1990). Cross-cultural differences in learning styles of elementary-age children from four ethnic backgrounds. *Journal of Multicultural Counseling and Development, 18*, 68–93.

Dunn, R. S., Beaudry, J. S., & Klavas, A. (1989). Survey of research on learning styles. *Educational Leadership, 46*, 50–58.

Dunn, R. S., & Dunn, K. J. (1978). *Teaching students through their individual learning styles: A practical approach.* Reston, VA: Reston Publishing.

Dunn, R. S., & Dunn, K. J. (1979). Learning styles/teaching styles: Should they . . . can they . . . be matched? *Educational Leadership, 36*, 238–244.

Edelman, M. W. (1989). Black children in America. In J. Dewart (Ed.), *The state of black America* (pp. 63–76). New York: National Urban League.

Education and gender (1994, June 3). *Congressional Quarterly Researcher, 4*(21), 482–503.

Elkind, D. (1984). Erik Erikson's eight stages of man. In H. E. Fitzgerald & M. G. Walveren (Eds.), *Human development* (pp. 11–18). Guilford, CT: Dushkin Publishing Group.

Ellington, L. (1998). Multicultural theorists and the social studies. *The Social Studies, 89*(2), 57–60.

English as a second language program: Benefits for your child. (1987). Austin, TX: Texas Education Agency.

Epstein, D. (1997). Boyz' own stories: Masculinities and sexualities in schools. *Gender and Education, 9*(1), 105–115.

Epstein, J. A., Botvin, G. J., & Diaz, T. (2000). Alcohol use among Hispanic adolescents: Role of linguistic acculturation and gender. *Journal of Alcohol and Drug Education, 45*(3), 18–32.

Erkut, S., Szalacha, L. A., Coll, C. G., & Alarcon, O. (2000). Puerto Rican early adolescents' self-esteem patterns. *Journal of Research on Adolescence, 10*(3), 339–364.

Espiritu, Y. L. (1997). Race, gender, and class in the lives of Asian Americans. *Race, Gender, and Class, 4*(3), 12–19.

Evans, K. M. (1997). Multicultural training needs for counselors of gifted African American children. *Multicultural Education, 5*(1), 16–19.

Fagella, K. (1994). Coming to America. *Instructor, 103*,(6), 42–43.

Faltis, C. J. (1993). *Joinfostering: Adapting teaching strategies for the multilingual classroom.* Columbus, OH: Merrill.

Faragallah, W. R., Schumm, W. R., & Webb, F. J. (1997). Acculturation of Arab American immigrants: An exploratory study. *Journal of Comparative Family Studies, 28*(3), 182–206.

Feng, J. (1994, June). Asian-American children: What teachers should know. *ERIC Digest*, 1–2.

Ferdman, B. M. (2000). "Why am I who I am?" Constructing the cultural self in multicultural perspective. *Human Development, 43*, 19–23.

Fish, L. S. (2000). Hierarchical relationship development: Parents and children. *Journal of Marital and Family Therapy, 26*(4), 501–510.

Fitzpatrick, J. P. (1987). *Puerto Rican Americans* (2nd ed.). Englewood Cliffs, NJ: Prentice-Hall.

Ford, D. Y., & Harmon, D. A. (2001). Equity and excellence: Providing access to gifted education for culturally diverse students. *The Journal of Secondary Gifted Education, 12*(3), 141–147.

Frisby, C. L. (1993). One giant step backward: Myths of black cultural learning styles. *School Psychology Review, 22*, 535–557.

Fuchs, D., & Fuchs, L. S. (1998). Competing visions for educating students with disabilities: Inclusion versus full inclusion. *Childhood Education 74*(5), 309–316.

Fuligini, A. J. (1997). The academic achievement of adolescents from immigrant families: The roles of family backgrounds, attitudes, and behavior. *Child Development, 68*(2), 351–363.

Gade, E., Hurlburt, G., & Fuqua, D. (1986). Study habits and attitudes of American Indian students: Implications for counselors. *The School Counselor, 34*, 135–139.

Gallagher, J. (1998). Multiculturalism at a crossroads: Can the push for pluralism in education survive the pull of America's melting pot? *Middle Ground, 1*(3), 10–14, 42.

Gallavan, N. P. (2000). Multicultural education at the academy: Teacher educators' challenges, conflicts, and coping skills. *Equity and Excellence in Education, 33*(3), 5–12.

Garcia, R. L. (1984). Countering classroom discrimination. *Theory into Practice, 22*, 104–109.

Gay, G., & Howard, T. C. (2000). Multicultural teacher education for the 21st century. *Teacher Educator, 36*(1), 1–16.

Geenen, S., Powers, L. E., & Lopez-Vasquez, A. (2001). Multicultural aspects of parent involvement in transitional planning. *Exceptional Children, 67*(1), 265–275.

Gerber, D. A. (2001). Forming a transnational narrative: New perspectives on European migrations to the United States. *The History Teacher, 35*(1), 61–77.

Gillespie, C. S., Powell, J. L., Clements, N. E., Swearingen, R. A. (1994). A look at the Newbery medal books from a multicultural perspective. *Language Arts, 48*(1), 40–50.

Gillette, M. D., & Chinn, P. C. (1997). Multicultural education: Responding to a mandate for equitable educational outcomes. *Teacher Education and Practice, 13*(1), 1–13.

Goldenberg, C. N. (1987). Low-income Hispanic parents' contributions to their first-grade children's word-recognition skills. *Anthropology & Education Quarterly, 18*, 149–179.

Gollnick, D. M., & Chinn, P. C. (2002). *Multicultural education in a pluralistic society* (6th ed.). Columbus, OH: Merrill.

Gollnick, D. M., Sadker, M. P., & Sadker, D. M. (1982). Beyond the Dick and Jane syndrome: Confronting sex bias in instructional materials. In M. P. Sadker & D. M. Sadker (Eds.), *Sex equity handbook for schools*. New York: Longman.

Gonzalez, E. (1989). Hispanics bring *corazon* and *sensibilidad*. *Momentum, 20*(1), 10–13.

Gordon, B. M. (1997). Curriculum, policy, and African American cultural knowledge: Challenges and possibilities for the year 2000 and beyond. *Educational Policy, 11*(2), 227–242.

Grant, C. A., & Sleeter, C. E. (1986, April). Race, class, and gender in educational research: An argument for integrative analysis. Paper presented at the meeting of the American Educational Research Association, San Francisco, CA.

Grant, N. (1997). Some problems of identity and education: A comparative examination of multicultural education. *Comparative Education, 33*(1), 9–28.

Grattet, Y. (2000). Hate crimes: Better data or increasing frequency? *Population Today, 28*(5), 1, 4.

Grossman, H., & Grossman, S. H. (1994). *Gender issues in education*. Boston: Allyn & Bacon.

Guild, P. (1994). The culture/learning style connection. *Educational Leadership, 51*(8), 16–21.

Guinn, B. (1997). Health locus of control and HIV/AIDS knowledge among Mexican American young adolescents. *Journal of Health Education, 28*(4), S-13—S-16.

Hakuta, K., & Garcia, E. E. (1989). Bilingualism and education. *American Psychologist, 44*, 374–379.

Haladyna, T., Haas, N., & Allison, J. (1998). Continuing tensions in standardized testing. *Childhood Education, 74*(5), 262–273.

Hale-Benson, J. E. (1986). *Black children: Their roots and their culture* (rev. ed.). Baltimore, MD: Johns Hopkins University.

Hall, E. T. (1981). *Beyond culture.* Garden City, NY: Anchor.

Halle, T. G., Kurtz-Costes, B., Mahoney, J. L. (1997). Family influences on school achievement in low-income, African American children. *Journal of Educational Psychology, 89*(3), 527–537.

Hamm, J. V. (2000). Do birds of a feather flock together? The variable bases for African American, Asian American, and European American adolescents' selection of similar friends. *Developmental Psychology, 36*(2), 209–219.

Haring, N. G. (1990). Overview of special education. In N. G. Haring & L. McCormick (Eds.), *Exceptional children and youth* (pp. 1–45). Columbus, OH: Merrill.

Hartman, J. S., & Askounis, A. C. (1989). Asian American students: Are they really a "model minority"? *The School Counselor, 37*, 109–111.

Hernandez, H. (1989). *Multicultural education: A teacher's guide to content and process.* Columbus, OH: Merrill.

Herring, R. D. (1989). Counseling Native American children: Implications for elementary school counselors. *Elementary School Guidance and Counseling, 23*, 272–281.

Herring, R. D. (1997). The creative arts: An avenue to wellness among Native American Indians. *Journal of Humanistics Education and Development, 36*(2), 105–113.

High, P. C., LaGasse, L. Becker, S., Ahlgren, I., & Gardner, A. (2000). Literacy promotion in primary care pediatrics: Can we make a difference? *Pediatrics, 105*(14), 927–945.

Hispanic Policy Development Project. (1997). The challenges of change. New York: The Hispanic Development Project.

Hispanic youth edging past blacks in number (1998). *Census and You, 33*(9), 3.

Ho, M. K. (1987). *Family therapy with ethnic minorities.* Newbury Park, CA: Sage.

Hodgkinson, H. (1998). The demographics of diversity. *Principal 78*(1), 26–32.

Hodgkinson, H. (2000/2001). Educational demographics: What teachers should know. *Educational Leadership, 58*(4), 6–11.

Hoover-Dempsey, K. V., Bassler, O. C., & Brissie, J. S. (1987). Parent involvement: Contributions of teacher efficacy, school socioeconomic status, and other school characteristics. *American Education Research Journal, 24*, 417–435.

Hope, W. C. (1999). Service learning: A reform initiative for middle school curriculum. *The Clearing House, 72*(4), 236–238.

Hourani, A. (1970). *Arabic thought in the liberal age: 1798–1939.* London, Oxford University Press.

Howard, T. C. (2001). Telling their side of the story: African American students' perceptions of culturally relevant teaching. *The Urban Review, 33*(2), 131–149.

Howard-Hamilton, M. F. (2000). Creating a culturally responsive learning environment for African American students. *New Directions for Teaching and Learning, 82*, 45–53.

Huang, S. L., & Waxman, H. C. (1997). Classroom behaviors of Asian American students in mathematics. (ERIC Document Reproduction Service No. ED 408 166.)

Huber, L. K. (2000). Promoting multicultural awareness through dramatic play centers. *Early Childhood Education Journal, 27*(4), 235–238.

Hudley, C. A. (1997). Teacher practices and student motivation in a middle school program for African American males. *Urban Education, 32*(2), 304–319.

Indian tribes, incorporated. (1988, December 5). *Newsweek*, pp. 40–41.

Iseke-Barnes, J. M. (2000). Ethnomathematics and language in decolonizing mathematics. *Race, Gender, & Class, 7*(3), 133–149.

Isen, H. G. (1983). Assessing the black child. *Journal of Non-White Concerns, 11*, 47–58.

Isom, B. A., & Casteel, C. P. (1997/1998). Hispanic literature: A fiesta for literacy instruction. *Childhood Education, 74*(2), 83–89.

Jackson, R. L. (1999). White space, white privilege: Mapping discursive inquiry into the self. *Quarterly Journal of Speech, 85*, 38–54.

Janzen, R. (1994). Melting pot or mosaic? *Educational Leadership, 51*(8), 9–11.

Jarolimek, J., & Foster, C. D. (1989). *Teaching and learning in the elementary school* (4th ed.). New York: Macmillan.

Jaynes, G. D., & Williams, R. M. (1989). *A common destiny: Blacks and American society.* Washington, DC: National Academy Press.

Jeffries, R., Nix, M., & Singer, C. (2002). Urban American Indians "dropping out" of traditional high schools: Barriers & bridges to success. *The High School Journal, 85*(3), 38–46.

Jenks, C., Lee, J. O., & Kanpol, B. (2001). Approaches to multicultural education in preservice teacher education: Philosophical frameworks and models for teaching. *The Urban Review, 33*(2), 87–105.

Jennings, W. B. (1989). How to organize successful parent involvement advisory committees. *Educational Leadership, 47*(2), 42–45.

Jensen, J. V. (1985). Perspective on nonverbal intercultural communication. In L. A. Samovar, & R. E. Porter (Eds.), *Intercultural communication: A reader* (4th ed.) (pp. 256–272). Belmont, CA: Wadsworth.

Johnston, R. C., & Viadero, D. (2000, March 15). Unmet promise: Raising minority achievement. Education Week. www.edweek.net/ew/ew_printstory.cfm?slug=27gapintro.h19.

Jones, K., & Ongtooguk, P. (2002). Equity for Alaska Natives: Can high-stakes testing bridge the chasm between ideals and realities? *Phi Delta Kappan, 83*(7), 499–503, 550.

Joshua, M. B. (2002). Inside picture books: Where are the children of color? *Educational Horizons, 80*(3), 125–132.

Kang, H., & Dutton, B. (1997). Becoming multicultural: Focusing on the process. *Multicultural Education, 4*(4), 19–22.

Keats, D. M. (2000). Cross-cultural studies in child development in Asian cultures. *Cross-Cultural Research, 34*(3), 339–350.

Keefe, J. W. (1987). *Learning style: Theory and practice.* Reston, VA: NASSP.

Keefe, J. W. (1990). Learning style: Where are we going? *Momentum, 21*(1), 44–48.

Ketter, J., & Lewis, C. (2001). Already reading texts and contexts: Multicultural literature in a predominantly white rural community. *Theory into Practice, 40*(3),175–183.

Killen, M., & Stangor, C. (2001). Children's social reasoning about inclusion and exclusion in gender and race peer group contexts. *Child Development, 72*(1), 174–186.

Kim, H., Rendron, L., & Valdez, J. (1999). Student characteristics, school characteristics, and educational apirations of six Asian American ethnic groups. *Journal of Multicultural Counseling and Development, 26*(3), 166–176.

Kitano, H. H. L. (1989). A model for counseling Asian Americans. In P. B. Pedersen, J. G. Draguns, W. J. Lonner, & J. E. Trimble (Eds.), *Counseling across cultures* (pp. 139–151). Honolulu: University of Hawaii Press.

Kitano, M. K., & Perkins, C. O. (2000). Gifted European American women. *Journal of the Education of the Gifted, 23*(3), 287–313.

Koff, E., Rierdan, J., & Stubbs, M. L. (1990). Gender, body image, and self-concept in early adolescence. *Journal of Early Adolescence, 10*, 56–68.

Kostelnik, M. J., Stein, L. C., Whiren, A. P., & Soderman, A. K. (1988). *Guiding children's social development.* Cincinnati, OH: Brooks/Cole.

Kreidler, W. J. (1995). Say good-bye to bias. *Instructor, 104*(5), 28.

Kulczycki, A., & Lobo, A. P. (2002). Patterns, determinants, and implications of intermarriage among Arab Americans. *Journal of Marriage and Family 64*, 202–210.

Latinos in school: Some facts and findings. (2001). *ERIC Digest No. 162.* (ERIC Clearinghouse on Urban Education No. ED 449288.)

Lawrence, V. J. (1997). Multiculturalism, diversity, cultural pluralism... "Tell the whole truth, and nothing but the truth." *Journal of Black Studies, 27*(3), 318–333.

Lee, C. C., & Lindsey, C. R. (1985). Black consciousness development: A group counseling model for Black elementary school students. *Elementary School Guidance and Counseling, 19*, 228–236.

Lee, E., Menkart, D., & Okazawa-Rey, M. (1998). *Beyond heroes and holidays: A practical guide to K–12 anti-racist, multicultural education and staff development.* Washington, DC: Network of Educators on the Americas.

Lee, E. S., & Rong, X. (1988). The educational economic achievement of Asian-Americans. *The Elementary School Journal, 88*, 545–560.

Lee, G. L., & Johnson, W. (2000). The need for interracial storybooks in effective multicultural classrooms. *Multicultural Education, 8*(2), 28–30.

Lee, G. L., & Manning, M. L. (2001). Working with Asian parents and families. *Multicultural Education, 9*, 23–25.

Lee, J. (2002). Racial and ethnic achievement gap trends: Reversing the progress toward equity? *Educational Researcher, 31*(1), 3–12.

Lee, O. (1997). Diversity and equity for Asian American students in science education. *Science Education, 81*(1), 107–122.

Lee, O., & Fradd, S. H. (1998). Science for all, including students from non-English-language backgrounds. *Educational Researcher, 27*(4), 12–20.

Lee, W. M. L. (1996). New directions in multicultural counseling. *Counseling and Human Development, 29*(2), 1–11.

Lefkowitz, E. S., Romo, L. P., & Corona, R. (2002). How Latino American and European American adolescents discuss conflicts, sexuality, and AIDS with their mothers. *Developmental Psychology, 36*(3), 315–325.

Leistyna, P. (2001). Extending the possibilities of multicultural professional development in public schools. *Journal of Curriculum and Supervision, 16*(4), 282–304.

Lems, K. (1999). The Arab world and Arab Americans. *Book Links, 9*(2), 1–13.

Leuthold, S. (1997). Crossing the lines: Toward a curriculum of comparative design. *Multicultural Education 5*(2), 16–19.

Lewis, J. B., deMarrais, K. B., & Prater, G. (1998). Teaching Navajo bilingual student special education students: Challenges and strategies. (ERIC Document Reproduction Service No: 417 895.)

Lewis, R. G., & Ho, M. K. (1989). Social work with Native-Americans. In D. R. Atkinson, G. Morten, & D. W. Sue (Eds.), *Counseling American minorities* (3rd ed.) (pp. 65–72). Dubuque, IA: W. C. Brown.

Lie, Gwat-Yong. (2000). Multicultural perspectives in working with families. *Families in Society: The Journal of Contemporary Human Services, 81*(5), 544.

Linton, T. E., & Foster, M. (1990). Powerful environments for underclass youth. *The Education Digest, 55*(7), 27–31.

Little, M. (1997). Teacher-parent cooperation: A Navajo perspective. *Journal of Navajo Education, 14*(1–2), 26–31.

Little Soldier, L. (1985). To soar with the eagles: Enculturation and acculturation of Indian children. *Childhood Education, 61*, 185–191.

Little Soldier, L. (1989). Cooperative learning and the Native American student. *Phi Delta Kappan, 71*, 161–163.

Locke, D. C. (1989). Fostering the self-esteem of African American children. *Elementary School Guidance and Counseling, 23*, 254–259.

Lomotey, K. (1989). Cultural diversity in the school: Implications for principals. *National Association of Secondary School Principals Bulletin, 73*, 81–88.

Lonner, W. J., & Ibrahim, F. A. (1989). Assessment in cross-cultural counseling. In P. B. Pedersen, J. G. Draguns, J. Lonner, & J. E. Trimble (Eds.), *Counseling across cultures* (3rd ed.) (pp. 299—333). Honolulu: University of Hawaii Press.

Lopata, H. Z. (1994). *Polish Americans.* New Brunswick, NJ: Transaction.

Low, J. M., & Wong, P. L. (1998). Effects of a Hmong intern on Hmong students. *Multicultural Education 5*(4), 12–16.

Lucal, B. (1996). Oppression and privilege: Toward a relational conceptualization of race. *Teaching Sociology, 24*, 245–255.

Lucero, E. L. (1997). Promoting multiculturalism in the early grades. *Principal, 76*(5), 5–6, 8, 10–11.

Luftig, R. L. (1983). The effect of schooling on the self-concept of Native American students. *The School Counselor, 30*, 251–260.

Lum, D. (1986). *Social work practice and people of color: A process-stage approach.* Monterey, CA: Brooks/Cole.

Lundeberg, M. A., Fox, P. W., & Puncochar, J. (1994). Highly confident but wrong: Gender differences and similarities in confidence judgments. *Journal of Educational Psychology, 86*, 114–121.

Lundy, B., Field, T., McBride, C., Field, T., & Largie, S. (1998). Same-sex and opposite-sex best friend interactions among high school juniors and seniors. *Adolescence, 33*(130), 279–289.

Lutz, T., & Kuhlman, W. D. (2000). Learning about culture through dance in kindergarten classrooms. *Early Childhood Education Journal, 28*(1), 35–40.

Macgillivray, I. K., & Kozik-Rosabal, G. (2000). Introduction. *Education and Urban Society, 32*(3), 287–302.

Machamer, A. M., & Gruber, E. (1998). Secondary school, family, and educational risk: Comparing American Indian adolescents and their peers. *Journal of Educational Research, 91*(6), 357–369.

Mahiri, J. (1998). Streets to schools: African American youth culture and the classroom. *The Clearing House, 71*(6), 335–338.

Manning, M. L. (1989). Multicultural education. *Middle School Journal, 21*(1), 14–16.

Manning, M. L. (1991). More than lipservice to multicultural education. *The Clearing House, 64*, 218.

Manning, M. L. (1993). Cultural and gender differences in young adolescents. *Middle School Journal, 25*(1), 13–17.

Manning, M. L. (1994). *Celebrating diversity: Multicultural education in middle level schools.* Columbus, OH: National Middle School Association.

Manning, M. L. (1995). Understanding culturally diverse parents and families. *Equity and Excellence in Education, 28*(1), 52–57.

Manning, M. L. (1996). Addressing the fears of diversity. *Kappa Delta Pi Record 33*, 4–7.

Manning, M. L. (1998). Gender differences in young adolescents' mathematics and science achievement. *Childhood Education 74*, 168–171.

Manning, M. L. (2002). *Developmentally appropriate middle level schools.* Olney, MD. Association for Childhood Education International.

Manning, M. L., & Baruth, L. G. (1991). Appreciating cultural diversity in the classroom. *Kappa Delta Pi Record, 27*(4), 104–107.

Manning, M. L., & Lucking, R. (1990). Ability grouping: Realities and alternatives. *Childhood Education, 66*, 254–258.

Manning, M. L., & Lucking, R. (1991). The what, why, and how of cooperative learning. *The Clearing House, 64*, 152–165.

Manning, M. L., & Lucking, R. (1993). Cooperative learning and multicultural classrooms. *The Clearing House, 67*, 12–16.

Marcell, A. V. (1994). Understanding ethnicity, identity formation, and risk behavior among adolescents of Mexican descent. *Journal of School Health, 64,* 323–327.

Marinoble, R. M. (1998). Counseling and supporting our gay students. *The Education Digest, 64*(3), 54–59.

Marion, R. (1981). *Educators, parents and exceptional children.* Rockville, MD: Aspen Systems.

"Married with children": More likely to describe Hispanic households. (1998). *Census and You, 33*(4), 3.

Martin, P., & Martin, S. K. (2001). U.S. immigration policy and globalization. *Insights on Law and Society, 1*(3), 4–6, 31.

Martinez, R. O., & Dukes, R. L. (1997). The effects of ethnic identity, ethnicity, and gender on adolescent well-being. *Journal of Youth and Adolescence, 26*(5), 503–516.

Martz, C. (1993). Educating European immigrants before World War I. *Educational Horizons, 71*(3), 139–141.

Mathews, R. (2000). Cultural patterns of South Asian and Southeast Asian Americans. *Intervention in School and Clinic, 36*(2), 101–104.

McAllister, G., & Irvine, J. J. (2000). Cultural competency and multicultural teacher education. *Review of Educational Research, 70*(1), 3–24.

McCollough, S. (2000). Teaching African American students. *The Clearing House, 74*(1), 5–6.

McCormick, L. (1990a). Cultural diversity and exceptionality. In N. G. Haring & L. McCormick (Eds.), *Exceptional children and youth* (pp. 47–75). Columbus, OH: Merrill.

McCormick, L. (1990b). Communication disorders. In N. G. Haring & L. McCormick (Eds.), *Exceptional children and youth* (pp. 327–363). Columbus, OH: Merrill.

McFalls, E. L., & Cobb-Roberts, D. (2001). Reducing resistance to diversity through cognitive dissonance instruction: Implications for teacher education. Journal of *Teacher Education, 52*(2), 164–172.

McFarlane, S. C., Fujiki, M., & Britton, B. (1984). *Coping with communicative handicaps.* San Diego: College-Hill Press.

McGoldrick, M. (1982). Irish families. In M. McGoldrick, J. K. Pearce, & J. Giordano (Eds.), *Ethnicity and family therapy* (pp. 310–339). New York: Guilford Press.

McInerney, D. M., Roche, L. A., McInerney, V., & Marsh, H. W. (1997). Cultural perspectives on school motivation: The relevance and application of goal theory. *American Education Research Journal, 34*(1), 207–236.

McIntyre, A. (1997). Constructing an image of a white teacher. *Teachers College Record, 98*(4), 653–681.

Menchaca, V. D. (2001). Providing a culturally relevant curriculum for Hispanic children. *Multicultural Education, 8*(3), 18–20.

Mendoza, J., & Reese, D. (2001). Examining multicultural picture books for the early childhood classroom: Possibilities and pitfalls. *Early Childhood Research and Practice, 3*(2), 1–30.

Midobuche, E. (2001). Building cultural bridges between home and the mathematics classroom. *Teaching Children Mathematics, 7*(9), 500–502.

Miller-Jones, D. (1989). Culture and testing. *American Psychologist, 44,* 360–366.

Miller-Lachmann, L. (1992). *Our family, our friends, our world: An annotated guide to significant multicultural books for children and teenagers.* Providence, NJ: R. R. Bowker.

Mindel, H. C., & Habenstein, R. W. (1981). Family lifestyles of America's ethnic minorities: An introduction. In C. H. Mindel & R. W. Habenstein (Eds.), *Ethnic families in America: Patterns and variations* (pp. 1–13). New York: Elsevier.

Minderman, L. (1990). Literature and multicultural education. *Instructor, 99*(7), 22–23.

Mirande, A. (1986). Adolescence and Chicano families. In G. K. Leigh, & G. W. Peterson (Eds.), *Adolescents in families* (pp. 433–455). Cincinnati, OH: Southwestern.

Mitchell, K., Bush, E. C., & Bush, L. (2002). Standing in the gap: A model for establishing African American male intervention programs with public schools. *Educational Horizons 80*(3), 140–146.

Mitchum, N. T. (1989). Increasing self-esteem in Native American children. *Elementary School Guidance and Counseling, 23,* 266–271.

Moitoza, E. (1982). Portuguese families. In M. McGoldrick, J. K. Pearce, & J. Giordano (Eds.), *Ethnicity and family therapy* (pp. 412–437). New York: Guilford Press.

Mondykowski, S. M. (1982). Polish families. In M. McGoldrick, J. K. Pearce, & J. Giordano (Eds.), *Ethnicity and family therapy* (pp. 393–411). New York: Guilford Press.

Montgomery, D. (2001). Increasing Native American Indian involvement in gifted programs in rural schools. *Psychology in the Schools, 38,* 467–475.

Moon, T. R., & Callahan, C. M. (2001). Curricular modifications, family outreach, and a mentoring program: Impacts on achievement and gifted identification in high-risk primary students. *Journal of Education of the Gifted, 24*(4), 305–321.

More, A. J. (1987). Native American learning styles: A review for researchers and teachers. *Journal of American Indian Education, 27*(1), 17–29.

Morganthau, T. (1993, August 9). America: Still a melting pot? *Newsweek,* pp. 16–25.

Multicultural teaching strategies. (1990). (Technical Assistance Paper No. 9). Tallahassee, FL: State Department of Education.

Mulvihill, T. M. (2000). Women and gender studies and multicultural education? Building the agenda for 2000 and beyond. *Teacher Educator, 36*(1), 49–57.

Murphy, D. S., & Sullivan, K. (1997). Connecting adolescent girls of color and math/science interventions. (ERIC Document Reproduction Service No. ED 410 106.)

Murray, C. B., & Clark, R. M. (1990). Targets of racism. *The American School Board Journal, 177*(6), 22–24.

Naber, N. (2000). Ambiguous insiders: An investigation of Arab American invisibility. *Ethnic and Racial Studies, 23*, 37–61.

National Assessment of Educational Progress. (1997). *NAEP 1996 science report card for the nation and the states.*

National Association of Secondary School Principals. (1979). *Student learning styles—diagnosing and prescribing programs.* Reston, VA: Author.

National Council for Accreditation of Teacher Education. (1986). *Standards, procedures and policies for accreditation of professional teacher education units.* Washington, DC: Author.

National Research Council. (1989). *Everybody counts: A report on the future of mathematics education.* Washington, DC: National Academy Press.

National Urban League. (1998). *The state of black America 1998.* New York: Author.

Nation's black families number 8 million. (1997). *Census and You, 32*(7), 3.

Nauman, A. K. (1987). School librarians and cultural pluralism. *The Reading Teacher, 41*(2), 201–205.

Nel, J. (1994). Preventing school failure: The Native American child. *The Clearing House, 67*, 169–174.

Nelson, C., & Keith, J. (1990). Comparisons of female and male early adolescent sex role attitude and behavior development. *Adolescence, 25*, 183–204.

Nieto, S. (2000). Affirming diversity: The sociopolitical context of multicultural education (3rd ed.). White Plains, NY: Longman.

Nieves, W., & Valle, M. (1982). The Puerto Rican family: Conflicting roles for the Puerto Rican college student. *Journal of Non-White Concerns in Personnel and Guidance, 4*, 154–160.

Norton, D. E. (1990). Teaching multicultural literature in the reading curriculum. *The Reading Teacher, 44*(1), 28–40.

Norton, D. E. (1999). *Through the eyes of a child.* (4th ed.). Columbus, OH: Merrill.

Ogbu, J. (1988). Class stratification, racial stratification, and schooling. In L. Weiss (Ed.), *Class, race,* *and gender in American education.* Albany: State University of New York Press.

Oliver, M. L., & Shapiro, T. M. (1998). The racial asset gap. In L. A. Daniels, D. McSween, & R. Jefferson-Franzier (Eds.), *The State of Black America 1998* (pp. 15–36). New York: National Urban League.

Olmedo, I. M. (1997). Family oral histories for multicultural curriculum perspectives. *Urban Education, 32*(1), 45–62.

Olney, M. F., & Kennedy, J. (2002). Racial disparities in VR use and job placement rates for adults with disabilities. *Rehabilitation Counseling Bulletin, 45*(3), 177–185.

Olsen, L. (1988). Crossing the schoolhouse border: Immigrant children in California. *Phi Delta Kappan, 70*, 211–218.

O'Malley, J. M., & Chamot, A. U. (1990). *Learning strategies in second language acquisition.* Cambridge: Cambridge University Press.

Ornstein, A. C., & Levine, D. U. (1989). Social class, race, and school achievement: Problems and prospects. *Journal of Teacher Education, 40*(5), 17–23.

Ovando, M. N., & Traxwell, D. (1997). Superintendents' multicultural competence. *Journal of School Leadership, 7*(4), 409–431.

Oyer, H. J., Crowe, B., & Haas, W. H. (1987). *Speech, language, and hearing disorders.* Boston: Little, Brown.

Paccione, A. V. (2000). Developing a commitment to multicultural education. *Teachers College Record, 102*(6), 980–1005.

Padilla, A. M. (1981). Pluralistic counseling and psychotherapy for Hispanic-Americans. In A. J. Marsella, & P. B. Pedersen (Eds.), *Cross-Cultural Counseling and Psychotherapy* (pp. 195–227). New York: Pergamon.

Pappamihiel, N. E. (2001). Moving from the ESL classroom into the mainstream: An investigation of English language anxiety in Mexican girls. *Bilingual Research Journal, 25* (1 & 2), 1–8.

Parette, H. P., & Petch-Hogan, B. (2000). Approaching families. *Teaching Exceptional Children, 33*(2), 4–10.

Park, C. (1997). Learning style preference of Asian American (Chinese, Filipino, Korean, and Vietnamese) students in secondary schools. *Equity and Excellence in Education, 30*(2), 68–77.

Patton, J. R., & Polloway, E. A. (1990). Mild mental retardation. In N. G. Haring & L. McCormick (Eds.), *Exceptional children and youth* (pp. 195–237). Columbus, OH: Merrill.

Payne, C. (1984). Multicultural education and racism in American schools. *Theory into Practice, 22*, 124–131.

Payne, C. R., & Welsh, B. H. (2000). The progressive development of multicultural education before and after the 1960s: A theoretical framework. *Teacher Educator, 36*(1), 29–48.

Pedersen, P. (1988). *A handbook for developing multicultural awareness.* Alexandria, VA: American Association of Counseling and Development.

Pence, D. J., & Fields, J. A. (1999). Teaching about race and ethnicity: Trying to uncover White privilege for a White audience. *Teaching Sociology, 27,* 150–158.

Perez, S. A. (1979). How to effectively teach Spanish-speaking children, even if you're not bilingual. *Language Arts, 56,* 159–162.

Perez, S. A. (1994). Responding differently to diversity. *Childhood Education, 70,* 151–153.

Perez, S. A. (2002). Using Ebonics or Black English as a bridge to teaching standard English. *Contemporary Education, 71*(4), 34–37.

Peterson, K. M., Cross, L. F., Johnson, E. J., & Howell, G. L. (2000). Diversity education for preservice teachers: Strategies and attitude outcomes. *Action in Teacher Education, 22*(2), 33–38.

Petty, W. T., Petty, D. C., & Salzer, R. T. (1994). *Experiences in language: Tools and techniques for language arts methods.* Boston: Allyn & Bacon.

Phinney, J. S. (2000). Identity formation across cultures: The interaction of personal, societal, and historical change. *Human Development, 43,* 27–31.

Pine, G. J., & Hilliard, A. G. (1990). Rx for racism: Imperatives for America's schools. *Phi Delta Kappan, 71,* 593–600.

Pope, M. (1995). The "salad bowl" is big enough for us all: An argument for the inclusion of lesbians and gays in any definition of multiculturalism. *Journal of Counseling and Development, 73,* 301–304.

Portman, T. A. A., & Herring, R. (2001). Debunking the Pocahontas paradox: The need for a humanistic perspective. *Journal of Humanistic Counseling, Education and Development, 40,* 185–199.

Purkey, W. W., & Novak, J. M. (1984). *Inviting school success: A self concept approach to teaching and learning.* Belmont, CA: Wadsworth.

Quinn, A. E. (2001). Moving marginalized students inside the lines: Cultural differences in classrooms. *English Journal, 90*(4), 44–50.

Ramos, I., & Lambating, J. (1996). Risk taking: Gender differences and educational opportunity. *School Science and Mathematics, 96*(2), 94–98.

Ramsey, P. G. (1987). *Teaching and learning in a diverse world.* New York: Teacher's College Press.

Rapoport, R. N. (1997). Families as educators for global citizenship: Five conundrums of intentional socialization. *International Journal of Early Years Education, 5*(1), 67–77.

Riccio, L. L. (1985). Facts and issues about ability grouping. *Contemporary Education, 57,* 26–30.

Richardson, E. H. (1981). Cultural and historical perspectives in counseling Indians. In D. W. Sue (Ed.), *Counseling the culturally different* (pp. 216–255). New York: John Wiley.

Rodriguez, A. P. (2000). Adjusting the multicultural lens. *Race, Gender, and Class, 7*(3), 150–177.

Rosario, M., Rotheram-Borus, M. J., & Reid, H. (1996). Gay-related stress and its correlates among gay and bisexual male adolescents of predominantly black and Hispanic backgrounds. *Journal of Community Psychology, 24,* 136–157.

Rotenberg, K. J., & Cranwell, F. R. (1989). Self-concepts in American Indian and white children. *Journal of Cross-Cultural Psychology, 20*(1), 39–53.

Rotheram-Borus, M. J., & Phinney, J. S. (1990). Patterns of social expectations among black and Mexican American children. *Child Development, 61,* 542–556.

Rotunno, M., & McGoldrick, M. (1982). Italian families. In M. McGoldrick, J. K. Pearce, & J. Giordano (Eds.), *Ethnicity and family therapy* (pp. 340–363). New York: Guilford Press.

Ruiz, S. Y., Roosa, M. W., & Gonzales, N. A. (2002). Predictors of self-esteem for Mexican American and European American youths: A reexamination of the influence of parenting. *Journal of Family Psychology, 16*(1), 70–80.

Sadker, M. P., & Sadker, D. M. (1982). Between teacher and student: Overcoming sex bias in classroom interaction. In M. P. Sadker & D. M. Sadker (Eds.), *Sex equity handbook for schools* (pp. 96–132). New York: Longman.

Sadker, M. P., Sadker, D. M., & Long, L. (1993). Gender and educational equity. In J. A. Banks & C. A. M. Banks (Eds.), *Multicultural education: Issues and perspectives* (2nd ed.) (pp. 111–128). Boston: Allyn & Bacon.

Sanders, D. (1987). Cultural conflicts: An important factor in the academic failures of American Indian students. *Journal of Multicultural Counseling and Development, 15,* 81–90.

Sanders, G. L., & Kroll, I. T. (2000). Generating stories of resilience: Helping gay and lesbian youth and their families. *Journal of Marital and Family Therapy, 26*(4), 433–442.

Santiestevan, H. (1986). Hispanics and education. *Social Education, 50,* 396.

Sapon-Shevin, M. (2000/2001). Schools fit for all. *Educational Leadership, 58*(4), 34–39. School practices to promote the achievement of Hispanic students. ERIC/CUE Digest No. 153. (2000). (ERIC Clearinghouse on Urban Education No. ED 439186.)

Schmuck, P. A., & Schmuck, R. A. (1994). Gender equity: A critical democratic component of America's high schools. *NASSP Bulletin, 78,* 22–31.

Schorr, L. (1998). Building community. In L. A. Daniels, D. McSween, & R. Jefferson-Franzier (Eds.), *The state of black America 1998* (pp. 37–51). New York: National Urban League.

Schwartz, W. (1999, March). Arab American students in public schools. *ERIC Digest* (EDO-UD-99-2), http://eric~web.tc.columbia.edu/digests/dig142. htnml. Retrieved July 22, 2002.

Schwartz, W. (2000). New trends in language education for Hispanic students. New York: ERIC Clearinghouse on Urban Education. (ERIC Docuementation Reproduction Service No. 442913.)

Schwartz, W. (2001). Strategies for improving the educational outcomes for Latinas. New York: ERIC Clearinghouse on Urban Education. (ERIC Document Reproduction Service No. ED 458344.)

Scourby, A. (1984). *The Greek Americans.* Boston: Twayne.

Scribner, A. P., & Scribner, J. D. (2001). High-performing schools serving Mexican American students: What they can teach us. Charleston, WV: ERIC Clearinghouse on Rural and Small Schools. (ERIC Documentation Reproduction Service No. 459048.)

Sendor, B. (1989). Root out racial bias in student placement. *American School Board Journal, 176*(3), 24–25.

Shade, B. (1982). Afro-American cognitive style: A variable in school success? *Review of Educational Research, 52,* 219–244.

Shafer, G. (2001). Standard English and the migrant community. *English Journal, 90*(4), 37–43.

Sharan, S. (1985). Cooperative learning and the multiethnic classroom. In R. Slavin, S. Sharan, S. Kagan, R. Lazarowitz, C. Webb, & R. Schmuck (Eds.), *Learning to cooperate, cooperating to learn* (pp. 255–276). New York: Plenum.

Shea, T. M., & Bauer, A. M. (1985). *Parents and teachers of exceptional children: A handbook for involvement.* Boston: Allyn & Bacon.

Sheridan, S. M. (2000). Considerations of multiculturalism and diversity in behavioral consultation with parents and teachers. *The School Psychology Review, 29*(3), 344–353.

Silva, C., & Patton, M. M. (1997). Multicultural education: Theory to practice. *Teacher Education and Practice, 13*(1), 22–38.

Simich-Dudgeon, C. (1987). Involving limited-English-proficient parents as tutors in their children's education. *ERIC/CLL News Bulletin, 10*(2), 3–4, 7.

Slavin, R. E. (1983). *An introduction to cooperative learning.* New York: Longman.

Slavin, R. E. (1987). *Cooperative learning* (2nd ed.). Washington, DC: National Education Association.

Slavin, R. E. (1996). Cooperative learning and middle and secondary schools. *The Clearing House, 69*(4), 200–204.

Sleeter, C. E. (2000). Creating an empowering multicultural curriculum. *Race, Gender, and Class, 7*(3), 178–196.

Sleeter, C. E. (2001). Preparing teachers for culturally diverse schools: Research and the overwhelming presence of whiteness. *Journal of Teacher Education, 52*(2), 94–106.

Sleeter, C. E., & Grant, C. A. (1999). *Making choices for multicultural education: Five approaches to race, class and gender* (2nd ed.). Columbus, OH: Merrill.

So, A. Y. (1987). Hispanic teachers and the labeling of Hispanic students. *The High School Journal, 71,* 5–8.

Southern Association for Children Under Six. (1988). *Multicultural education: A position statement.* Little Rock, AR: Author.

Sparks, S. (2000). Classroom and curriculum accommodations for Native American students. *Intervention in School and Clinic, 35*(5), 259–263.

Spaulding, S. (1994). 4 Steps to effective parent conferences. *Learning, 23*(2), 36.

Steinberg, L., Blinde, P., & Chan, K. (1984). Dropping out among language minority youth. *Review of Educational Research, 54,* 113–132.

Stewart, W. J. (1990). Learning-style-appropriate instruction: Planning, implementing, evaluating. *The Clearing House, 63,* 371–374.

Stormont, M., Stebbins, M. S., & Holliday, G. (2001). Characteristics and educational support needs of underrepresented gifted adolescents. *Psychology in the Schools, 38*(5), 413–423.

Struchen, W., & Porta, M. (1997). From role-modeling to mentoring for African American youth: Ingredients for successful relationships. *Preventing School Failure, 41*(3), 119–123.

Studer, J. R. (1993/1994). Listen so that parents will speak. *Childhood Education, 70,* 74–76.

Sue, D. W. (1981). *Counseling the culturally different.* New York: John Wiley.

Sue, D. W. (1989). Ethnic identity: The impact of two cultures on the psychological development of Asians in America. In D. R. Atkinson, G. Morten, & D. W. Sue (Eds.), *Counseling American minorities: A cross-cultural perspective* (3rd ed.) (pp. 103–115). Dubuque, IA: Wm. C. Brown.

Sue, D. W., & Sue, S. (1983). Counseling Chinese Americans. In D. R. Atkinson, G. Morten, & D. W. Sue (Eds.), *Counseling American minorities: A cross-cultural perspective* (2nd ed.) (pp. 97–106). Dubuque, IA: Wm. C. Brown.

Sue, D. W., & Sue, D. (1999). Counseling the culturally different (3rd. ed.). New York: John Wiley.

Suleiman, L. M. (2001). Image making of Arab Americans: Implications for teachers in diverse settings. Paper presented Annual Meeting of the California Association for Bilingual Education, January

31–February 1, 2001. (ERIC Document Reproduction Service No. ED 452310.)

Swisher, K., & Deyhle, D. (1989, August). The styles of learning are different, but the teaching is just the same: Suggestions for teachers of American Indian youth. *Journal of American Indian Education, Special Issue,* 1–11.

Tamura, E. H. (2001). Asian Americans in the history of education: An historical essay. *History of Education Quarterly, 41*(1), 58–71.

Tan, A., Fujioka, Y., & Lucht, N. (1997). Native American stereotypes, TV portrayals, and personal contact. *Journalism and Mass Communication Quarterly, 74*(2), 265–284.

Taylor, S. V. (2000). Multicultural is who we are: Literature as a reflection of ourselves. *Teaching Exceptional Children, 32*(3), 24–29.

Ten quick ways to analyze children's books for racism and sexism. (1974, November 3). *Interracial Books for Children, 5*(3), 6–7.

TESOL (Teachers of English to Speakers of Other Languages). (1976). Position paper on the role of English as a second language in bilingual education. Washington, DC: Author.

Texeira, M. T., & Christian, P. M. (2002). And still they rise: Practical advice for increasing African American enrollments in higher education. *Educational Horizons, 80*(3), 117–124.

Thompson, G. L. (2000). What students say about bilingual education. *Journal of At-Risk Issues, 6*(2), 24–32.

Tiedt, P. L., & Tiedt, I. M. (1999). *Multicultural teaching: A handbook of activities, information, and resources* (2nd ed.). Boston: Allyn & Bacon.

Toepfer, C. F. (1988). What to know about young adolescents. *Social Education, 52,* 110–112.

Trentacosta, J., & Kenney, M. J. (Eds.) (1997). *Multicultural and gender equity in the mathematics classroom.* Reston, VA: National Council of Teachers of Mathematics.

Trumbull, E., Rothstein-Fisch, C., & Greenfield, P. M. (2001). Ours and mine. *Journal of Staff Development, 22*(2), 10–14.

Tsai, J. L., Mortensen, H., & Wong, Y. (2002). What does "being American" mean? A comparison of Asian American and European American young adults. *Cultural Diversity and Ethnic Minority Psychology, 8*(3), 257–273.

Tyler, R. W. (1989). Educating children from minority families. *Educational Horizons, 67*(4), 114–118.

Uno, D., Florsheim, P., & Uchino, B. N. (1998). Psychosocial mechanisms underlying quality of parenting among Mexican American and white adolescent mothers. *Journal of Youth and Adolescence, 27*(5), 585–605.

U.S. Bureau of the Census. (1990). *Persons of Hispanic origin in the United States.* C 3.223.10: 1990. CP-3–3. Washington, DC: Author.

U.S. Bureau of the Census. (1992). *Statistical abstracts of the United States* (112th ed.). Washington, DC: Author.

U.S. Bureau of the Census. (1993a, September). *We the American . . . Asians.* Washington, DC: Author.

U.S. Bureau of the Census. (1993b, September). *We the American . . . Blacks.* Washington, DC: Author.

U.S. Bureau of the Census. (1993c, September). *We the . . . first Americans.* Washington, DC: Author.

U.S. Bureau of the Census. (1993d, September). *We the American . . . Foreign born.* Washington, DC: Author.

U.S. Bureau of the Census. (1993e, November). *We the American . . . Hispanics.* Washington, DC: Author.

U.S. Bureau of the Census. (1993f, September). *We the American . . . Pacific Islanders.* Washington, DC: Author.

U.S. Bureau of the Census. (1996, September). Almost half of the nation's chronic poor are children. *Census and You, 31*(9), 7.

U.S. Bureau of the Census. (1997a). *Statistical abstracts of the United States* (117th ed.). Washington, DC: Author.

U.S. Bureau of the Census. (1997b). More recent immigrants are generally younger. *Census and You, 32*(6), 1.

U.S. Bureau of the Census. (2001). *Statistical abstracts of the United States* (121st ed.). Washington, DC: Author.

U.S. Commission on Civil Rights. (1975). *A better chance to learn: Bilingual-bicultural education.* Washington, DC: Author.

Valdes, G. (1998). The world outside and inside schools: Language and immigrant children. *Educational Researcher, 27*(6), 4–18.

Valero-Figueria, E. (1988). Hispanic children. *Teaching Exceptional Children, 20,* 47–49.

Vander Zanden, J. W. (1989). *Human development* (4th ed.). New York: Knopf.

Vare, J. W., & Norton, T. L. (1998). Understanding gay and lesbian youth: Sticks, stones, and silence. *The Clearing House, 71*(6), 327–331.

Vera, H., Feagin, J. R., & Gordon, A. (1995). Superior intellect? Sincere fictions of the White self. *Journal of Negro Education, 64*(3), 295–306.

Viadero, D. (2000, March 22). Lags in minority achievement defy traditional expectations. *Education Week,* www.edweek.net/ew/ew_printstory.cfm?slug=28causes.h19.

Viadero, D., & Johnston, R. C. (2000). Lifting minority achievement: Complex answers. *Education Week, 19*(30), 1, 14–16.

Vogl, B. D., & Jaros, G. G. (1998). Can we achieve a celebration of diversity. *The Educational Forum, 62,* 334–340.

Vontress, C. E. (1976). Counseling the racial and ethnic minorities. In G. S. Belkin (Ed.), *Counseling: Directions in theory and practice* (pp. 277–290). Belmont, CA: Wadsworth.

Wade, R. C. (2000). Service learning for multicultural teaching competency: Insights from the literature for teacher educators. *Equity and Excellence in Education, 33*(1), 21–29.

Walker, J. L. (1988). Young American Indian children. *Teaching Exceptional Children, 20,* 50–51.

Wallace, B. C. (2000). A call for change in multicultural training at graduate schools of education: Educating to end oppression and for social justice. *Teachers College Record, 102*(6), 1086–1111.

Warren, S. R. (2002). Stories from the classrooms: How expectations and efficacy of diverse teachers affect the academic performance of children in poor urban schools. *Educational Horizons, 80*(3), 109–116.

Weaver, H. N. (2000). Culture and professional education: The experiences of Native American social workers. *Journal of Social Work Education, 36*(3), 415–428.

Weeber, J. E. (2000). What could I know of racism? *Journal of Counseling and Development, 77,* 20–23.

Welts, E. P. (1982). Greek families. In M. McGoldrick, J. K. Pearce, & J. Giordano (Eds.), *Ethnicity and family therapy* (pp. 269–288). New York: Guilford Press.

Wertsman, V. F. (2001). A comparative and critical analysis of leading reference sources. *Multicultural Review, 10*(2), 42–47.

West, B. E. (1983). The new arrivals from Southeast Asia. *Childhood Education, 60,* 84–89.

White, J. J. (1998). Helping students deal with cultural differences. *The Social Studies, 89*(3), 107–111.

Wiest, L. R. (2001). Teaching mathematics from a multicultural perspective. *Equity & Excellence in Education, 34*(1), 16–25.

Wilder, L. K., Jackson, A. P., & Smith, T. B. (2001). Secondary transition of multicultural learners: Lessons from the Navajo Native American experience. *Preventing School Failure, 45*(3), 119–124.

Williams, D. L., & Chavkin, N. F. (1989). Essential elements of strong parent involvement programs. *Educational Leadership, 47*(2), 18–20.

Williams, R. L. (1997). The Ebonics controversy. *Journal of Black Psychology, 23*(3), 208–214.

Williams, S. (2001). Trends among Hispanic children, youth, and families. Washington, DC: Child Care Trends. (ERIC Documentation Reproduction Service No. ED 453313.)

Willis, A. I., & Lewis, K. C. (1999). Our known everydayness: Beyond a response to White privilege. *Urban Education, 43*(2), 245–262.

Willis, S. (1994). Teaching language-minority students. *ASCD Update, 36*(5), 1–5.

Wilson, R. (1989). Black higher education: Crisis and promise. In J. Dewart (Ed.), *The state of Black America 1989* (pp. 121–135). New York: National Urban League.

Winawer-Steiner, H., & Wetzel, N. A. (1996). German families. In M. McGoldrick, J. K. Pearce, & J. Giordano (Eds.), *Ethnicity and family therapy* (2nd ed.) (pp. 496–516). New York: Guilford Press.

Wingfield, M., & Karaman, B. (1995). Arab stereotypes and American educators. *Social Studies and Young Learners, 7*(4), 7–10.

Winter, S. M. (1994/1995). Diversity: A program for all children. *Childhood Education, 71*(2), 91–95.

Winzer, M. A., & Mazurek, K. (1998). *Special education in multicultural contexts.* Columbus, OH: Prentice-Hall.

Wolf, J. S. (1990). The gifted and talented. In N. G. Haring & L. McCormick (Eds.), *Exceptional children and youth* (pp. 447–489). Columbus, OH: Merrill.

Wolfe, M. M., Tang, P. H., & Wong, E. C. (2001). Design and development of the European American values scale for Asian Americans. *Cultural Diversity and Ethnic Minority Psychology, 7*(3), 274–283.

Wrigley, T. (1997). Raising achievement for Asian pupils. *Multicultural Teaching 16*(1), 21–25.

Yager, T. J., & Rotheram-Borus, M. J. (2000). Social expectations among African American, Hispanic, and European American adolescents. *Cross-Cultural Research, 34*(3), 283–305.

Yao, E. L. (1985). Adjustment needs of Asian immigrant children. *Elementary School Guidance and Counseling, 19,* 222–227.

Yao, E. L. (1988). Working effectively with Asian immigrant parents. *Phi Delta Kappan, 70,* 223–225.

Yarborough, B. H., & Johnson, R. A. (1983). Identifying the gifted: A theory-practice gap. *Gifted Child Quarterly, 27,* 125–138.

Yee, L. Y. (1988). Asian children. *Teaching Exceptional Children, 20*(4), 49–50.

Yetman, N. R., & Steele, C. H. (Eds.). (1975). *Majority and minority: The dynamics of racial and ethnic relations* (2nd ed.). Boston: Allyn & Bacon.

Young, J. L. (1994). Sapphires-in-transition: Enhancing personal development among black female adolescents. *Journal of Multicultural Counseling and Development, 22*, 86–95.

Youngman, G., & Sandongei, M. (1983). Counseling the American Indian child. In D. R. Atkinson, G. Morten, & D. W. Sue (Eds.), *Counseling American minorities: A cross-cultural perspective* (pp. 73–76). Dubuque, IA: Wm. C. Brown.

Yurkovich, E. E. (2001). Working with American Indians toward educational success. *Journal of Nursing Education, 40*(6), 259–269.

Zehr, M. A. (1999, September 22). Hispanic students "left out" by high stakes tests, panel concludes. *Education Week, 19*(3), 5.

Zehr, M. A. (2000, November 8). Un dia nuevo for schools: Overview. *EducationWeek, 20*(10), 1.

Zychowicz, M. J. (1975). American Indian teachings as a philosophical base for counseling and psychotherapy. Unpublished doctoral dissertation. Northern Illinois University, De Kalb.

NAME INDEX

SUBJECT INDEX